THE MOTHERHOOD BUSINESS

THE MOTHERHOOD BUSINESS

Consumption, Communication, and Privilege

EDITED BY
Anne Teresa Demo
Jennifer L. Borda
Charlotte Kroløkke

THE UNIVERSITY OF ALABAMA PRESS
Tuscaloosa

The University of Alabama Press
Tuscaloosa, Alabama 35487-0380
uapress.ua.edu

Typeface: Bembo and Museo Sans

Manufactured in the United States of America
Cover photograph: Baby socks on clothesline with dollar bills; © Ginasanders | Dreamstime.com
Cover design: Mary-Francis Burt

∞

The paper on which this book is printed meets the minimum requirements of American National Standard for Information Sciences—Permanence of Paper for Printed Library Materials, ANSI Z39.48–1984

Cataloging-in-Publication data is available from the Library of Congress
ISBN: 978-0-8173-1890-1
E-ISBN: 978-0-8173-8908-6

Library of Congress Cataloging-in-Publication Data

The motherhood business : consumption, communication, and privilege / edited by Anne Teresa Demo, Jennifer L. Borda, and Charlotte Krolokke.
pages cm. — (Rhetoric, culture, and social critique)
Includes bibliographical references and index.
ISBN 978-0-8173-1890-1 (cloth : alk. paper) — ISBN 978-0-8173-8908-6 (ebook)
1. Motherhood—Economic aspects. 2. Mothers. 3. Consumption (Economics)—Social aspects. I. Demo, Anne Teresa, 1968– II. Borda, Jennifer L., 1973– III. Krolokke, Charlotte, 1965– .
HQ759.M8734165 2015
306.874'3—dc23

2015013786

We would like to dedicate this book to our mothers:
Mary P. Demo, Patricia Borda, and Anna Marie Halmø Nielsen.

We also gratefully acknowledge all who collaboratively mother
their own children and the children of others, and,
in doing so, empower us all.

Contents

Acknowledgments

The Motherhood Business was conceived in 2008 during a National Communication Association (NCA) preconference. Since that time, the contributors have collectively celebrated and offered one another generous support and patience through births, adoptions, relocations, promotions, diagnoses, and passings. As our authors transitioned through various phases of their lives, this book project benefited from evolving insights, the addition of new contributors, and three NCA panel presentations, as well as many conversations with generous colleagues who added more nuanced perspectives along the way. We also had the opportunity to incorporate the rapidly developing interdisciplinary literature into our project, as well as respond to the challenging and enlightening recommendations of two anonymous reviewers, which we feel enriched the project tremendously.

Academic labor not only bears the imprint of insights from colleagues who listen and read attentively but also (for parents) the aid of those who care for our children. The editors, in particular, would like to thank Bradford Vivian, Erin Rand, Vanessa Beasely, Karma Chávez, Willem Verweij, the teachers at Live and Learn Early Learning Center, and Michael Warnock. We also are very grateful for the support of Dan Waterman, Vanessa Rusch, Jennifer M. Rogers, and the publishing team at the University of Alabama Press. We would also like to thank the Danish Research Council for generously granting us support towards the indexing of this book.

THE MOTHERHOOD BUSINESS

Introduction

Reframing Motherhood: Factoring in Consumption and Privilege

Anne Teresa Demo

Consumption and consumer culture shape parenting in ways unimagined even a decade ago. Internationally, fertility tourism now spans over one hundred countries as infertile couples travel abroad for reproductive procedures unavailable or too expensive in their own countries.[1] Domestically, the rise of over four million mommy bloggers across North America has transformed the marketing landscape for toy companies that have shifted their focus to the blogosphere. Whereas corporations such as Disney and Hasbro once sent their free marketing samples to broadcast and print media outlets, the majority (70 percent) are now sent to bloggers.[2] The prerecession rise of lavish nurseries, over-the-top birthday parties, and commercialized educational spaces fueled a counter-industry of books and back-to-basics toys seeking to decommercialize play and minimize the impact of branding. Despite the historic economic downturn in 2009, markets serving parents and targeting children, from organic baby food producers to the toy industry, were relatively recession-proof.[3] As Alison Pugh found, even under financial constraint, parents sacrificed to provide the goods and experiences that act as a passport to peer belonging.[4] Parents not only continued to spend during the recession, they also transformed the marketplace by adding new products and services. The growing trend of mompreneurs, women who develop new products and home-based businesses in response to needs unaddressed in the marketplace, show how consumption can lead to production and a vision of entrepreneurship seemingly more responsive to a family-work balance.[5] The relationship between parenting and consumption has, in other words, never been more multifaceted and conflicted.

This collection of essays explores how consumption and consumer culture both constrain and empower contemporary parenting. The following chapters purposefully focus on motherhood and the emerging industries associated with becoming and doing the work of mothering. Despite the diversity in family composition and the growing involvement of fathers in all aspects of parenting, women are responsible for 85 percent of family purchasing decisions whether or not they also work outside the home.[6] Mothers also increasingly provide the primary source of income for families. According to a 2013 Pew Research Center report, "A record 40% of all households with children under the age of 18 include mothers who are either the sole or primary source of income for the family," up from 11 percent in 1960.[7] Recognition of the conflation of mothering and consuming is evident in the emerging media frame of mothers as the family or household CFO.[8] Frequent references to the "nesting instinct," described in popular pregnancy literature as a uniquely gendered biological impulse to buy and organize, normalize the relationship between buying and mothering. From pregnancy forward, women tend to not only determine what to buy but also rely on particular products and brands to help establish their identity as mothers and signal it to others.[9] The subject-positions of mother and consumer now overlap in unprecedented ways.

Recognition that the market activity of mothers challenges extant scholarship about consumption has led to an emerging line of interdisciplinary inquiry to which this volume adds. Although we draw from related fields engaged in this inquiry, our critical approach is based in rhetoric and communication studies, which we argue enriches interdisciplinary literature on consumption, motherhood, and privilege as both individual and linked concepts. As a whole, the collection makes three overarching contributions. First, we delineate the rhetorical dynamics of consumption and show how consumption is both engendered by and judged according to contradictory discourses that circulate about motherhood. Second, we demonstrate the value of approaching class privilege as discursive markers that not only compound marginalization but also maximize advantage by either deflecting privilege or conferring cultural and social capital to children. Finally, we trace how the market activity of mothers (encompassing consumption, entrepreneurship, and commodification) has both altered and reinscribed key norms of contemporary mothering. Before outlining our contributions in more depth, I situate the project in the context of rhetoric of motherhood scholarship and the cross-disciplinary work on motherhood and capitalism.

The Rhetoric of Motherhood

Despite established lines of inquiry related to motherhood, the scope of scholarship in rhetorical studies has been limited in significant ways. Indeed, Linda Buchanan concludes her 2013 book *Rhetorics of Motherhood* by arguing: "Although motherhood is both powerful and pervasive, its construction and implications for women have been little studied within rhetoric to this point."[10] The most recurrent rhetorical concepts employed in scholarship published over the last twenty years divide into two major clusters. The first cluster documents the longstanding constraints women faced in the public sphere that positioned maternal appeals as one of the few available means of persuasion during the nineteenth and early twentieth century. Karlyn Kohrs Campbell's delineation of the feminine style has been particularly generative for work on the maternal persona.[11] Invoking moral status based on maternity typically coincides with the use of a personal tone, familial anecdotes, and a standpoint grounded in values of interconnection and nurturance. Studies of maternal persona and/or feminine style of diverse public figures (from Mary Harris Jones and Ann Richards to Judge Judy and Sarah Palin) trace how political authority has been derived through maternal appeals even as such appeals have the potential to unintentionally normalize regressive gender norms. Katie Gibson and Amy Heyse's work on the maternal persona of Sarah Palin is characteristic of trends within this first cluster. Their analysis attends carefully to the complexities of how motherhood is "experienced and expressed" but emphasizes the limitations of maternal appeals in an effort to illuminate shifting norms in political rhetoric rather than motherhood.[12] In comparison, Sara Hayden's analysis of the material politics of the Million Mom March contests the totalizing quality of most scholarly critiques of maternal appeals. She argues that the effectiveness of the "nation-as-family" metaphor tempers "overarching indictments" regarding the risks and impotency of material appeals: "That maternal appeals will not directly effect change in every situation does not negate their potential to effect positive and progressive change in many arenas."[13] Instead of examining such appeals as a gendered lens for understanding political rhetoric more generally, Hayden's analysis places scholarship on maternal appeals at the foreground. This shift is atypical and helps explain how Buchanan can claim a dearth of research on motherhood within rhetorical studies despite numerous studies on the feminine style and maternal appeals.

The second cluster of scholarship relevant to this volume is more conceptually diffuse than the first, but thematically consistent in its findings that popular media narratives about motherhood disempower women. Such scholarship bridges rhetoric and media/cultural studies, encompassing a range of concepts that fall under the broad classification of discursive formations—including cultural scripts, media frames, social types, and cultural codes. Focused primarily on mainstream media coverage and mothering advice books, the scholarship in this cluster delineates how postfeminist and neoliberal themes increasingly overlap to define contemporary motherhood. Described as a "depoliticizing ideology" or "backlash ideology," postfeminism assumes gender equity has been achieved, disregards lasting structural inequality, and assigns blame for the social and economic struggles on individual choices.[14] A primary vehicle for postfeminist renderings of motherhood is the rhetoric of choice, which appropriates feminist connotations of choice but strips away any type of collective action and empowerment. Mary Douglas Vavrus, for example, examines the rhetoric of choice in media coverage about mothers who "opt out" of the workforce. She finds that the rhetoric of choice in such stories "subtly suggests that women exercising their choices are themselves to blame for sex discrimination" and, in so doing, opt-out stories "play a role in the discursive legitimation of neoliberalism."[15] Similarly, Lynn O'Brien Hallstein's analysis of celebrity mom profiles finds that "like the super mom ideal, celebrity mom profiles also work to reentrench the new post-second wave ideal that women can choose to have it all, while also incorporating a neoliberal version of individual responsibility that eviscerates the second wave politics of choice."[16] The merger of a postfeminist logic that assigns blame to women for their limited choices and the neoliberal emphasis on privatization and entrepreneurship is an example of what Hallstein describes as the "ongoing refinement" of a "sophisticated backlash ideology" that requires sustained critical attention.[17] Our volume explores how the business of motherhood shapes this "ongoing refinement" and the increasing entanglement of neoliberalism with postfeminist gender regimes.

The essays in this volume rely on conceptual tools employed more often in the second cluster than the first; however, our understanding of the complexities of motherhood derives in part from the careful work tracing how maternal appeals have, in the history of American politics, cut both ways. To be sure, the rhetoric of motherhood remains a source of authority and delegitmation, a basis for solidarity and individuation, and a potent "available means of persuasion" to both challenge and normalize the status quo. Because we foreground the dynamics of consumption that situate mothers in the space between the public and private spheres, our contributors trouble the conflation of woman and mother. As Hayden argues in her analysis of SavvyAuntie.com, an online community founded by "auntrepreneur" Melanie Notkin, "the definition of woman continues to be conflated with mother, creating limited options for women to enact identities that call on their multifaceted abilities, passions, needs, and desires."[18] Hayden proves this claim (in part) through an analysis of how childless women enact their subject position as "savvy aunties" through the purchase of trendy gifts that not only facilitate peer belonging for the child but also convey a "cool status" to the adult.

Previous works such as Buchanan's *Rhetorics of Motherhood* focused on public figures such as Mother Theresa who have been defined not only by childlessness and work-life but also values of selflessness, altruism, and compassion. In comparison, our volume traces how changes in and recalcitrance to such binaries occur through everyday decisions over not only what mothers buy and sell but also how mothers justify and are judged by their engagement with the marketplace. Are the toys we buy and the choice to pay for private school examples of materialism or forms of protection? How do momprenuers and mommy bloggers demarcate the dividing line between work and home? Is the decision to pursue surrogacy in another country self-indulgence or self-sacrifice? Our volume approaches the business of motherhood as a definitive factor in the lives of women and as a nodal point for contemporary capitalism and family life.

Motherhood, Capitalism, and the Commodity Frontier

Debates over the economic status of mothers and the value of domestic labor are not unique to our era. Seemingly contemporary issues such as the separation of family life from the corrupting commercialism of the marketplace and the gendered division of housework emerged in the early stages of industrial capitalism. In *Origins of the Family*, Engels directly challenged women's relegation to domestic work: "The emancipation of women will only be possible when women can take part in production on a large, social scale, and domestic work no longer claims anything but an insignificant amount of her time."[19] Yet, even as domestic labor was commonly understood to be outside the realm of commodity production, mothers played a foundational role in the rise and maintenance of capitalism into the twentieth century. As Kathryn Russell notes, "Women's contributions are crucial in the domestic sphere, because they maintain the daily subsistence of the labor force and give birth to and socialize future workers."[20]

The devaluation of housework and childrearing by a system that increasingly depended on such labor incited second-wave feminists to characterize households as sites of economic exploitation.[21] Whereas socialist feminist literature examined how housework and childcare functioned as labor processes, our volume focuses on what Arlie Hochschild describes as the "commodity frontier" of free market capitalism where families are "outsourcing more functions" and the tasks associated with mothering are increasingly "monetized and impersonalized."[22] Exploring the relationship between motherhood and capitalism through the lens of consumption is justified in part by the decrease in domestic labor that results from the availability of goods and services targeted toward mothers. In her assessment of the "unfinished" scholarship on domestic labor, Lise Vogel acknowledges the shift from housework to consumption: "By the early 1900s, food preparation was less time-consuming, laundry was in some ways less onerous . . . More recently, frozen food, microwaves, laundromats, and the increased availability of day care, nursery, kindergarten, and after-school programs have decreased domestic labor even further."[23] The transformation of care work into a commodity market has only continued to accelerate with the feminization of the US labor force and the decline of social services triggered by neoliberal economic policies.[24]

The influence of neoliberalism on the changing nature of motherhood in contemporary capitalism is an emerging focus for feminist scholars in sociology, anthropology, and communication studies (broadly conceived).[25] The basic philosophy of neoliberalism assumes that the social good is maximized when states embrace free markets, dismantle social programs, and ease regulatory constraints. According to David Harvey, interventions by the state "must be kept at a bare minimum" because "human well-being can best be advanced by liberating individual entrepreneurial freedoms and skills within an institutional framework characterized by strong private property rights, free markets, and free trade."[26] Within communication studies, analyses of neoliberalism and motherhood adopt what Melinda Vandenbeld Giles describes as a culturalist approach to neoliberalism, which emphasizes how discursive meanings and social practices normalize our relationship to markets and the state: "A culturalist perspective investigates how neoliberalism is altering our understanding of self, life, social relationships, and material realities thereby incorporating analysis of lifestyle, institutions, economics structures, symbols, and intergenerational relations."[27] Media lifestyle profiles of mothers (from women who opt out of the workforce to yummy mommies and the celebrity mom) have proven to be a consistent resource for fusing postfeminist and neoliberal narratives that individualize or obscure the problem of unfair workplace practices and childcare policies.[28] Moreover, when paid work or unpaid domestic labor is addressed explicitly in such lifestyle profiles, it is increasingly framed in entrepreneurial terms. As Jo Littler notes, "There is a trend for celebrity mothers to emphasize their working lives in relation to their maternal identity . . . and the gungho attitude to valorizing enterprise in all of these narratives translates their activity into new variants of the neoliberal maternal."[29] This trend toward the "neoliberal maternal" also informs lifestyle paradigms such as attachment parenting and "back-to-basics" books targeted at new mothers. These paradigms normalize child-centric philosophies associated with "intensive mothering" but reframe the domestic and emotional labor associated with such approaches as a form of optimization, not sacrifice.[30] While the relationship of neoliberalism to motherhood is not the main focus of our volume, it provides the context for our approach to consumption and entrepreneurship featured across the case studies.

Similarly, although our primary contribution is to illuminate the interrelationship between motherhood, consumption, and privilege, our volume also connects to broader inquiries regarding how the social dynamics of communication underwrite capitalism.[31] Our attention to the cultural and moral implications of market activity responds in part to Ronald Walter Greene's call to "be sensitive to how capitalism incorporates rhetorical communication into its regime of accumulation and its mode of regulation."[32] Just as Greene emphasizes the overlap between economics and politics, our volume demonstrates that the market and private family life (even biological reproduction) are "no longer unique domains of social action."[33] Moreover, Greene's claim that capitalism relies on communicative labor for its success is borne out in our volume. However, the notion of communicative labor is not only maximized by the ways in which we talk, write, and speak about jobs but also by the ways that consumption defines our homes, families, and mothering practices.

Our volume thus follows the work of Phaedra Pezzullo, John Sloop, and Christine Harold, who provide the grounding for a consumption-focused approach to political economy in communication studies.[34] Rhetorical approaches to political economy have, as Greene notes, been "hard to find" and generally limited to five primary areas: (1) the rhetoric of economics, (2) studies of economic policy debates, (3) scholarship on anticapitalism/prounion activism, (4) studies of corporate communication, and (5) the somewhat ambiguous designation of "links between rhetorical pedagogy and class."[35] Although consumption and consumer culture have served as a recurrent backdrop for exploring the interplay between commercial and social life over the last decade, a majority of those works do not explicitly engage theories of consumption.[36]

Consumption as Communication

Consumption has become a multidisciplinary focus of inquiry that spans the humanities and social sciences—ranging from the Marxist underpinnings of cultural studies to the quantifiable metrics of consumer research. Although consumption and consumerism are often key terms of analysis, their meanings overlap in contradictory ways even within a particular disciplinary tradition. An enduring constraint in distinguishing these terms is the etymology linking consumption to destruction or wastefulness. As Daniel Miller notes, "Most academics who have written about consumption have adopted this unusually moral or normative aspect compared to the study of most other phenomena."[37] The emerging focus on anticonsumerism and ethical consumption in cultural studies, which has begun to influence work in communication studies, reflects Miller's point to a degree but also indicates a shift away from the narrowing of consumption to exploitation or depletion.[38] For example, Jo Littler concedes the tendency to refer to consumption as "the general 'using up' of an object, good or service regardless of the kind of economic or ideological context" whereas Jeremy Gilbert acknowledges the prevalent view of consumption as a "necessary evil" as well as a potential form of creative practice.[39] The "consuming is bad, don't consume" stance is, according to Juliet Schor, untenable: "People have to consume. Consuming is a very legitimate, and very important, life activity."[40] In day-to-day buying practices, the use-value and symbolic value of a good or service typically eclipses ethical repercussions associated with a purchase. If we are to understand its intersection with privilege, however, analyzing consumption requires an attention to use-value, symbolic value, and the social and environmental repercussions of market activity.[41]

Consumerism is also a contested term encompassing both paradigms that normalize consumption and consumer rights activism that challenges it. Within communication studies, the rhetoric of consumer activism has received more attention than the rhetoric of consumerism, with few works that explicitly engage consumerism or consumer culture as a conceptual focus.[42] The essays in the volume, however, emphasize the synergy between consumption (what individuals buy) and consumerism (the social paradigm that normalizes consumption). Sociologist Zygmunt Bauman defines consumerism as a "principal propelling and operating force of society" and "type of social arrangement that results from recycling mundane, permanent and so to speak 'regime-neutral' human wants, desires, and longings into . . . a force that coordinates systematic reproduction, social integration, social stratification and the formation of human individuals."[43] Although the use-value of particular goods and services (such as those related to infertility) complicate the consumer/merchant norm associated with consumerism, the paradigm is typically sustained by the planned obsolescence of products (i.e., new models with more safety features) and the symbolic obsolescence of brands. As Bauman notes, "Consumer society thrives as long as it manages to render the non-satisfaction of its members . . . perpetual. The explicit method of achieving such an effect is to denigrate and devalue consumer products shortly after they have been hyped into the universe of consumers' desires."[44] As an outgrowth of consumerism, commodification describes a reductive process that transforms an experience, activity, or event into a purchasable commodity. The obvious examples relevant to this volume include surrogacy and egg donation, in which money is exchanged for a biological service or reproductive material, a practice that has been critiqued for exploiting poor women and treating children as commodities.

The recognition that consumption (at some level) is not only necessary but also constitutes identities, relationships, and sources of agency motivates our focus on the social dimensions of consumption. Anthropologists such as Mary Douglas and Daniel Miller called attention to the limits of individualistic economic models of consumption. Douglas's early work introduced the idea of a "communication approach to consumption" that redefined consumption as a "series of rituals" and commodities as "a nonverbal medium for the human creativity faculty."[45] Her 1979 book with Baron Isherwood, *The World of Goods,* established the productive role of material goods in forming social relationships and marking divisions: "We start with the general idea that goods are coded for communication. They have other practical uses, but the one we need to investigate is how they allow one consumer to engage with others in a series of exchanges."[46] Like Douglas, Miller examines everyday objects and considers how the mundane activities of consumption such as routine shopping are "significant, deep, creative, laden with responsibilities, and richly polysemic with diverse meanings."[47] We begin with a similar assumption but instead foreground the moral and ideological entailments of public discourses about market activity and motherhood.

Despite the commercial and marketing attention on mothers as consumers, scholarship on consumption and consumer culture has (with notable exceptions such as Miller) persistently under-theorized the consumer lives of children and mothers. Daniel Thomas Cook attributes this failing to an individualized model borrowed from economics that obscures "co-consumption" practices—purchases made "in the name of, or with someone in mind other than the shopper."[48] Recognition of this relational model of consumption and the centrality that children and mothers play in economic life alters "the entire landscape of social and cultural consumption theory."[49] By contrasting studies of the commercial products, spaces, and services, this volume argues that even the relational model suggested by "co-consumption" may be insufficient given the public scrutiny that a mother's decision to either buy or boycott receives. That is, mothers not only shop "in the name of" others but also within streams of moral discourse about consumption. Within this context, consumption can be viewed as dialogic at the levels of both self and discourse.

Conceptualizing consumption as dialogic calls attention to the competing discourses and multiplicity of subject positions within the self that are activated when buying for a child. As our volume will show, mothers make consumption decisions and defend their choices with an acute awareness that buying, like speaking, does not occur in a vacuum.[50] The decision to purchase a name-brand, generic, or green laundry detergent is shaped by the clash of competing popular and expert discourses "and an awareness of previous exchanges, whether with a family member, friend, or imagined like-minded shoppers.[51] Our approach to consumption emphasizes this interplay of context, discourse, and subjectivity inherent to communication and rhetorical studies.

Axes of Privilege and the Consumer Life of Mothers

The consumer life of mothers and emerging entrepreneurship associated with motherhood also dramatize how privilege and oppression intersect across axes of gender, race, class, sexuality, nationality, and ability. As the subtitle of our volume suggests, we hope that the contributions provide a preliminary pathway toward understanding how contemporary discourses related to market activity (consumerism, neoliberalism, etc.) draw on, normalize, and reproduce hierarchies of class, race, sexuality, and nationality. Our project is aligned with feminist communication scholarship on intersectionality that seeks to mark and interrogate the multidimensional nature of privilege and subjectivity. The study of intersectionality derives from the activism of women of color marginalized by second-wave feminist organizing. In response to the racism, classism, and homophobia of the feminist movement, the Combahee River Collective drafted what Karma Chávez and Cindy Griffin describe as "one of the foundational statements that names and advocates an intersectional approach to feminism."[52] Kimberlé Crenshaw later coined the term "intersectionality" and argued for its scholarly relevance based on the "multidimensionality of marginalized subjects" and their lived experiences.[53] Within communication studies, intersectional analyses have complicated notions of gender, race, sexuality, and citizenship status that fail to account for the reciprocal and compounding relationship among these categories in the lives of women.[54] Our contribution to that conversation is to foreground class as a consistent axis of analysis. If what we buy (or do not buy) increasingly defines child-rearing, then studies of motherhood and mothering practices require a more agile vocabulary for conceptualizing how class status is either marked or obscured in discourses related to consumption and market activity.

Given the legacy of Crenshaw's emphasis on "marginalized subjects" in subsequent scholarship, there has been some question about whether the study of intersectionality encompasses all subject positions impacted by the intersection of gender, race, class, sexuality, nationality, and ability. As Jennifer Nash notes, "Generally, intersectional literature has excluded an examination of identities that are imagined as either wholly or even partially privileged."[55] Given the history of erasure in communication studies, there was an urgent need to study "marginalized subjects" previously ignored in scholarship and to complicate approaches that failed to account for the "multidimensionality" of oppression. To be sure, exigencies for doing so still exist.

In the context of motherhood and consumption, studying the "multidimensionality" of women *with* privilege also helps us understand how structural inequalities are normalized. By delineating how and when class is marked or unmarked, we better understand its role in narratives about economic mobility and definitions of women's labor. Contributors to our volume such as Kroløkke, Hvidtfeldt Madsen, Ducre, and Flores thus address how class, race, and nationality (particularly in relation to fertility and education) compound the marginalization experienced by the poor and/or women of color. Other contributors, however, explore how women with economic and social capital seek to maximize privilege by commodifying their mothering practices into brands (Borda and Dillard) or by conferring it to their children through consumption choices that foster mobility (Gordon and Harold). In either case, our volume begins with the assumption that reducing motherhood to a single-axis framework based only on gender is insufficient. Additionally, we contend that identifying strategies used to maximize, confer, or deflect class privilege also enriches our understanding of subjectivity and power.

The concept of privilege has been instrumental for understanding how mundane language choice and practices normalize inequality. Members of privileged groups—whether based on race, nationality, gender, class, ability, legal status, or sexual preference—conform with societal norms so they are often unaware of, or actively deny, the "unearned assets" that come with being part of the norm. Peggy McIntosh established a defining metaphor for understanding privilege as "an invisible weightless knapsack of special provisions, maps, passports, codebooks, visas, clothes, tools and blank checks."[56] Whereas McIntosh's oft-quoted passage explicitly refers to race, economic privilege also functions via unmarked pathways to mobility and an unacknowledged safety net that frames middle-class achievements as the result of merit, not advantage. Because economic and social disparities are sustained through this invisible infrastructure of daily life, our volume illuminates how different forms of privilege are deployed, conferred, and maintained through the "maps" and "codebooks" of mothering.

Although the option to buy certainly hinges on having the resources to pay, economic status is an unpredictable marker of difference when it comes to spending on children. Pugh found, for example, that both rich and poor parents buy to protect their children from social isolation. Both also refer to consumption decisions as a common basis for evaluating their parenting. Affluent parents affirmed their parenting by referencing examples of "symbolic deprivation"—products or experiences they denied their children.[57] Low-income parents, in comparison, referenced examples of "symbolic indulgence" to affirm their parenting, citing instances when they purchased products or experiences that required sacrifice because of their "significant symbolic value for the children's social world."[58] Given such complex and counter-intuitive relationships to buying, economic privilege cannot be reduced to a class-based determinism—the rich buy and the poor do not—because what we buy, borrow for, or boycott is informed by intersecting norms of consumer culture and motherhood within particular communities and cultures. Our volume thus approaches privilege by considering how class, race, and nationality are either marked or unmarked in discourses about motherhood, consumption, entrepreneurship, mobility, and leisure.

The unearned advantages of economic privilege are often recognized as augmenting racial and gender privilege but rarely serve as the anchoring concept within communication scholarship.[59] Sociology and education provide a precedent for foregrounding economic privilege, as each has a well-developed literature on the formative role of social class and parental involvement in educational success.[60] To privilege class, or at least attend to it as a concept equally determinative as race in the context of parenting and consumption, requires an analysis that moves beyond broad classifications such as "middle class" to consider contributing factors to social class such as the cultural, social, and emotional capital that augment or compensate for diminishing economic capital. These concepts, drawn from Pierre Bourdieu's work on class distinctions, emphasize the role of social knowledge and family life in transferring economic privilege. Our volume shares this focus on social knowledge but contends that the relationship between class privilege and family life is shaped in significant ways by public discourses about motherhood and consumption. The volume thus shows how economic privilege not only informs other axes of privilege but also is performed and resisted in ways that differ from strategies of racial privilege that have been more fully explored in communication studies.

Four categories of capital—economic, cultural, social, and emotional—signpost the broad dimensions of class privilege explored in *The Motherhood Business*. As sociologist Diane Reay notes, "all capitals are interwoven in the transfer of privilege . . . economic capital augmenting social capital, emotional compounding cultural capital."[61] Economic capital describes the available monetary resources (wages or salary, investments, and assets) that determine classifications such as income status. Having access to financial resources is an obvious necessity whether the product or service purchased is baby food or college tuition; however, the concept of economic capital is particularly relevant in the context of the fertility industry, which is the opening focus of the volume. Economic capital also provides means for acquiring cultural capital through decisions about schooling (i.e., the purchase of a house in a particular school district, enrollment in private school, or even participation in enrichment programs), as well as the purchase of status objects that act as a passport into peer groups. The resulting cultural competency and social mobility informs where families are comfortable shopping, what mothers buy, and why (and how) their choices are praised or criticized. Class privilege has been closely tied to cultural capital across scholarly literatures, and the analysis of school choice and food consumption within this volume underscores its relevance to communication studies. Social capital, the resources and advantages that originate from social connections, was also one of the forms of capital developed by Bourdieu and has been studied extensively in offline contexts such as the primary school setting.[62] Read collectively, however, the case studies of commercial and noncommercial blogs in our volume indicate social capital may increasingly be cultivated online.

Finally, class privilege may also be secured through emotional capital, a concept that encompasses a mixture of intense and emotionally involved care work as well as prolonged, unpaid time investments. Intensive mothering ideology, for example, normalizes a range of emotions—affection, patience, empathy, pride, worry, and love—as authentic, capable of accruing value, and productive for the child or family in question. The ideology also deploys a secondary range of emotions—guilt, envy, shame, and contempt—as disciplining tools. Popular neuroscience texts on childhood development similarly seek to regulate and discipline a mother's emotional life. As Davi Johnson Thorton shows, such texts associate "requisite affective repertoires" and "emotional management" as essential to mothering in a neoliberal context.[63] The potential for affective practices to accrue value and transfer privilege is situational. "There are," argues Margaret Wetherell, "likely to be complicated mixes of affective repertories available to any one individual or social group at any one moment, including some affective practices that are widespread . . . and some which are very local and exceedingly transient, specific to . . . quite particular historical moments."[64] Our current historical moment is marked by significant changes in the gender dynamics of family life. Women are increasingly the primary sources of economic capital for their families even as emotional capital remains (culturally at least) something that mothers nourish and that others consume. As the economics and care of family life continues to evolve, however, the negotiation of economic, cultural, social, and emotional capital, as well as the rhetorical frames used to facilitate the transfer of privilege, will only become more critical in the interdisciplinary study of motherhood and consumption.

Consumption and Intensive Mothering

The publication of Adrienne Rich's 1986 *Of Woman Born* established a foundational distinction between *mothering* as the empowering lived experiences of women and *motherhood* as a patriarchal institution imposed on women. The opposition introduced by Rich has informed feminist mothering practices and the emerging subfield of motherhood studies pioneered by Andrea O'Reilly and advanced in key works by Sharon Hays as well as coauthors Susan Douglas and Meredith Michael.[65] Our volume, however, follows the work of Lynn O'Brien Hallstein, who challenges the viability of this binary in a post–second wave context.[66] We also find that Rich's division has become increasingly untenable in a commercial landscape shaped by social media. Our focus thus rests on the synergy between institutional motherhood (a source of oppression for women) and mothering (a source of empowerment for women) in the context of consumption and entrepreneurship.

To be sure, the disparities in caregiving first described by Rich persist. However, the dynamics of power underwriting such disparities have shifted from patriarchy to neoliberalism and its logic of entrepreneurship and market solutions. Claims associated with patriarchal motherhood, such as the denial of selfhood and women's powerless responsibility are increasingly difficult to reconcile with the rise of mothers as a powerful market force. What endures, and even proliferates, are ways to ascribe the moral responsibility of childrearing to women. Despite women's "inroads in the workforce," Cook argues, "they are increasingly held morally and socially responsible for virtually every aspect of the lives of their children. As such, many have become actively engaged in influencing the kinds of products available for their children by making use of Web 2.0 technologies and social media, which, in turn, is making mothers' practices, skills and networks part of the marketing resources for many companies."[67] Our volume thus explores motherhood in the context of a significant ontological shift as mothers with class privilege increasingly approach consumption and market activity as a building block for their identities and empowerment. As Cook concludes, "Mothers make their own motherhoods even if the motherhoods available to them are not of their own making."[68] For the last half century (at least), the primary means for making motherhood and controlling women has been the ideology of intensive mothering.

Widely identified as the animating force of patriarchal motherhood and norm for contemporary maternity, the ideology of intensive mothering has been remarkably adaptive to economic and societal shifts. Sharon Hays traced the emergence of intensive mothering to the period immediately prior to World War II and showed how the three core beliefs of intensive mothering shaped mothering practices during the economic growth of the early 90s. The first belief identified by Hays holds "that the child absolutely requires consistent nurture by a single primary caretaker," preferably the mother or other female "temporary substitutes."[69] Drawn from eighteenth- and nineteenth-century views of motherhood, this gendered obligation was also foundational to popular twentieth-century child-rearing manuals (Spock, Brazelton, and Leach) that normalized the second and third core beliefs of intensive mothering. These manuals not only reaffirmed *who* is responsible for childcare but also delineated *how* mothers (or their female surrogates) should raise children. According to Hays, the ideology of intensive mothering promotes approaches that are "child-centered, expert-guided, emotionally absorbing, labor-intensive, and financially expensive."[70] Finally, the "priceless" status of the child within the ideology of intensive mothering frames "decisions regarding their rearing completely distinct from questions of efficiency or financial profitability."[71] Case studies in our volume show, however, that intensive mothering has been adapted to and strengthened by its rearticulation in the context of consumption and market activity.

Intensive mothering also provides the foundation for what Susan Douglas and Meredith Michaels describe as "new momism," a supermom ideal promoted in celebrity profiles, popular press accounts, and television shows from the mid-80s forward.[72] As with intensive mothering, new momism similarly insists that "no woman is truly complete or fulfilled unless she has kids, that women remain the best primary caretakers of children, and that to be a remotely decent mother, a woman has to devote her entire physical, psychological, emotional, and intellectual being, 24/7 to her children."[73] Co-opting the rhetoric of choice from the feminist movement, this vision of motherhood encourages women to channel their political and educational gains to family life. As Lynn O'Brien Hallstein concludes, "new momism requires mothers to develop professional-level skills, such as therapists, pediatricians, consumer product safety instructor, and teacher, in order to meet and treat the needs of their children." [74] Our volume explores two further adaptations to intensive mothering ideology emerging in the context of market activity. First, discourse surrounding the rise of the momprenuer (what perhaps should be called supermom 2.0) reveals new ways that intensive mothering circumscribes the rhetoric of choice. Second, Douglas and Michaels identified an emerging contradiction regarding the ways that motherhood and consumption are reconciled: "Our homes are supposed to be havens from the . . . everyone-is-defined-by-commodities values of the marketplace. . . . And yet, our devotion as mothers . . . our kid's own self-worth . . . all have been measured by how many and what kinds of goods and services we buy for them."[75] *The Motherhood Business* documents how that relationship has been reconciled, and in some cases synergized, across diverse sites of consumption and commodification.

Overview of the Volume

Our inquiry into the relationship between motherhood, consumption, and privilege begins with the rapidly expanding global fertility market. The fertility and biotourism industry is a particularly important starting point for the volume given the reinscription of colonial patterns between childless couples from first-world countries and their egg donors and surrogates from third-world countries. Although later sections of the volume concentrate on the US context, the fertility industry requires an international focus because its primary growth sectors reside outside US borders. In "The Golden Egg: The Business of Making Mothers through Egg Donation," Charlotte Kroløkke examines transnational reproductive networks that fuel fertility travel within Europe by comparing marketing campaigns that frame IVF treatments as a reproductive holiday with firsthand accounts from Danish women who reluctantly traveled to other countries for egg donation procedures. As Kroløkke notes, even as national restrictions and health care systems differ, consumers of fertility markets in the United States and Europe share a recalibration of the foundational nature/nurture binary. Within the context of transnational egg donation in particular and Assisted Reproductive Technology (ART) in general, intent increasingly trumps biology as the defining marker of maternity. More broadly, Kroløkke's chapter also establishes that dominant theories of gift and commodity exchange are insufficient in the context of a global reproductive market. The second chapter analyzes marketing appeals for fertility and adoption services from the perspective of an African American woman who once sought reproductive assistance. Kishi Animashaun Ducre's "Race(ing) to the Baby Market: The Political Economy of Overcoming Infertility" contextualizes her experience on the "baby train" in relation to the legacy of sacrifice by women of color whose bodies have been devalued. Her intersectional analysis demonstrates that "theory in the flesh" is an important lens for a political economy of consumption.[76] She concludes that any analysis of alternative paths to motherhood requires close attention to racial privilege and the subtle ways that whiteness informs the differential social valuing of prospective parents, surrogates, and donor gametes. Karen Hvidtfeldt Madsen also examines the global fertility industry but compares how various stakeholders frame the surrogacy experience. In "A Baby Made in India: The Transnational Surrogacy Business and New Metaphors of Motherhood," she contrasts recurrent metaphors used by prospective parents who blog about the process with narrative frameworks used by Indian surrogates. Hvidtfeldt Madsen finds that, despite fundamental disparities in agency and resources, both surrogate mothers and prospective parents challenge the binary opposition of altruism versus commercialism.

The next four chapters consider how the class dynamics of intensive mothering shape consumption in the United States. They show how key tenants of intensive mothering, such as the requirement that mothering be "child-centered, expert-guided, emotionally absorbing, labor-intensive, and financially expensive," have adapted to the changing media environment and dramatic growth of momprenuers.[77] More specifically, the chapters demonstrate that intensive mothering withstands a broadening definition of expertise. In "'We Were Introduced to Foods I Never Even Heard Of': Parents as Consumers on Reality Television," Cynthia Gordon examines how the TLC show *Honey, We're Killing the Kids* portrays parents as "compulsory consumers" of expert nutritional advice. Recurrent show segments reinscribe the authority of experts and present parents who fail to be "expert-guided" as blameworthy. By tracing how parents and experts are framed across these segments, Gordon demonstrates that diet, social class, and morality become entangled and shows why food consumption constitutes an increasingly important site for how new mothers signal their identity to others. In "Cultivating Community in the Commercial Marketplace: Blurred Boundaries in the 'Mommy' Blogosphere," Jennifer Borda examines the increasing role of consumerism in the influential and expanding mommy blogosphere. Her analysis of twenty prominent blogs not only finds significant resistance to expert-guided, authoritative parenting advice but also a growing preference for mommy blogs as a meaningful parenting resource.[78] Borda concludes that the drive to develop a marketable brand often comes at the cost of community. In so doing, the ideologies initially challenged in blogs are reified, thus mitigating their radical potential to redefine motherhood beyond the notion of the white, middle-class, and heteronormative mother/consumer. Kara Dillard's chapter, "Mompreneurs: Homemade Organic Baby Food and the Commodification of Intensive Mothering," identifies how the emerging momprenuer category alters the intensive mothering paradigm by establishing the mother-turned-entrepreneur as an authoritative expert. Comparing the websites of five leading organic baby food companies run by self-identified mompreneurs, Dillard outlines the risk-based appeals used to first legitimate the labor-intensive approach to baby food preparation and then market the products nationally. She concludes that the commodification of intensive mothering and rise of the momprenuer circumscribe problems women face regarding a work/family balance around middle-class interests. In "Maternal Crime in a Cathedral of Consumption," Sara Hayden reveals how the rules of intensive mothering and norms of middle-class consumption align to form a relatively strict code of conduct for highly educated and relatively affluent professional women. Hayden traces responses to a *New York Times* online commentary about Bridget Kevane, a Montana mother charged with child endangerment in 2007 for allowing her three children (then eight-, seven-, and three-year-olds) to accompany two twelve-year-old friends to a shopping mall without an adult. Reactions to the case not only reflected media-generated anxiety over the safety of children in public sites but also legitimated hypervigilance as a necessary risk management strategy for mothers, particularly those with class privilege. Although this case study stands as a counterpoint to previous chapters, in that Kevane put her needs before those of her children by choosing self-care over shopping with them, the punitive state response and biting online critiques of her actions documented by Hayden underscore the "powerful hold of intensive mothering and rules of consumption" witnessed across the volume.

The remaining essays explore how the marketplace imperative to maximize outputs not only informs the goods, services, and investments purchased on a child's behalf but also overvalues child-rearing practices and modes of play that frame consumption as a form of productivity. In "'Don't Worry, Mama Will Fix It!': Playing with the Mama Myth in Video Games," Shira Chess analyzes how practices of mothering are commodified into a form of play via the emerging market of video games designed for women. Chess analyzes how games such as *Cooking Mama: Chop and Shop* and *Babysitting Mama* rely on and perpetuate the philosophy of intensive mothering associated with new momism. "Mama" (the game's avatar) models a hypermomism that privileges self-sacrifice, care-giving, and domesticity over biology. As Chess concludes, "It ceases to matter whether the player is a mother in the real world, or for that matter is female, male, adult or child," because all are trained to reproduce the idealized white, middle-class Mama Myth in the gamespace and beyond. Although products such as video games and baby food clearly differ from the investment consumption associated with purchasing a home in a particular school district, a consistent economic logic underwrites the desire for such commodities: strategic inputs (e.g., food, toys, and schools) yield children who can compete educationally and become productive citizen-consumers. In "Motherhood and the Necessity of Invention: The Possibilities of Play in a Culture of Consumption," Christine Harold examines the notion of agency that defines the outcomes-based imperative motivating popular child-rearing philosophies and the proliferation of achievement toys. Despite key differences between attachment parenting (associated with William Sears) and structured or "tough love" parenting (associated with Richard Ferber), Harold argues that each philosophy "assumes that agency is something that is gifted to the child, bequeathed so to speak, through the implement of proper parenting." This assumption fuels the marketing and consumption of educational toys and services. Harold concludes by outlining an alternative view of agency offered by advocates of creative play (associated with Rudolf Steiner) that shifts focus from strategic inputs (flashcards) to imagination (found objects) and, in so doing, challenges the logic of consumption. Finally, the relationship between agency, consumption, and education is also explored by Lisa Flores in "Choosing to Consume, Choosing Whiteness: School Vouchers and the Racialized Politics of the Education 'Crisis.'" Focusing on pro-voucher discourse in debates over failing public schools, she argues that public support for private education is justified through narratives that highlight structural inequalities facing poor and nonwhite students while individualizing and privatizing the solution. According to Flores, the coupling of choice and mobility in the voucher debate should be ascribed to such broader cultural shifts as the rise of neoliberal multiculturalism. Layering her chapter with autoethnographic reflections that reveal how access to class and race privilege will shape the schooling of her own children, Flores seeks to denaturalize the rebranding of education from a "public good" to a "consumer good" and encourages further analysis of the relationship between neoliberalism and consumption.

Conclusion

At least since the nineteenth century, the division between mothering and the marketplace has been more a turnstile than a wall. As Victoria de Grazia notes, "It is the capacity of commodities to move between the customarily female spaces of the market and the household, between the world of production and the world of reproduction . . . that have forged modern definitions of motherhood."[79] The synergy between mothering and the marketplace demonstrated in our volume suggests that the division is, at this point, more rhetorical than structural, particularly for those with economic privilege. In the context of reproduction, if your country of origin prohibits access to fertility treatments due to age or sexuality, take an "IVF vacation." Regarding work/family balance, if your professional commitments make it difficult to achieve the norms of intensive mothering, outsource care-work or commodify it for others so you can work from home. Education is an investment that begins accumulating at birth (if not before) and increasingly accrues value through privatization. These mergers of mothering and commerce, public goods and consumer goods, define the business of motherhood, and a goal of our volume has been to understand how social inequality is a subsidiary product.

We thus approached the study of motherhood, consumption, and privilege with a number of questions. What markets and industries most define the business of motherhood and why? How is the relationship between mothering and marketplace reconciled? What aspects of market life are featured and obscured? What ideologies does the business of motherhood rely on and reinforce? In addressing such questions, our volume makes a case for analyzing consumption through the lens of communication studies. Our focus on axes of privilege, particularly social class, prompted a series of additional questions. In what ways do industries linked to reproduction, mothering, and childhood normalize and challenge hierarchies of race, nationality, and class? What narratives of privilege underwrite neoliberal motherhood and how are they contested? Other than economic capital, how are other types of capital (cultural, social, and emotional) leveraged to justify privilege and confer advantage? Such questions underscore the consequences of how we frame the business of motherhood and its role as an evolving life force of capitalism.

Notes

1. "Being a Smart Consumer When Choosing Fertility Tourism," *Global IVF Medical Fertility Tourism*, accessed September 27, 2014, http://globalivf.com/2013/06/21/traveling-abroad-for-fertility-tourism/.

2. Ira Basen, "Monetizing Mommy-hood," *The Sunday Edition*, Canadian Broadcast System, January 3, 2012, accessed May 1, 2012, http://www.cbc.ca/thesundayedition/coming-up/2012/01/03/coming-up—-monetizing-mommy-hood/.

3. For example, see: Claire Courchane, "For American Girl, Dolls Spell Dollars." *Washington Times*, June 16, 201, accessed May 1, 2012, http://www.washingtontimes.com/news/2011/jun/16/for-american-girl-dolls-spell-dollars/; Jane Bainbridge, "Feeding Off the Baby Boom," *Marketing* (June 3, 2009): 30–31.

4. Allison J. Pugh, *Longing and Belonging: Parents, Children, and Consumer Culture* (Berkeley, CA: University of California Press, 2009).

5. Amanda Bower, "Meet the Mompreneurs," Time Magazine, April 25, 2005, accessed May 1, 2012, http://www.time.com/time/magazine/article/0,9171,1053667,00.html#ixzz1zQHbxSFL.

6. Marissa Miley and Ann Mack, *The New Female Consumer: The Rise of the Real Mom*, Advertising Age White Paper, November 16, 2009, accessed September 1, 2013, http://adage.com/trend-reports/report.php?id=10.

7. "Breadwinner Moms," *Pew Social & Demographic Trends*, accessed August 28, 2013, http://www.pewsocialtrends.org/2013/05/29/breadwinner-moms/.

8. For example, see: Stefanie Ilgenfritz, "Another Role For Mom: Chief Financial Officer," *Wall Street Journal*, Oct 3, 2008, accessed May 1, 2012, http://blogs.wsj.com/juggle/2008/10/03/another-role-for-mom-chief-financial-officer/; Caryn Medved and Erika L. Kirby, "FAMILY CEOS: A Feminist Analysis of Corporate Mothering Discourses," *Management Communication Quarterly* 18, no. 4 (May 2005): 435–78.

9. Thyra Uth Thomsen and Elin Brandi Sørensen, "The First Four-wheeled Status Symbol: Pram Consumption as a Vehicle for the Construction of Motherhood Identity," *Journal Of Marketing Management* 22, no. 9/10 (November 2006): 907–27.

10. Linda Buchanan, *Rhetorics of Motherhood* (Carbondale; Edwardsville: Southern Illinois University Press, 2013), 115.

11. Karlyn Kohrs Campbell, *Man Cannot Speak for Her: Volume I; A Critical Study of Early Feminist Rhetoric* (New York: Praeger, 1989); Bonnie J. Dow and Mari Boor Tonn, "'Feminine Style and Political Judgement in the Rhetoric of Ann Richards," *Quarterly Journal of Speech* 79, no. 3 (August 1993): 286; Mari Boor Tonn, "Millitant Motherhood: Labor's Mary Harris 'Mother' Jones," *Quarterly Journal of Speech* 82, no. 1 (February 1996): 1; Christina R. Foust, "A Return to Feminine Public Virtue: Judge Judy and the Myth of the Tough Mother," *Women's Studies in Communication* 27, no. 3 (Fall 2004): 269–93; Katie L. Gibson and Amy L. Heyse, "'The Difference Between a Hockey Mom and a Pit Bull': Sarah Palin's Faux Maternal Persona and Performance of Hegemonic Masculinity at the 2008 Republican National Convention," *Communication Quarterly* 58, no. 3 (July 2010): 235–56.

12. Gibson and Heyse, "'The Difference Between a Hockey Mom and a Pit Bull,'" 253.

13. Sara Hayden, "Family Metaphors and the Nation: Promoting a Politics of Care through the Million Mom March," *Quarterly Journal of Speech* 89, no. 3 (August 2003): 212.

14. Mary Douglas Vavrus, "Opting Out Moms in the News," *Feminist Media Studies* 7, no. 1 (March 2007): 49; D. Lynn O'Brien Hallstein, "She Gives Birth, She's Wearing a Bikini: Mobilizing the Postpregnant Celebrity Mom Body to Manage

the Post–Second Wave Crisis in Femininity," *Women's Studies in Communication* 34, no. 2 (September 2011): 114.

15. Vavrus, "Opting Out Moms in the News," 52.

16. O'Brien Hallstein, "She Gives Birth, She's Wearing a Bikini," 115.

17. Ibid., 130.

18. Sara Hayden, "Constituting Savvy Aunties: From Childless Women to Child-Focused Consumers," *Women's Studies in Communication* 34, no. 1 (2011), 16, 17, 19.

19. Friedrich Engels and Tristram Hunt, *The Origin of the Family, Private Property and the State*, Reissue edition (London; New York: Penguin Classics, 2010), 199.

20. Kathryn Russell, "A Value-Theoretic Approach to Childbirth and Reproductive Engineering," in *Materialist Feminism: A Reader in Class, Difference, and Women's Lives*, ed. Chrys Ingraham and Rosemary Hennessy, 1st ed. (New York: Routledge, 1997), 330.

21. Silvia Federici, *Revolution at Point Zero: Housework, Reproduction, and Feminist Struggle* (PM Press, 2012); Lise Vogel, *Woman Questions: Essays for a Materialist Feminism* (New York: Routledge, 1995); Ellen Malos, *The Politics of Housework* (London; New York: Allison & Busby; distributed in the US by Schocken Books, 1980).

22. Arlie Russell Hochschild, *The Commercialization of Intimate Life: Notes from Home and Work* (Berkeley: University of California Press, 2003), 31.

23. Lise Vogel, "Domestic Labor Revisited," *Science & Society* 64, no. 2 (July 1, 2000), 163.

24. Melinda Vandenbeld Giles, *Mothering in the Age of Neoliberalism*, 1st ed. (Bradford, Ontario: Demeter Press, 2014), 5.

25. Ibid.; Jennifer A. Reich, "Neoliberal Mothering and Vaccine Refusal Imagined Gated Communities and the Privilege of Choice," *Gender & Society*, May 9, 2014, 0891243214532711; Jo Littler, "The Rise of the 'Yummy Mummy': Popular Conservatism and the Neoliberal Maternal in Contemporary British Culture," *Communication, Culture & Critique* 6, no. 2 (June 1, 2013): 227–43, doi:10.1111/cccr.12010; Davi Johnson Thornton, "Neuroscience, Affect, and the Entrepreneurialization of Motherhood," *Communication and Critical/Cultural Studies* 8, no. 4 (2011): 399–424, doi:10.1080/14791420.2011.610327.

26. David Harvey, *A Brief History of Neoliberalism*, 1st ed. (Oxford; New York: Oxford University Press, 2007), 2.

27. Vandenbeld Giles, *Mothering in the Age of Neoliberalism*, 15.

28. Vavrus, "Opting Out Moms in the News"; Littler, "The Rise of the 'Yummy Mummy'"; O'Brien Hallstein, "She Gives Birth, She's Wearing a Bikini."

29. Littler, "The Rise of the 'Yummy Mummy,'" 239.

30. Thornton, "Neuroscience, Affect, and the Entrepreneurialization of Motherhood."

31. Ronald Walter Greene, "Rhetoric and Capitalism: Rhetorical Agency as Communicative Labor," *Philosophy & Rhetoric* 37, no. 3 (August 2004): 188–206; Ronald Walter Greene, "Rhetorical Capital: Communicative Labor, Money/Speech, and

Neo-Liberal Governance," *Communication & Critical/Cultural Studies* 4, no. 3 (September 2007): 327–31, doi:10.1080/14791420701472866.

32. Greene, "Rhetorical Capital," 328.

33. Greene, "Rhetoric and Capitalism," 189.

34. Although Sarah Banet-Weiser and Roopali Mukherjee situate their 2012 book, *Commodity Activism,* within the "nascent field of critical consumer studies" rather than communication studies, their focus on consumption, subjectivity, and activism aligns with Pezzullo in particular. Phaedra C. Pezzullo, "Resisting 'National Breast Cancer Awareness Month': The Rhetoric of Counterpublics and Their Cultural Performances," *Quarterly Journal of Speech* 89, no. 4 (November 2003): 345–65; John M. Sloop, "People Shopping," in *Rhetoric, Materiality, & Politics*, ed. Barbara A. Biesecker and John Louis Lucaites (Peter Lang, 2009), 67–98; Christine Harold, "On Target: Aura, Affect, and the Rhetoric of 'Design Democracy,'" *Public Culture* 21, no. 3 (Fall 2009): 599–618, doi:10.1215/08992363-2009-010; Roopali Mukherjee and Sarah Banet-Weiser, *Commodity Activism: Cultural Resistance in Neoliberal Times* (New York: NYU Press, 2012). Also, see Sara Hayden, "Constituting Savvy Aunties: From Childless Women to Child-Focused Consumers," *Women's Studies in Communication* 34, no. 1 (2011): 116, doi:10.1080/07491409.2011.566531.

35. Greene, "Rhetorical Capital," 327.

36. While Dana Cloud identifies private consumption as characteristic of therapeutic discourse, her primary goal is to delineate the therapeutic as a strategy of contemporary capitalism. Similarly, Greg Dickinson has examined the relationship between consumer culture and citizenship following September 11 and the materiality of consumption in commercial sites such as Starbucks, Wild Oats Marketplace, and the FlatIron Crossing mall but places primacy on citizenship, materiality, and rhetorics of place over consumption. Dana L. Cloud, *Control and Consolation in American Culture and Politics: Rhetoric of Therapy*, 1st ed. (Thousand Oaks: SAGE Publications, Inc, 1997), 161; Dickinson, "Joe's Rhetoric Finding Authenticity at Starbucks;" Greg Dickinson and CM Maugh, "Placing Visual Rhetoric: Finding Material Comfort in Wild Oats Market," in *Defining Visual Rhetoric*, ed. Charles A Hill and Marguerite Helmers (Mahwah, NJ: Lawrence Erlbaum Associates, 2004), 259–76; Dickinson, "Selling Democracy"; Jessie Stewart and Greg Dickinson, "Enunciating Locality in the Postmodern Suburb: FlatIron Crossing and the Colorado Lifestyle," *Western Journal of Communication* 72, no. 3 (July 2008): 280–307, doi:10.1080/10570310802210148.

37. Daniel Miller, "Consumption," in *Handbook of Material Culture*, ed. Chris Tilley et al. (SAGE, 2006), 34.

38. See, Pezzullo, "Contextualizing Boycotts and Buycotts"; Plec and Pettenger, "Greenwashing Consumption."

39. Jo Littler, "What's Wrong with Ethical Consumption?," in *Ethical Consumption: A Critical Introduction*, ed. Tania Lewis (London: Routledge, 2011), 28; Jeremy Gilbert, "Against the Commodification of Everything," *Cultural Studies* 22, no. 5 (2008): 553.

40. Juliet Schor, "Tackling Turbo Consumption," *Cultural Studies* 22, no. 5 (2008): 594.

41. Research within marketing, for example, examines the role of consumption objects in identity construction during key life transitions such as motherhood, divorce, and when adult children move out of the home. This research draws distinctions between a product's "signal value," what it expresses about the self to others, and its "experiential value" based on a consumer's personal history with the product. The cases studies in this volume, however, expand that focus by also exploring the relational value associated with consumption. What, for example, does a mother's purchase communicate to and about a child? How does the process of consumption foster or forestall relationships between the consumer and merchant or service provider? Such questions have particular relevance for nutritional and educational consumption as well as the international fertility industry examined by our contributors. See, Margaret Hogg, Carolyn F. Curasi, and Pauline Maclaran, "The (Re-)Configuration of Production and Consumption in Empty Nest Households/Families," *Consumption, Markets & Culture*, 7, no. 4 (2004): 239–59; Margaret Hogg, Pauline Maclaran, and Carolyn F. Curasi, "Consumption, Role Transitions and the Re-construction of the Self: An Exploratory Study of Social Capital within the Context of Transitional Consumers," *European Advances of Consumer Research* 6 (2003) 258–62; Thyra Uth Thomsen and Elin Brandi Sørensen, "The First Four-wheeled Status Symbol: Pram Consumption as a Vehicle for the Construction of Motherhood Identity," *Journal Of Marketing Management* 22, no. 9/10 (November 2006), accessed May 1, 2012: 907–27. *Business Source Elite*, EBSCO*host.*

42. As the preceding discussion of Peuzzlo, Sloop, and Harold notes, consumption is beginning to be addressed more directly in communication studies. For example, Christine Harold's 2007 book, *OurSpace*, examined evolutions in anticorporate activism—contrasting formative culture jammers such as Adbusters and the Yes Men with emerging efforts around the Creative Commons movement. Her more recent work shifts from tracing critiques of corporate branding to analyzing the role of product design in fostering relationships between consumers and corporations. Other notable exceptions include the emerging scholarship on environmental consumption and consumer activism. See, Pezzullo, "Resisting 'National Breast Cancer Awareness Month'"; Pezzullo, "Contextualizing Boycotts and Buycotts"; Sloop, "People Shopping"; Harold, *OurSpace*; Harold, "On Target"; Tinnel, "Scripting Just Sustainability"; Plec and Pettenger, "Greenwashing Consumption"; Powell, "The Great American Meatout"; Hayden, "Constituting Savvy Aunties."

43. Zygmunt Bauman, *Consuming Life* (Cambridge; Malden, MA: Polity Press, 2007).

44. Ibid., 47

45. Mary Douglas and Baron C. Isherwood, *The World of Goods: Towards an Anthropology of Consumption (1979; repr.*, London: Routledge, 1996), 41.

46. Ibid., xxi.

47. Mark Gottdiener, *New Forms of Consumption: Consumers, Culture, and Commodification* (Lanham, MD: Rowman & Littlefield Publishers, 2000), 78.

48. Daniel Thomas Cook, "The Missing Child in Consumption Theory," *Journal of Consumer Culture* 8, no. 2 (2008): 234.

49. Ibid., 237.

50. Mikhail Bakhtin, *The Dialogic Imagination: Four Essays*. Ed. Michael Holquist. Trans. Caryl Emerson and Michael Holquist. Austin and London: University of Texas Press, 1981, 279–80.

51. Ibid., 280.

52. Karma R. Chávez and Cindy L. Griffin, *Standing in the Intersection: Feminist Voices, Feminist Practices in Communication Studies* (Albany: SUNY Press, 2012), 6.

53. Kimberle Crenshaw, "Demarginalizing the Intersection of Race and Sex: A Black Feminist Critique of Antidiscrimination Doctrine, Feminist Theory and Antiracist Politics," *The University of Chicago Legal Forum* 140 (1989), 139; Also, see Kimberle Crenshaw, "Mapping the Margins: Intersectionality, Identity Politics, and Violence against Women of Color," *Stanford Law Review* 43, no. 6 (July 1991): 1241, doi:10.2307/1229039.

54. For a summary of recent intersectional scholarship, see Chávez and Griffin, *Standing at the Intersection.*

55. Jennifer C. Nash, "Re-Thinking Intersectionality," *Feminist Review* 89, no. 1 (2008), 10.

56. Peggy McIntosh, "White Privilege: Unpacking the Invisible Knapsack," *Peace and Freedom* (August 1989): 10.

57. Allison J. Pugh, *Longing and Belonging, 85–86.*

58. Ibid., 124.

59. Indeed, Chávez and Griffin note, "Although related fields in sociology, linguistics, and political science regularly talked of social class, communication scholars rarely address social class." Of the recent scholarship that acknowledges the intersectionality of class and race privilege, Lester Olson and Joan Faber McAlister offers the most direct call to encourage further study of social class as a relevant axis of privilege. See Chavez, *Standing in the Intersection, 14*; Lester Olson, "Intersecting Audiences: Public Commentary Concerning Audre Lorde's Speech, 'Uses of the Erotic: The Erotic as Power,'" in *Standing in the Intersection: Feminist Voices, Feminist Practices in Communication Studies*, ed. Karma R. Chávez and Cindy Griffin (Albany: SUNY Press, 2012), 125–46; Helene A. Shugart, "Sumptuous Texts: Consuming 'Otherness' in the Food Film Genre," *Critical Studies in Media Communication* 25, no. 1 (2008): 68–90, doi:10.1080/15295030701849928; Danielle Endres and Mary Gould, "'I Am Also in the Position to Use My Whiteness to Help Them Out': The Communication of Whiteness in Service Learning," *Western Journal of Communication* 73, no. 4 (October 2009): 418–36, doi:10.1080/10570310903279083; Joan Faber McAlister, "Good Neighbors: Covenantal Rhetoric, Moral Aesthetics, and the Resurfacing of Identity Politics," *Howard Journal of Communications* 21, no. 3 (2010): 273–93, doi:10.1080

/10646175.2010.496674; Christopher R. Groscurth, "Paradoxes of Privilege and Participation: The Case of the American Red Cross," *Communication Quarterly* 59, no. 3 (July 2011): 296–14, doi:10.1080/01463373.2011.583498.

60. See, Reay, *Class Work*; Gillies, "Raising the 'Meritocracy' Parenting and the Individualization of Social Class"; Madeleine Leonard, "Children, Childhood and Social Capital: Exploring the Links," *Sociology* 39, no. 4 (October 1, 2005): 605–22; Nixon, "Working-class Lesbian Parents' Emotional Engagement with Their Children's Education"; Joshua Freistadt and Lisa Strohschein, "Family Structure Differences in Family Functioning Interactive Effects of Social Capital and Family Structure," *Journal of Family Issues* 34, no. 7 (July 1, 2013): 952–74.

61. Reay, *Class Work, 82.*

62. Refer to endnote 60.

63. Thornton, "Neuroscience, Affect, and the Entrepreneurialization of Motherhood."

64. On the need to develop an intersectional model for affect and emotional capital, see Margaret Wetherell, *Affect and Emotion a New Social Science Understanding* (Los Angeles; London: SAGE, 2012), http://site.ebrary.com/id/10568231.

65. Andrea O'Reilly, *Mother Outlaws: Theories and Practices of Empowered Mothering* (Toronto: Women's Press, 2004); Andrea O'Reilly, *From Motherhood to Mothering: The Legacy of Adrienne Rich's Of Woman Born* (Albany: State University of New York Press, 2004); Andrea O'Reilly, *Maternal Theory: Essential Readings* (Toronto: Demeter Press, 2007); Andrea O'Reilly, *Feminist Mothering* (Albany: State University of New York Press, 2008); Andrea O'Reilly, *Twenty-First-Century Motherhood: Experience, Identity, Policy, Agency* (New York: Columbia University Press, 2010); Andrea O'Reilly, *Encyclopedia of Motherhood* (Thousand Oaks, Calif.: Sage Publications, 2010); Sharon Hays, *The Cultural Contradictions of Motherhood* (New Haven: Yale University Press, 1996); Susan J. Douglas and Meredith W. Michaels, *The Mommy Myth: The Idealization of Motherhood and How It Has Undermined All Women* (New York: Free Press, 2005).

66. Although O'Reilly holds that, "Any discussion of maternal empowerment must begin with the distinction," Lynn O'Brien Hallstein has begun to challenge its viability in a post–second wave context. She delineates the numerous limitations in maintaining the strict binary including the failure to "recognize how contemporary maternity is constituted by both institutionalized motherhood and empowered mothering." See, O'Reilly, *Mother Outlaws*; D. Lynn O'Brien Hallstein, *White Feminists and Contemporary Maternity: Purging Matrophobia* (New York: Palgrave Macmillan, 2010).

67. Daniel Thomas Cook, "Introduction: Specifying Mothers/Motherhoods," *Journal of Consumer Culture* 13, no. 2 (July 1, 2013): 77.

68. Ibid., 77.

69. Hays, *The Cultural Contradictions of Motherhood.*

70. Ibid., 8.

71. Ibid., 54.

72. Douglas and Michaels, *The Mommy Myth.*

73. Ibid., 4.

74. Lynn O'Brien Hallstein, "New Momism," in *Encyclopedia of Motherhood*, ed. Andrea O'Reilly (SAGE, 2010), 915.

75. Douglas and Michaels, *The Mommy Myth.*

76. Chavez, *Standing in the Intersection, 7.*

77. Hays, *The Cultural Contradictions of Motherhood, 8.*

78. Although Nathanson and Tuley offer a compelling feminist critique of the advice industry, they fail to account for the rise of mommy blogs as a preferred and authoritative source of advice. Jessica Ann Nathanson and Laura Camile Tuley, *Mother Knows Best: Talking Back to the Experts* (Toronto: Demeter Press, 2008), 1.

79. Victoria de Grazia and Ellen Furlough, *The Sex of Things: Gender and Consumption in Historical Perspective* (Berkeley: University of California Press, 1996), 7–8.

1
The Golden Egg

The Business of Making Mothers through Egg Donation

Charlotte Kroløkke

Determined to give pregnancy one more chance, Rita, at the age of fifty, with money from her divorce settlement, went to Spain for egg donation and fertility treatment.[1] She is not alone. Divergent national legislation on access and availability of infertility treatments combined with cheap flights and a generation of women who are used to—and can afford to—travel all contribute to the willingness to seek fertility treatment abroad.[2] As noted by one British woman in a newspaper account about her choice to go to Spain for egg donation and fertility treatment: "I trekked across South Africa in the back of a truck. I can do Spain, for God's sake."[3] The above two cases, and cases like them, illustrate how privilege—not only financial privilege but privileges linked to the cultural capital associated with previous travel experiences—make going abroad for treatment a choice accessible to some.

Rooted in feminist communication scholarship,[4] this chapter discusses the interplay of consumption with discourses on fertility as it unfolds in a select facet of the European market for assisted reproduction. Similar to the fertility market in the United States,[5] the European market is stratified along categories of age, gender, race, and education, while also complicated by divergent national legislation, different health care systems, and cultural and linguistic differences. To provide the reader with a conceptual frame, I first situate the European market in fertility by linking fertility travel and reproductive privilege with nationality, and then turn to a feminist communication approach to discuss the ways that oocytes are gendered and discursively framed as gifts. The material included for analysis centers on the mediated representations of Spanish gamete donors, including the construction of IVF holidays in Spain and the Czech Republic. In the second half of the chapter, I turn to interviews with three Danish women who negotiate their choice to travel as a form of entrepreneurship, thereby framing fertility travel as well as oocyte donation as an acceptable and potentially empowering choice that not only fulfills their "natural" desire for a child but also, through economic compensation, empowers a Spanish or Czech woman. Fertility travelers depart in important ways from the marketing of fertility travel as a type of "fertility holiday," however. Instead, they foreground the trauma and emotional upheavals involved and, in so doing, these Danish women rhetorically position fertility travel as a resistance strategy.

Framing the Issue: Passport to Motherhood

The travel undertaken for fertility treatments is not unlike the traveling involved in search of medical treatments. In a recent special issue on medical migrations, Elizabeth Roberts and Nancy Scheper-Hughes define medical travel as situated in the nexus between globalization, mobility, neoliberalism, and global health care.[6] It involves the movement of bodies and body parts, such as that undertaken in transplant tourism, in which not only the recipient but also donor bodies travel to donate an organ. Moreover, it makes particular destinations such as India, Barbados, Spain, or California into hub destinations for different fertility treatments.[7]

The transnational business in motherhood relies on a conventional set of gendered stratifications.[8] Feminist intersectional theorists such as Kimberlé Crenshaw and Patricia Hill Collins make explicit how gendered stratifications including different forms of privilege associated with, for example, race, gender, class, sexuality, and nationality intersect.[9] Similarly, Karen Barad develops the concept of intra-action, which also can be used to illustrate how phenomena such as race, gender, and class intra-act in sometimes surprising ways.[10] In the case of traveling for egg donation, the European market is characterized by a desire and even a legal requirement to match recipient and donor phenotypes.[11] This frequently privileges fair skinned and educated donors, and this is especially true in cases of Northern European fertility travelers. Motherhood is, thus, created through the reinstatement of inequalities between privileged women (and men) in the globalized North or West and comparatively poorer women in the South or East who become, as Margaret Jolly notes, the (new) reproductive assistants.[12] Young, attractive, fair-skinned women currently attending a university and/or already mothers (who have proven fertility) are particularly attractive to the Northern European traveler, and thus, to the fertility industry at large.

The business of making motherhood through transnational egg donation clearly underscores economic privilege as a key to fertility travel. While some Danish women can afford to travel abroad for egg donation, others cannot. And while some Spanish and Czech women can afford fertility treatment in their own countries, others cannot. Other forms of privilege include access and availability of the reproductive technique, which constrain some, while others are able to cross not only, at times, legal and moral but also national borders.[13] Lesbian couples are, for example, denied treatment in some countries (e.g., Italy), while permitted treatment in others (e.g., Denmark). In Norway, the fertilized egg has to be returned to the woman that it came from, and thus, Norwegian women in need of egg donation have to go elsewhere. Women older than forty-six years of age are denied treatment in Denmark yet welcomed in Spain or the Czech Republic. Reproductive privilege, therefore, is intricately linked to not only economic privilege but also privilege related to nationality, sexuality, and age. While reasons to travel vary greatly, fertility travel is often framed by travelers as a "forced" experience.[14]

Positioning fertility travel within a global nexus of reproduction, Marcia Inhorn develops the concept of *reproflows*.[15] Reproflows refers to the ways that reproductive matter and reproductive assistants, as well as receivers, move or flow in an increasingly transnational market in reproductive services. For example, white American egg donors fly to the Middle East to donate eggs intended for economically privileged Middle Eastern couples.[16] The concept of reproflows captures, Inhorn argues, the transnational movements that unfold when technologies, bodies, knowledge, and reproductive cells cross nation states and enter the sphere of commerce, while also illustrating how these are frequently gendered and crisscross in interesting and even unpredictable ways.[17] Reproflows play with the imaginations of bodily fluids flowing—extracted from and inserted into other bodies—while also presenting a framework for understanding the transnational dynamics at stake, including how technological and clinical expertise flow across nation states and how old and new stratifications reappear.

Fertility travel, like medical travel, draws on this rhetoric of entrepreneurship. Laura Mamo, for example, links the contemporary transnational business of making mothers with late-modern notions of entrepreneurship.[18] Historically, the individualist and entrepreneurial ethos of the West (including the notion that the body is privately and individually owned) has worked to cement women's rights over their own bodies. The rhetoric of choice is now, however, used to make egg donation and fertility travel legitimate reproductive choices that individual women can make.[19] Transnational egg donation is, however, doubly situated—not only in the nexus of globalization and in the neoliberal marketplace but also frequently as a form of gifting while, simultaneously, made into a commodity.[20] I, therefore, now turn to feminist communication perspectives to illustrate the ways in which oocytes in the European market in fertility are rhetorically constructed as both commodities and gifts.

Consuming the Priceless: Eggs as Commodities, Eggs as Gifts

Feminist communication scholarship helps illustrate how some cells are rhetorically framed as more attractive than other cells.[21] The commoditization of gametes is facilitated by several key developments that also rhetorically draw on the notion of gifting: for one, new reproductive technologies make it possible for human oocytes to be harvested, frozen, banked, and, importantly, thawed for later use;[22] yet commoditization is linked to the spread of global capitalism and the speed at which (in)fertile individuals and biomatter now move.[23] In this section, I wish to outline the feminist communication issues at stake—advancing the idea that when biogenetic substances move from the realm of reproduction to the commodity sphere, specific ideas and values are assigned to particular gametes.

The commoditization of gametes is connected to earlier discourses on the rhetoric of desire and scarcity: Why, for example, "waste" human eggs, when they can give someone else the "gift of life"?[24] To Rene Almeling, conventional gender ideologies intersect with discourses on altruism and commodification. Not only does this rhetoric shape the US fertility market, it also sets the stage through which egg and sperm donors come to understand their reproductive contributions.[25] Sperm donation gets framed as "a job," she argues, while egg donation becomes discursively constructed as "a gift" or, as she states: "It is possible that women donating eggs will be perceived as altruistic helpers who want nothing more than for recipients to have families, while men donating sperm will be construed as employees performing a job with little care for the bank's customers."[26] In this manner, gamete donation is rhetorically framed to fit conventional understandings of gender.

The ways in which reproductive cells become particular commodities illustrate the workings of a postmodern consumer culture in which sperm and eggs are commodities infused with cultural meanings.[27] In fact, Catherine Waldby and Robert Mitchell argue that gametes are always embedded with cultural values, or rather, "bodies *bring with them* variously ontological values."[28] Human eggs cannot be understood as stable entities or simply reproductive cells, but rather they must be seen as dynamic cells imploded with varying and shifting "biovalues,"[29] as they cross not only time and space but also "varying cultural terrains."[30] Reproductive cells are not only products for sale but are also marketed as particular types of commodities: "One never buys sperm, but 'Caucasian' or 'Hispanic,' 'Muslim' or 'Jewish' sperm," for example.[31] The commoditization and objectification of reproductive cells reveal, in interesting ways, how youth and intelligence combined with attractiveness and race are important in the selection and marketing of gamete donors. Clinics as well as oocyte recipients expect a racial match, while the recipients' desire for an "intelligent" donor produces requests for donors currently attending university.

Reproductive cells exist, as noted by Elizabeth Roberts, in the uncomfortable zone between the home/market, the private/public, value/dignity, and subject/object.[32] This is especially the case with oocyte donation. As Almeling notes: "It may be cultural norms associated with the family, not the workplace, that influence processes of valuation in this market, as these bodily goods are intended to help people have children. Traditionally, ideals of femininity and motherhood have portrayed women as denizens of the private sphere who are selfless, caring, and devoted to others, while ideals of masculinity and fatherhood situate men as hardworking, emotionally distant breadwinners who inhabit the public sphere."[33] The processes involved in extraction and insertion of human ova involves removing what has the appearance of something private, and perhaps even sacred, and positioning it into the market economy. Danish national debates on oocyte donation illustrate a general discomfort with this move while also underscoring the gendered dimensions. For example, in the Danish debates, sperm is narrated as "naturally" traveling outside of the male body, while oocytes are framed as not only inside the individual woman but also, to a higher extent, mirroring her identity.[34]

Oocytes are in fact often framed as too priceless to enter the commodity sphere.[35] Altruism and, consequently, the rhetoric of gifting is the dominant narrative of not only the Scandinavian countries but also the fertility industry at large.[36] It works to remove oocytes from the market sphere and repositions donation in light of a higher purpose.[37] The altruistic narrative resolves the potentially unfeminine motivations, while facilitating a narrative that is also preferred by the intended parents.[38] Janice Raymond situates this in light of conventional gendered roles: "It is the language of selflessness and responsibility toward others in which women's very possibilities are framed."[39] Moreover, Raymond notes that altruism cements women's status as reproductive consumers/assistants, whether it concerns producing eggs (as maternal donors) or producing babies (as mothers).[40]

Few scholars have systematically studied the commodity/gift framework from the perspective of the donors.[41] Yet, in a rare ethnographic study on US egg donors, Anne Pollock illustrates how egg donors themselves engage in the commodity/gift sphere by strategically exchanging one commodity/gift (their ova) for another (money).[42] In her study, the US donors used egg donation to maintain a middle-class lifestyle, such as pay off credit card debt or go on an expensive trip, for example.[43] In a similar study, albeit with Spanish donors, Gemma Orobitg and Carles Salazar found that egg donors rework economic interests and altruism, moving between objectification and subjectification, thereby becoming what the authors describe as "cultural bricoleurs."[44] Becoming a donor thus involves not only administering medical treatments and exchanging eggs out of a desire to help others, but it also involves enabling a particular lifestyle or fulfilling particular dreams and desires.

Consequently, egg donation continues to confuse the gift/commodity dichotomy while collapsing conventional distinctions between nature/nurture, and biology/culture; meanwhile, in the case of transnational egg donation, it also challenges our notion of the making of nationality and kin.[45] I agree with Waldby and Roberts when they point to the limitations of the gift/commodity dichotomy: "Ideas of gift and commodity are inadequate to conceptualize exhaustively their technicity, and the ways this technicity mediates the values and relations associated with particular kinds of tissues."[46] Meanwhile, gifting is, as Mauss notes, a particular mode for circulating commodities.[47] The Danish women traveling to clinics in Spain both express a sense of indebtedness to their anonymous and gift-giving Spanish donors while also hoping to be recipients of at least two "good-looking" eggs.[48]

Turning now to the empirical framework, I wish to apply a feminist communication perspective to illustrate how the business of making mothers through egg donation draws on conventional assumptions related to maternity, nationality, and class. I focus my attention first on the clinical discourses, including the development of IVF holidays, while also paying attention to the presentation and mediation of egg donation and the imagined donor. Toward the end of the analysis, I center my discussion on the business of making biological mothers and do so in light of the narratives told by three Danish women. These are women who are part of a larger interview study and women who have already traveled to Spain for egg donation because Spanish and Czech clinics have almost no waiting lists on egg donation.[49] The choice to center my analysis on Spain and the Czech Republic is made because they are the two countries chosen for egg donation by Danish women.

The Mediation and Commoditization of Oocytes and Fertility Travel

With a reported 187 IVF facilities, Spain is a prominent European center for fertility treatments and egg donation. Especially prominent, in the Spanish context, is the Instituto Valenciano de Infertilidad (IVI). IVI exemplifies the workings of a transnational market in fertility by offering expert fertility treatments in all major Spanish cities (including the coastal city of

Alicante) and collaborating with the World Egg Bank—the world's largest online and US based registry of eggs. At the clinic in Alicante, foreign patients receive egg donation and fertility treatments at a lower price than in the United States, while the clinic's success rate matches or is even superior to the success rates of other Western European and North American clinics. Access, availability, and location (including a comfortable climate, tourist attractions, and the reputation of warm and friendly locales) all make Spain a desirable destination for fertility travel.

In the marketing of the partnership between IVI and the World Egg Bank, traveling to Spain is positioned not as a last resort but as the best choice. A trip to Spain involves the highly administered reproflows of infertile bodies and frozen or fresh biogenetic substance that move in sync—thawed and made fertile in the warm (friendly) climate of Spain—an already desirable tourist destination. As noted by the program: "You travel to Spain for your donor egg thaw, fertilization, and embryo transfer,"[50] and in this way, egg donation is made to appear more like a treatment than reproductive work already (and naturally) directed toward the intended parent ("*your* donor thaw"). In addition to what is framed as expert fertility treatment, patients reiterate the holiday feel in their own descriptions of oocyte donation in Spain. As noted by one traveler: "It's been a very nice experience and we spent our summer holidays in the Costa Daurada."[51]

Traveling to Spain for fertility treatment is, in the marketing of the different clinics, rhetorically intertwined with other forms of traveling. For example, IVF Spain, which is also located in Alicante, places their advertisements in the inflight magazine of the airline Norwegian, transforming their treatment into holistic and ecofriendly fertility services based on "respect for life" and a "natural balance." Placed in the inflight magazine and thus, addressed to the traveler who is already on the go, the clinic positions itself as engaged in "ethical practice," welcoming future clients to their clinic in Alicante, offering their care and treatment in Norwegian, English, and German.

Dr. Juan Garcia Velasco, director of IVI Madrid, attributes the Spanish success in transnational reproduction to what he refers to as its high quality reproductive healthcare, a liberal legal framework, and the large availability of oocyte donors, thus, short waiting lists.[52] According to the director of IVI Valencia, Dr. Carlos Perez, permissive legislation that allows for the donation of unneeded tissues and organs is an important facet of the Spanish success.[53] As noted by Dr. Velasco, "Spain is the leading country in the world for all organ donation"—speaking not only to what he frames as "genuine" altruism—authentically Spanish, but also to the aforementioned notion of scarcity/desire, reinstating here a narrative of giving away what otherwise is not needed.[54] Nowhere is the current Spanish recession, including high unemployment rates among young women, including young immigrant women in Spain,[55] framed as an economic motivator for donation, and this is in spite of the fact that a majority of egg donors say that financial compensation is an important, if not the only, reason for donating.[56]

IVI Spain does not allow the intended parents to pick the egg donor of their choice. Instead, as required by Spanish law, recipients and donors are matched along ethnicity, hair color, height, and body type. Aware of the importance of the Internet in marketing the services available, however, IVI engages in visual representations of what could be "your" egg donor. While the information is mostly directed at attracting future donors, it is also information to which intended parents turn. As noted by Tober,[57] it is a representation that potentially reproduces reproductive stratifications depicting who the most desirable donor is likely to be.

On their website, IVI Spain plays up images of modern, urban facilities with attractive donors.[58] The IVI logo with the blue soft line next to the "I" is, according to IVI, a visual representation of the pregnant belly. Meanwhile, the image of a state-of-the-art facility is strengthened not only by IVI's reported international clientele[59] but also by its reported presence of medical doctors from different countries.

As depicted on the IVI website, the imagined or model IVI donors are not only young but seemingly urban (in dress), and not particularly Spanish "looking"—representing instead a new Spain in which the differences between the intended parents, frequently arriving from the UK, Germany, and Scandinavia, and the donors are both minimized and interestingly, also exoticized. Rather than representing a traditional Spain, they represent a global, modern Spain while articulating conventional gendered aesthetics as well: The egg donor positions her head in a classical feminized pose—smiling, inviting, and seemingly forthcoming to the onlookers. Meanwhile, the sperm donor is made to appear more masculine—looking straight at the onlookers, more solemn, and with face stubble. The more urban aesthetics and almost pan-European white and heterosexed appearance reinforces the assumption that the donor could be from anywhere in Western Europe, perhaps a university student, while the gendered aesthetics work to enhance her attractiveness. Economically less privileged, perhaps, the potential donor performs gender in a legitimate and eligible way and is made to appear to match the intended parents. In the visual representation, attractiveness and happiness go hand in hand symbolically signifying a donor who is healthy and empowered. This is a donor who willingly and happily (not desperately) donates biogenetic substance.

Egg donation is, in the online material, constructed in light of altruism and solidarity both: Women helping women. Donation is, thus, made to appear within a single-sexed model in which Spanish women, in this case, help other (European) women achieve what is constructed as their "natural" desire for motherhood. The donors are not only young and healthy but, in this construction, they are sensitive to other women's needs and, thus, the donors perform a recognizable and legitimate feminine (and heteronormative) performance. While advanced maternal age and poor response to ovarian stimulation are the most frequent reasons for egg donation,[60] the online marketing material focuses on early menopause and illnesses as not only primary but also perhaps more acceptable reasons likely to foster donor sympathy with the infertile woman. This representation supports more conventional and heteronormative ideals of motherhood including what may appear as acceptable maternal age.

While new reproductive technologies have the potential to deconstruct essentialist understandings of femininity and masculinity, not surprisingly, the online representation of the imagined Spanish donor is conformist in supporting the institutions of femininity and masculinity both.[61] Moreover, while the bodies presented on the website are clearly constructed bodies, the representations privilege not only youth and attractiveness but also, through groomed appearance and forthcoming performance, imagination of a friendly Spanish culture and perhaps even the intellectually gifted, thus stratifying donation in terms of not only race (light skin) and sexuality (heterosexed, feminine bodies) but also in terms of intra-actions related to appearance (attractiveness, height, weight, eye color, hair color) as well as class (education and the presumption of intelligence). The visual representation also illustrates how a donor preferably performs a coherent representation of herself, including an emphasis on a conventionally gendered aesthetics.

Journeys to Motherhood: The Rhetorical Construction of IVF Holidays

The marketing of fertility travel plays not only on the dreamscapes of future parenthood but reframes what may be uncomfortable fertility treatments to pleasurable, transformative experiences. The development of European brokerage companies attentive only to managing the practical needs of the foreign clientele speak to this. IVF Spain is a company designed to meet the needs of the international patients.[62] On their website, Spanish classical guitar music is combined with images of palm trees, photos of the collaborating clinics, pristine Alicante beaches, 3D fetal images, blue skies, and the image of an already existing blond blue-eyed baby, made into a puzzle, only missing one piece—the egg which is carefully positioned by the doctor's hand into the puzzle, thus completing this seductive image. In the textual presentation, the company reassures us that their outmost concern is stress reduction, and one potential hurdle to pregnancy is made to disappear. This brokerage company, run by a British family, introduces Northern comforts and cultural values to the warm, friendly South: air-conditioned transportation, British drivers, punctuality, and a free phone. Thus, the foreignness involved in traveling to Spain is constrained to a warm climate, pleasant music, beautiful beaches, friendly people, and great food.[63]

The marketing material of "Your IVF Vacation" in the Czech Republic similarly combines fertility treatments with the comforts of creating a home away from home.[64] Here the visual representations and the rhetorical strategies rest with old historic cities and scenic landscapes. Nowhere does this provider feature the treatments that it sells or mediates. The traces of the matter, including perhaps uncomfortable treatments, sterilized containers, stirrups, and needles, are reworked into sophisticated technology and most saliently, in this context, personalized and comfortable care. Here a prospective client can become pregnant while also enjoying the historic sites of the Czech Republic and perhaps even, once again, fall in love.

This reworking of infertility illustrates an interesting ambivalence in which treatments are for sale yet also largely invisible and repackaged in light of a romantic holiday theme or cultural tourism—visiting historic chateaus or comfortable spas, for instance. This Czech brokerage company communicatively manages the insecurities involved in traveling for fertility treatments with a visit to, as noted in the marketing material, the "Mother of Cities"[65]—Prague—and the creation of new personal relations, rewritten into "your" Czech family. The family theme is present, not only as far as the clients' desire for pregnancy is concerned, but also in the company's self-representation. Pictures of the owner's own family including her two sons are substantiated with her own personal history: her move away from the Czech Republic to Australia during the Communist years (another form of fleeing), and their later return to the Czech Republic, is retold. The narratives serve to connect at a more personal level with the clients' own reproductive travel or, as framed by them, a form of reproductive fleeing.

The testimonials available on the agency's website are supportive of this framing and position a trip to Brno as one engaged in multiple forms of family building. As noted by one client, a trip to the Czech Republic enabled new forms of relatedness: "On our last day, Richard picked us up from our hotel and drove us back to Vienna. Again the time just seemed to fly by as we talked and laughed. When we said our goodbye's it felt like I was saying goodbye to a family member. Richard and his Mother Marcela made the trip to Brno so warm and comforting and my husband and I know that we have truly made friends for life."[66]

In the marketing material, a trip to the Czech Republic is not only cheaper, offering more expedient treatments, but also has the added advantage of being a pleasant experience. In this manner, the rhetoric of "family," "romance," and "vacation" blends together and positions infertility as a temporary, fixable state while transforming traveling for infertility treatment into a comfortable, safe, kin-producing journey.

Throughout the marketing material, the fertility traveler is mobilized rhetorically to become an online browser, perusing the catalogue loaded with images of beautiful locations, holistic treatments, and historic cities. Not only is the trip, in the above case, to Brno in the Czech Republic itself a vacation, but additionally the fertility treatments along with pregnancy are rhetorically framed as "special journeys."[67] Comfort and care characterize the treatments offered in Spain as well as in the Czech Republic, positioning the fertility traveler as customer and tourist both. Moreover, as a central European nation, the Czech Republic is repositioned as in the "heart of Europe,"[68] rich in history, well-trained doctors, and beautiful cities.

In contrast, the Spanish clinics reiterate a more well-known image of a beautiful coastline, wonderful food (tapas, paellas, and more), welcoming people, and a great climate—adapting the image and rhetoric of mass tourism to personalized reproductive care, even frequently employing other doctors as international consultants. IVF Spain in Alicante, for example, employs a German doctor who oversees the holistic treatments offered at this clinic, while the clinic Clinica Fertia, located in Costa del Sol, promises international experience and "Scandinavian expertise," employing three Finnish doctors, framed now as "medical consultants."[69]

In sharp contrast to the marketing material, which emphasizes customer care and a holiday theme, traveling for treatment is, by the infertile, framed as forced. In interviews with Danish women who travel to Spain for egg donation, the reproductive traveler is not a privileged tourist who combines oocyte donation with a beach trip but is rather an "exiled" hero who is forced abroad by her "understandable" desire for a child. As noted by one of the interviewees who, at the age of fifty, traveled to IVI Barcelona to receive an egg donation: "It was extremely challenging for me [to go to Spain], because I was all alone, and because I have been raised as, well, as I have . . . to be a good girl. . . . You don't do something like that. It is illegal. . . . So the first ticket I bought for Spain and [I] went down to them. [W]ell, I was almost feeling like I had to tiptoe around to not get caught; then after a while, you get more professional. But it is really humiliating."[70]

In going to Spain, Rita crossed not only national but also in her case legal borders and gendered expectations. Faced with the Danish legislation that sets the legal age for receiving fertility treatment at 46, thus privileging youthfulness for women, Rita was, in Danish law, too old to become a mother.[71] Numerous times expressing her anger with Danish legislation, Rita positions herself as a "reproductive refugee." The trauma involved with infertility combined with a long list of unsuccessful infertility treatments takes center stage. In her narrative, her choice-making abilities are limited by national legislation. While the forced nature involved in this kind of traveling is clearly present in the above interview and in the comments made by infertile individuals in general, popular accounts and the marketing material of some fertility clinics nevertheless continue to situate fertility travel in light of other forms of medical tourism—trips that frequently combine treatments with more touristic pleasures, such as the sun and beaches in Spain.[72]

A feminist communication perspective illustrates how privilege is present in the mediation and commoditization of oocytes and in the rhetorical construction of IVF holidays. While Spanish clinics work to privilege youthful, fair-skinned, attractive, and seemingly happy donors, the construction of fertility travel into reproductive holidays privileges the economic mobility of certain types of patients—frequently, international patients. This rhetorical construction is, however, in conflict with the travelers' own accounts in which experiences with the trauma of infertility, unsuccessful fertility treatments, the economic stress of seeking help in the private fertility industry, and legal barriers take center stage. In the following section, I turn to the interviewees' accounts to discuss how the positioning of maternal intent and entrepreneurship play an integral part in these women's stories.

Biology Revisited: Maternal Intent and Entrepreneurship as the New Biology?

> This is a child who has me. . . . I call it a biological mother—not a genetic mother—yes that is how I view it. I am the one who initiated it all. I am the one who carried the child and ensured that it went from the point of two cells meeting, creating an embryo, and it then became a baby. And I have given birth to her using my own power, nursed her, and taken care of her . . . and all of this stuff when she was little, right? I don't know if I would have said this before she came but that is how I feel now.[73]

Anne is, in the above narrative, positioned not as a gestational surrogate but as a biological mother. Her biological motherhood is manifested in several ways: she initiated the process, and her daughter would not have been created if it had not been for her decision to go to Spain. The pregnancy, and the shared space and fluids, is constructed as a more significant contribution to Anne's understandings of biological motherhood than genetic material. Anne carried the developing baby, gave birth to her ("using her own power"), nursed, and cared for her. Not only does she engage in the conventional requirements for maternity (nurture), but she also employs a rhetoric of "nature" in her description: "I have given birth to her using my own power"—thus, suggesting that natural childbirth confers maternity. Moreover, her strong desire for a child underlines her central argument that she is not only a mother—she is, in fact, a "real" and "biological" mother.

The narrative illustrates how kinship and biology are "made" rhetorically. In fact, theorizing this aspect, Charis Thompson notes that while gestational surrogacy and egg donation are identical clinical and reproductive procedures, they are rhetorically constructed very differently.[74] Thompson uses the concept of "strategic naturalizing" to illustrate how motherhood is rhetorically and strategically constructed to always match the intent to mother. In Anne's narrative, technological developments enable her motherhood-without-genes, separating maternity from reproductive cells and "liberating" Anne from her infertile and aging body. In her narrative, Anne draws upon a culturally conservative approach—the Roman principle of *Mater semper certa est*, or "the mother is always certain." In cases of egg donation, the pregnant body is renaturalized as the one upon which motherhood is conferred. To this extent, egg recipients strategically shift and at different times blur categories valuing "nature" (the shared blood system, for example) with categories valuing "nurture" (caring for the baby in utero and later nursing the baby), while simultaneously reinstating procreational intent and choice as the crucial markers of maternity.

Moreover, in the above narrative, Anne takes up a neoliberal subject position. She departs from the more passive "patient" position made available to her within the Nordic welfare states,[75] and instead turns to the more active citizen position. She becomes an "entrepreneur of the self."[76] Anne's story is not unique but is characteristic of the interviewees' stories in general. I agree with Nikolas Rose,[77] however, when he argues that the neoliberal subject is neither "better" nor more "freeing"; rather, becoming a neoliberal subject involves the calculated acts and investments made by individuals who regulate themselves: "The citizen is to become a consumer and his or her activity is to be understood in terms of the activation of rights of the consumer in the marketplace."[78] The interviewees construct a "model of action" based on economic enterprise and transnational mobility. As a result, they transform themselves from the more passive position as a Scandinavian welfare health system "patient" into that of a neoliberal "consumer," making procreation a matter of choice.

Traveling for egg donation is, in the interviewees' accounts, reframed as a needed and justified fertility service. As they note, they travel not to "buy" eggs but to receive a "service" or "treatment." Meanwhile, the interviewees strategically position egg donors as unattached to their eggs and with no intent to procreate. Neither altruism nor commerce seemingly creates kinship bonds; rather, the babies are legitimately the children of the recipient woman's investment, including her consumption, longing, and entrepreneurship directed at this particular child. Or as noted by Anne, this child would not have been created if it had not been for her choice and decision to mother.

The Danish recipients frame egg donors rhetorically as having agency—empowered, much like themselves, to make their own consumption choices, as well as being altruistic (read: good-hearted) women. In this narrative of intent and entrepreneurship, the commercial compensation given to women for egg donation in Spain as well as the Czech Republic[79] is reframed as a form of reward, simultaneously taking the economic compensation out of the realm of exchange and the market, and making it appear more reciprocal. The Danish recipients merge the gift/commodity frame in their understanding of transnational egg donation while simultaneously embracing entrepreneurship and positioning fertility travel and egg donation within a well-known Danish gender equality frame in which egg donation becomes an empowerment for women to, just like men, "spread their genes."[80]

Intimate Mommy Markets: Concluding Comments

A feminist communication analysis of the privatization and commoditization of biogenetic substance raises interesting issues pertaining to our understanding of motherhood and consumption. As evidenced in the material, the rhetoric of commoditization is mixed with the notion of eggs as "gifts of life." The analyses illustrate how oocytes become both particular types of commodities (bright and attractive university students, for example), excess material (oocytes that otherwise would have gone to waste), gifts (precious genetic material), and necessary reproductive cells (the missing piece to the puzzle). In the interviews, these shifting meanings facilitate an important move away from the consumption of oocytes—and the potential moral dilemmas—to the making of pregnancy and, most notably, also to the making of motherhood. In what follows, a few concluding observations will be made on how conventional assumptions related to reproductive privilege including maternity, nationality, and class are rhetorically reworked in the marketing material and by the Danish women traveling to Spain.

Clearly, fertility travel blurs our understanding of motherhood; the nature/nurture dichotomy is, by the Danish recipients as well as in the marketing material of the clinics, replaced with "intent" and with the privileging of shared space as the defining categories for biological motherhood. This discourse aligns itself in interesting ways with other debates, most notably the abortion debate, and thus intentionality draws upon an already existing framework for understanding motherhood and reproductive choice. For example, women can in Denmark choose to abort an unwanted pregnancy prior to the twelfth week on the basis that they do not intend to mother. In turning to the marketing material and the interviews, it becomes clear that motherhood and intentionality become intertwined again. Motherhood becomes an entrepreneurial choice, or as noted by Mamo, a do-it-yourself project.[81] In this narrative, donation (giving) as well as receiving is a choice that individual women legitimately can make and a choice that importantly, in the Scandinavian framework, supports notions of gender equality (in this case, between egg and sperm donors), while a rhetoric of altruism and giving helps restore equality between recipients and donors.

The material centers egg donation and fertility travel in light of a rhetoric of entrepreneurship, thus ethical quandaries center on women's abilities to become entrepreneurs. The narratives included in this study privilege the voices of the infertile and the ways in which fertility travel is both a form of forced travel yet liberating as well. The fact that oocyte donors in Spain as well as in the Czech Republic are anonymous further contributes to the invisibility of donor stories while repositioning parental intent and the making of choices as vital. In the narratives as well as in the online marketing material the traumas associated with infertility take center stage, while egg donation and the experiences associated with donation (including uncomfortable hormonal treatments as well as the structural inequalities associated with the donor's age and socioeconomic status) are reframed as an act of altruism, while commercial compensation is framed as a reward. Thus, some reproflows (the infertile, traveling bodies) are made to appear more visible than other flows (the donating, domestic bodies).

The marketing of IVF vacations remakes fertility treatments into journeys not only into motherhood but also to a comfortable healthcare facility in Spain or the Czech Republic. Fertility travelers are positioned as entrepreneurs more so than patients. Not only are eggs, perhaps, enterprised-up;[82] each treatment is personalized and custom-made to fit the individual woman's or couple's needs. Fertility travelers not only search the Internet for clinical options, they also choose facilities in countries that they medically trust and in countries that they either already have a knowledge of (as is often the case with Spain) or a country that they would like to visit (as is the case with the Czech Republic). The attractiveness of Prague is reiterated when one Czech consultant in an interview notes, "Why not stay in a beautiful city like Prague, in a country with 'civilized people,' if you have to be someplace else for a few weeks?"[83]

Moreover, the analysis demonstrates how the opposition between motherhood and the marketplace persists in several ways. While Danish ethicists ponder that developments in reproductive technologies lead to "commoditizing children into designer products,"[84] this dilemma is, by the interviewees, resolved in the continued construction of an individualist, pan-entrepreneurial ethos and in the altruist narrative. Infertile Danish women travel to Spain, for instance, and pay for a *service* offered by the Spanish clinic. In their narratives, they do not pay for human oocytes but for a necessary treatment. They are simultaneously thankful to the donor (and the country) who made it possible, and they are angry toward the country that made it difficult (in this case, Denmark). To this extent, consumerism and entrepreneurship are endowed and reframed in light of what becomes constructed as a "biological" and "natural" urge to mother. In so doing, fertility travel is transformed into a form of reproductive choice. This narrative allows the Danish women, who can afford the treatment abroad, to have their desire for motherhood fulfilled, simultaneously naturalizing their desire while making their own privileges, such as economic and transnational mobility, disappear.

On a concluding note, the material reveals the troubling relationship between reproduction (the making of kin; the social) and economics (the market)—a relationship that is becoming even more pronounced in an era of globalization. As noted by Igor Kopytoff: "The threat lies in the possible invasion of human and sacralized world of kinship by economistic principles deemed appropriate only to the world of things."[85] Clearly, transnational egg donation arouses cultural anxiety and produces debate. Egg donation furthers the privileges of some women (women from the North and the West), leading feminist critics to frame it as akin to trafficking in organs,[86] while women's bodies become resources in the production of "men's babies."[87] Interestingly, the Danish women included in this study engage in this line of thinking when they express relief that they—and not their husbands—suffer from infertility. In so doing, they reinstate a heteronormative and patriarchal understanding of kinship ties in which male genetic material (sperm) and female bodily space make up "own" children.[88] In sharp contrast, the importance of female genetic material shifts from a rhetoric of "nature" to "nurture" and then again, gets renaturalized to a new understanding of "nature," namely pregnancy and natural birth-giving. The material illustrates how biological motherhood is rhetorically reinvented and undergoes a process of both de- and renaturalization.[89]

Transnational egg donation opens up for not only the de- and renaturalization of biology/culture, it also introduces the importance of parental intent and choice as kinship-conferring elements. Egg donation, as it unfolds on the global stage, involves a highly specialized marketplace in which foreign clinics compete and women donate their eggs in the production of Danish babies. In the process, love and care—in sharp contrast to money and greed—are reiterated in the business of making motherhood-without-genes. Simultaneously, transnational egg donation and fertility travel blur these distinctions. As noted by Janelle Taylor: "Reproductive technologies and the controversies that swirl around them clearly suggest that such distinctions—between persons and objects, bodies and commodities, mothers and consumers—are not so clear-cut."[90] The business of making motherhood through egg donation enters the commodity sphere, while it is strategically also rewritten to fit a rhetoric of gift-giving and family-making, on the outset at least, thus softening the commercial aspect while also situating egg donation in light of both altruism and entrepreneurship.

Notes

1. Danish legislation permits infertility treatment of women until their forty-sixth birthday while no age limit exists as far as male infertility treatments are concerned. "Rita" is a pseudo name given to one of the interviewees included in this chapter.

2. For more information on fertility travel in the European context, the most updated research is available in Shenfield, de Mouzon, Pennings, Ferraretti, Nyboe Andersen, de Wert, and Groossens (The ESHRE Taskforce on Cross Border Reproductive), "Cross Border Reproductive Care in Six European Countries," *Human Reproduction* 25, 6 (2010): 1361–68.

3. Louise France, "Passport, Tickets, Suncream, Sperm," *The Observer* January 15, 2006, accessed March 10, 2012, http://observer.theguardian.com/woman/story/0,,1684149,00.html.

4. See also Charlotte Kroløkke, "West is Best. Affective Assemblages and Spanish Oöcytes," *Journal of European Women's Studies*, 21, 1 (2014): 57–71; Anne Pollock, "Complicating Power in High-Tech Reproduction: Narratives of Anonymous Egg Donors," *Journal of Medical Humanities* 24 nos ¾ (2003): 241–63.

5. Rene Almeling, *Sex Cells: The Medical Market for Eggs and Sperm* (Berkeley: University of California Press, 2011).

6. Elizabeth Roberts and Nancy Scheper-Hughes, "Introduction: Medical Migrations," *Body & Society* 17 nos 2 & 3 (2011): 1–30.

7. Whereas India and California are known for surrogacy, Barbados is becoming known for affordable yet exlusive fertility holidays and Spain is a key destination in the European fertility market.

8. Shelee Colen, "'Like a Mother to Them': Stratified reproduction and West Indian Childcare Workers and Employers in New York," in *Conceiving the New World Order: The Global Politics of Reproduction*, ed. Faye Ginsburg and Rayna Rapp (Berkeley: University of California Press, 1995), 78–103.

9. Kimberlé Crenshaw, "Demarginalizing the Intersection of Race and Sex: A Black Feminist of Antidiscrimination Doctrine, Feminist Theory and Antiracist Politics," *University of Chicago Legal Forum* (1989): 139–67.

10. Karen Barad, "Getting Real: Technoscientific Practices and the Materialization of Reality," *Differences. A Journal of Feminist Cultural Studies* 10 no. 2 (1998): 801–31.

11. According to Spanish law, Spanish clinics are required to match the phenotypes of the donor with those of the recipient.

12. Margaret Jolly, "Divided Mothers: Changing Global Inequalities of 'Nature,'" in *The Globalization of Motherhood: Deconstructions and Reconstructions of Biology and Care*, ed. Maher and Chavkin (New York: Routledge, 2010), 154–79.

13. According to Shenfield et al., oocyte donation was the single most likely reason that Europeans travelled (22.8 percent). Shenfield, "Cross Border Reproductive Care in Six European Countries."

14. Danes travel for egg donation while Swedes, for instance, travel for anonymous sperm donation and Norwegians travel for both anonymous egg and sperm donation. Several issues seem to be at stake: Denmark upholds the option for donors to be anonymous while other countries such as Norway, Sweden, and the United Kingdom only allow known donation.

15. Marcia Inhorn, "'Assisted' Motherhood in Global Dubai: Reproductive Tourists and Their Helpers," in *The Globalization of Motherhood: Deconstructions and Reconstructions of Biology and Care*, ed. Maher and Chavkin (New York: Routledge, 2010, 180–202. A different yet similar concept is that of "care-chains" developed by Arlie Hochchild and Barbara Ehrenreich, *Global Woman: Nannies, Maids, and Sex Workers in the New Economy* (New York: Metropolitan Press, 2002).

16. Inhorn, "Assisted' Motherhood."

17. Ibid.

18. Laura Mamo, *Queering Reproduction. Achieving Pregnancy in the Age of Technoscience* (Durham: Duke University Press, 2007).

19. Barbara K. Rothman, "Motherhood Under Capitalism," in *Consuming Motherhood*, ed. Taylor, Layne, and Wozniak (New Brunswick, New Jersey, London: Rutgers Press, 2004), 19–30.

20. Almeling, *Sex Cells: The Medical Market for Eggs and Sperm.*

21. D. Tober, "Semen as Gift, Semen as Goods: Reproductive Workers and the

Market in Altruism." in *Commodifying Bodies*, ed. Scheper-Hughes and Wacquant (London, Thousand Oaks, New Delhi: Sage, 2005), 137–60, Kroløkke, "West is Best."

22. Gamete banking is estimated by fertility doctors to increase in importance—enabling individuals who can afford the service to "bank" or "invest" their reproductive cells for future use. The fact that frozen gametes can now be used in IVF has greatly facilitated for more transnational crossings to take place.

23. Nancy Scheper-Hughes, "Bodies for Sale—Whole or in Parts," in *Commodifying Bodies*, ed. Scheper-Hughes and Wacquant (London, Thousand Oaks, New Delhi: Sage, 2005), 1–8.

24. Scheper-Hughes, "Bodies for Sale."

25. Almeling, *Sex Cells: The Medical Market for Eggs and Sperm.*

26. Almeling, *Sex Cells. The Medical Markets for Eggs and Sperm*, 10.

27. Daniels, *Exposing Men: The Science and Politics of Male Reproduction* (Oxford: Oxford University Press, 2006); Charlotte Kroløkke, "Click a Donor: Viking Masculinity on the Line," *Journal of Consumer Culture*, Vol. 9 no. 1 (2009): 7–30.

28. Daniels, *Exposing Men*, 34

29. Catherine Waldby and Robert Mitchell, *Tissue Economies. Blood, Organs, and Cell Lines in Late Capitalism* (Durham: Duke University Press, 2006).

30. Aditya Bharadwaj, "Biosociality and Bocrossings: Encounters with Assisted Conception and Embryonic Stem Cells in India," in *Biosocialities, Genetics and the Social Sciences: Making Biologies and Identitiesm, ed.* Gibbon and Novas (Oxon: Routledge, 2008), 103.

31. Daniels, *Exposing Men*, 104.

32. Roberts, *The Traffic Between Women*, 119.

33. Almeling, *Sex Cells. The Medical Markets for Eggs and Sperm*, 10.

34. Charlotte Kroløkke, "West is Best. Affective Assemblages and Spanish Oöcytes," *Journal of European Women's Studies*, forthcoming 2014.

35. This is for instance true in Denmark when egg donation is done altruistically. Currently, the egg donor receives no financial compensation.

36. Almeling, *Sex Cells. The Medical Markets for Eggs and Sperm.*

37. Tober, "Seman as Gift."

38. Anne Pollock, "Complicating Power in High-Tech Reproduction: Narratives of Anonymous Egg Donors," *Journal of Medical Humanities* 24 nos ¾ (2003): 241–63.

39. Janice Raymond, *Women as Wombs* (San Francisco: HarperSanFrancisco, 1993), 51.

40. Ibid.

41. Another exception includes Almeling, *Sex Cells. The Medical Markets for Eggs and Sperm.*

42. Pollock, "Complicating Power."

43. Ibid.

44. Orobitg and Salazar, "The Gift of Motherhood: Egg Donation in a Barcelona Infertility Clinic," *Ethnos* 70 no. 1 (2005): 31–52.

45. Kroløkke, "West Is Best."

46. Waldby and Roberts, *Tissue Economies*, 182.

47. Marcel Mauss, *The Gift. The Form and Reason for Exchange in Archaic Societies* (New York, London: W. W. Norton & Co. Inc., 1954).

48. Kroløkke, "West Is Best."

49. The interviewees included in this chapter are part of a larger research project: Two of the three women are in their late forties and early fifties who are single women requiring egg and sperm donation both. The youngest participant is in her early thirties and married. Two of them have already travelled for fertility treatment while the third (and younger) woman has gone to visit different clinics in Spain and is now in the decision phase about which clinic to choose. They all have degrees from institutions of higher learning, are heterosexual, and are economically positioned as either middle class or upper middle class.

50. World Egg Bank, "Donor Eggs." http://www.theworldeggbank.com/ivi.html (accessed May 2011).

51. "Anyone tried ivf with donor eggs in spain?" (http://forum.sofeminine.co.uk/forum/maternite2/__f154_maternite2-Anyone-tried-ivf-with-donor-eggs-in-spain.html (accessed May 2011).

52. Juan Antonio Garcia Velasco, "Egg Donation in Spain," ESHRE *Reproduction* (2007): 27.

53. Velasco compares the altruistic motivations of oocyte donors to the "genuine altruism" of the Spanish people. Spain is, he argues, the leading country in the world as far as organ donation is concerned. That coupled with a more permissive legislation has made Spain a popular country for fertility travel. Velasco, "Egg Donation in Span."

54. Ibid.

55. Interview with the donor department in a prominent Spanish fertility clinic made it clear that donors are not only Spanish women but also immigrant women from Russia and Ukraine.

56. According to Velasco, 22 percent of the donors questioned said that their reason for donating was altruistic, 35 percent said economic, and 43 percent said both. Velasco, "Egg Donation in Spain."

57. Tober, "Seamen as Gift."

58. IVI, "About." http://www.ivi.es/en/donors/semen-and-egg-donors.aspx (accessed May 2011).

59. According to IVI's own video material (available in not only Spanish but also in Italian, French, and English), as many as 50 percent of their patients come from countries other than Spain.

60. Velasco, "Egg Donation in Spain," 28.

61. See also Elizabeth Roberts, "The Traffic Between Women: Female Alliance and Familial Egg Donation in Ecuador," in *Assisting Reproduction, Testing Genes. Global Encounters with New Biotechnologies*, ed. Birenbaum-Carmeli and Inhorn (New York: Berghahn Books, 2009), 113–43.

62. IVF Spain, "About." http://www.ivfspain.com/, (accessed May 2011).

63. Ibid.

64. Two medical assistants from Praga Medico were interviewed during a visit to Prague in May, 2011.

65. My IVF Alternative, accessed May 2011, http://www.yourivfvacation.cz/.

66. My IVF Alternative, accessed May 2011, http://www.yourivfvacation.cz/testimonials.html.

67. My IVF Alternative, accessed May 2011, http://www.yourivfvacation.cz.

68. Online marketing material of Praga Medica. As noted on their website: "Prague means treatment in the heart of Eruope, with direct flights to over 100 destinations in 50 countries. The Czech Republic, EU member state since 2004, boasts with superior medical facilities, world-class English speaking specialists and low medical costs." Praga Medica, "Welcome," accessed May 2010, http://www.medicalservicesprague.com/.

69. Clica Fertia, "About," accessed January 2012, http://www.clinicafertia.com/en.html.

70. Interview with Rita, September 2010.

71. The age limit for women in Spain is fifty-one.

72. World Egg Bank, accessed May 2010, http://www.theworldeggbank.com/.

73. Interview with Anne, August 2010.

74. Charis Thompson, *Making Parents: The Ontological Choreography of Reproductive Technologies* (Cambridge: MIT Press, 2005).

75. Nikolas Rose, *Governing the Soul: The Shaping of the Private Self* (London and New York: Free Association Books, 1999.)

76. Walkerdine and Bansel, "Neoliberalism, Work, and Subjectivity: Towards a More Complex Account," in *The Sage Handbook of Identities*, ed. Wetherell and Mohanty (Los Angeles, London, New Delhi, Singapore, Washington, DC: Sage, 2010), 494.

77. Rose, *Governing the Soul.*

78. Rose, *Governing the Soul*, 164–65.

79. The commercial compensation for egg donation is in Spain approximately 900 Euros while in the Czech Republic it is an estimated 500 Euros. Donors living in Prague are, according to a Czech clinic, likely to receive a higher compensation than donors from rural areas. While this difference may reflect different costs of living, it may also speak to the idea that urban donors are, by and large, viewed as more attractive. In talking with one of the leading Czech clinics, they made it quite clear that the economic compensation was the most important motivator to the donors.

80. Interview with Line, August 2011.

81. Laura Mamo, *Queering Reproduction: Achieving Pregnancy in the Age of Technoscience* (Durham: Duke University Press, 2007).

82. Mamo, *Queering Reproduction: Achieving Pregnancy in the Age of Technoscience*

83. Interview with Zdenek Dvorak, Praga Medica, conducted May, 2011 in Prague.

84. Igor Kopytoff, "Commoditizing Kinship in America," in *Consuming Mother-*

hood, ed. Taylor, Layne, and Wozniak (New Brunswick, New Jersey, London: Rutgers Press, 2004), 271–78 .

85. Kopytoff, 272.

86. "No to eggsploitation" is a British activist group opposed to egg donation and equates egg donation to organ trafficking. More information and examples of this particular rhetoric can be found at http://no2eggsploitation.wordpress.com/2009/09/28/no2eggsploitation/. Retrieved April, 2010.

87. Rothman, "Motherhood Under Capitalism," 19.

88. Ibid.

89. Sarah Franklin, Celia Lury, Jackie Stacy, *Global Nature, Global Culture* (London, Thousand Oaks, New Delhi: Sage Publications, 2000).

90. Janelle Taylor, "Introduction," in *Consuming Motherhood*, ed. by Taylor, Layne, and Wozniak (New Brunswick, New Jersey, London: Rutgers Press, 2004), 11.

References

Almeling, Rene. *Sex Cells: The Medical Market for Eggs and Sperm*. Berkeley: University of California Press, 2011.

Barad, Karen. "Getting Real: Technoscientific Practices and the Materialization of Reality," *Differences. A Journal of Feminist Cultural Studies* 10 no. 2 (1998): 801–31.

Bharadwaj, Aditya. "Biosociality and Bocrossings: Encounters with Assisted Conception and Embryonic Stem Cells in India." In *Biosocialities, Genetics, and the Social Sciences: Making Biologies and Identities*, edited by Gibbon and Novas, 98–116. Oxon: Routledge, 2008.

Colen, Shelee. "'Like a Mother to Them': Stratified reproduction and West Indian Childcare Workers and Employers in New York." In *Conceiving the New World Order: The Global Politics of Reproduction*, edited by Faye Ginsburg and Rayna Rapp, 78–103. Berkeley: University of California Press, 1995.

Crenshaw, Kimberlé. "Demarginalizing the Intersection of Race and Sex: A Black Feminist of Antidiscrimination Doctrine, Feminist Theory, and Antiracist Politics," *University of Chicago Legal Forum* (1989): 139–67.

Daniels, Cynthia. *Exposing Men: The Science and Politics of Male Reproduction*. Oxford: Oxford University Press, 2006.

France, Louise. "Passport, Tickets, Suncream, Sperm," *The Observer* January 15, 2006.Accessed March 10, 2012, http://observer.theguardian.com/woman/story/0,,1684149,00.html.

Franklin, Sarah, Celia Lury, and Jackie Stacy. *Global Nature, Global Culture*. London, Thousand Oaks, New Delhi: Sage Publications, 2000.

Hochchild, Arlie, and Barbara Ehrenreich. *Global Woman: Nannies, Maids, and Sex Workers in the New Economy*. New York: Metropolitan Press, 2002.

Inhorn, Marcia. "'Assisted' Motherhood in Global Dubai: Reproductive Tourists and Their Helpers." In *The Globalization of Motherhood: Deconstructions and Recon-*

structions of Biology and Care, edited by Maher and Chavkin, 180–202. New York: Routledge, 2010.

Jolly, Margaret. "Divided Mothers: Changing Global Inequalities of 'Nature.'" In *The Globalization of Motherhood: Deconstructions and Reconstructions of Biology and Care,* edited by Maher and Chavkin, 154–79. New York: Routledge, 2010.

Kopytoff, Igor. "Commoditizing Kinship in America." In *Consuming Motherhood*, edited by Taylor, Layne, and Wozniak, 271–78. New Brunswick, New Jersey, London: Rutgers Press, 2004.

Kroløkke, Charlotte. "West is Best. Affective Assemblages and Spanish Oöcytes," *Journal of European Women's Studies* 21, no. 1 (2014): 57–71.

Kroløkke, Charlotte. "Click a Donor: Viking Masculinity on the Line," *Journal of Consumer Culture* 9 no. 1 (2009): 7–30.

Mamo, Laura. *Queering Reproduction. Achieving Pregnancy in the Age of Technoscience.* Durham: Duke University Press, 2007.

Mauss, Marcel. *The Gift. The Form and Reason for Exchange in Archaic Societies*. New York, London: W. W. Norton & Co. Inc., 1954.

Orobitg, Gemma, and Carles Salazar. "The Gift of Motherhood: Egg Donation in a Barcelona Infertility Clinic," *Ethnos* 70 no. 1 (2005): 31–52.

Pollock, Anne. "Complicating Power in High-Tech Reproduction: Narratives of Anonymous Egg Donors," *Journal of Medical Humanities* 24 nos ¾ (2003): 241–63.

Raymond, Janice. *Women as Wombs*. San Francisco: Harper SanFrancisco, 1993.

Roberts, Elizabeth. "The Traffic Between Women: Female Alliance and Familial Egg Donation in Ecuador." In *Assisting Reproduction, Testing Genes. Global Encounters with New Biotechnologies*, edited by Birenbaum-Carmeli and Inhorn, 113–43. New York: Berghahn Books, 2009.

Roberts, Elizabeth, and Nancy Scheper-Hughes. "Introduction: Medical Migrations," *Body & Society* 17 nos 2 & 3 (2011): 1–30.

Rose, Nikolas. *Governing the Soul: The Shaping of the Private Self.* London and New York: Free Association Books, 1999.

Rothman, Barbara K. "Motherhood Under Capitalism." In *Consuming Motherhood*, edited by Taylor, Layne, and Wozniak, 19–30. New Brunswick, New Jersey, London: Rutgers Press, 2004, 19–30.

Scheper-Hughes, Nancy. "Bodies for Sale—Whole or in Parts." In *Commodifying Bodies*, edited by Scheper-Hughes and Wacquant, 1–8. London, Thousand Oaks, New Delhi: Sage, 2005.

Shenfield, Francoise, Jacques de Mouzon, Guido Pennings, Anna P. Ferraretti, Anders Nyboe Andersen, Guido de Wert, and V. Groossens. (The ESHRE Taskforce on Cross Border Reproductive), "Cross Border Reproductive Care in Six European Countries," *Human Reproduction* 25 no. 6 (2010): 1361–68.

Taylor, Janelle. "Introduction." In *Consuming Motherhood*, edited by Taylor, Layne, and Wozniak, 1–18. New Brunswick, New Jersey, London: Rutgers Press, 2004.

Thompson Charis, *Making Parents: The Ontological Choreography of Reproductive Technologies*. Cambridge: The MIT Press, 2005.

Tober, Diane M. "Semen as Gift, Semen as Goods: Reproductive Workers and the Market in Altruism." In *Commodifying Bodies*, edited by Scheper-Hughes and Wacquant, 137–60. London, Thousand Oaks, New Delhi: Sage, 2005.

Velasco, Juan Antonio Garcia. "Egg Donation in Spain," ESHRE *Reproduction* (2007): 27.

Waldby, Catherine, and Robert Mitchell. *Tissue Economies. Blood, Organs, and Cell Lines in Late Capitalism*. Durham: Duke University Press, 2006.

Walkerdine, Valerie, and Peter Bansel. "Neoliberalism, Work and Subjectivity: Towards a More Complex Account." In *The Sage Handbook of Identities*, edited by Wetherell and Mohanty, 494. Los Angeles, London, New Delhi, Singapore, Washington DC: Sage, 2010.

2
Race(ing) to the Baby Market

The Political Economy of Overcoming Infertility

K. Animashaun Ducre

"*You . . . are . . . a . . . mother*," the bereavement counselor said to me, softly but emphatically. I was among a group of mothers who had recently experienced baby loss, and we were contemplating how to deal with the upcoming Mother's Day holiday in 2008. Two months prior, I had a stillborn baby girl at 22 weeks. The counselor was trying to affirm my rights to claim motherhood.

I went through two phases following my baby loss: I vowed that I could never go through that uncertainty again, and I eschewed all efforts to discuss another attempt at pregnancy. By the following year, I became determined, frenzied even, to become a parent. Initially, I looked into domestic adoption with a public agency. Then, my doctor referred me to a fertility specialist. After two cycles of drug therapy followed by intrauterine insemination, I became frustrated and returned to adoption as an option. This time, I contacted a private agency. At some point during the conversation, the counselor suggested that I look into international adoption and Ethiopia in particular. I refer to this era as my time on the *baby train*: conception, to loss, to adoption information sessions, to Clomid pills, to counting my eggs, to transporting sperm samples in a cup, to browsing adoption brochures and websites, to combing the State Department's website for visa information. Needless to say, I became overwhelmed. I had to get off that train.

My recollections of the journey on the baby train renewed my sense of how aggressively those who are unable or unwilling to have a child by conventional means have been courted and wooed by those in the baby market. Advertisements abound of glowing women cradling their swollen bellies; adorable, smiling babies; and loving family portraits. Like those commercials featuring ice-cold beer, mouth-watering sandwiches, and gorgeous models, these temptations tap into our biological and psychological hungers and desires. However, there can be real problems with the images around children and family. As an African American woman from a working-poor background, I was immediately struck by the limited frames around race, class, and sexuality that inform visual and narrative constructions of alternative family planning. First, these ads hide the exorbitant financial and human costs of assisted reproductive technologies (ART) and adoption. Secondly, the contexts for these images are framed by white, upper-middle-class, and heteronormative ideals.[1] Finally, these images and the pursuit of parenthood via these alternatives fail to acknowledge the structural inequalities that lead to the formation of the baby market. This paper critiques the baby market from a political economic perspective. I contend that despite its allure, the market as an emerging alternative path to parenthood is fraught with problems associated with race, class, and global gender inequalities. Central to this analysis is the subtle means by which whiteness becomes a salient identity assumed by the market's consumers. And, in the case of international adoption, nonwhite infants and children become its products. The high costs associated with infertility treatment and adoption, along with their insular marketing strategies that focus on white couples, limit access to those who are less affluent and/or nonwhite. Moreover, a critical macroperspective on the link between reproductive medical interventions and international adoption reveals an uncomfortable fact that we must face: poverty, operating both globally and domestically, spurs the growth of both options.

My project aligns with intersectional work in feminist communication studies that makes explicit how scholars are positioned within discourses of marginalization. As Karma Chávez and Cindy Griffin note, "This theory requires that scholars identify, and give voice to, the interconnected nature of being silenced, in multiple ways, and the lived (bodily) manifestations of those silencings."[2] In my recent book, *A Place We Call Home*, I argue that along with intersectionality, personal narrative is an essential tool used by Black feminists to highlight multiple and interlocking oppressions resulting from discrimination due to race, class, gender, and sexual orientation. Invoking the work of both bell hooks and Audre Lorde, I conclude: "[Their] words seem to throw off the cloak of oppression and invisibility that women of color face. . . . The reliance upon the incorporation of a personal narrative into a research project challenges this personal-objective divide. This contestation is validated by the use of feminist epistemology, and centering a gendered (and raced) way of knowing that privileges marginalized voices."[3] Across this essay, I interrogate the ways that reproductive options rely upon and reproduce privilege, particularly race- and class-based privilege. In what follows, I weave together stories of other women of color with my own experiences both within and against the medical industry while navigating the baby market. Employing personal narrative is deliberate and wholly connected to understanding the baby market from a Black feminist perspective. In this way, I follow the work of Ellis, Bochner, Boylorn, and McClaurin by invoking personal narratives to address the erasure of women of color and their experiences as both consumers and exploited labor in the fertility market.[4]

According to the most recent annual statistics from the Society for Assisted Reproductive Technology, there were approximately 61,740 children born as a result of ART in 2012.[5] The number of international adoptions over the last decade has ranged from a high of 22,991 annually in 2004 to a low of 7,092 in 2013 following stricter policies in Russia and China.[6] Thus, a discussion about the consumption of motherhood must pay attention to alternative forms of achieving parenthood. In fact, increasing reliance upon international adoption and ART for family formation, along with the significant costs related to such endeavors, have led many scholars to call these strategies part of a *baby market*.[7] Michele Goodwin proposed four conditions on why fertility treatments and adoption should be considered markets: 1) these activities are unregulated, 2) both industries adhere to principles of supply and demand, 3) the social valuations of adoptive parents, and 4) there is a correlational relationship between the international adoption and domestic adoption. The following sections detail these conditions, along with a critical analysis of how the impacts of ART and adoption are compounded by race, class, gender, and sexuality.

Unregulated Industries of ART and Adoption

Prior to my own trip on the baby train, I did not know much about infertility treatment and adoption. In my first year of researching the subject, I had to learn all of its nuances. Assisted reproductive technology can run from the minimally invasive procedures (like taking oral hormones) to those requiring a series of lab visits (ovulation induction, IVF, embryonic transfer, among others). In the adoption world, there are public and private agencies, international and domestic adoptions, full service adoption agencies versus child placement agencies. In addition, there are also surrogacy arrangements, along with egg and sperm donor banks. The American-based systems of ART and adoptions have become global with the growth of medical tourism. It is important to note that these agencies and independent services are not all licensed, nor is there a sustained monitoring of their activities. While the issue of money exchanges for children is a very uncomfortable topic for most, it is the basis for exchange for all ART services and private adoptions. Therefore, it is fair to conclude that the baby market—a multibillion-dollar global industry—is unregulated and largely commercial. Episodic scandals in both the ART and adoption industries prompt repeated calls for regulation. Interestingly, both opponents and proponents of regulating the industry often borrow rhetoric in the debates over the legalization of abortion. *At what point are the embryos considered "a life" with inalienable rights? How much should the state intervene on personal choices of families to pursue ART and adoption?* When an American woman sent her adopted son back to his native Russia alone on a transcontinental flight in 2010, the United States was forced to revise its bilateral adoption agreement with Russia with stricter guidelines. Despite these regulatory fits and starts, the industries remain largely unregulated. Furthermore, piecemeal attempts at regulation only foster growth of black market sources of family planning.[8]

Supply, Race-Based Demand, and Throw Away Women

The second condition of the baby market is its similarity to other markets where supply and demand influence cost. I would argue that those costs are not only financial as there are real human costs when alternative family planning intersects with race and class.

The irony is that I had been ambivalent about motherhood most of my life. It seemed that as my fertility became more elusive, my desire to have a child became stronger. Upon my gynecologist's recommendation, I found myself making an appointment with the area's top fertility specialists. Upon entering the office (one of three regional fertility centers owned by the multimillionaire doctor), I was struck by its ambience. My prior experience with gynecological services was the intimate surroundings of a small doctor's office and the cramped and busy waiting rooms of the local perinatalogist during my high-risk pregnancy. The fertility center's waiting room transported me to a rustic, but posh, hotel resort lobby. The walls were painted with warm, soothing colors of rust and orange. A fireplace flanked one wall of the waiting room dotted with plush leather sofas, chenille covered couches, and even a rocking chair. A large armoire housed coffee for waiting patients. Instead of the generic coffee pot common to medical waiting rooms, there was one of those specialty brew machines where you select the flavor of coffee or tea for a custom beverage. This brew station signaled that my trip to the fertility doctor would be an expensive one.

Our first appointment consisted of two consultations: one with an actual doctor and the other with the clinic's billing representative. During our consultation, she gave me a price menu: a one-page document that lists the procedures on the left side of the sheet and their corresponding prices on the other. The least expensive procedure was ovulation monitoring, which cost

$250. Insemination would cost an additional $50. Insemination with lab and monitoring (associated with taking Clomid, a hormonal drug therapy), would cost even more. ART treatments like IVF were priced at nearly $6,000 per cycle. There were additional costs related to sperm storage and freezing. At the time, I did not even understand what all of those procedures meant, but at least I knew how much they cost. Later, when I found myself writing a $500 check for lab work at the fertility center, I thought to myself, "If you're broke and infertile, you are shit out of luck." After all, fertility treatments are not covered under most private health insurance plans, and it is certainly not covered under public health insurance, or Medicaid. Only fifteen states have mandates for coverage of infertility treatments.[9]

For five consecutive days, I took Clomid to spur my egg production, underwent monitoring, and finally intrauterine insemination of my husband's sperm. As previously noted, one of the most expensive and invasive treatments for infertility is IVF, which can cost thousands of dollars per cycle. Perhaps the vexing part about opting for fertility treatment is that positive outcomes are uncertain. In fact, the success rates of fertility treatments are relatively low. Deborah Spar presents a listing of pregnancy success and live birth by age, starting at age twenty-two until forty-six.[10] The optimal age for the greatest success was between twenty-six and thirty, with pregnancy success rates of 43 percent and 41 percent, respectively. Live births, as a result of these conceptions by reproductive technologies, are slightly lower. However, we might imagine that a significant number of the women seeking infertility treatment (and able to afford to do so) are over thirty-five, which medical professionals describe as *advanced maternal age*. Chances of pregnancy for such women are lower than 30 percent. The costs, coupled with the uncertainty, were some of the reasons that compelled me to opt out of further fertility treatment cycles and to seriously consider adoption.

In addition to the more obvious financial costs to overcoming infertility, there are historical human costs. The history of medical advances that led to the discovery and marketing of ART technologies is rooted within the tragic case of Henrietta Lacks, a poor Black woman who died of cervical cancer in 1951 in the colored ward of Johns Hopkins Hospital in Baltimore. Rebecca Skloot's *New York Times* bestselling book, *The Immortal Life of Henrietta Lacks,* chronicles the discovery of the HeLa cells at the intersection of racism and breach of medical ethics.[11] One of the doctors took a sample of Lacks's cervix without her consent during one of her trips to the hospital to receive radiation treatment. Miraculously, her cells were the first human cells to survive in culture. From that point on, the cell line *HeLa* was born, mass-produced, and distributed across the world. Henrietta Lacks's immortal cancerous cells transformed the use of cell biology to research disease and the effectiveness of pharmaceuticals. HeLa is credited with the discovery of such medical breakthroughs as the polio vaccine as well as advances in cellular research that laid the foundation for medical strides in IVF. HeLa is also responsible for the exponential growth of today's pharmaceutical industry. All of these advances, both scientific and financial, occurred without the knowledge and consent of Lacks's family: her widowed husband and her surviving four children. In fact, Skloot points out that numerous scientists had made significant advances in their professional careers and millions of dollars had been spent directly on the acquisition of HeLa cells for research and for drugs derived from work on these cells, while some members of the Lacks's family had little to no health insurance. The fact that HeLa cell production, use, and distribution occurred during rampant racial segregation adds even greater irony to the case of Henrietta Lacks and her miraculous cells. Many whites, who would have been appalled to sit, worship, swim, and dine near "Negroes," were the benefactors to medical advances spurred by the body of a Black woman. Moreover, cells harvested from Lacks's *womb* spawned these medical interventions—cells had been cut from the core of her body, leading to medical advances in disease prevention and vaccines. To add insult to injury, there was a concerted effort at misinformation following the increase in media exposure to the scientific importance of the HeLa cell research. First, the HeLa cells were attributed to a fictitious name, *Helen Lane,* and it was reported that the cells were taken after her death. There is a poignant moment in Skloot's book where lab assistant Mary Kubicek, who had been working with Henrietta's cell culture prior to her death, had been asked to attend her autopsy: "She wanted to run out of the morgue and back to the lab, but instead, she stared at Henrietta's arms and legs—anything to avoid looking into her lifeless eyes. Then Mary's gaze fell on Henrietta's feet, and she gasped: Henrietta's toenails were covered in chipped bright red nail polish. 'When I saw those toenails,' Mary told me years later, 'I nearly fainted. I thought, Oh jeez, *she's a real person.* I started imagining her sitting in her bathroom painting those toenails, and it hit me for the first time that those cells we'd been working with all this time and sending all over the world, they came from a live woman. I'd never thought of it that way.'"[12]

The fact that biological samples taken from the womb of an African American woman without her consent would eventually lead to boutique fertility centers to benefit scores of mostly white, upper-middle-class women is a testament to what Raymond articulates as *throw away women*: the sacrifice of women of color's bodies for scientific advancement and predominantly white, affluent desires.[13]

While lacking Goodwin's attention to the racialized context of the baby business, Deborah Spar does offer a brief account of Dr. James Marion Sims (1813–1883) and his exploitation of another throw away woman, a slave named Anarcha. Sims is regarded as the father of modern gynecological practice and surgery.[14] Born in South Carolina, and trained in Pennsylvania and Alabama, Sims became a world-renowned gynecological surgeon. However, feminist and social historians are quick to point out that Sims perfected his surgical methods through trial and error with enslaved Black females in his first medical practice in Montgomery, Alabama.[15] One of the first corrective surgeries was on a slave woman named Anarcha in 1849. Anarcha endured thirty operations within four years for a condition called vesicovaginal fistulas, which is severe urinary incontinence as a result of protracted labor.[16] Sims's apologists point out the unfairness of judging his presumed inhumanity by contemporary sensibilities, but they fail to confront the political-economic context upon which medical innovations arose.[17] First, the enslaved women were not treated out of altruism but out of their instrumental value as property. While there are debates about whether consent was given by the women prior to surgery, even Sims's apologists note that consent was obtained from the slave owner. Combining the peculiar institution of slavery with rigorous medical training resulted in an endless supply of Black bodies for anatomical dissections and experiments.[18] If there are to be monuments to Sims (indeed, there is one in Central Park, in New York), should not there also be a memorial to Anarcha? Sims received global acclaim and moved to New York to establish the State Hospital for Women, where he and his medical team continued inhumane practice upon and disregard for immigrant Irish women's and Black women's bodies. As Spar notes, "They operated on hundreds, maybe even thousands, of women, removing ovaries or clipping cervixes to fix what they described as the purely physical impediments to reproduction. Sadly most of these 'cures' proved as ineffectual as their medieval predecessors. Records from Simm's Women's Hospital show virtually no evidence of subsequent pregnancies, and modern medical knowledge suggests that Sims was almost certainly operating far from the source of his patients' problems."[19]

The term throwaway women also refers to the devaluation of Black mothers in the racialized baby market. A more recent example of this concept is the case of Anna Johnson. In 1990, Black single mom Anna Johnson was paid $10,000 to serve as a gestational surrogate for a middle-class couple, Mark and Crispina Calvert. Mark was white, and Crispina was of Filipina ancestry. By the time Anna gave birth to baby Christopher, relations between her and the Calverts had soured. Anna had filed for custody of the newborn, and her case marked the first of its kind in the nation in which a nongenetically linked, gestational surrogate sued for custody of the baby she carried to term. In the end, the Calverts were granted full custody of baby Christopher, but the resulting judicial decision and the media storylines surrounding the case were charged with racialized discourse. Deborah Grayson's account of the ensuing trial and publicity demonstrated prevailing notions of the subordinated status of surrogacy in its reduction to alienated labor in general, but more specifically the disregard for Black women's claims to motherhood in particular.[20] Evoking the roles of Black women as wet nurses and nannies during and after enslavement, she concludes, "Black women have long been asked to raise white children without having any parental rights to them. Now, it would seem, they can be asked to birth white children and have no claim to them."[21] Like Henrietta Lacks, Anna Johnson's body was reduced to a means to an end, separating her humanity from her body for the benefit of others. The racialized nature of the baby market devalues Black women as mothers, as well as Black infants.

In the case of the baby market for adoption, the demand for healthy white newborns has exceeded the supply. Scholars point to the scarcity in healthy white babies as a result of the confluence of several progressive cultural forces: societal acceptance of single motherhood, the birth control pill, and the legalization of abortion.[22] However, Goodwin dismisses the significance of these factors. Instead, she proposes that "fee structures based on race give evidence that adoption is subject to the free market forces of supply, demand, and preference."[23] This race-based demand results in a valuation of children, in which higher fees are associated with the adoption of white and biracial children and the lowest fees are associated with the adoption of Black children. These differentials must be associated with a market, rather than a charitable service whose first goal is to "act in the best interests of the child." She notes:

> But for the racialized nature of adoption, the market in babies and children might be less detectable. If US adoptions were primarily focused on child welfare and charity, rather than adult need and desire, the costs associated with adopting white children would not exceed black children. . . . Even if the rate of adoption for white babies exceeded that of their black counterparts, black children might nevertheless be second in line to foreign adoption, if the fulfillment of the best interests of US babies was the reality. But sadly, it is not. According to the Department of Health and Human Services, many couples

> wait more than eighteen months, and spend as much as thirty thousand dollars, to adopt children from abroad, bypassing the less "expensive" and less desired black babies.[24]

Prior to my trip on the baby train, I was unaware of the multiple paths to adoption: public and private adoption, along with domestic and international adoptions. I was also unaware of the differential fee structure in private adoptions (based on the infant's race) until I witnessed it firsthand when comparing which agency to use. In the case of public adoption of American infants and children, arrangements are made through public social services agencies, typically through their foster programs. Private adoption is an avenue for adoption of both US-born as well as international infants and children. These adoption arrangements are made between prospective parents and an independent agency. Just as there are various means to adopt, the costs associated with adoption also varies. As the critique by Goodwin cited earlier notes, there are different costs of adoption based upon valuation of infants and children on the basis of skin color, hair texture, or perceived characteristics due to cultural stereotypes. In the end, the adoption agency I chose was the one that explicitly stated, "Our fees are consistent regardless of the infant's race." The fact the agency featured this principle as part of their mission statement confirms that racial differentiation remains a standard operating procedure in the industry.

White Privilege, Citizenship, and the Social Valuation of Adoptive Parents

Typically, I found myself to be the only woman of color in the waiting room at the fertility center. Likewise, the brochures and website advertising fertility treatment typically featured white infants and white families. The smiling infants that dot the advertising have fair features and light-colored eyes and hair. The families depicted are almost exclusively white, middle class, and heterosexual. There are also snapshots of pregnant models: all are young, attractive, and typically white. These pregnant models are often presented wearing white, with their expanded bellies exposed. Perhaps the strangest circumstance is that the pregnant models are often featured among natural settings like standing in a field, or reclining in the grass. The Madonna-like depictions in nature are a far cry from the sterilized hair caps, open-backed robes, catheters, monitors, and test tubes that dominate the landscape of a fertility center. Charis Thompson's fieldwork describes the ontological choreography of fertility-clinic physicians and staff as they navigate complicated relationships of kinship and science.[25] Her research reveals clinic-staff discussions about the suitability of certain clients to a parent on the basis of class, sexual orientation, and ethnicity, thereby restricting access to those who did not fit white, heterosexual, and middle- and upper-income ideals. She points out that despite no racial and class differences among rates of infertility, most clients of fertility clinics are from one demographic group. As a client of the fertility center, I did feel managed. At one point, I was called back to the center after having left two hours earlier, because the staff questioned my assertion that I was ovulating. Indeed, I was ovulating, but the process required lab confirmation.

Christine Ward Gailey implicates the marketing of adoption agencies in preserving the right of prospective adoptive parents to have the baby they want.[26] Her book's title, *Blue Ribbon Babies*, refers to 1970s adoption language for a healthy white baby. She notes that "the neoliberal emphasis on choice, for who can afford it, is unvarnished in these promotional materials, although the language used is often that of altruism" and she equates the search for "Baby Right" akin to the search for Mr. Right, with adopters armed with a list of favorite traits for the prospective child.[27] Indeed, the registration form that I completed for my adoption agency featured a section with demographic and financial questions about our family. Following that section was one on our adoption preferences. Would we prefer an infant? Would we be amenable to adopting a child with special needs? There was a special note attached to the question of our gender preference that read, "Gender preferences are strongly discouraged." Paradoxically, the next question asks registrants to select the race(s) of adoptees that we would prefer, with options that included Black, Biracial (including Black), Caucasian (non-Hispanic), Caucasian (including Hispanic), Asian, Native American, and East Indian. No caveat accompanied the questions about racial preference.

The third condition met by the baby market is the valuation on the other end of the consumption chain: the "social valuing" of adoptive parents. For many adoption agencies, the financial status of adoptive parents is prioritized in the selection and adoption process.[28] As evidence, Goodwin points to scholarship that not only chronicles Black families' financial obstacles to adoption but also the link between marginalized status and greater risk of losing parental rights to one's offspring. The sheer costs of ART limit the potential clients that are able to utilize these measures. In the case of adoption, priority is given to parents who have good credit rating, higher incomes, are homeowners, and so forth. However, these social valuations are not sufficient proxies for good parenting, merely measures for middle-class identification.

A visit to my local library on international adoption yielded a book by

Dawn Davenport, *The Complete Book of International Adoption,* but it assumed that its readers were white families considering transracial adoption.[29] Even when I was browsing adoption sites online, under the search term for adopting Black infants, I would come across white families with Black or biracial adopted children in the website images and online testimonials. These forms of media sent an unwelcome message to me as an African American woman who sought alternative means to family formation on the baby train. In the case of domestic adoption, the advertising is disingenuous, for there are significantly more Black infants awaiting adoption than white infants. A glance at the web page for the Children's Home Society in New Jersey clearly states that, "There are a very small number of Caucasian infants available for adoption. We have an ongoing need for families wishing to adopt African-American infants and toddlers."[30] However, the picture that anchors the text on the website features a young white woman with a white child. Of the six couples who offer family photos in the testimonials featured on the web site for Adoption Associates, all appear to be in heterosexual relationships, and only one couple appears where partners are both African American.[31] It is presumed that most users of this site are not African American, because further down the page, it offers "transracial adoption play groups" as well as a DVD for African American Hair Care, which reads: "Have you adopted transracially? You may sometimes wonder how you'll ever meet the challenge of hair care for your African-American or Biracial child. Wonder no longer—in our African-American and Biracial Hair Care DVD, master stylists use live models to help you work with a texture that is different than your own, with practical advice and suggestions for new styling techniques. Visit the Adoption Accents web site for more information."[32]

An online adoption forum directed me to the weblog, *Chocolate Hair, Vanilla Care* designed by a white mother who adopted a Black daughter. In addition to posting You Tube videos and editorials about styling her daughter's hair, you can "shop" for T-shirts that read "Chocolate Hair, Vanilla Care" and buy African American children's books that value multiculturalism, skin tone, and "nappy" hair, as well as adult books on transracial adoption.[33] It should be noted that this is not simply a site about natural hair care; it is site designed specifically for white caretakers ("Vanilla Care") of Black children and provides paid advertising for hair products and instruments. This website, and the instructional hair care DVD, suggest an emergent consumer market designed to capitalize on the cultural illiteracy of white adopters in transracial adoptions.

Many scholars on adoption refer to the 1972 decision of the National Association of Black Social Workers to oppose the interracial domestic adoption of African American children by white families.[34] The statement equated this practice of adoption as tantamount to cultural genocide. Despite condemnation from Black social workers, race-matching policies in domestic adoption were prohibited. And, despite politicized debates over domestic interracial adoptions between both the left and the right, the number of domestic interracial adoptions, particularly between Black children with white adoptive families, represents about 20 percent of all private domestic adoptions in 2007.[35] However, the data does not account for the adoption of biracial children. Dorothy Roberts supposes that white potential adopters simply do not want Black children.[36] This point is further evidenced by the differential valuation of adoptees within the baby market. While Volkman connects the trends toward open adoption and the Black Social Workers' stance on interracial adoption as significant moments, others highlight US domestic policies that make Black families more vulnerable to state intervention and, ultimately, dissolution.[37]

Roberts attributes three trends that threaten poor Black families, especially children: 1) the legislative shift from family preservation as the central theme in the welfare of children to the termination of parental rights, 2) welfare reform that pushed more women and children off of the welfare rolls and made them more vulnerable to poverty, and 3) tougher criminal penalties, which institutionalize both parents and children.[38] The shift that she refers to is encapsulated in the Child Welfare Act of 1980 to the Adoption and Safe Families Act in 1997, which legislated an expedited process for parental rights' termination for an efficient transition of those children into adoption. Rousseau chronicles the pathologizing of Black women and Black motherhood from 1996–2009, which created the image of the welfare queen.[39]

This connection between US welfare reform, criminalization, and adoption resulted in elevated risks of dissolution for poor, urban Black families and a surge in rates of African American youth into state custody.[40] As a result, African American children represent more than half of all foster children, when African Americans only constitute 13 percent of the American population. Ortiz and Briggs interrogate the "crack baby crisis" of the 1980s and those distinctions made between the deserving poor of the Third World and the pathological "culture of poverty" framework used to describe the poor (and Black) urban underclass.[41] Most claims about the long-term compromised health and life outcomes of newborns with drug-addicted mothers have been persistently debunked by medical literature. Nonetheless, the notion of a biologically determined cohort of "crack babies" codified the conservative agenda of the late 1980s and early 1990s. This is the same agenda that culminated in the War on Drugs, which led to the criminalization, rather than rehabilitation, of poor, Black pregnant drug users. Moreover, it is the same agenda, the Republican's "Contract with America," upon which adoption reform prohibited race-based matching in domestic adoptions. Ortiz and Briggs explain how policy reform was demarcated along racial and economic lines: "Even as welfare reform all but eliminated federal transfer payments to help working-class women raise their own children, the 1996 adoption reform provided a $6,000 tax break to (implicit white) families who adopted a 'special needs' child—with nonwhite a subcategory of the definition of special needs. . . . Combined with the 1980 Adoption Assistance and Child Welfare Act . . . the Adoption Promotion Act meant that the federal government would provide upward of a $13,000 bonus for middle-class white people to raise the same children."[42] The preceding discussion provides evidence of Goodwin's third condition of the baby market, which casts being black and poor as pathological while placing a premium on being white and middle class.

The differential valuation of infants extends to international adoption and dominant frames of who is worthy of rescue. The case of Chinese adoption is particularly instructive. Dorow interweaves the individual desires of the adopted families that she interviews with the immutable racial attitudes and immigration histories of Chinese Americans.[43] She concludes that the increasing desire for Chinese adoptees is based upon what potential adopters perceive as the "rescuability of Chinese children along with their imagined racial flexibility." To this end, decisions about Chinese adoption are made in relation to what she refers to as "black abjectness," evoking Ortiz and Brigg's points about distinctions between deserving and undeserving poor. She shares the sentiments of one parent of a Chinese adoptee:

> Jackie had just finished telling me how important it was to teach her daughter about Chinese culture, when she continued, "I mean, look at the black community. If they truly had pride in who they were, the community wouldn't be disintegrating. . . .I think the reason why the Asian communities have excelled in our society is that they *do* have pride in who they are." Simultaneously referencing discourses of the culture of poverty (associated with blacks), the model minority (associated with Asians), and globalized humanism (associated with whites), Jackie imagines what her daughter is and can be against what she is not and will not be. A racially and culturally proud, desirable, redeemable Asian child is distinguished from the racially and culturally abject, marginalized, and possibly irredeemable black (collective) body.[44]

The issues of race and class in adoption are connected through our notion of citizenship. Through the power of American citizenship, potential adopters are given choices in the baby market. The path to family formation is not only a marker for citizenship; it is a tenet of the American middle-class ideal of citizenship. Our history of American racial relations has been charged with limiting the rights and access for full citizenship for African Americans, and for other racial and ethnic minorities. A major source for American immigration and full citizenship has come in the form of international adoption, which is not always framed around issues related to immigration. The contradiction comes when the right of citizenship counters the prevailing principles of "the best interests of the child" within all forms of adoption. As white adoptive families assert their race and class privileges associated with citizenship, the baby market caters to those families, rather than acting in the interests of the children. Moreover, African Americans must wage the persistent battle for citizenship amidst a hostile climate of Black pathology and the criminalization of poor Black women. Covert questions arise in the adoption: *Are these children worthy of the rights and entitlements of American citizenship? Are these parents worthy of the rights and entitlements of American citizenship?*

The Political Economy of the Baby Market: International Adoption and Medical Tourism as Neocolonialism

The fourth and final condition of baby markets is the presence of "unrestrained international markets," which impact the domestic baby market. Gailey notes that 15 percent of all adoptions in the United States are intercountry (international) adoptions.[45] She also discusses the role of the political economy in adoption both domestic and international, private and public, invoking the notion of "the personal is political" espoused by C. Wright Mills, along with feminist activists:

> Although many adopters might disagree, adoption in the United States is not a private matter. As both policy and practice, adoption involves people with different degrees of social power in a society of ever-increasing wealth differences, racial and ethnic hierarchies, and uneven but persistent discrimination by gender and sexual orientation. We must situate adoption practices in national and global contexts: neoliberal policy shifts away from social services and social welfare in the last quarter of the twentieth century, the collapse of the Soviet bloc, the economic and social reforms in China, and the proliferation of capi-

> talist markets through-out the world . . . episodically creates a practice of adoption that in effect trafficks in children.[46]

Adoption scholars situate the practice of international, transracial adoptions as part of increasing American militarization and occupation. Briggs conjures an interesting frame of "Madonna and child" images as an appeal to American support for humanitarian relief abroad, especially in the wake of military intervention.[47] In her chapter entitled, "Client, Ambassador, and Gift," Dorow highlights the ways in which Chinese adoptees are framed in these three manners—all in an attempt to distance the adoption process from its commoditization.[48] Riley refers to this phenomenon as a "privileged obliviousness" of the adopter: this divorce between the social and economic forces that force birth parents to give up their children and their adopted child.[49] I find Dorow's discussion of an *adoptee as gift* to be most relevant within a political economic context, because the actions are so clearly channeled in one direction—from poor women (often of color) who give up their children for adoption to childless women with means from the West.[50] Approaching an adoptee as gift relies upon the articulation of fate or destiny. As Darrow notes, however, the adoption of an abandoned Chinese girl to Western parents complicates the notion of preordination: "the sex of the child casts doubts on narrations of predestination by standing as a testament to the material structures that shaped abandonments. I would therefore argue that the language of fate tends to suppress the histories of patriarchy and state policy that loosen girls from the "giving" birth family and that make them gifts *unfreely* given."[51]

Some connect today's baby markets to other historical moments predicated upon the resource exchange of human relations: Goodwin connects baby markets with slavery, referring to a picture that she keeps in her office, which depicts a slave auction sign that reads, "two mulatto wenches for sale." Spar connects the travails of infertility with concubinage during the Biblical era, as exemplified by the plight of Sarah and Abraham in the Old Testament. Eng equates transnational adoption with the solicitation of war brides and mail-order brides, thereby connecting contemporary practices of gendered commodification and exploitation.[52] Lovelock traces the history of intercountry adoption for the United States, as well as comparative studies of Canada and New Zealand.[53] She argues that the manner that adoption patterns for these nations were balanced with the national concerns regarding immigration. In the 1940s and 1950s, European orphans arising from the devastation of World War II represented a significant number of adoptees. Next, there was an era marked by a rise in adoption of Asian children, then those from Latin America, then the former Soviet Union (especially Romania), and more recent trends have turned back toward Asian countries. Lovelock identifies two successive waves that characterize international adoptions, where attitudes shifted from "*finding families for children*" to "*finding children for families.*" Embedded within these actions is a deliberate discourse on American humanitarianism and "rescue," or what Gailey refers to as "salvation imagery." For example, in the wake of Haiti's January 2010 earthquake, members of the Central Valley Baptist Church in Idaho were accused of abducting Haitian children. Ten members of this Christian group tried to smuggle thirty-three children out of Haiti through the Dominican Republic. This international incident made some question, "When does adoption become child trafficking?"[54]

Like the understanding of an adopted child as a "gift," the association of adopted children as "rescues" is equally problematic. It negates the role played by the history of colonialism and contemporary globalized programs that produce inequalities through national debt, structural adjustment programs by world lending agencies, and unregulated global capital that drive global poverty and the inability of parents (mostly women) to care for their children.

While many are familiar with the increase in international adoption, there is also a small but growing number of global fertility centers that offer lower costs related to ART. The largest sperm bank in the world is Cryos Denmark, which guarantees shipment virtually anywhere in the world.[55] Euphemistically referred to as "procreation vacations," destination ART programs are designed to combine leisure and the scientific enterprise of IVF. The Czech Republic has emerged as an innovator in this field. While living in the Caribbean, I came across an advertorial with the headline, "A vacation that really delivers." It was a sponsored article chronicling Dr. Julia Skinner, who founded the Barbados fertility clinic in 2002. While the article relies on testimonial from a Trinidadian woman and her experience, the text is quick to point out the Clinic's advantages of lower costs, accelerated egg donation, and a relaxing Caribbean atmosphere for potential American and European clients.[56] India has emerged as a global leader in IVF procedures. In 2010, India had more than 550 registered IVF centers and was expected to surpass both the United States and China in the number of IVF cycles.[57] An episode on the Oprah show entitled *Wombs for Rent* brought Indian surrogacy to mainstream audiences in 2006.[58] Viewers witnessed dorm-style living of impregnated Indian women acting as surrogates to childless couples from the United States and abroad. Despite a critical backlash of Dr. Nayna Patel, the doctor featured on that episode, a *Nation* magazine article revealed that her Akansha Infertility and IVF Clinic has experienced unprecedented success since the taping of the segment.

In the context of discussions about the macro and microlinkages shaping ART and transnational adoption, Rothman offers an important caveat: "There is an enormous difference between what works at an individual level and what works as social policy. As a public policy, adoption cannot be the long-range solution for infertility, even though it obviously works for many individuals. It does not work as a social policy because it makes us dependent upon the grief of one group of people to solve the problems of another group of people."[59] I know that this research and writing project has deeply affected the ways in which I considered the very private choice within a racialized and politicized context.

* * *

On March 28, 2014, the baby train that I had boarded five years prior reached its final destination: my husband and I welcomed the arrival of a baby boy we named Ellis Julian via private adoption. My quest finally led me to a private agency whose mission statement stressed that it would not differentiate the costs of adoption based on the race of the infant. My research and experience confirm that inequality defines the baby train. Given access to the resources that I have, my son's birth mother would have not had to make an adoption plan for her child. Still, I rest in the knowledge that *she* chose me; that we are forever linked and that we hold a bond, however young and fragile, in our open adoption.

Notes

1. While this paper focuses almost exclusively on issues related to race, class, and gender, it is important to note the frames of heteronormativity in discourse around family planning. For more emphases around heternormativity, please see D. D. Eng (2003) "Transnational Adoption and Queer Diasporas," Social Text 21(3):1–37, and S. Dorow and A. Swiffen, (2009) "Blood and Desire: The Secret of Heteronormativity in Adoption Narratives of Culture," American Ethnologist 36(3): 563–73.

2. Karma R. Chavez, *Standing in the Intersection: Feminist Voices, Feminist Practices in Communication Studies* (Albany: SUNY Press, 2012), 7.

3. K. Animashaun Ducre, *A Place We Call Home: Gender, Race, and Justice in Syracuse* (Syracuse: Syracuse University Press, 2012), 5.

4. Carolyn S. Ellis and Arthur Bochner, "Autoethnography, Personal Narrative, Reflexivity: Researcher as Subject," 2000, http://works.bepress.com/carolyn_ellis/49/; Carolyn Ellis, *The Ethnographic I: A Methodological Novel about Autoethnography* (Rowman Altamira, 2004), http://books.google.com/books?hl=en&lr=&id=

h-KgTdh8H24C&oi=fnd&pg=PP2&dq=carolyn+ellis+and+autoethnography&ots=4uENrANlZ5&sig=GsomE9ugMGynYaAC84NNz4sKc7M; Irma McClaurin, *Black Feminist Anthropology: Theory, Politics, Praxis, and Poetics* (Rutgers University Press, 2001); Robin M. Boylorn, "As Seen On TV: An Autoethnographic Reflection on Race and Reality Television," *Critical Studies in Media Communication* 25, no. 4 (October 2008): 413–33, doi:10.1080/15295030802327758.

5. "IVF and Infertility By The Numbers," *Forbes*, accessed June 21, 2014, http://www.forbes.com/sites/davidsable/2014/04/24/ivf-and-infertility-by-the-numbers/; Rachel L. Swarns, "U.S. Adoptions From Abroad Decline Sharply," *The New York Times*, January 24, 2013, sec. World, http://www.nytimes.com/2013/01/25/world/us-adoptions-from-abroad-decline-sharply.html.

6. Kimberly Krawiec, "Price and Pretense in the Baby Market," in *Baby Markets: Money and the New Politics of Creating Families*, ed. Michele Goodwin (Cambridge [U.K.]; New York: Cambridge University Press, 2010): 41–55.

7. Ibid.; Michele Goodwin, *Baby Markets: Money and the New Politics of Creating Families* (Cambridge [U.K.]; New York: Cambridge University Press, 2010); Debora L Spar, *The Baby Business: Elite Eggs, Designer Genes, and the Thriving Commerce of Conception* (Boston; London: Harvard Business School; McGraw-Hill [distributor], 2006).

8. Sharon Kirkey, "Fertility Laws Push Canadian couples into the Black Market: Reformed Needed Now, Critics Argue," *Edmonton Journal*, December 12, 2010.

9. Kaiser Family Foundation, "Mandated Coverage of Infertility Treatment," January 2010, accessed September 22, 2013, http://kff.org/womens-health-policy/state-indicator/infertility-coverage/.

10. Spar, *The Baby Business*.

11. Rebeccca Skloot, *The Immortal Life of Henrietta Lacks* (New York: Crown Publishers, 2010).

12. Ibid., 90.

13. J. G. Raymond, "The International Traffic in Women: Women Used in Systems of Surrogacy and Reproduction." Reprod Genet Eng 2, no. 1 (1989): 51–57.

14. Spar, *The Baby Business*.

15. D. Ojanuga, "The Medical Ethics of the 'Father of Gynaecology', Dr J Marion Sims," *Journal of Medical Ethics* 19, no. 1 (March 1993): 28–31.

16. Caroline M. de Costa, "James Marion Sims: Some Speculations and a New Position," *The Medical Journal of Australia* 178, no. 12 (June 16, 2003): 660–63.

17. I. H. Kaiser, "Reappraisals of J. Marion Sims," *American Journal of Obstetrics and Gynecology* 132, no. 8 (December 15, 1978): 878–84; L. Lewis Wall, "The Medical Ethics of Dr J Marion Sims: a Fresh Look at the Historical Record," *Journal of Medical Ethics* 32, no. 6 (June 2006): 346–50; L. Lewis Wall, "Did J. Marion Sims Deliberately Addict His First Fistula Patients to Opium?," *Journal of the History of Medicine and Allied Sciences* 62, no. 3 (July 2007): 336–56.

18. Stephen C. Kenny, "'I Can Do the Child No Good': Dr Sims and the Enslaved Infants of Montgomery, Alabama," *Social History of Medicine: The Journal of the Society for the Social History of Medicine / SSHM* 20, no. 2 (August 2007): 223–41; Harriet A. Washington, *Medical Apartheid: The Dark History of Medical Experimenta-*

tion on Black Americans from Colonial Times to the Present (New York: Harlem Moon, 2006).

19. Spar, *The Baby Business, 13.*

20. Deborah R. Grayson, "Mediating Intimacy: Black Surrogate Mothers and the Law," *Critical Inquiry* 24, no. 2 (January 1, 1998): 525–46.

21. Ibid., 540–41.

22. Spar, *The Baby Business*; Christine Ward Gailey, *Blue-Ribbon Babies and Labors of Love: Race, Class, and Gender in U.S. Adoption Practice* (Austin: University of Texas Press, 2010).

23. Goodwin, *Baby Markets, 6.*

24. Ibid., 8.

25. Charis Thompson, *Making Parents: The Ontological Choreography of Reproductive Technologies* (Cambridge: MIT Press, 2005).

26. Gailey, *Blue-Ribbon Babies and Labors of Love.*

27. Ibid., 88.

28. Nancy E. Riley, "American Adoptions of Chinese Girls: The Socio-political Matrices of Individual Decisions," *Women's Studies International Forum* 20, no. 1 (1997): 87–102.

29. Dawn Davenport, *The Complete Book of International Adoption: A Step-by-Step Guide to Finding Your Child* (New York: Broadway Books, 2006).

30. The Children's Home Society of New Jersey, "Domestic Adoption," http://www.chsofnj.org/adopt_domestic.html (accessed September 22, 2013).

31. Adoption Associates, "African-American Infant Adoption," accessed September 22, 2013, http://www.adoptionassociates.net/domestic/african_american/.

32. Ibid.

33. *Chocolate Hair, Vanilla Care, "About,"* September 22, 2013 http://www.chocolatehairvanillacare.com/p/about.html (accessed September 22, 2013).

34. Sara K. Dorow, *Transnational Adoption: A Cultural Economy of Race, Gender, and Kinship* (New York: New York University Press, 2006); Mary Ann Davis, "Intercountry Adoption Flows from Africa to the U.S.: A Fifth Wave of Intercountry Adoptions?," *International Migration Review* 45, no. 4 (2011): 784–811; Dorothy E Roberts, *Shattered Bonds: The Color of Child Welfare* (New York: Basic Books, 2002).

35. Sharon Vandivere, Karin Malm, and Laura Radel, *Adoption USA: A Chartbook Basedon the 2007 National Survey of Adoptive Parents* (Washington, DC: The U.S. Department of Health and Human Services, Office of the Assistant Secretary for Planning and Evaluation, 2009), accessed September 22, 2013, http://aspe.hhs.gov/hsp/09/NSAP/chartbook/.

36. Roberts, *Shattered Bonds.*

37. Toby Alice Volkman et al., *Cultures of Transnational Adoption* (Durham: Duke University Press Books, 2005).

38. Roberts, *Shattered Bonds.*

39. Nicole Rousseau, *Black Woman's Burden: Commodifying Black Reproduction* (New York: Palgrave Macmillan, 2009).

40. Gailey, *Blue-Ribbon Babies and Labors of Love.*

41. Ana Teresa Ortiz and Laura Briggs, "The Culture of Poverty, Crack Babies, and Welfare Cheats: The Making of the 'Healthy White Baby Crisis,'" *Social Text* 21, no. 3 (2003): 39–57.

42. Ibid., 51–52.

43. Dorow, *Transnational Adoption.*

44. Ibid., 38.

45. Gailey, *Blue-Ribbon Babies and Labors of Love.*

46. Ibid., 3–4.

47. Laura Briggs, "Mother, Child, Race, Nation: The Visual Iconography of Rescue and the Politics of Transnational and Transracial Adoption," *Gender & History* 15, no. 2 (2003): 179–200.

48. Dorow, *Transnational Adoption.*

49. Riley, "American Adoptions of Chinese Girls."

50. Marcia C. Inhorn, *Reproductive Disruptions: Gender, Technology, and Biopolitics in the New Millennium* (Oxford: Berghahn Books, 2008).

51. Dorow, *Transnational Adoption, 141.*

52. David L. Eng, "Transnational Adoption and Queer Diasporas," *Social Text* 21, no. 3 (n.d.): 1–37.

53. Lovelock, Kirsten. "Intercountry Adoption as a Migratory Practice: A Comparative Analysis of Intercountry Adoption and Immigration Policy and Practice in the United States, Canada and New Zealand in the Post W.W. II Period." International Migration Review 34, no. 3 (2000): 907–49.

54. Matthew Clark, "Haiti Orphan Rescue Mission: Adoption or Child Trafficking?" Christian Science Monitor, February 1, 2010, accessed September 22, 2013, http://www.csmonitor.com/World/Global-News/2010/0201/Haiti-orphan-rescue-mission-Adoption-or-child-trafficking.

55. Cryos Denmark, accessed September 22, 2013, http://dk.cryosinternational.com/home.aspx.

56. Debbie Jacobs, "Advertorial: A Vacation That Really Delivers," *Caribbean Beat, Inflight Magazine for Carribean Airlines,* January/February 2011, 57–61.

57. Emily Wax, "In India, Age Often Not an Impediment to Pregnancy," *The Washington Post,* August 13, 2010, A01

58. Lisa Ling, "*Wombs for Rent,*" *Oprah* January 1, 2006, accessed September 22, 2013, http://www.oprah.com/world/Wombs-for-Rent/5.

59. Barbara Katz Rothman, *Recreating Motherhood,* 2nd edition (New Brunswick, NJ: Rutgers University Press, 2000).

References

Adoption Associates, Inc. "African American Infant Adoptions." Accessed September 22, 2013. http://www.adoptionassociates.net/domestic/african_american/.

Anagnost, Ann. "Maternal Labor in a Transnational Circuit." In *Consuming Mother-*

hood, edited by Janelle S. Taylor, Linda L. Layne and Danielle F Wozniak, 139–67. New Brunswick: Rutgers University Press, 2004.

Boylorn, Robin. "As Seen on TV: An Autoethnographic Reflection on Race and Reality Television." *Critical Studies in Media Communication* 25, no. 4 (2008): 413–33.

Briggs, Laura. "Mother, Child, Race, Nation: The Visual Iconography of Rescue and the Politics of Transnational and Transracial Adoption." *Gender & History* 15, no. 2 (2003): 179–200.

Bureau of Consular Affairs. "FisalYear 2010 Annual Report on Intercountry Adoptions." 6: US Department of State, 2010.

Carney, Scott. "Inside India's Rent-a-Womb Business." *Mother Jones*. April 8, 2010. Accessed September 22, 2013. http://m.motherjones.com/politics/2010/02/surrogacy-tourism-india-nayna-patel.

Cartwright, Lisa. "Images of 'Waiting Children': Spectatorship and Pity in the Representation of the Global Social Orphan in the 1990s." In *Cultures of Transnational Adoption*, edited by Toby Alice Volkman, 185–212. Durham: Duke University, 2005.

Chávez, Karma R., and Cindy L. Griffin, eds. *Standing in the Intersection: Feminist Voices, Feminist Practices in Communication Studies*. Albany: SUNY Press, 2012.

The Children's Home Society of New Jersey. Accessed September 22, 2013. http://www.chsofnj.org/adopt_domestic.html.

Chocolate Hair, Vanilla Care. "About." Accessed September 22, 2013. http://www.chocolatehairvanillacare.com/p/about.html.

Clark, Matthew. "Haiti 'Orphan' Rescue Mission: Adoption or Child Trafficking?" *Christian Science Monitor/Global News Blog*. February 1, 2010. Accessed September 22, 2013. http://www.csmonitor.com/World/Global-News/2010/0201/Haiti-orphan-rescue-mission-Adoption-or-child-trafficking.

Clarke, Alison J. "Maternity and Materiality: Becoming a Mother in Consumer Culture." In *Consuming Motherhood*, edited by Janelle S. Taylor, Linda L. Layne, and Danielle F. Wozniak, 55–71. New Brunswick: Rutgers University Press, 2004.

Cryos Denmark. Accessed September 22, 2013. http://dk.cryosinternational.com/home/aspx.

Davenport, Dawn. *The Complete Book on International Adoption—A Step-by-Step Guide to Finding Your Child*. New York Three Rivers Press, 2006.

Davis, Mary Ann. "Intercountry Adoption Flows from Africa to the U.S.: A Fifth Wave of Intercountry Adoptions?". *International Migration Review* 45, no.4 (2011): 784–811.

De Costa, Caroline M. "James Marion Sims: Some Speculations and a New Position." *Medical Journal of Australia* 178, no. 12 (2003): 660–63.

Dorow, Sara K. *Transnational Adoption: A Cultural Economy of Race, Gender, and Kinship*. New York: New York University Press, 2006.

Ducre, K. Animashaun. *A Place We Call Home: Gender, Race, and Justice in Syracuse*. Syracuse: Syracuse University Press, 2012.

Ellis, Carolyn S. *The Ethnographic I: A Methodological Novel about Autoethnography*. Lanham, MD: Rowman/Altamira Press, 2004.

Ellis, Carolyn S., and Arthur Bochner. "Autoethnography, Personal Narrative, Reflexivity: Researcher as Subject." In *The Handbook of Qualitative Research,* edited by Norman Denzin and Yvonna Lincoln. 733–68. Thousand Oaks: Sage, 2000.

Eng, David L. "Transnational Adoption and Queer Diasporas." *Social Text* 21, no. 3 (2003): 1–37.

Farquhar, Dion. *The Other Machine: Discourse and Reproductive Technologies*. Thinking Gender, New York: Routledge, 1996.

Gailey, Christine Ward. *Blue-Ribbon Babies and Labors of Love*. Louann Atkins Temple Women & Culture Series. Austin: University of Texas Press, 2010.

Goodwin, Michele Bratcher, ed. *Baby Markets: Money and the New Politics of Creating Families*. Cambridge: Cambridge University Press, 2010.

Grayson, Deborah R. "Mediating Intimacy: Black Surrogate Mothers and the Law." *Critical Inquiry* 24, no. 2 (1998): 525–46.

Inhorn, Marcia C. *Reproductive Disruptions: Gender, Technology, and Biopolitics in the New Milennium*. Oxford: Berghahn Books, 2008.

Jacobs, Debbie. "Advertorial: A Vacation That Really Delivers " *Caribbean Beat, Inflight Magazine for Carribean Airlines*, January/February 2011, 57–61.

Kaiser Family Foundation. "Mandated Coverage of Infertility Treatment, January 2010. Access date September 22, 2013. http://kff.org/womens-health-policy/state-indicator/infertility-coverage/.

Kaiser, I. H. "Reappraisals of J. Marion Sims." *American Journal of Obstetrics and Gynecology* 132, no. 8 (1978): 878–84.

Kendall, Laurel. "Birth Mothers and Imaginary Lives." In *Cultures of Transnational Adoption*, edited by Toby Alice Volkman, 162–83. Durham: Duke University Press, 2005.

Kenny, Stephen C. "'I Can Do the Child No Good': Dr Sims and the Enslaved Infants of Montgomery, Alabama." *Social History of Medicine* 20, no. 2 (2007): 223–41.

Kirkey, Sharon. "Fertility Laws Push Canadian Couples into the Black Market: Reformed Needed Now, Critics Argue." *Edmonton Journal*, December 12, 2010.

Kirsch and Kirsch, P. C. "Meet Families Waiting for African American and Mixed Race Babies." http://www.indianaadoption.com/CM/Custom/Meet-Families-Waiting-for-Babies-of-Mixed-Race.asp. Accessed September 22, 2013.

Kopytoff, Igor. "Commoditizing Kinship in America." In *Consuming Motherhood*, edited by Janelle S. Taylor, Linda L. Layne, and Danielle F Wozniak. New Brunswick, 2004: 270–271.

Krawiec, Kimberly D. "Price and Pretense in the Baby Market." In *Baby Markets: Money and the New Politics of Creating Families*, edited by Michele Bratcher Goodwin. Cambridge: Cambridge University Press, 2010.

Layne, Linda L. "Making Memories: Trauma, Choice, and Consumer Culture in the Case of Pregnancy Loss." In *Consuming Motherhood*, edited by Janelle S. Taylor,

Linda L. Layne, and Danielle F. Wozniak. New Brunswick: Rutgers University Press, 2004: 122–138.

Ling, Lisa. "Wombs for Rent. *Oprah*. January 1, 2006," Accessed September 22, 2013. http://www.oprah.com/world/Wombs-for-Rent/5.

Lovelock, Kirsten. "Intercountry Adoption as a Migratory Practice: A Comparative Analysis of Intercountry Adoption and Immigration Policy and Practice in the United States, Canada and New Zealand in the Post W.W. II Period." *International Migration Review* 34, no. 3 (2000): 907–49.

McLaurin, Irma. *Black Feminist Anthropology: Theory, Politics, Praxis, and Poetics*. New Brunswick: Rutgers University Press, 2001.

Ojanuga, D. "The Medical Ethics of the 'Father of Gynaecology', Dr J Marion Sims." *Journal of Medical Ethics* 19, no. 1 (1993): 28–31.

Ortiz, Ana Teresa, and Laura Briggs. "The Culture of Poverty, Crack Babies, and Welfare Cheats: The Making of the 'Healthy White Baby Crisis.'" *Social Text* 21, no. 3 (2003): 39–57.

Raymond, J. G. "The International Traffic in Women: Women Used in Systems of Surrogacy and Reproduction." *Reprod Genet Eng* 2, no. 1 (1989): 51–57.

Riley, Nancy E. "American Adoptions of Chinese Girls: The Socio-Political Matrices of Individual Decisions." *Women's Studies International Forum* 20, no. 1 (1997): 87–102.

Roberts, Dorothy E. *Killing the Black Body: Race, Reproduction, and the Meaning of Liberty*. 1st ed. New York: Pantheon Books, 1997.

——. *Shattered Bonds: The Color of Child Welfare*. New York: Basic Books, 2002.

Rory. "Chocolate Hair, Vanilla Care." http://www.chocolatehairvanillacare.com/. Accessed Septemeber 22, 2013.

Rothman, Barbara Katz. "Caught in the Current." In *Consuming Motherhood*, edited by Janelle S. Taylor, Linda L. Layne and Danielle F Wozniak. New Brunswick: Rutgers University Press, 2004.

——. "Motherhood under Capitalism." In *Consuming Motherhood*, edited by Janelle S. Taylor, Linda L. Layne and Danielle F Wozniak. New Brunswick: Rutgers University Press, 2004.

Rousseau, Nicole. *Black Woman's Burden: Commodifying Black Reproduction*. New York: Palgrave McMillan, 2009.

Sable, David. "IVF and Infertility By the Numbers." *Forbes*, April 4, 2014. Accessed June 21, 2014. http://www.forbes.com/sites/davidsable/2014/04/24/ivf-and-infertility-by-the-numbers/

Scruby, Airan. "Bills to Tighten in Vitro Rules." *San Bernardino County Sun (California)*, 2009.

Skloot, Rebecca. *The Immortal Life of Henrietta Lacks*. New York: Crown Publishers, 2010.

Smith, Andrea. "Beyond Pro-Choice Versus Pro-Life: Women of Color and Reproductive Justice." *NWSA Journal* 17, no. 1 (2005): 119–40.

Spar, Debora L. *The Baby Business: How Money, Science and Politics Drive the Commerce of Conception*. Boston: Harvard Business School Publishing Corporation, 2006.

Swarns, Rachel L. "U.S. Adoptions from Abroad Decline Sharply," *The New York Times*, January 24, 2013. Accessed June 21, 2014. http://www.nytimes.com/2013/01/25/world/us-adoptions-from-abroad-decline-sharply.html

Taylor, Janelle S. "Introduction." In *Consuming Motherhood*, edited by Janelle S. Taylor, Linda L. Layne, and Danielle F. Wozniak, 1–18. New Brunswick: Rutgers University Press, 2004.

Thompson, Charis. *Making Parents: The Ontological Choreography of Reproductive Technologies*. Inside Technology. Edited by Wiebe E. Bijker, W. Bernard Carlson, and Trevor Pinch Cambridge: MIT Press, 2005.

Vandivere, Sharon, Karin Malm, and Laura Radel. "Adoption USA: A Chartbook Based on the 2007 National Survey of Adoptive Parents." Washington, DC: The U.S. Department of Health and Human Services, Office of the Assistant Secretary for Planning and Evaluation, 2009. Accessed September 22, 2013. http://aspe.hhs.gov/hsp/09/NSAP/chartbook/

Volkman, Toby Alice, ed. *Cultures of Transnational Adoption*. Durham: Duke University Press, 2005.

Wall, L. L. "Did J. Marion Sims Deliberately Addict His First Fistula Patients to Opium?". *Journal of the History of Medicine and Allied Sciences* 62, no. 3 (2007): 336–56.

——. "The Medical Ethics of Dr J Marion Sims: A Fresh Look at the Historical Record." *Journal of Medical Ethics* 32, no. 6 (2006): 346–50.

Washington, Harriet A. *Medical Apartheid: The Dark History of Medical Experimentation on Black Americans from Colonial Times to the Present*. 1st ed. New York: Doubleday, 2006.

Wax, Emily. "In India, Age Often Not an Impediment to Pregnancy." *The Washington Post*, August 13, 2010, A01.

Yngvesson, Barbara. "Going 'Home': Adoption, Loss of Bearings, and the Mythology of Roots." In *Cultures of Transnational Adoption*, edited by Toby Alice Volkman. Durham: Duke University Press, 2005.

3

A Baby "Made in India"

Motherhood, Consumerism, and Privilege in Transnational Surrogacy

Karen Hvidtfeldt Madsen

Websites with domain names such as havingababyinindia.blogspot.com, millionrupeebaby.blogspot.com, and tajmababy.blogspot.com are just some of the numerous weblogs (blogs) on the subject of surrogacy in India available on the Internet. The bloggers are Western parents or intended parents seeking transnational fertility treatments that combine egg donation and the service of one or more surrogate mothers in India. Some are infertile couples that have tried every other available option in their home country; others are singles or male couples from countries where the legislation prohibits their access to such treatments.

The aim of this chapter is to address how motherhood, kinship, consumerism, and privilege develop in relation to transnational surrogacy through a comparative analysis of the virtual motherhood of prospective parents from the West and the surrogate motherhood of Indian women who carry a child for fees and medical service. First, I examine how prospective parents seeking surrogacy in India use weblogs as a venue for identity work by identifying recurrent themes and rhetorical strategies used to describe their experience.[1] Specifically, my analysis focuses on the journey metaphors used to describe the surrogacy process and traces how bloggers confront various fears, challenges, and frustrations through the language of kinship and agency. Second, I draw on a variety of sources (ethnographies, documentary films, and news accounts) that feature Indian surrogates commenting on their experience. Focusing on the intersection of motherhood and privilege,[2] I identify the religious and mythological frameworks that shape their daily enactments of kinship. Finally, I delineate how the binary opposition of altruism versus commercialism that typically characterize public media and research work on transnational surrogacy is challenged,[3] and how the Western bloggers' statements compare to our knowledge of Indian surrogate mothers' experiences. In so doing, my chapter explores the rhetorical dynamics of what Marcia Inhorn describes as global *reproflows*, which encompasses the complex mixture of bodies, cells, money, and information on the move in the transnational reproduction industry.[4] My analysis is also informed, however, by the growing body of work in gender and science studies regarding how reproduction technologies are framed for stakeholders,[5] and seeks to illuminate how issues of consumerism and privilege are discussed in relation to transnational surrogacy in a late-modern neoliberal context.[6]

Assisted Reproduction and Surrogacy in India

An increasing number of Indian fertility clinics have specialized in offering surrogacy services over the last decade.[7] The clinics not only serve Indian citizens but also NRIs (Nonresident Indians) and patients from Europe, Australia, and North America with no direct connection to India other than their impression of India as a global leader for international surrogacy. Besides the lower costs, private Indian clinics offer expertise and international standards, shorter waiting periods, doctors educated in the United States or the United Kingdom, and extensive use of digital communication, which reduces the isolation caused by geographical distance.[8] Diverse treatments are available and, until recently, the necessary visa requirements had few restrictions regarding marital status or sexuality.

The surrogate industry is a growing part of India's medical tourism industry, which was estimated to contribute $2 billion to its GNP in 2012. Estimates of the number of Indian fertility clinics vary between 350 to over 3,000; however, a UN-backed study in July 2012 assessed the surrogacy business at more than $400 million a year.[9] In 2014, *The Indian Express* estimated the current number of surrogacy cases in India to be between four hundred and five hundred, with about 30 percent involving international patients.[10] Some clinics have a much higher percentage. For example, the Akanksha Clinic in Anand in Gujerat boasts more than five hundred surrogate babies born since 2004. Of those cases, two-thirds involved clients from more than thirty different countries. The Mumbai-based fertility bank, Surrogacy India, boasts more than 295 surrogate babies born since it opened in 2007. Of those cases, 90 percent involved international clients and 40 percent were same-sex couples.[11]

Indian laws on assisted reproductive technologies legalized commercial surrogacy in 2002 and have since left the market operating on a more or less unregulated basis. A number of problematic cases concerning citizenship of children born by surrogates in India led the Ministry of Health and Family Welfare to draft the Assisted Reproductive Technology Regulation Bill in 2010.[12] The bill aimed to regulate the central issues of assisted reproduction and required the establishment of advisory boards of experts at both national and state levels with the task of recommending future modifications to the rules. Registration and accreditation of fertility clinics is required, and in the specific area of surrogacy, the bill sought to clarify both rights and duties of the parties involved: the commissioning parents (referred to as 'patients'), surrogates, donors, and children. According to the bill, conception by surrogacy shall only be available to patients for whom a normal pregnancy would not be possible. Additionally, the restrictions stipulated that a couple or an individual shall not, as hitherto, be allowed to have the service of more than one surrogate at any given time.[13] Furthermore, the number of oocytes or embryos that may be placed in a woman will be regulated by the National or State boards.[14] The bill also requires that the future citizenship of the child or children is clarified in advance and that a local guardian is appointed with the obligation to take care of the child's well-being in case the foreign party does not claim the child. In this case, the child will be given Indian citizenship.[15]

The bill has yet to pass and therefore only has status as a set of guidelines. But in July 2013, the Indian government updated visa regulations, and the process to obtain a specific surrogate visa now requires a valid (heterosexual) marriage certificate showing that parents have been married for at least two years and a formal letter from the home country stating that surrogacy is recognized and legal. The new regulation excludes all applicants from countries that do not officially recognize transnational surrogacy, and the entire gay community, the sum of which, according to Adrienne Vogt, accounted for 60 to 70 percent of the total volume. Singles coming from abroad also are excluded by the regulation.[16]

In response to these new restrictions in India, surrogacy destinations are opening in Mexico, Thailand, and Nepal, and thus the global market of surrogacy moves constantly. To maintain its competitive edge in these emerging markets, the Indian government has (in 2014) decided to allow the import of frozen human embryos for artificial reproduction. This makes possible a more flexible and swift procedure to bring in or ship human embryos that are already prepared for implantation in the surrogate womb, and may make the surrogacy experience in India more attractive for foreign couples.[17]

Virtual Motherhood

The Internet plays a crucial role for intended parents from countries such as the United States, the United Kingdom, and Australia, which are commonly identified as the primary source countries for foreigners seeking surrogacy services in India.[18] The blogs allow prospective parents to follow the Indian surrogate's pregnancy checkups on Skype and regularly communicate with the doctors and surrogates through the use of digital media. An excited intended mother describes on her blog how she performs "long-distance motherhood" where the electronic device metaphorically replaces the fetus far away: "I did not sleep a wink last night, slept with my phone on the pillow next to my ear and with a laptop next to the bed. I'm losing it!"[19]

The existence of digital networks fostered by the rise of blogs also has been a decisive factor in the professionalization of the intended parents, who share information and experiences worldwide within seconds. The bloggers often express a feeling of solidarity toward each other and an obligation to disseminate relevant factual information about Indian clinics, their procedures, and how to deal with Indian and domestic authorities. They share and discuss the numerous and often highly emotional aspects of the process. They describe, for example, the pain of infertility, stressful waiting periods, and the joy that accompanies the arrival of long-desired children.

Blogs on surrogacy have all the characteristics of new digital media and multimodal ways of integrating text-based sequential stories with graphics, photos, and film. A central element of the blogging activity concerns the possibility of sharing a visual chronicle of their journey: the ultrasound pictures of the fetus's growing, "belly shots" of the pregnant surrogate, and portraits of newborn babies and children (often with dark hair and brown eyes bearing witness to their Indian genes) are uploaded among many tourist images from trips to India, although it is obvious that the bloggers are not regular tourists. The purpose of traveling is to bring home one or more children and thus, transform oneself and one's partner into parents and establish a "normal" family.

As a medium, the blog genre gives users the opportunity to create a familial origin story. Reproduction is obviously a process extended in time: the bloggers hope and wish for a pregnancy, often over several attempts. The chronological structure of the blog makes it possible to express the details of waiting and the countdown of days until the expected time of birth. The diary-like form of communication that characterizes a blog often seems to have a therapeutic purpose for the bloggers. Writing on *So How Does It Feel to Be Pregnant?*, Shannon notes, "It is a lot to wrap your head around. . . . While I'm over the moon to be pregnant, it's just hard accepting that it's not happening inside my body." Tracy expresses a similar dilemma: "I feel like I am in pregnancy limbo. Pregnant, but not really pregnant."[20] The virtual community gives the intended parents the possibility of narrating the pregnancy, if not physically experiencing it. In so doing, the blog compensates for the lack of embodiment and proximity, as well as the feeling of isolation and loneliness often experienced by prospective parents.

Surrogacy blogs also reveal how the virtual ties fostered through the process can be more meaningful than conventional family relations. Some bloggers express a fear of being condemned by family and friends outside their virtual surrogacy community and they exchange thoughts on the blog about how and when it is wise to disclose the surrogate's pregnancy. Some bloggers even use pseudonyms to maintain their privacy. For example, "CharlieCat" writes on *Surrogacy Pains*, "Unlike any other pregnancy, our support comes from strangers from around the world."[21] The author of *Surrogacy Circle* similarly evokes the feeling of intimacy and solidarity among bloggers: "When one of our 'own' surro-buddy has a baby we ALL get so involved and excited."[22] Thus, just as the line between being pregnant and not-pregnant is blurred in the flow of reproductive fluids, body parts, intentions, and desires, the relations between the social and the genetic are also blurred. In several cases, bloggers refer to each other as "blog family" and express the feeling of being more closely connected to peers in the blog world than they are to their biological families.

Blog titles like *Made in India*, *Procreated in India*, and *Million Rupee Baby* reflect the need of the intended parents to disarm the commercial aspects of transnational surrogacy by appropriating symbols of Indian culture through humor and irony.[23] Through domain names (e.g., www.tajmababy.blogspot.com), cultural terms like "chai" and "masala," or strategic cover images such as colorful sarees, the blogs signify the cultural flows that accompany the repoflows.[24] The blog *A Distant Miracle* makes the journey an explicit focus with a cover image of the Taj Mahal and a subtitle that dramatizes the effort involved in the surrogacy process: "Traveling 7,500 Miles to Grow Our Family."

The blog *Out of India* not only frames the surrogacy process as a gift from one nation to another through its domain name (www.fromindia-withlove.blogspot.com) but also as a gift from God through its subtitle: "A Miracle of Life Will Bud in Delhi and Blossom in California As a Gift From God Through Egg Donation and Gestational Surrogacy."[25] In so doing, the blog introduces a religious discourse that includes metaphors of nature ("bud," "blossom") and a medical discourse ("egg donation" and "gestational surrogacy"). The notion of "donation" inscribes the act of gifting as a central element.

A variety of metaphoric frames are used across the surrogacy blogs created by intended parents. The "journey" is a well-established metaphor for a surrogacy process that is used extensively. As a metaphoric frame, the journey encompasses a number of related terms. For example, infertile parents choose different "routes" in the process of becoming parents, and all family members need to be "on board" for the journey. The reliance on metaphors among these prospective parents echoes the work of Emily Martin, who found that women's demands for autonomy and "natural" birth procedures (in the sense that they are physically active and possibly without medical intervention) resulted in a corresponding set of metaphors for the birth procedure. Martin identified the "journey" as a key metaphor used by women because it could capture "the sense of acting and doing" by comparing the act of giving birth to running a marathon or climbing a mountain.[26] The metaphor of traveling, according to Martin, was used in the sense of an "inner journey," as women reinterpreted birth as an opportunity for psychological development and learning. Within the field of transnational surrogacy, the journey thus has multiple meanings, as it refers to the psychological challenges, concrete traveling to India, and process of coming to terms with the commercial aspects involved.

In the surrogacy weblogs, the reliance on the journey metaphor dramatizes emotional investment over the financial investment made by intended parents. CharlieCat has brought home twins from New Delhi to Australia and emphasizes the great efforts and costs the infertility has meant for the couple: "My journey, like many others, comes after 15 years of infertility treatments, miscarriages, invasive treatments, hormone therapies that never worked." During the lengthy process, she and her partner gave up their initial plan of using a surrogate in the United States with their own biological embryo after they realized that the combination of CharlieCat's age and personal medical history left only a slight chance of achieving a viable pregnancy. So, they decided instead to buy donor eggs and to secure an Indian surrogate.[27] Similarly, Meg from Perth in Western Australia became the mother of a son in 2010 "after three tries, two miscarriages and four trips to India" and with help from both egg donation and a surrogate. In *Chai Baby*, CharlieCat lists the distresses that bloggers typically mention in relation to their surrogacy journeys: "The miscarriages, the missed attempts, the failed attempts, the exotic flus and whooping coughs, the dead sperm, paying for surrogates & egg donor we didn't use, the grief of using an egg donor, the hurt, the sorrow, the anxiety, the fights, the worry, the bureaucracy—these are *our birthing pains.*"[28]

CharlieCat uses the physical pain of labor as a metaphor for the challenges that the prospective parents of surrogate children face. By creating a homology between physical and emotional pain, the metaphor also naturalizes the surrogacy process. The blogger behind *Million Rupee Baby* (a mother from California whose daughter was born in 2009) also seeks to normalize surrogacy and legitimate her status as a mother by dramatizing the emotional labor involved in the surrogacy process. Citing a "declaration by an unknown author" that was recirculated throughout the surrogacy blogosphere, the blog indicates how prospective parents reframe notions of agency and labor. Using moral terms, the text stresses the efforts that the intended parents undergo to get their children: "I will be better not because of genetics or money . . . but because I have struggled and toiled for this child." "I will be a better mother for all that I have endured. I am a better wife, a better aunt, a better daughter, neighbor, friend, and sister because I have known pain."[29]

Surrogacy bloggers often define themselves and each other as particularly dedicated parents by virtue of what they have endured. Indeed, other common metaphors include references to their "marathon," which signals both the lengthy process involved and the emotional strength required for transnational surrogacy.[30] Thus surrogacy bloggers also argue that parents who have experienced infertility have invested much more than those who "just" get pregnant without help. Even though they have not experienced the actual physical pregnancy, they have felt and lived through a pain comparable with an actual birth. Following this argument, they are made legitimate parents despite not having gone through pregnancy or having genetic relatedness to the child.

Intended parents often position the surrogate mothers as unreal and supernatural, describing them as "angels." These narratives compare to the traditional fairytale where the hero meets a number of complications before succeeding and living happily ever after. For example, descriptions of the setting for Indian surrogacy borrow from traditional fairytales and magical realism in that bloggers often characterize their journey as an adventure in a distant and foreign land. On the blog *A Distant Miracle*, Shannon summarizes her experiences in a fairytale manner when she says that "dreams DO come true."[31]

The bloggers stress (both) their own (and the surrogate mother's) active efforts as significant, and they argue that their own intentionality is crucial in establishing kinship with the child. Emily Martin argues that the metaphors of the female body and reproduction during the twentieth century were influenced by the industrial society (e.g., efficiency, regularity), and that they have since moved into what she describes as a theoretical framework of chaos, where the unpredictable and flexible count as ideals. Similarly, the bloggers seem to develop metaphors that in many ways reflect late-modern ideals in the era of globalization. The global community, for example, is celebrated when Megan welcomes the transnational opportunities made available for them through Internet communications: "So, here we have an egg donor from South Africa, a surrogate in India and a couple in Australia making a family. Wow. It is such an honour to be the instigator of this process and make friends with people from across the world, who only have our best interests at heart."[32] Similarly, the blogger Tracy compares her experience of the Indian reproduction process with a sports team, in a way that also addresses the rhetoric in late modern business management where coaching, project management, and team building are key words: "Anyone pursuing surrogacy should know that it is the ultimate team effort. M is the captain—the glue (literally) that holds us all together. I am the quarterback—in charge of distributing the ball (or eggs, if you will). B is on special teams—usually on the sidelines, but an indispensible part of the team. Dr. Patel is the coach—writing the play book and leading us all to victory. We have learned to trust in and have created a lifelong bond with our new teammates."[33] Here, Meg chooses to present her 'team' as solely driven by altruistic motives while Tracy highlights the more emotional aspects. In the discourse, the surrogate mother M 'stars' as 'Captain,' the doctors become 'coaches,' while the recipient couple takes on more peripheral positions.

The bloggers distance the act of transnational surrogacy from a commercial transmission of buying or hiring a womb by virtue of these metaphors of global connection. The relationship to the Indian surrogates is narrated as a late-modern global teamwork where all stakeholders are granted agency and respectability. Thus, globalization is both the basis for the Internet-based community of bloggers and a theme in the construction of virtual motherhood. From the point of view of the intended parents, surrogacy is described as an emotional investment where the journey metaphor underlines the intensity of the process.

Surrogate Motherhood

The surrogacy process looks quite different for surrogate mothers. First, they do not have weblogs and their views are not as readily available as those of the prospective parents. However, a glimpse into these essential perspectives can be found by culling ethnographies, documentary films, and news accounts. In the documentary stage play *Made in India*, based on fieldwork in India, surrogate mother Puja provides the following commentary on the experience of motherhood:

> How do we do it? people ask. Don't we feel as consumables, like pack mules? They put a burden on us for a while, pat us on the shoulder, takes the burden and go on. What kind of mothers are we? Don't we

> feel any pain when we give away the baby? Some couples behave like this: They treat the surrogate mother as a princess while she is carrying the child, gives her a mobile phone and call her each day to hear how it goes. After delivery we are hardly allowed to touch the baby. They say the baby will get an infection. While it was inside us, we did not pass the infection? I'm not sure how I feel about giving the baby to her. I know it's not her fault that she could not raise her own child or breast-feed him. But she does not seem to have any emotional ties to him either. Did you see when the baby started crying, she kept talking to you without paying any attention to him? When he cries, I want to start crying as well. I have felt him growing and moving inside me. I have gone through stomach aches, back aches and over five month of no appetite at all.[34]

This extended passage isolates several of the key themes that characterize how understandings of motherhood are negotiated in cases of transnational surrogacy. The play reenacts the surrogate's feelings of attachment to the surrogate child, including how she deals with sadness when having to hand the baby over to the intended parents. Similarly, a feature article in the Norwegian magazine *Plot*[35] refers to an interview with the surrogate mother Diksha who says: "For seven days I was inconsolable" about the separation from her first surrogate child whom she breast-fed for two months before the separation.[36]

In these accounts, physical pain is expressed as well. Surrogate mother Jagruti Rameshbhai Vasawa positions the labor process, including the pain involved in Caesarean section, as especially important: "It is natural to think of a child you have carried for nine months. I gave birth to my own three children in the normal way, but the surrogate child was taken by Caesarean section. This is more painful. We have had to cut up the stomach to deliver them, therefore we have a closer connection. And we find it horrible to give away the child. But that's how it is. No pain—no gain."[37] Thus the surrogates, like the Western bloggers, transform the physical pain they have experienced into feelings of connectedness toward the child as the painful pregnancy treatments and the Caesarean transform into emotions of love and care. The article refers to doctors, however, who state that it is the intended parents who impose their Western ideals of motherhood on the surrogates: "Surrogate mothers rarely want to see the baby and they never want to keep it. They are mentally prepared. What makes them sad is that that surrogacy journey is over."[38] In contrast to the surrogate comments and the *Made in India* play, these doctors position surrogates as enjoying the experience so much that any sadness in fact relates to the fact that the process comes to an end. In a similar vein, Anita Soni, a physician at Hiranandani Hospital in Mumbai, states that the foreign couple's demand for communication and meetings with the surrogates creates problems: "Honestly, I think that some Western parents are quite selfish when they want contact with the surrogate mother. It just makes it more complicated for all parties."[39] From the point of view of the Indian medical professionals, the surrogates handle the issues of pregnancy better without the influences of the intended parents. In this framing, the emotional communication serves the need of the Western intended parents, not the Indian surrogates.

According to sociologist Amrita Pande, surrogates draw on a variety of rhetorical strategies to define their relation to surrogate children. First, they extend their framework of kinship. Pande notes that Indian surrogate mothers from the surrogate hostel in Gujerat[40] refer to "everyday forms of kinship" formed from both the "shared substance" (e.g., sharing blood and producing milk) and "shared company" with the unborn child (during pregnancy). They also refer to "the labor of gestation and giving birth." Pande also identifies different strategies used by the surrogate mothers in order to come to terms with the separation from the child. As the Christian Bible contains examples of surrogate mothers, Indian women also refer to mythological and religious frameworks, for example the foster mother of Lord Krishna.[41] They compare those stories to the cultural practices of giving their own daughters away and how those children will be missed. In several cases, the interviewed surrogates mention that they feel a special closeness to the intended mother, "a special bond . . . like a family."[42] Thus, the Indian surrogate mothers express different opinions on the investments they make along the surrogate process. Some get to feel strongly attached to the child through pregnancy, especially if they get to take care of the children after birth, and others express full contentment with the arrangement.

More Than Money

The strategies used to destigmatize the fees associated with surrogacy within the blogs further emphasize the relationship of medical specialists and technology over the relationship between the surrogate and child. Even when the surrogate is mentioned explicitly, she is contextualized in relation to the team of specialists. For example, the blogger CharlieCat argues that the surrogate mother obviously has a right to be paid just as a doctor would: "Everyone else gets paid: the doctors, the lawyers, the psychologist, the infertility specialist, but not the one person who is being poked and prodded and is actually doing the work and carries the risk?" Thus, the intended parents affirm the acceptability of paying for surrogacy: "No one can ever say that our babies were an afterthought or a fashionable accessory come to us on a whim. Like many of my peers, homes have been remortgaged, loans undertaken, decisions made that will impact on our financial future for many years to come."[43] While the surrogate gains the financial means to purchase a home, the prospective parents may experience financial pressure in order to gain access to the specialists and technology required for them to create a family. Within such accounts, the stress of financial insecurity serves as a parallel burden to the stress of bearing a pregnancy. Other prospective parents argue that it is the service of surrogacy that they pay for, not the child: "How is this any different to a woman who becomes pregnant in the 'natural' way, who buys the services of medical professionals in order to have her baby? If she decides to give birth in a private hospital, she purchases the services of her OBGYN, nursing staff, a private room and other goods and services required for her to give birth. Are these not commodities? Because she is paying for these services does this then mean she is buying her baby, or that her medical team are selling the baby to her? With surrogacy, there is just one more step in the process to have a baby, the services of a woman willing to carry the baby."[44] As this quote suggests, the surrogate mother (in the minds of prospective parents) does not stand apart from the medical and technological services a pregnancy or childbirth requires today. All (Western) women are currently serviced during pregnancy by doctors and health professionals, and therefore, the difference between a "natural" and a "non-natural" pregnancy is deconstructed and redeveloped within a new metaphorical framework.

On the blogs, the Western intended parents construct the argument that their payments cover the service of carrying out a pregnancy, not the actual child. Following a neoliberal frame of mind, the surrogate's ability and right to dispose of her own body are highlighted, including, for example, her right to make money on surrogate motherhood as a service. They downplay the money they pay and instead highlight the mental effort that parenthood has "cost" them, and the blog can be seen as a way of documenting these efforts and legitimizing the creation stories. Names, metaphors, and the visual expression of the blogs reveal that the intended parents use a "gift economy" framework, and that the gift is the child. While you typically do not pay for a gift, the intended parents understand their payment as symbolically consisting of intentionality combined with the pain and worries they have felt during the long waiting period.

In reality though, it is without doubt the paying parents who put together and lead "the team." The surrogate mother has nowhere near the same degree of influence. After agreeing to the surrogate arrangement, she is typically not allowed to reject medicine, caesarian section, or fetal reduction. In some cases the surrogates are required to stay in surrogacy hostels throughout the pregnancy, where the clinic decides what the surrogates are allowed to eat and how often they can see their families and children. Ultimately, she will be replaced if she does not meet the intended parents' expectations, as is the case for the doctor and the clinic.

For the reasons outlined above, Sayantani DasGupta and Shamita Das Dasgupta critique popular and marketing discourse about surrogacy in which the surrogate is framed as an altruistic relationship instead of a commercial one. Specifically, they argue that Indian surrogacy has been steeped in the language of altruism: "The very rhetoric of global gestational surrogacy in India reflects a sort of cultural and physically invasive colonialization. Indeed, media reports, medical brokerage websites, blogs written by infertile American couples, and infertility forums reveal multiple, interlocking rhetoric that not only obfuscate the commercial and exploitative aspects of this industry, but also uphold Western constructions of motherhood, agency and bodily ownership."[45]

Although this is without doubt true for many weblogs, the abovementioned blogs do (to some extent) confront commercial issues of transnational surrogacy. And as the 2013 documentary *Ma Na Sapna* (A Mother's Dream) notes, surrogates have complex views on the process. The Indian surrogates featured in *Ma Na Sapna* define a "good couple" as being one who pays their respect to the surrogate by sending her regular updates on the child, but possibly also by undertaking her future living costs. Surrogate Parul expresses the experience of feeling disrespected, as she receives her payment from the commissioning parents together with a contact phone number, which proves to be false ("Maybe they're worried that I'd call them a lot. They don't want anyone to know the truth. They want everyone to believe that their mother gave birth to them. Not a surrogate mother.")[46] The Indian surrogates focus on maximizing their earning, typically led by the wish of buying a house of their own. However, they also value the respectful relation to the intended parents. In *Ma Na Sapna*, the surrogates are shown negotiating their payments through their doctor, Nayana Patel. A broker, Madhu, is introduced in the film. She complains that the surrogates no longer earn enough to buy a house as the real estate prices have gone up more than their payments ("If they can they do surrogacy twice and then buy a house after that."). In *Made in India* surrogate Puja says that "Our house ended up double price, almost 5 lakhs. That's why I had to borrow the money from my father. I became surrogate mother again to pay that debt. . . . The money I earn this time, I will spend for a donation for my daughter's education. No schools are free anymore, you have to pay. This time is my last one." Puja describes a vicious circle where an imbalance between expectations and the level of income keeps her in the surrogacy business. At the same time the preference of doing cesareans on the surrogate means a health risk if the procedure is performed more than a few times.

According to Pande, the Indian surrogates often challenge traditional patrilinear understandings of kinship, as they redefine their efforts of treatments, pregnancy, and giving birth as kinship ties toward the child and the intended mother. This evidence points to an understanding of kinship as an active 'kin-work' next to the more passive 'kin-ship,'[47] which can be said to correspond with the rhetoric of 'business management' found on the weblogs. The notion of the surrogacy process as a business commitment (where the level of income is crucial) and a respectful relationship to the intended parents as business partners does not exclude attachment to and care for the actual child.

Conclusions

This analysis leaves no doubt that Indian surrogates and prospective parents from the West operate on very unequal terms within the global fertility industry. While the economically privileged intended parents travel across continents several times during the process, the Indian surrogates typically do not leave their local environment. Most surrogates do not speak English. They do not have a weblog and do not participate in the intended parents' Internet-based communication. Agency on the Internet is not equitably distributed; there is a clear hierarchy and direction of power in the global movements, meaning that Indian surrogate mothers do not have the same opportunities to influence their situation as the Western childless intended parents, for whom blogs are just one of many ways in which to develop and exchange views. The Western bloggers draw on rhetorical strategies of normalization and naturalization as recognizable and conventional ways in which understandings of motherhood and kinship are applied, and the chronological structure of the weblog is suitable for this piece of identity work. The multimodal possibilities and temporal building of the blog make it suitable for sharing updated factual knowledge, and the bloggers can develop and discuss complex issues as well as intense emotions.

Nevertheless, both Western intended parents and Indian surrogates de- and reconstruct the transnational surrogacy process according to structures of globalization. The blog communication facilitates changing ideas of kinship and family formations at a micro level. The dissemination of images, narrations, and metaphors on the blogs provide a view into how traditional values are confronted with a globalized and postmodern way of family making. The weblog is a forum both for family narratives that legitimize kinship and affiliation but at the same time construct narratives that downplay the unpleasant fact of very unequal levels of privilege within transnational surrogacy. Thus both parties negotiate and nuance issues of consumerism and privilege in relation to transnational surrogacy and global family making. At the same time, they also challenge the binary opposition of altruism versus commercialism by demonstrating the development of intrusive paradoxes: for example, how the child is experienced as a gift, although in a sense it can be said to have been designed and paid for, and that the child feels like 'your own,' long before it is born. Rather than emphasizing genetic connections, both surrogate mothers and intended parents in different ways construct a sense of belonging to the child and argue that 'blood ties' are something you can create by intention, offering new meanings to the experiences, struggles, and pain connected to the surrogacy process.

Notes

1. I have tracked a blog community consisting of around twenty weblogs that are intimately connected through their interest for or experience with surrogacy in India between 2007 and 2009 until 2011, and a few are still posting. More than half of the bloggers are situated in the United States, while the rest write from Canada, Australia, Greece, and Great Britain. All except one blogger have succeeded in becoming parents, quite a few have twins, and one couple has been able to bring home three children at the same time with the help of two surrogate mothers. In this chapter, I turn to blogs in which women specifically address the question of motherhood. I have obtained consent from all the bloggers whom I quote and include screen prints from. On the rise of blogs and their evolving forms, see Greg Meyers, *The Discourse of Blogs and Wikis* (London/New York: Continuum, 2010); Todd Stauffer, *Blog On: The Essential Guide to Building Dynamic Weblogs* (New York: McGraw-Hill/Osborn, 2002); Michael Keren, *Blogosphere. The New Political Arena* (Lanham, Maryland: Lexington Books, 2006). On the rise of blogs related to motherhood, see Borda in this volume.

2. Pande, A., "It May Be Her Eggs But It's My Blood": Surrogates and Everyday Forms of Kinship in India. (*Qualitative Sociology, 32*(4), 2009), 379; Pande, A., Transnational Commercial Surrogacy in India: Gifts for Global Sisters? (*Reproductive BioMedicine Online, 23*(5), 2011), 618–25. Valerie Gudenus, *Ma Na Sapna. A Mothers Dream* (2013) www.manasapna.com.

3. Susan Markens suggests two overall competing rhetorical frameworks in her work on the understanding of surrogacy in the United States, one referred to as "the plight of the infertile couples" and the other as "baby-selling." The baby-selling framework focuses on the commodification of the child and positions the fertility industry as a baby factory, the surrogate mother as a worker, and the intended parents as privileged and self-indulgent consumers. In contrast, the rhetorical frame-

work of "the poor infertile" has the narratives of the infertile as point of departure and thereby legitimize the choice of a surrogate mother, including the commercial transactions. Markens, S., *Surrogate Motherhood and the Politics of Reproduction*. (Berkeley: University of California Press, 2007). Also Berend, Z. "The Romance of Surrogacy" (Sociological Forum, Vol. 27, No.4, December 2012: 913–36)

4. Marcia Inhorn, "Assisted Motherhood in Global Dubai: Reproductive Tourists and Their Helpers," in *The Globalization of Motherhood: Deconstructions and Reconstructions of Biology and Care*, ed. JaneMaree Maher and Wendy Chavkin (New York: Routledge, 2010), 183–84.

5. E. Martin, *The Woman in the Body: A Cultural Analysis of Reproduction* (Boston: Beacon Press, 2001); A. Appadurai, *Modernity at Large: Cultural Dimensions of Globalization* (Minneapolis: University of Minnesota Press, 1996); Marcia Inhorn, "Assisted Motherhood in Global Dubai: Reproductive Tourists and Their Helpers," in *The Globalization of Motherhood: Deconstructions and Reconstructions of Biology and Care*, ed. JaneMaree Maher and Wendy Chavkin (New York: Routledge, 2010), 183–84. See also Maren Knecht, Maren Klotz, Stefan Beck, *Reproductive Technologies as Global Form* (Frankfurt am Main/New York: Campus Verlag, 2012); Sarah Franklin and Helena Ragoné, *Reproducing Reproduction. Kinship Power and Technological Innovation* (University of Pennsylvania Press, 1998); Faye D. Ginsburg and Rayna Rapp, *Conceiving the New World Order. The Global Politics of Reproduction* (University of California Press, Berkeley: 1995), Marcia Inhorn, *Quest for Conception: Gender, Infertility, and Egyptian Medical Traditions* (University of Pennsylvania Press, Philadelphia, 1994); Helena Ragoné, *Surrogate Motherhood. Conception in the Heart* (Westview Press Inc, Boulder, 1994); Barbara K. Rothman, *Recreating Motherhood: Ideology and Technology in a Patriarchal Society* (W. W. Norton, New York, 1989); Deborah L. Spar, *The Baby Business. How Money, Science, and Politics Drive the Commerce of Conception* (Harvard Business School Press, Boston, 2006); Charis Thompson, *Making Parents. The Ontological Choreography of Reproductive Technologies* (The MIT Press, Cambridge, 2005); Laura Mamo, *Queering Reproduction: Achieving Pregnancy in the Age of Technoscience* (Duke University Press, Durham, 2007).

6. C. H. Kroløkke and S. Pant, "I Only Need Her Uterus": Neo-liberal Discourses on Transnational Surrogacy. (*NORA: Nordic Journal of Women's Studies, 20*(4), 2012), 233

7. The technological procedure of IVF makes it possible for the surrogate mother to gestate a pregnancy without having a genetic connection to the child, as an already fertilized egg from an egg donor is transferred to the uterus. From a genetic point of view, she is therefore not involved in the pregnancy she gestates. In gestational surrogacy, the egg or sperm (or both) can be provided from a donor, thus the intended parents can be the genetic mother as well as the father of the child or children. If the intended parent is a single male or a same sex male couple, an egg donor will necessarily be involved—which can be either a known or an anonymous egg donor. And when a male-female couple's infertility is related to lack of egg production—due to, for instance, illness or age—egg donation is also often used. Surrogacy is often referred to as being either 'altruistic' (only costs related to the pregnancy are

covered) or commercial. Commercial surrogacy is allowed in a number of US states but not in Australia or most European countries. Nita Bhalla et al., "Foreigners Are Flocking To India To Rent Wombs And Grow Surrogate Babies," *Business Insider*, accessed June 21, 2014, http://www.businessinsider.com/india-surrogate-mother-industry-2013-9.

8. André Jansson and Jesper Falkheimer, *Geographies of Communication*. Nordicom, 2006; Charlotte H. Kroløkke and Karen Hvidtfeldt Madsen, "Også respektabel? Retoriske konstruktioner af fleksible (u)frugtbare kroppe," *Rhetorica Scandinavica* 56 (2010): 31–48

9. Arlie Hochschild, "Childbirth at the Global Crossroads," *The American Prospect* October 2009, accessed March 12, 2014, http://prospect.org/cs/articles?article=childbirth_at_the_global_crossroads; accessed March 11, 2014, http://www.reuters.com/article/2013/09/30/us-india-surrogates-idUSBRE98T07F20130930.

10. Surabhi Abantika Ghosh, "In Boost to Infertility Treatment, Govt Allows Import of Frozen Embryos," *The Indian Express*, accessed June 21, 2014, http://indianexpress.com/article/technology/science/in-boost-to-infertility-treatment-govt-allows-import-of-frozen-embryos/.

11. Nita Bhalla and Mansi Thapliyal, "India Seeks to Regulate Its Booming 'Rent-A-Womb' Industry." *Reuters*, September 30, 2013, accessed March 11, 2014, http://www.reuters.com/article/2013/09/30/us-india-surrogates-idUSBRE98T07F20130930.

12. The bill is currently awaiting the approval of the Indian law ministry. The Assisted Reproductive Technology (Regulation) Bill—2010. Ministry of Health & Family Welfare. Govt. of India, New Delhi: 34 (19)

13. The Assisted Reproductive Technology (Regulation) Bill—2010: 34 (20).

14. The Assisted Reproductive Technology (Regulation) Bill—2010: 23 (2).

15. The Assisted Reproductive Technology (Regulation) Bill—2010: 34 (19).

16. Adrienne Vogt, "The Rent-a-Womb Boom," *Daily Beast—Women in the World*, March 1, 2014, accessed June 14, 2014, http://www.thedailybeast.com/witw/articles/2014/03/01/the-rent-a-womb-boom-is-india-s-surrogacy-industry-empowering-or-exploitative.html.

17. "In Boost to Infertility Treatment, Govt Allows Import of Frozen Embryos."

18. "In India, a Rise in Surrogate Births for West," *Washington Post*, July 26, 2013, accessed June 21, 2014, http://www.washingtonpost.com/world/in-india-a-rise-in-surrogate-births-for-west/2013/07/26/920cb5f8-efde-11e2-8c36-0e868255a989_story.html.

19. A Distant Miracle, "So How Does It Feel To Be Pregnant?" September 30, 2010, accessed November 21, 2011, http://adistantmiracle.blogspot.com.

20. Million Rupee Baby, "All You Need To Know About Parenthood" August 11, 2008, http://millionrupeebaby.blogspot.com (accessed November 21, 2011).

21. Chai Baby, "Surrogacy Pains," August 29, 2011, accessed December 3, 2011, http://havingababyinindia.blogspot.com.

22. Our Magical Journey, "Surrogacy Circle," August 17, 2011, accessed March 21, 2014, http://ourmagicaljourney.blogspot.com.

23. For example, see Procreated in India, accessed March 17, 2014, http://

procreatedinindia.blogspot.com and Million Rupee Baby. http://millionrupeebaby.blogspot.com.

24. For example, see Cocoa Masala, accessed November 21, 2013, http://cocoamasala.blogspot.com/, and Taj Ma Baby, accessed November 21, 2013, http://tajmababy.blogspot.com. A Distant Miracle, "My Farewell," October 27, 2011, accessed November 21, 2011, http://adistantmiracle.blogspot.com. Christmas Eve Boys, *"Terry and Steve + 2,"* November 21, 2011, accessed November 21, 2011, http://christmaseveboys.blogspot.com/.

25. From India With love, "Out of India," http://fromindia-withlove.blogspot.com, accessed November 21, 2011.

26. Martin, *The Woman in the Body*, 158.

27. Chai Baby, "Why NSW Surrogacy Laws Are Not Good Policy and Other Things," November 1, 2011, accessed November 2011, http://havingababyinindia.blogspot.com..

28. Chai Baby, "Surrogacy Pains," August 29, 2011, accessed March 19, 2014, http://havingababyinindia.blogspot.com.

29. Million Rupee Baby, "I Will Be A Wonderful Mother—Author Unknown," October 26, 2008, accessed March 19, 2014, http://millionrupeebaby.blogspot.dk/2008/10/i-will-be-wonderful-mother-author.html.

30. Chai Baby, "'UPDATED: Blokes and Their Tackle Or: 'Men's Egos Around Fertility Are as Fragile as Chooks Eggs with Calcium Deficiency," May 30, 2010, accessed March 21, 2014, http://havingababyinindia.blogspot.com.

31. A Distant Miracle, "My Farewell," October 27, 2011, accessed November 21, 2011, http://adistantmiracle.blogspot.com.

32. Amani and Bob's Indian Surrogacy, "Thunderbirds Are GO!," September 28, 2008, accessed November 22, 2011, http://amaniandbobsurrogacy.blogspot.com.

33. Million Rupee Baby, "Play Like a Champion Today," August 3, 2008, accessed November 22, 2011, http://millionrupeebaby.blogspot.com.

34. Global Stories: "Made in India" Odense, Copenhagen Denmark, 2013.

35. Synnøve Skei Fosse, Amalie Kvame Holm and Eivind H. Natvig. "Tjenestepikerne," (*Magasinet Plot* 1, Stavanger: Dybdeforlaget A/S, 2011), 12–49.

36. Fosse et al., 24.

37. Ibid., 25.

38. Ibid., 16.

39. Sandeep Mane, "Surrogacy India: fertility clinic in Mumbai," Fosse et al., 28.

40. Amrita Pande conducted field studies in Anand in Gujerat in 2006–2008, where she observed the surrogate mothers' living conditions and conducted interviews with surrogate mothers and other stakeholders. The Danish theater company Global Stories production *Made in India* (2012–13) was based on Amrita Pande's research, and she herself was an actress in the play.

41. A. Pande, "At Least I Am Not Sleeping with Anyone," 308.

42. A. Pande, "Commercial Surrogacy," 986; see also E. Teman, *Birthing a Mother: The Surrogate Body and the Pregnant Self* (Berkley: University Of California Press, 2010).

43. Chai Baby, "Why NSW Surrogacy Laws Are Not Good Policy and Other Things," Novermber 1, 2011, accessed March 19, 2014, http://havingababyinindia.blogspot.com.

44. Amani and Bob's Indian Surrogacy, "Supreme Court India Enters Surrogacy Debate," November 16, 2009, accessed November 21, 2011, http://amaniandbobsurrogacy.blogspot.com..

45. DasGupta and Dasgupta, "Motherhood Jeopardized," 139.

46. Valerie Gudenus, *Ma Na Sapna. A Mothers Dream*, Switzerland 2013 (www.manasapna.com).

47. A. Pande, "Commercial Surrogacy in India."

References

Appadurai, Arjun. *Modernity at Large: Cultural Dimensions of Globalization*. Vol. 3. print., *Public worlds, 1*. Minneapolis: University of Minnesota Press, 1996.

Berend, Zsuzsa. "The Romance of Surrogacy." *Sociological Forum* 27 (2003): 913–36.

Falkheimer, Jesper, and André Jansson. *Geographies of Communication: The Spatial Turn in Media Studies*. Göteborg: Nordicom, 2006.

Franklin, Sarah, and Helene Ragoné, eds. *Reproducing Reproduction: Kinship, Power, and Technological Innovation*. Philadelphia: University of Pennsylvania Press, 1998.

Ginsburg, Faye D., and Rayna Rapp. *Conceiving the New World Order. The Global Politics of Reproduction*. Berkeley: University of California Press, 1995.

Inhorn, Marcia C. *Quest for Conception: Gender, Infertility, and Egyptian Medical Traditions*. Philadelphia: University of Pennsylvania Press, 1994.

———. "'Assisted' Motherhood in Global Dubai: Reproductive Tourists and Their Helpers." In *The Globalization of Motherhood: Deconstructions and Reconstructions of Biology and Care*, edited by JaneMaree Maher and Wendy Chavkin. 180–202. New York: Routledge, 2010.

Keren, Michael. *Blogosphere: The New Political Arena*. Lanham, Md.: Lexington Books, 2006.

Kroløkke, Charlotte H., and Karen Hvidtfeldt Madsen. "Også respektabel?: retoriske konstruktioner af fleksible (u)frugtbare kroppe." *Rhetorica Scandinavica* 56 (2010): 31–48.

Kroløkke, Charlotte Halmø, and Saumya Pant."'I only need her uterus': Neo-liberal Discourses on Transnational Surrogacy." *NORA: Nordic Journal of Women's Studies* 20 (2012): 233.

Mamo, Laura. *Queering Reproduction: Achieving Pregnancy in the Age of Technoscience*. Durham: Duke University Press, 2007.

Markens, Susan. *Surrogate Motherhood and the Politics of Reproduction*. Berkeley: University of California Press, 2007.

Martin, Emily. *The Woman in the Body: A Cultural Analysis of Reproduction*. Boston: Beacon Press, 2001.

Michi Knecht, Maren Klotz, Stefan Beck, eds. *Reproductive Technologies as Global Form: Ethnographies of Knowledge, Practices, and Transnational Encounters*. Edited by Michi

Knecht, Stefan Beck, and Maren Klotz, *Eigene und fremde Welten, 19*. Frankfurt: Campus Verlag, 2012.

Myers, Greg. *The Discourse of Blogs and Wikis, Continuum Discourse Series*. London: Continuum, 2010.

Pande, Amrita. "'It May Be Her Eggs But It's My Blood': Surrogates and Everyday Forms of Kinship in India." *Qualitative Sociology* 32 (2009): 379.

——. "Transnational commercial surrogacy in India: gifts for global sisters?" *Reproductive BioMedicine Online* 23 (2011): 618–25.

Ragoné, Helena. *Surrogate Motherhood: Conception in the Heart, Institutional Structures of Feeling*. Boulder: Westview Press, 1994.

Rothman, Barbara Katz. *Recreating Motherhood: Ideology qnd Technology in a Patriarchal Society*. New York: Norton, 1989.

Spar, Debora L. *The Baby Business: How Money, Science, and Politics Drive the Commerce of Conception*. Boston: Harvard Business School Publishing Corporation, 2006.

Stauffer, Todd. *Blog On: The Essential Guide to Building Dynamic Weblogs*. New York: McGraw-Hill/Osborne, 2002.

Thompson, Charis. *Making Parents: The Ontological Choreography of Reproductive Technologies*. 2005.

4
"We Were Introduced to Foods I Never Even Heard Of"

Parents as Consumers on Reality Television

Cynthia Gordon

In the family health makeover reality show, *Honey, We're Killing the Kids*, private family life and expert interventions become a product for public consumption. By attributing children's everyday health practices (food consumption and activity patterns) and the "epidemic" of childhood obesity to specific lifestyle choices, rather than to sociological factors, the show constructs identities for the people it features.[1] Of particular interest is how language is used to create identities for the participating parents who are ostensibly "killing their kids" through their practices (e.g., feeding their children too much processed food) in the context of a program wherein a nutrition expert stages a family health intervention to "save" the children. In this chapter, I use theories and methods of discourse analysis to examine how parents—and in particular mothers—are discursively portrayed as compulsory consumers of expert advice when it comes to feeding their children. In analyzing how families are depicted, especially when purchasing and preparing food, I also show how these consumer identities are situated within ideologies of middle-class privilege and individual agency, and couched in assumptions about gender and whiteness.

Specifically, I analyze the language that constitutes the program, especially in scenes wherein parents are confronted about their children's health, are given expert advice about food, and attempt to put that advice into practice. The show's nutritionist and the parents draw on and are connected differently to ideologies about parenting and food: The nutritionist talks about children's health in terms of parental responsibility and orients to food through the lens of nutrition science. The parents, and particularly the mothers, are depicted as blameworthy and as unknowledgeable about healthy foods (but redeemable, if they properly consume the advice of the expert).

Reality television increasingly represents and scrutinizes the behaviors, competence, and identities of "ordinary" people—such as parents—while simultaneously elevating the status of "experts" of various types.[2] Reality television's expert advice is also made available for audiences at home. While perhaps aiming to be helpful, these practices contribute to contemporary conceptualizations of everyday activities (from preparing food and exercising to getting dressed) as requiring the consumption of expert-provided guidance. Family-help shows, as Galit Ferguson argues, "tie together discourses of parenting, transformation, class, expertise, race, gender, the nation, worth, and shame."[3] Indeed, cultural studies scholars have repeatedly identified reality television as a site for ideological reproduction and social identity construction, highlighting its role as a potential influence on how viewers orient to various aspects of their social worlds.[4] My sociolinguistic discourse analysis of *Honey, We're Killing the Kids* offers a different, but complementary, perspective: It gives microlevel insights into how parental identities in general, and maternal identities in particular, are linguistically portrayed on reality television, and how consumerism and middle-class (and, largely, white) ideals are promoted through such constructions. In other words, it aims to show how important cultural ideologies related to family life, parenting, and food consumption are realized through the details of the language of reality television.

Theoretical Background: Identities and Ideologies

Discourse analysts and other scholars that understand communication through a social constructionist lens have established that identities, while presumably having some relatively "fixed" elements, are interactionally co-constituted.[5] They have shown how people use language, and other communicative means, to portray themselves and others as particular kinds of people at specific interactional moments through taking up *alignments* toward themselves, others, and topics of talk;[6] through *positioning* themselves and others in socially meaningful *storylines*;[7] and through performing culturally recognized *acts* and taking up social *stances* that *index* identities.[8] Individually and in combination these notions are widely utilized in discourse analytic inquiry into identity construction; collectively they have been conceptualized as part of a larger, interdisciplinary approach that Mary Bucholtz and Kira Hall call a "sociocultural linguistic approach."[9] Scholars adopting this approach conceive of identity as a product of culturally contextualized social interaction rather than as primarily psychological. They also view identities as existing on multiple levels, including interaction-specific and more broadly cultural. The approach suggests that identities are constructed through direct naming (e.g., through referring to someone as "doctor") as well as indexed through social stances, linguistic styles, and other means. It additionally acknowledges the importance of the self-other relationship in identity creation. Finally, scholars using this approach view identity construction as in part habitual, in part conscious or strategic, and as related to larger ideological structures.[10] In other words, contemporary discursive understandings of identity offer means of connecting microlevel language use and identity construction, and identity construction to broader social, cultural, and ideological phenomena.

Numerous ideologies shape the everyday talk that constitutes family life. A primary ideology in American culture is that parents, and especially mothers, are responsible for their children's behaviors.[11] Thus, when a child misbehaves, a mother might tell an account that manifests this sense of responsibility.[12] The ideology of "intensive mothering"—identified and described by Sharon Hays as one where "the methods of appropriate child rearing are construed as *child-centered, expert-guided, emotionally absorbing, labor-intensive*, and *financially expensive*"—also affects many parent-child interactions, especially in the American middle class.[13] This ideology is drawn upon to create gendered parental identities in family conversations; Shari Kendall for example shows how in two dual-income families mothers are linguistically construed as "primary caregivers" and fathers as "breadwinners," though both parents work outside the home and report shared co-parenting ideologies.[14]

Further, in the specific context of childhood obesity, the word "parent" is often a stand-in for "mother." As Tanya Zivkovic, Megan Warin, Michael Davies, and Vivienne Moore explain, "It is mothers, but not fathers, who are deemed to be primarily culpable, both legally and morally, for childhood obesity."[15] JaneMaree Maher, Suzanne Fraser, and Jan Wright's analysis of media representations of childhood obesity demonstrates how mothers are constructed as "managers of children's bodies," for instance through news reporting that emphasizes actions of mothers but not fathers.[16]

Intensive mothering and the idea that parents (and mothers especially) are responsible for children's outcomes are also situated within wider consumerist ideologies and practices. Parenting does not happen in a vacuum (despite how it is sometimes depicted on reality television). As Ellen Seiter remarks, "Contemporary parenthood is always already embedded in consumerism."[17] And the assumption that food shopping and preparation is primarily a female domain persists, creating what Amelia Lake and colleagues call an "enduring gender divide in food responsibility."[18] As Marjorie DeVault's classic sociological study showed, it is women who are responsible for "feeding the family."[19]

The ideology that parents in general, and mothers in particular, should consume in the best interest of their children is underpinned by the assumption of privilege. However, not all people have the financial means, time availability, or access to be consumers of goods like organic foods and low-fat cookbooks, or of services like nutrition counseling and swimming lessons for children. In addition, within consumerism, individual agency is emphasized at the expense of other dimensions. For instance, in the context of obesity, macrosocietal problems (like lack of access to fresh foods, or lack of safe places for children to play) are downplayed, with issues of individual drive and aspiration being highlighted, as is the case in *Honey, We're Killing the Kids*.

Given the show's focus and the role of food in family life, it is not surprising that ideologies of food also emerge in the show; food can be read there as "a sign of appropriate parental authority."[20] Food ideologies also appear more broadly in everyday (family) talk. As Wynne Wright and Elizabeth Ransom point out, food "has increasingly become a signifier of social class and cultural capital for a growing number of Americans."[21] Fast food restaurant density has been found to be higher in African American and low-income neighborhoods, for example.[22] Not only the kinds of foods people eat, but also the words used to talk about and describe food, index social class identities. Menus that use foreign languages and exotic ingredients, for instance, are assumed to come from upper-class restaurants, whereas those that emphasize simplicity and low prices are perceived as directed toward a lower-class clientele.[23]

Previous research suggests that how families not only consume but also orient to and talk about food in their everyday lives, relates to, and constructs, cultural identities,[24] racial identities,[25] and individual family-role identities such as "nutrition gatekeeper."[26] The contemporary "obesity epidemic" that affects many countries also comes into play: A "good parent," Riina Kokkonen observes, "is somehow able to be in control of the prevailing 'obesogenic' environment filled with easy time-saving convenience food and to choose only the healthy food."[27] Food and food-related talk thus can work to create morally charged identities such as "good parent," in addition to doing work to index gender, social class, and race.

Honey, We're Killing the Kids

I examine how consumer identities are created for parents in the context of the first season of *Honey, We're Killing the Kids* (*Honey*), which aired in the United States in 2006.[28] A show that fits into the "makeover" reality television genre, it can also be classified as what Laurie Ouellette and James Hay call "life intervention" programming, because it "mobilize[s] resources to help ordinary people overcome problems."[29] As Tania Lewis explains, *Honey* "offers parents and in particular their children a complete lifestyle makeover" and "combines social observational elements and melodramatic spectacle with a strongly didactic approach to issues of diet, health, and family relations."[30] It has elements in common with other programs focused on modifying everyday family life practices, be it behaviors related to parenting (*Supernanny*), diet and exercise (*The Biggest Loser: Family Edition*), or housecleaning (*Clean House*). In such shows, everyday family dynamics and behaviors are judged unacceptable and in need of modification by an outsider who is identified as an "expert." As Peter Lunt explains, "experts of every description"—including therapists, home organization specialists, dietitians, and trainers—"now appear on our screens to offer analysis, advice and criticism to individuals concerned to improve themselves."[31] This has the effect of "taking aspects of the private sphere"—including, I would suggest, participants' identities—"and placing them in the context of public scrutiny."[32]

In *Honey*, each episode features one family whose private life—in particular, their health behaviors—is assessed and modified by a nutrition expert. Participating families include ten white families, two African American families, and one Hispanic family.[33] This distribution is fairly typical; as Beth Montemurro remarks, "many reality shows are disproportionately cast with white men and women."[34] All of the families are headed by wife-husband pairs, with the exception of one African American family headed by a single mother. Families live in various parts of the United States, and each includes at least two children. Some of the children (and the parents) appear to be overweight or obese, while others do not. It is revealed, however, that all of the families have less-than-ideal health habits (and in many cases, shockingly so), including disordered patterns of eating, exercise, and rest.

A TLC press release explains the nature of the program, and what effect it aims to have on members of these families:

> *HONEY, WE'RE KILLING THE KIDS!* offers a startling look at the causes of America's childhood obesity epidemic and issues a critical wake-up call for parents. In the series, nutrition expert Dr. Lisa Hark shows how everyday choices can have long-term impacts on children, and offers both the motivation and the know-how to help turn these families' lives around. Using state-of-the-art computer imaging and certified assessments based on measurements and statistics, Dr. Hark first gives Mom and Dad a frightening look at the possible future faces of their children—and a dramatic reality check. Then, introducing her new guidelines and techniques, Dr. Hark works with parents to reverse

> course and give their kids a healthy diet and active lifestyle. But will they stray the course and revert back to their unhealthy ways?[35]

In this press release, the "state-of-the-art computer imaging" refers to morphing images that show how the expert predicts the children will physically age and develop from the present until age forty (the predictions are grim). These are shown to parents in a "confrontation" scene and are used to "shock" the parents (and likely the audience); the parents respond in ways that suggest that their identities as parents are threatened, which I explore elsewhere.[36] The televised "intervention" phase then unfolds; as Ouellette and Hay explain: Dr. Hark "arrives at the home, observes the family in their natural habitat, diagnoses their problems, locks up all the junk food, introduces a set of rules. . . . Cameras capture initial resentments, mid-episode slip-ups, and the eventual mastering of the 'healthy' lifestyle that they have come to desire as their own."[37] Like many such programs, everyday practices and personal accountability are foregrounded, while social and economic factors are almost completely neglected, as suggested by scholarship in cultural studies on reality television.[38] However, there is minimal discourse analytic research considering how the language of health-based reality television shows constructs ideologies such as personal responsibility.

My own prior research in this area suggests that identity construction on reality television must be explored within the context of an understanding that reality television is a multi-layered context, or involves multiple "frames."[39] According to Erving Goffman, a frame can be understood as a definition of a situation.[40] In Deborah Tannen's words, the notion captures "what people think they are *doing* when they talk to each other," or what kind of activity they are engaged in at a given moment.[41] Frames that constitute reality television include "ordinary" conversations held between co-present participants, "confessionals," or statements made seemingly in private directly to the camera, and a narrator's running commentary. In previous work on the show, I demonstrate how the nutritionist's highly direct, "impolite" language (e.g., "You are killing your kids") in her first encounter with the parents contributes to framing the entire process as a life-saving intervention for the children (rather than a typical nutrition counseling or health encounter); it is clear that the success of the intervention depends fully on the parents. The analysis that follows considers the "ordinary conversations" that constitute the show (such as conversations between the nutritionist and the parents), statements made to the camera, and the narrator's commentary in investigating the identity construction that constitutes not only the entertainment and identity performance of reality television,[42] but also sends ideological messages.

Portraying Parental Identities: Responsibility and Knowledge

Parents participating in *Honey* are portrayed as responsible for their children's shortcomings (thus, as blameworthy) and as lacking knowledge about health, in particular how to purchase (and even identify) healthy foods, as well as how to prepare these foods in their homes. In what follows, I suggest that parents' (especially mothers') identities are constructed in juxtaposition to that of the nutritionist, who uses her expertise to intervene and "save" the families. In contrast to parents, when orienting to food, Dr. Hark uses language from nutrition science, thus demonstrating her knowledge. The analysis also reveals an uneven depiction of parental knowledge in the white versus nonwhite families, which is relevant for *Honey*, which, it is argued, has built into it "an acculturation toward middle-class values."[43] Gender differences—in terms of blame and knowledge—are less pronounced, but mothers appear to take the most responsibility across families, reinforcing traditional (but enduring) cultural assumptions that mothers are ultimately responsible for children.

Responsibility: Parents as Blameworthy, but Redeemable

The ideology of parental responsibility—which is interconnected to ideologies of intensive mothering/parenting, individual agency, and consumerism—underlies *Honey*. In previous work, I examine, across all episodes, the pivotal confrontation scene in which Hark blames the parents for their children's present and future health, with a focus on how parents respond.[44] In this scene, Hark evokes the commonly held idea in American culture that parents are responsible for children's behavior[45] and physical appearance.[46] She also animates the belief that parents are responsible for properly caring for children, including nourishing them, which, it has been suggested, is primarily viewed as the responsibility of mothers.[47]

As part of the confrontation scene's "wake up call" to parents, Hark shows computer-generated images that show the children aging poorly (looking not only overweight but also increasingly unkempt and unhappy); in Brenda Weber's words, the images "promise that chubby kids will turn into burnout losers with sallow faces, mullets, missing teeth, paunches, and a general air of felonious misery."[48] Not surprisingly then, these images usually upset the parents. In some cases, the predicted images resemble the parents' current appearance; as noted by Beverley Skeggs, this identifies the parents as "the real problem now in the present."[49]

Hark also uses notably direct language to assign parental responsibility and blame. Her "impolite" language emphasizes the parents' pivotal role in the life-saving intervention for their children.[50] Hark makes explicit statements about the children's unhealthy status and poor habits. For example, she tells the parents of a nine-year-old son that he "is already *fifty pounds* overweight. And that's because he eats *way* too much of the *wrong foods*," (episode 1).[51] Speaking of a ten-year-old girl, Hark tells her parents, "What I found *most shocking* about her diet, was that over three days, she hardly ate any vegetables, and she didn't eat a single piece of fruit!," (episode 4). Hark also makes accusations; for instance she explicitly states, in all episodes, "You are *killing* your kids." Further, she elicits statements of parental responsibility, asking parents questions such as, "Do you feel at all responsible for the way he ((the child)) looks as an adult?" (episode 5) and "How much blame do you take for this image ((of what the child is depicted looking like at age 40))?" (episode 7).

Such utterances effectively call up the ideology of parental responsibility through various linguistic and paralinguistic strategies—including apologies and emotional displays such as crying —used by mothers and fathers to repair their damaged parental identities.[52] For example, one mother, upon seeing the image showing the predication of how her son will look as an adult, starts to cry, saying, "I feel like it's—it's my fault," (episode 11). Parents' uses of such strategies "highlight their awareness and acceptance of parental responsibilities relating to children's dietary, exercise, and rest patterns," while also providing the emotionality expected on reality television.[53]

While my previous research did not uncover a marked difference in the blaming of mothers versus fathers in the confrontation scene, I noted how their verbal participation differs: Of the 968 words spoken by parents in the two-parent families as they respond to Hark, fathers produce 383 words (40 percent) and mothers speak 585 words (60 percent). Yet, there is a great deal of variation. For example, the fathers' words spoken ranged from four (episode 6) to 62 (episode 2), and the mothers' 26 (episode 2) to 82 (episode 1). In general, mothers' greater verbal participation in this scene wherein parents accept and deflect blame could reflect the ideology that holds mothers, more so than fathers, responsible for nourishing children, although this is only a speculation.

In addition to being highlighted in the confrontation scene, the ideology of parental responsibility is made apparent by the show's narrator (who is heard but not seen). He observes, for instance, that the single mother featured in episode 11 "cooks with love, but she's drowning her family in grease." The narrator notes, of the family featured in episode 1, that "both boys get no structured exercise, and spend over six hours a day watching TV, and playing video games. Terrence Senior ((the boys' father)) works nights, driving dumpsters, and barely sees his boys." The implication here is that part of the boys' failure to get exercise is due to their father's failure to spend time with them, because he must serve as the family's breadwinner; also implied is that the mother has done nothing to address this problem.

Parental responsibility also, of course, underpins the program's name; the "we" in *Honey, We're Killing the Kids* refers to the parents. (The show is not called *Honey, Socioeconomic Factors Like Lack of Adequate Grocery Stores in Our Neighborhood Are Killing Our Kids*.) The parents, both mothers and fathers, in all the episodes, accept responsibility for their children's health. They agree to be consumers (at least in the context of the program), accepting Hark's negative assessment of their family, and agreeing to participate in her health intervention program. It is made clear, by the narrator and Hark, that this is how parents can redeem themselves and save their children from an unhealthy and perhaps unhappy life. A prototypical example of this acceptance is shown in the following extract, which occurs near the end of the confrontation scene in episode 12, where Dr. Hark gives the parents hope of redemption:

Dr. Hark: But the good news is, that you can quickly start to offer them ((*the children*)) a better future.
Now I'm offering to introduce an intensive three-week health and fitness routine.
It's not gonna be easy.
But remember, what's at stake is the children's future health.
Are you prepared to rise to the challenge.
Mom: Yes.
Dad: We are.
Dr. Hark: That's great news.

In extracts such as this one, parents accept blame for their children's poor health and commit themselves to Hark's regime, which she will institute in their homes over a three-week period (and which will be video recorded). Across episodes, the narrator notes the parents' commitment to reform, yet he wonders, "But will they succeed at changing the face of their children's future?" Again, the responsibility for the children's health is place squarely on the shoulders of the parents, and, arguably, "parents" can be viewed as a stand-in for "mothers" in the childhood obesity context.[54]

As the responsible party, parents must consume Hark's knowledge and expertise. They accept that their parenting must be expert-guided and centered on the children, characteristic of intensive mothering, an ideology that has middle-class connotations. They especially need guidance when it comes to food. I consider this in detail in the next section.

Knowledge: Orienting to Food

One of the primary goals of the health intervention is to reform the eating habits of these families. Before, the foods eaten (especially by children) are primarily "processed foods" like "cookies, candies, soda, hot dogs, fried foods, and pizza," as Hark points out across episodes. Children are depicted eating pizza in front of the television, eating candy by the handful, drinking giant glasses of soda, and squirting whipped cream into their mouths. Parents are depicted deep-frying, bringing home take-out, and eating in front of the television. Hark, however, will teach families how to purchase, prepare, and consume healthy foods. Her identity as expert vis-à-vis food provides a contrastive touchstone for how the parents are presented while also quietly advocating middle-class values. And her degradation of the families' food consumption helps construct their behavior as in need of an upgrade.

In the confrontation scene, Dr. Hark talks about food from the perspective of nutrition science. Thus food is dealt with in its component scientific parts—nutrients, vitamins, and calories—and discussed in terms of how children's intake of these fails to match up with their biological requirements. For example, a seven-year-old in episode 1 is, according to Dr. Hark, eating "nearly a thousand calories a day *more* than he needs" and a teen in episode 11 is "consuming 30 percent more calories than her body needs." Dr. Hark remarks to one boy's parents that "his food diaries"—which she and her team of experts collected as part of the data-gathering phase on the family—"revealed some *serious* vitamin deficiencies. He also eats more processed sugar in a year than his own body weight!" A boy in episode 2 is proclaimed to be "clinically undernourished," which, she explains, "means his body is deprived of essential nutrients."

When Hark meets the children and their parents at home to initiate her health intervention, she again makes remarks about the children's poor diets, for instance noting that they are failing to consume healthy things such as "water, fruits, and vegetables." She also lectures children and parents as she introduces three rules they need to adopt that week in order to reform their behaviors.[55] In episode 1, for example, she remarks that the hot dogs the children typically eat "are about eighty percent fat," and, while showing the family a stick of butter, remarks, "It's like eating *butter*." She then notes that the family will have to give up foods like hot dogs that not only increase risks of developing high-blood pressure and type 2 diabetes, but also have lots of "sugar, salt, fat, and artificial coloring." They will be replaced with "lean meat"; the family will also eat "fruits and vegetables."

Similarly, in episode 3 after commenting that the children are eating "a *hundred and thirty teaspoons of sugar* day," she tells the family:

Dr. Hark: The most sugar that EACH child needs in a day is TEN TEASPOONS.
It rots your teeth, it can cause diabetes.
Now this has GOT TO STOP.
The first rule for this week, we're calling SACK THE SUGAR, meaning anything with lots of sugar on it is OFF THE MENU.
You're still going to have sugar, but this sugar will be in the form of fruit.

Here Hark conceptualizes the food the children are eating into its constituent parts, most notably as high in sugar. In so doing, she lectures the family from her position as expert. The show has a "didactic" quality that Hark's talk helps create.[56] While constructing her identity and professional role, she also creates a marked contrast between the family's typical food consumption and how they will eat after they implement her changes.

Whereas Hark's identity as expert stays relatively stable throughout the episode—she always is depicted as knowledgeable about food, for instance—the parents' identities necessarily change somewhat as they come to embrace her recommendations (fitting in with the transformative narrative typical of makeover reality television). However, throughout much of the episode, and especially at the beginning, the parents and mothers especially are portrayed as lacking knowledge about food and nutrition and therefore desperately in need of Hark's expertise. Perhaps most notably, in every episode one or more parents are shown struggling to identify, pronounce, and/or prepare the new healthy foods. This not only has implications for their parental identities—in particular for mothers, who are culturally viewed as responsible for nourishing children—and their need of expert guidance, but also regarding socioeconomic class.

The shopping lists that Dr. Hark provides to the families as part of a manual containing her rules and guidelines include items like tofu, clams, bok choy, squid, avocado, and Jerusalem artichoke—quite a contrast from the sugary cereals, sodas, and candies the families have been shown emptying from their cupboards. This contrast, and even the idea of reforming one's diet, is imbued with class implications: As an article in *The Guardian* notes, "real awareness of what we eat—food that is better for us, and for the environment—is essentially a middle-class preoccupation."[57] Further, scientific studies have linked higher-quality diets—including foods such as fresh fruits and vegetables, fish, whole grains, low-fat dairy, and lean meats— with more affluent, better-educated people.[58] Although the exact causes, and the causal nature of the relationship between food and social class, are unclear, the new foods introduced can be read as a middle-class array. In contrast, processed foods can be read as lower class.

In fact, families have some problems identifying some of the new foods. To reinforce this, when the families (most commonly: mother and children) are shopping, the narrator emphasizes that the healthy foods are unfamiliar to the family members, because the parents have never brought them into the home. For example, the narrator points out that one family "heads off to the supermarket to fill their now empty kitchen with vegetables and fruits that the kids have never seen before, let alone eaten" (episode 11). Similarly, when the mother in another family is shown shopping at a grocery store with her sons, as was directed by Hark, the narrator remarks, "This is the first time the boys have touched real fresh vegetables for years" (episode 1). While likely hyperbole, this statement again indirectly implies that this mother has been shirking her parental responsibility of properly feeding her children and further, that she does not embrace the middle-class value of eating fresh fruit. Similarly, in episode 8, when the mother and son are shopping, the narrator says, "Mom knows her way around the aisles of packaged and processed foods, but in the healthy section, she's soon wandering, lost, and bewildered."

In some episodes (but not all), this lack of familiarity with healthy foods is also enforced by parents' own commentaries. For example, in episode 4, the mother is shown grocery shopping; in voice-over the mother explains how frustrating it is "trying to look for things I've never seen before, never heard of before." She is shown not knowing where to find avocados or alfalfa sprouts. She utters "avocados" while selecting several papayas; as the narrator explains (condescendingly, I would suggest) in voice-over, "Sorry Mom, those are papayas, not avocados." In a parallel example in episode 8, a child and his father are unpacking the groceries at home and when the child asks his father if a leek is asparagus, the father says (seemingly without looking at the vegetable in question), "Yes, if it's green," the narrator comments in voice-over in a chastising way, "No dad, that's a leek." These comments position the parents as unknowledgeable about healthy fruits and vegetables (which, it is implied, is unacceptable), to the point of not recognizing them. This exaggerates their lack of knowledge.

The mother in episode 9 is depicted as having particular trouble identifying foods at the store. As the narrator explains of the family, "Looking for fresh foods leads them into uncharted territory.... Problems arise when they don't recognize a thing." Then, the mother is shown in the grocery store saying, "What's that big long green stuff everybody eats on TV?" The mother looks at one item and says, "I think that's a Brussel sprout." She also wonders aloud, "What does a pita look like?" and in voice-over, is shown saying to the camera, "I didn't know some of this stuff existed. I've never seen it before, never heard of it, don't know what to do with it." This mother, again, has knowledge of processed, so-called lower-class foods, but not the fresh foods of the middle class.

Hark's menu of meals to prepare using the items (which are eventually located by family members) includes dishes that are quite "exotic" for these families. Menu dishes include fish stuffed with shrimps and artichokes; smoked salmon vegetable breakfast; wheatgrass shakes; pan-seared tuna; steamed salmon wrapped in cabbage leaves with beet salad; pinach bhaji (an Indian dish); a Japanese sushi and miso soup dinner; red potatoes, baked flounder, and borscht (a Ukrainian soup made out of beets); and seafood paella (a Spanish dish whose name is mispronounced by the mother in episode 5). While less "exotic" foods—like a vegetable pizza—are included in the menu, these are typically introduced later in the family's week. Thus the families are shown early on grappling with buying unfamiliar ingredients and using them to prepare unfamiliar dishes. Again, there are class implications here; for example, a recent qualitative interview study in Britain found that the middle-class families ate more "ethnic" foods than did working-class families.[59] Further, middle-class parents were more likely to attempt to shape their children's (especially older children's) food preferences, which is what Hark is asking of the parents.

Interestingly, there are some subtle differences across families that relate to race/ethnicity, and also speak to the role of gender: Two of the ten white families are shown having trouble identifying one or more healthy food items (avocados in episode 4 for the mother; and Brussels sprouts and pita in episode 9 for the mother) and one is shown having trouble preparing the food (squid in episode 3 for the mother—she has trouble finding its head). One white mother (episode 5) mispronounces paella. (For one white family, a grocery clerk is shown explaining what Jerusalem artichokes are, but it is not clear if the parents are familiar with this or not.) In contrast, two of the three nonwhite families are shown having trouble identifying vegetables (leeks for the father in the Hispanic family in episode 8; bok choy for the African American single mother in episode 11, which she also mispronounces several times); and the third has trouble preparing food (clams for the mother in the African American family in episode 1, which she washes using dishwasher fluid, a gaffe which is pointed out by her husband and—delightedly—by the narrator). Thus, procuring and preparing foods—both thought to be a parental responsibility—are generally portrayed as being more difficult for parents in the nonwhite families. Mothers are especially shown struggling; this is perhaps only because they seem to do most of the cooking in many of the participating families, but could also be linked to the assumption that mothers are ultimately responsible for feeding children. In several of the episodes, Dr. Hark explicitly attempts to increase paternal involvement in food preparation and in mealtime more generally, such as in the family where the son explains, "My mom usually does all the work and Dad really gets home late and never does anything." The struggles depicted on the show thus portray mothers as having been primarily responsible for food in the families, though it is suggested that fathers should help out more. The struggles depicted also suggest that the nonwhite families have to work harder to reach Hark's ideals, which match up with middle-class ways of orienting to and consuming food.

The mother in the episode that centers around a single-parent African American family (episode 11) is portrayed as particularly unknowledgeable about food, both in terms of identification and preparation. (This is the only single-parent family featured in an episode across the season.) In the extract below, the mother is shown attempting to prepare dinner using one of Hark's recipes. Her daughter Alexis (age thirteen) and her son Shakur (age nine) are also in the kitchen and try to help out. The mother does not appear to know how to identify a clove of garlic; nor does she seem to be familiar with steps of food preparation such as slicing vegetables. The narrator's comments are used throughout to reinforce that the mother's utterances and behaviors are indicative of lack of knowledge about healthy, or middle-class, food.

Mom: What is two cloves of garlic? Finely chop.
Narrator: Mom is lost at sea with the new healthy ingredients and the kids aren't helping.
Mom: ((*picks a head of garlic out of a basket*)) What's two cloves?
Is this a clove?
Bamboo shoots. ((*rolls eyes*))
Okay we're looking for bamboo shoots.
((*children look in cupboard*))
Shakur: How do you spell bamboo shoots?
Mom: B A B B something.
Shakur: <*quietly*> Bamboo.>
Narrator: Cooking is turning into a treasure hunt.

Shakur: ((*finds the jar*)) Bamboo shoots!

Narrator: Slicing and dicing is a shock for Mom.

Mom: I know it's a LOT more work than I'm usually doing.

Narrator: For dinner she usually opens up a can, orders takeout, or deep fries everything.

Here the mother is depicted as having trouble identifying a clove of garlic; she cannot spell bamboo; and because of her lack of experience cooking for her children, basic food preparation steps (like slicing) are a "shock for Mom."

As the interaction continues, the mother's talk to the camera is spliced into the scene to emphasize her lack of access to the newly introduced foods. In particular, the mother and the daughter are depicted as not being at all familiar with bok choy (Chinese cabbage)—they don't even know how to pronounce it. The narrator's comments again contribute to constructing the mother as lacking key knowledge.

Mom: ((*speaking to camera*)) We were introduced to foods I never even heard of.

Mom: ((*in kitchen, with children*)) What's one small head of pork chop?
Or bok cha?
What is that?

Narrator: They don't know their bok choy from a pork chop.

Alexis: Chop.

Mom: Chop or bok choy.

Shakur: Pork chop!

Mom: ((*speaking to camera*)) Bok cha whatever, bok choo whatever <*smiles*>
<*chuckling*> What's a bok cha? I don't know!
((*speaking to son*)) Look in the refrigerator and see if anything says that.

Alexis: ((*reading recipe*)) One small bow ow,
I don't know how you pronounce it.

Mom: I don't know about this bok chow stuff.
What part of this do I cook?
Like what do I chop this thing?

Again, here we see a parent's troubled interactions with food—as she wonders what "a small head of pork chop" is and how to pronounce bok choy—being reinforced by the narrator, saying, "They don't know their bok choy from a pork chop." It seems possible that the family is playing with these words—bok and pork are phonetically similar; Mom's "bok chow" rhymes with daughter Alexis's "bow ow"—rather than truly struggling, but this interpretation is not taken by the narrator.[60] And, the mother explicitly states lack of familiarity with these items (uttering, "I don't know," and asking questions). Later in the episode, Hark sends the family to a cooking class to improve their knowledge of cooking techniques (such as how to peel garlic). In so doing, she is improving not only the family's eating habits but also the mother's parenting skills. The family is moving closer to middle-class ideals as they accept the expert's advice, and learn to consume it, along with the new foods.

Changing and Contesting Identities

While all the parents, prior to their adoption of Hark's rules, are depicted as failing to live up to their responsibilities as parents and as unknowledgeable especially about healthy foods, all parents are generally demonstrated to have good intentions and eventually "transform" through interaction with Hark, both of which fit into the broader narrative of makeover reality television while also reflecting consumerist ideologies. For example, the mother in episode 8 tells the camera during the first week of the intervention, "I don't want to fail." Elsewhere in this episode, the narrator notes, "Mom's full of conviction." Thus, while she may lack knowledge and expertise, the mother is determined and persistent. Also in episode 8, the father is shown cleaning out the family's cupboards (at the direction of Hark); while discarding a box of processed food, he remarks, "Four hundred and forty milligrams of sodium." This father thus displays growing expertise thanks to Hark, who, as the narrator notes, has led him to read nutritional information on food boxes for the first time. The parents are positioned throughout the program in reference to the ideologies of parental responsibility; over its course, they make strides in becoming more responsible—although still not experts of health the way Hark is.

While all families transform in the program, and parental identities thereby change for the better, it is not the case that all families were satisfied with the experience. Follow-up interviews tend to highlight mothers and their perspectives. For instance, one mother highlights the class bias of the program, remarking in a newspaper interview that the computer-generated images predicting the children's future physical appearance "made the kids look dirty and scraggly. Just because you're overweight doesn't mean you're dirty or scraggly or have no job."[61] She also remarks that the "before" predicted images showed her sons having tattoos (while the "after" did not), and that, "Not everybody who has a tattoo is a bad person or doesn't take care of themselves. . . . I have five of them."[62] Thus, she notices that her family's lifestyle before the intervention is indirectly connected with lower-class stereotypes. A second mother interviewed for the article (from episode 4) called the entire program "garbage" while noting that she was asked to prepare food her children refused to eat, like squid and couscous. However, these mothers are exceptional. On the show, of course, socioeconomic class—along with race, and gender—are not explicitly addressed (except when Hark identifies mothers as overworked and invites fathers to help out more around the house and/or be more active in food preparation).

In summary, Hark's expert identity in the realm of food is created through how she approaches food through the lens of nutrition science, and how the narrator talks about her. The parents are constructed by both Hark and the narrator as failing to live up to expectations regarding parental responsibility, and their own talk and the talk of the narrator further position them as unknowledgeable about healthy food. The parents, and especially the mothers who are expected to feed the family, desperately need Hark's guidance. In accepting it—becoming concerned with food as an issue, developing familiarity with "middle-class" and "exotic" foods, and attempting to shape their children's tastes—the parents also reinforce middle-class values and the upward mobility message that is built—mostly invisibly— into the show and its underlying theme of consumerism.

In fact, the parents' acceptance of Hark's rules represents upward mobility in a visually striking way. At the end of each episode, Hark shows new computer-generated images depicting her predication of how the children will look as they mature into adulthood. The predications are radically improved, because of Hark's intervention: Instead of having a "felonious" air, dirty clothing, and dated hairstyles, the children at age forty appear as "clear-skinned, well-groomed, smiling, and, vitally, thin."[63] The clothing they are wearing is typically in the realm of white-collar business or business-casual wear. As Ferguson explains, "The televisual configurations of such transformations contain within them judgments about social class and self-comportment"—the children were initially aged into working-class people; after the makeover, they appear to be middle class.[64]

While each family featured in the program is different—in most families the mother is the primary cook, but in several it is the father, and in others it varies by meal—it appears mothers more so than fathers, and nonwhite more so than white families, are held up for scrutiny, at least in the realm of food. This reinforces ideologies that mothers are ultimately responsible for "feeding the family."[65] And, supplementary materials for the show that are available online through TLC's website suggest that mothers are the primary target of *Honey*. For example, short educational videos featuring the expert in season 2 (dietician Felicia Stoler replaced Hark) called *Sneak Peeks*, are addressed to mothers.[66] In a *Sneak Peek* episode titled "Keeping A Healthy Home," Stoler encourages children to help with food preparation, because people learn to cook by "watching mom and helping mom prepare meals." Stoler begins "Grocery Shopping" by noting that "Moms often complain that it's hard to keep unhealthy foods out of their shopping baskets." There is even a video entitled "Exercise for Busy Moms," which suggests that mothers do squats, lunges, and push-ups in the kitchen while preparing dinner. It seems expected that mothers, more so than fathers, will consume the information *Honey* provides, and will use it to shape their everyday shopping, food preparation, and other habits.

The episodes I have examined not only seem more targeted at altering mothers' behaviors than fathers' but also position the white more so than nonwhite families as closer to the idealized middle-class eating habits encouraged by Hark. In fact, cultural diversity amongst the families is not explicitly addressed on *Honey*. For example, Hark criticizes the token Hispanic mother's "hoarding" of bacon fat (episode 8). To the camera, the mother remarks that the bacon fat is "like the staple of our family," something she regularly uses for cooking. The fact that this may be linked to her Latin American background, and might have social or emotional value, is not addressed; instead, the cooking fat is relegated to an unacceptable habit.

Conclusion

As Skeggs argues, reality television "presents the possibility of a better life as a matter of labour, opportunity and choice, dependent upon the self's willingness to invest in its self."[67] The parents on *Honey* are depicted as responsible for their children's health behaviors. Through expert intervention, they more closely approximate middle-class ideals of child rearing and food consumption. Ultimately, I want to suggest that identity construction in reality television programs such as *Honey, We're Killing the Kids* itself (re)constructs a dominant, contemporary ideology: that parents and in particular mothers — not only on the show, but those viewing at home too—need to consume information provided by experts. By consuming such information, mothers and fathers will know how to properly consume at the grocery store. Unlike shows such as *The Biggest Loser*, where specific brand name products are touted by the show's experts, Hark did not advertise particular products nor did her replacement (perhaps in part due to the show's short-lived success). Instead, they advocate a type of shopping, food preparation, and family life that reinforces middle-class values more generally.

In creating contrastive identities for experts and parents, and establishing experts as authoritative and parents as failing to live up to their responsibilities, life intervention reality television puts forth a view of parents as consumers—participating parents need to rely on expert advice, and viewers at home should do so as well—to be truly competent. This is of course couched in a larger ideology that health problems such as obesity are primarily related to individual choices and behaviors (especially by mothers, in the childhood obesity context), not wider sociological and socioeconomic factors such as access to fresh produce. It also overlooks the idea that food is imbued with symbolic and cultural value. The show thus offers parents who participate (and those who watch at home) a one-dimensional understanding of a complex health epidemic, as do accompanying materials such as the online "Exercise for Busy Moms" video. While the show may be well intentioned, and it very well may be designed to help parents and families as a form of "edutainment," it necessarily presents an incomplete picture, and one that emphatically highlights the shortcomings of mothers and fathers and their need for expert-provided information to achieve not only good health, but upward socioeconomic mobility. Whether or not parents and others viewing such programming "buy" the messages presented by the show, how reality television packages the identities of parents, especially mothers, and experts merits further academic investigation as well as public scrutiny. In exploring the microlinguistic features of reality television shows, we can achieve insights into how such messages are created, and into how viewers are being asked to consume them.

Notes

1. Tania Lewis, "Changing Rooms, Biggest Losers and Backyard Blitzes: A History of Makeover Television in the United Kingdom, United States and Australia," *Continuum: Journal of Media & Cultural Studies* 22, no. 4 (2008): 452.

2. See Tania Lewis, *Smart Living: Lifestyle Media and Popular Expertise* (New York: Peter Lang, 2008).

3. Galit Ferguson, "The Family on Reality Television: Who's Shaming Whom?" *Television & New Media* 11, no. 2 (2010): 88.

4. See, for example, Laurie Ouellette and James Hay, *Better Living through Reality TV* (Malden, MA: Blackwell, 2008) and Tania Lewis, *Smart Living: Lifestyle Media and Popular Expertise* (New York: Peter Lang, 2008).

5. For a useful discussion, see Karen Tracy, *Everyday Talk: Building and Reflecting Identities* (New York: Guilford Press, 2002).

6. See Erving Goffman, "Footing," in *Forms of Talk* (Philadelphia: University of Pennsylvania Press, 1981), 124–59.

7. See Bronwyn Davies and Rom Harré, "Positioning: The Discursive Production of Selves," *Journal for the Theory of Social Behavior,* 20 no. 1 (1990): 43–63.

8. See Elinor Ochs, "Indexing gender" in *Rethinking Context: Language as an Interactive Phenomenon*, ed. Alessandro Duranti and Charles Goodwin (Cambridge: Cambridge University Press, 1992), 335–58. See also Elinor Ochs, "Constructing Social Identity: A Language Socialization Perspective," *Research on Language and Social Interaction* 26, no. 3 (1993): 287–306.

9. Mary Bucholtz and Kira Hall, "Identity and Interaction: A Sociocultural Linguistic Approach," *Discourse Studies* 7, no. 4–5 (2005): 585–614.

10. Ibid., 585.

11. Barry R. Schlenker, *Impression Management: The Self-concept, Social Identity, and Interpersonal Relations* (Montery: Brooks/Cole Publishing Co., 1980).

12. Cynthia Gordon, "'I Just Feel Horribly Embarrassed When She Does That': Constituting a Mother's Identity," in *Family Talk: Discourse and Identity in Four American Families*, ed. Deborah Tannen, Shari Kendall, and Cynthia Gordon (New York: Oxford University Press, 2007), 71–101.

13. Sharon Hays, *The Cultural Contradictions of Motherhood* (New Haven and London: Yale University Press, 1996), 8.

14. Shari Kendall, "Father as Breadwinner, Mother as Worker: Gendered Positions in Feminist and Traditional Discourses of Work and Family," in *Family Talk: Discourse and Identity in Four American Families*, ed. Deborah Tannen, Shari Kendall, and Cynthia Gordon (New York: Oxford University Press, 2007), 123–63.

15. Tanya Zivkovic, Megan Warin, Michael Davies, and Vivienne Moore, "In the Name of the Child: The Gendered Politics of Childhood Obesity," *Journal of Sociology* 46, no. 4 (2010): 377.

16. JaneMaree Maher, Suzanne Fraser, and Jan Wright, "Framing the Mother: Childhood Obesity, Maternal Responsibility and Care," *Journal of Gender Studies* 19, no 3 (2010): 234, 236.

17. Ellen Seiter, *Sold Separately: Parents and Children in Consumer Culture* (New Brunswick: Rutgers University Press, 1993), 3. See also Daniel Thomas Cook, "Semantic Provisioning of Children's Food: Commerce, Care and Maternal Practice," *Childhood* 16, no. 3 (2009): 317–34.

18. Amelia A. Lake, Robert M. Hyland, John C. Mathers, Andrew J. Rugg-Gunn, Charlotte E. Wood, and Ashley J. Adamson, "Food Shopping and Preparation among 30-somethings: Whose Job is It? (The ASH30 Study)," *British Food Journal* 108, no. 6 (2006): 475.

19. Marjorie L. DeVault, *Feeding the Family* (Chicago: University of Chicago Press, 1991).

20. Rachel Kendrick, "'We Can Change the Face of This Future': Television Transforming the Fat Child," *Australian Feminist Studies* 23, no. 57 (2008): 393.

21. Wynne Wright and Elizabeth Ransom, "Stratification on the Menu: Using Restaurant Menus to Examine Social Class," *Teaching Sociology* 33, no. 3 (2005): 310.

See also Julie Guthman, "Fast Food/Organic Food: Reflexive Tastes and the Making of 'Yuppie Chow'," *Social & Cultural Geography* 4, no. 1 (2010): 45–58.

22. Jason P. Block, Richard A. Scribner, and Karen B. DeSalvo, "Fast Food, Race/Ethnicity, and Income: A Geographic Analysis," *American Journal of Preventive Medicine* 27, no. 3 (2004): 211–17.

23. Wynne Wright and Elizabeth Ransom, "Stratification on the Menu."

24. Elinor Ochs, Clotilde Pontecorvo, and Alessandra Fasulo, "Socializing Taste," *Ethnos* 61, no. 1–2 (1996): 7–46.

25. Psyche Williams-Forson, "More Than Just the Big Piece of Chicken: The Power of Race, Class, and Food in American Consciousness," in *Food and Culture: A Reader* (2nd edition), ed. Carole Counihan and Penny Van Esterik (New York: Routledge, 2008), 342–53.

26. Alexandra Johnston, "Gatekeeping in the Family: How Family Members Position One Another as Decision Makers," in *Family Talk: Discourse and Identity in Four American Families*, ed. Deborah Tannen, Shari Kendall, and Cynthia Gordon (New York: Oxford University Press, 2007), 165–93.

27. Riina Kokkonen, "The Fat Child—A Sign of 'Bad' Motherhood? An Analysis of Explanations for Children's Fatness on a Finnish website," *Journal of Community and Applied Social Psychology* 19, no. 5 (2009): 345.

28. *Honey* is a BBC original program; subsequently made and aired were versions in the US (aired on TLC [The Learning Channel] and, in Canada, on The Food Network) and in Australia. My analysis is on the thirteen episodes of the first season aired in the US; the patterns I identify, however, emerge in similar ways in the other versions as well.

29. Laurie Ouellette and James Hay, "Makeover Television, Governmentality and the Good Citizen," *Continuum: Journal of Media & Cultural Studies* 22, no. 4 (2008): 475.

30. Tania Lewis, "Changing Rooms, Biggest Losers and Backyard Blitzes," 452.

31. Peter Lunt, "*Little Angels*: The Mediation of Parenting," *Continuum: Journal of Media & Cultural Studies* 22, no. 4 (2008): 538.

32. Ibid.

33. This information is provided to the viewers by the nutritionist: After confronting the parents about their children's poor health, she states the life expectancy for the child, given his or her sex, ethnic group (using the term *white*, *African American*, or *Hispanic*), and current health habits and status.

34. Beth Montemurro, "Toward a Sociology of Reality Television," *Sociology Compass* 2, no. 1 (2008): 97.

35. "Press Release—TLC," accessed March 22, 2012, http://www.lisahark.com/presstlc.pdf.

36. See Cynthia Gordon, "Impression Management on Reality TV: Emotion in Parental Accounts," *Journal of Pragmatics* 43, no. 14 (2011): 3551–64.

37. Laurie Ouellette and James Hay, *Better Living through Reality TV* (Malden, MA: Blackwell, 2008), 89.

38. Ibid., 91–92.

39. My understanding of reality television as multilayered context is inspired by Joanna Thornborrow and Deborah Morris, "Gossip as Strategy: The Management of Talk About Others on the Reality TV Show 'Big Brother'," *Journal of Sociolinguistics* 8, no. 2 (2004): 246–71. I more fully explicate this understanding in Cynthia Gordon, "'You Are Killing Your Kids': Framing and Impoliteness in a Health Makeover Reality TV Show," in *Real Talk: Reality Television and Discourse Analysis in Action*, eds. Nuria Lorenzo-Dus and Pilar Garcés-Conejos Blitvich (Basingstoke, UK: Palgrave Macmillan, 2013), 245–65.

40. See Erving Goffman, *Frame Analysis* (New York: Harper & Row, 1974), and Erving Goffman, "Footing," in *Forms of Talk* (Philadelphia: University of Pennsylvania Press, 1981), 124–59.

41. Deborah Tannen, "What's in a Frame? Surface Evidence for Underlying Expectations," in *Framing in Discourse*, ed. Deborah Tannen (New York: Oxford University Press, 1993), 6.

42. See Jonathan Bignell, *Big Brother: Reality TV in the Twenty-first Century* (Basingstoke: Palgrave Macmillan, 2005). See also Zala Volčič and Mark Andrejevic, "*That's Me*: Nationalism and Identity on Balkan reality TV," *Canadian Journal of Communication* 34, no. 1 (2009): 7–24.

43. Emma Rich, "'I See Her Being Obesed!': Public Pedagogy, Reality Media and the Obesity Crisis," *Health* 15, no. 3 (2011): 3–21.

44. Cynthia Gordon, "Impression Management on Reality TV."

45. Gordon, "'I Just Feel Horribly Embarrassed When She Does That,'" and Barry R. Schlenker, *Impression Management.*

46. Jessica L. Collett, "What Kind of Mother Am I? Impression Management and the Social Construction of Motherhood," *Symbolic Interaction* 28, no. 3 (2005): 327–47.

47. See Daniel Thomas Cook, "Semantic Provisioning of Children's Food." See also Marjorie L. DeVault, *Feeding the Family* (Chicago: University of Chicago Press, 1991).

48. Brenda R. Weber, *Makeover TV: Selfhood, Citizenship, and Celebrity* (Durham: Duke University Press, 2009), 140.

49. Beverley Skeggs, "The Moral Economy of Person Production: The Class Relations of Self-Performance on 'Reality' Television," *The Sociological Review* 57, no. 4 (2009), 635.

50. Cynthia Gordon, "'You Are Killing Your Kids.'"

51. In this and other transcribed, verbatim extracts from the data, capital letters indicate emphatic stress. A period indicates a falling, final intonation. A comma indicates continuing intonation. A hyphen indicates self-interruption. A colon indicates an elongated vowel sound. Angle brackets indicate manner of speaking or a vocal noise. Material appearing in double parentheses indicates a transcriber comment. These conventions, designed to capture not only what was said but also how it was said, are adapted from Deborah Tannen, Shari Kendall, and Cynthia Gordon (eds.),

Family Talk: Discourse and Identity in Four American Families (New York: Oxford University Press, 2007).

52. Gordon, "Impression Management on Reality TV."

53. Ibid., 3560.

54. JaneMaree Maher, Suzanne Fraser, and Jan Wright, "Framing the Mother: Childhood Obesity, Maternal Responsibility and Care."

55. In Ochs' terms, the nutritionist performs meaningful social acts. See Elinor Ochs, "Constructing Social Identity."

56. Tania Lewis. "Changing Rooms, Biggest Losers and Backyard Blitzes," 452.

57. Jon Henley, "Britain's Food Habits: How Well Do We Eat?," *The Guardian*, May 9, 2011, accessed September 2, 2013, http://www.guardian.co.uk/lifeandstyle/2011/may/10/britains-food-habits-well-eat.

58. Nicole Darmon and Adam Drewnowski, "Does Social Class Predict Diet Quality?" *American Journal of Clinical Nutrition* 87, no. 5 (2008): 1107–17.

59. Wendy Wills, Kathryn Backett-Milburn, Meil-Li Roberts, and Julia Lawton, "The Framing of Social Class Distinctions through Family Food and Eating Practices," *The Sociological Review* 59, no. 4 (2011): 725–40.

60. Discourse analytic studies in fact suggest that language play can be an important part of family life and child learning. Marjorie Harness Goodwin, "Occasioned Knowledge Exploration in Family Interaction," *Discourse and Society* 18, no. 1 (2007): 93–110.

61. Rob Owen, "Tuned in: Families on TLC Diet Makeover Show Report Bitter Aftertaste," Pittsburgh Post-Gazette, April 10, 2006, accessed September 2, 2013, http://www.post-gazette.com/pg/06100/680907-114.stm.

62. Ibid.

63. Rachel Kendrick, "'We Can Change the Face of This Future'."

64. Galit Ferguson, "The Family on Reality Television," 92.

65. See Marjorie L. DeVault, *Feeding the Family*.

66. See "Portion Control," accessed April 19, 2014, http://www.tlc.com/tv-shows/other-shows/videos/honey-were-killing-the-kids-portion-control.htm.

67. Beverly Skeggs, "The Value of Relationships: Affective Scenes and Emotional Performances," *Feminist Legal Studies* 18, no. 2 (2010): 35.

References

Bignell, Jonathan. *Big Brother: Reality TV in the Twenty-first Century*. Basingstoke: Palgrave Macmillan, 2005.

Block, Jason P., Richard A. Scribner, and Karen B. DeSalvo. "Fast Food, Race/Ethnicity, and Income: A Geographic Analysis." *American Journal of Preventive Medicine* 27 (2004): 211–17.

Bucholtz, Mary, and Kira Hall. "Identity and Interaction: A Sociocultural Linguistic Approach." *Discourse Studies* 7 (2005): 585–614.

Collett, Jessica L. "What Kind of Mother Am I? Impression Management and the Social Construction of Motherhood." *Symbolic Interaction* 28 (2005): 327–47.

Cook, Daniel Thomas. "Semantic Provisioning of Children's Food: Commerce, Care and Maternal Practice." *Childhood* 16 (2009): 317–34.

Darmon, Nicole, and Adam Drewnowski. "Does Social Class Predict Diet Quality?" *American Journal of Clinical Nutrition* 87 (2008): 1107–17.

Davies, Bronwyn, and Rom Harré, "Positioning: The Discursive Production of Selves." *Journal for the Theory of Social Behavior* 20 (1990): 43–63.

DeVault, Marjorie L. *Feeding the Family*. Chicago: University of Chicago Press, 1991.

Ferguson, Galit. "The Family on Reality Television: Who's Shaming Whom?" *Television & New Media* 11 (2010): 87–104.

Goffman, Erving. *Frame Analysis*. New York: Harper & Row, 1974.

——. "Footing." In *Forms of Talk*, 124–59. Philadelphia: University of Pennsylvania Press, 1981.

Goodwin, Marjorie Harness. "Occasioned Knowledge Exploration in Family Interaction." *Discourse and Society* 18 (2007): 93–110.

Gordon, Cynthia. "'I Just Feel Horribly Embarrassed When She Does That': Constituting a Mother's Identity." In *Family Talk: Discourse and Identity in Four American Families*, edited by Deborah Tannen, Shari Kendall, and Cynthia Gordon, 71–101. New York: Oxford University Press, 2007.

——. "Impression Management on Reality TV: Emotion in Parental Accounts." *Journal of Pragmatics* 43 (2011): 3551–64.

——. "'You Are Killing Your Kids': Framing and Impoliteness in a Health Makeover Reality TV Show." In *Real Talk: Reality Television and Discourse Analysis in Action*, edited by Nuria Lorenzo-Dus and Pilar Garcés-Conejos Blitvich, 245–65. Basingstoke, UK: Palgrave Macmillan, 2013.

Guthman, Julie. "Fast Food/Organic Food: Reflexive Tastes and the Making of 'Yuppie Chow'." *Social & Cultural Geography* 4 (2010): 45–58.

Hays, Sharon. *The Cultural Contradictions of Motherhood*. New Haven and London: Yale University Press, 1996.

Henley, Jon. "Britain's Food Habits: How Well Do We Eat?" *The Guardian*, May 9, 2011. Accessed September 2, 2013. http://www.guardian.co.uk/lifeandstyle/2011/may/10/britains-food-habits-well-eat.

Johnston, Alexandra. "Gatekeeping in the Family: How Family Members Position One Another as Decision Makers." In *Family Talk: Discourse and Identity in Four American Families*, edited by Deborah Tannen, Shari Kendall, and Cynthia Gordon, 165–93. New York: Oxford University Press, 2007.

Kendall, Shari. "Father as Breadwinner, Mother as Worker: Gendered Positions in Feminist and Traditional Discourses of Work and Family." In *Family Talk: Discourse and Identity in Four American Families*, edited by Deborah Tannen, Shari Kendall, and Cynthia Gordon, 123–63. New York: Oxford University Press, 2007.

Kendrick, Rachel. "'We Can Change the Face of This Future': Television Transforming the Fat Child." *Australian Feminist Studies* 23 (2008): 389–400.

Kokkonen, Riina. "The Fat Child—A Sign of 'Bad' Motherhood? An Analysis of Explanations for Children's Fatness on a Finnish website." *Journal of Community and Applied Social Psychology* 19 (2009): 336–47.

Lake, Amelia A., Robert M. Hyland, John C. Mathers, Andrew J. Rugg-Gunn, Charlotte E. Wood, and Ashley J. Adamson. "Food Shopping and Preparation among 30-somethings: Whose Job is It? (The ASH30 Study)." *British Food Journal* 108 (2006): 475–86.

Lewis, Tania. "Changing Rooms, Biggest Losers and Backyard Blitzes: A History of Makeover Television in the United Kingdom, United States and Australia." *Continuum: Journal of Media & Cultural Studies* 22 (2008): 447–58.

——. *Smart Living: Lifestyle Media and Popular Expertise*. New York: Peter Lang, 2008.

Lunt, Peter. "*Little Angels*: The Mediation of Parenting." *Continuum: Journal of Media & Cultural Studies* 22 (2008): 537–46.

Maher, JaneMaree, Suzanne Fraser, and Jan Wright. "Framing the Mother: Childhood Obesity, Maternal Responsibility and Care." *Journal of Gender Studies* 19 (2010): 233–47.

Montemurro, Beth. "Toward a Sociology of Reality Television." *Sociology Compass* 2 (2008): 84–106.

Ochs, Elinor. "Indexing gender." In *Rethinking Context: Language as an Interactive Phenomenon*, edited by Alessandro Duranti and Charles Goodwin, 335–58. Cambridge: Cambridge University Press, 1992.

——. "Constructing Social Identity: A Language Socialization Perspective." *Research on Language and Social Interaction* 26 (1993): 287–306.

Ochs, Elinor, Clotilde Pontecorvo, and Alessandra Fasulo. "Socializing Taste," *Ethnos* 61 (1996): 7–46.

Ouellette, Laurie, and James Hay. *Better Living through Reality TV*. Malden, MA: Blackwell, 2008.

——, "Makeover Television, Governmentality and the Good Citizen." *Continuum: Journal of Media & Cultural Studies* 22 (2008): 471–84.

Owen, Rob. "Tuned in: Families on TLC Diet Makeover Show Report Bitter Aftertaste." Pittsburgh Post-Gazette, April 10, 2006, accessed September 2, 2013, http://www.post-gazette.com/pg/06100/680907-114.stm.

Rich, Emma. "'I See Her Being Obesed!': Public Pedagogy, Reality Media and the Obesity Crisis." *Health* 15 (2011): 3–21.

Schlenker, Barry R. *Impression Management: The Self-concept, Social Identity, and Interpersonal Relations*. Montery: Brooks/Cole Publishing Co., 1980.

Seiter, Ellen. *Sold Separately: Parents and Children in Consumer Culture*. New Brunswick: Rutgers University Press, 1993.

Skeggs, Beverley. "The Moral Economy of Person Production: The Class Relations of Self-Performance on 'Reality' Television." *The Sociological Review* 57 (2009): 626–44.

——. "The Value of Relationships: Affective Scenes and Emotional Performances." *Feminist Legal Studies* 18 (2010): 29–51.

Tannen, Deborah, "What's in a Frame? Surface Evidence for Underlying Expectations." In *Framing in Discourse*, edited by Deborah Tannen, 137–81. New York. Oxford University Press, 1993.

Tannen, Deborah, Shari Kendall, and Cynthia Gordon, eds. *Family Talk: Discourse and Identity in Four American Families*. New York: Oxford University Press, 2007.

Thornborrow, Joanna, and Deborah Morris."Gossip as Strategy: The Management of Talk About Others on the Reality TV Show 'Big Brother.'"*Journal of Sociolinguistics* 8 (2004): 246–71.

TLC. "Portion Control." Accessed April 19, 2014. http://www.tlc.com/tv-shows/other-shows/videos/honey-were-killing-the-kids-portion-control.htm.

——. "Press Release." Accessed March 22, 2012. http://www.lisahark.com/presstlc.pdf.

Tracy, Karen. *Everyday Talk: Building and Reflecting Identities*. New York: Guilford Press, 2002.

Volčič, Zala, and Mark Andrejevic. "*That's Me*: Nationalism and Identity on Balkan reality TV." *Canadian Journal of Communication* 34 (2009): 7–24.

Weber, Brenda R. *Makeover TV: Selfhood, Citizenship, and Celebrity*. Durham: Duke University Press, 2009.

Williams-Forson, Psyche. "More Than Just the Big Piece of Chicken: The Power of Race, Class, and Food in American Consciousness." In *Food and Culture: A Reader* (2nd edition), edited by Carole Counihan and Penny Van Esterik, 342–53. New York: Routledge, 2008.

Wills, Wendy, Kathryn Backett-Milburn, Meil-Li Roberts, and Julia Lawton. "The Framing of Social Class Distinctions through Family Food and Eating Practices." *The Sociological Review* 59 (2011): 725–40.

Wright, Wynne, and Elizabeth Ransom. "Stratification on the Menu: Using Restaurant Menus to Examine Social Class." *Teaching Sociology* 33 (2005): 310–16.

Zivkovic, Tanya, Megan Warin, Michael Davies, and Vivienne Moore. "In the Name of the Child: The Gendered Politics of Childhood Obesity." *Journal of Sociology* 46 (2010): 375–92.

5
Cultivating Community within the Commercial Marketplace

Blurred Boundaries in the "Mommy" Blogosphere

Jennifer L. Borda

When *The New York Times* featured an article on the new phenomenon of "baby blogs" in January 2005, approximately 8,500 people, including mothers, fathers, and grandparents, were writing "Web logs" about their offspring.[1] That number had doubled from the previous year and, with a new blog popping up on the Internet every 4.7 seconds, author David Hochman observed what he believed set "baby blogs" apart from the rest of the blogosphere: "the way that blogging about parenthood seems to have become part of parenthood itself."[2] Three years later, Technorati's "State of the Blogosphere" estimated that the total number of blogs had reached approximately one hundred thirty-three million. Of those bloggers, 36 percent of women and 16 percent of men were focusing on family updates.[3] Forward to October 2011, and the number of "mommy blogs" had increased to an estimated 3,900,000, and 14 percent of American women with at least one child either contributing to or reading a mommy blog regularly.[4]

These mommy blogs have been described as a way for women to connect with one another and share the truths of motherhood not found in the mainstream media or often even within one's own network of familial and personal relationships.[5] On the whole, mommy blogs seem inclined to chart the daily messiness of mothering, both in terms of the literal down in the trenches dirt and the more figurative emotional and psychological hurdles that come along with birthing, raising, and loving your children. Some of the most successful blogs also have addressed the acutely painful and even less discussed challenges that have come to define the motherhood experience for many women, such as postpartum depression, infertility, miscarriage, disability, family tragedy, and, in particular, the sudden loss of a child.

While only an estimated five hundred mommy bloggers have amassed enough of an online presence to exert considerable influence, the impact of mothers on the blogosphere is undeniable and, not surprisingly, has garnered intense interest by the media, marketers, and political campaigns in the last few years. Most notably, this growing Internet phenomenon has opened up possibilities for unprecedented access to a coveted consumer demographic, since women with children are estimated to make 80 percent of household purchasing decisions and spend more than $2 trillion a year on their families.[6] In February 2007, *Advertising Age* identified mommy blogs as "a marketer's dream," describing them as "a word-of-mouth network run by tech-savvy media pros who work cheap and have a direct line" to a loyal demographic. This consumer market is made up of savvy shoppers who are both affluent and eager for buying recommendations and mother-tested product picks.[7]

For the lucky few who have cultivated a loyal Internet following by blogging about their home and family life (probably less than 2 percent of the total mommy blogger population), their daily musings have developed into a new and unique media business model in which proven social media influence among mothers translates into enviable financial success. Two of the blogs that have consistently made the top of the most influential mommy blogger lists for the last few years, Dooce (published by Heather Armstrong) and Pioneer Woman (published by Ree Drumond), are estimated to generate ad revenue of between $40,000 and $60,000 per month. As a result of their blogs' successes, these and a number of other high-profile mommy bloggers have expanded their brand into various related enterprises, including television shows, publishing deals, consulting, and spokesperson opportunities, which have resulted in six figure, if not multi-million-dollar, incomes. For these mothers, blogging has become a way to manage the work/life balance that plagues so many working mothers. These mothers largely work at home, and their professional identities and endeavors appear to blend seamlessly with their home life, including their experience of motherhood.

But what happens when motherhood, community, business, and consumption collide together in the blogosphere? Does the shared wisdom, setbacks, insight, and humor found in mommy blogs offer an alternative model for the legions of mothers who have found themselves floundering in a sea of expert advice (mostly offered by prominent male physicians)? Do these moms speaking from the trenches open up new definitions and possibilities for twenty-first-century motherhood? And how does the insertion of consumption into this dynamic affect their ability to reenvision motherhood, foster community, and function as a collaborative resource—the very aspects that made mommy blogs so popular in the first place? Do community and commercialization clash when a mommy blogger "sells out" to advertisers in order to sustain her family and her work financially?

In an effort to tease out answers to some of these questions, I will first chronicle the rise of the mommy blog over the last decade. Specifically, I provide an overview of the defining features of mommy blogs and outline a typology of twenty of the top-ranked US and Canadian mommy blogs. Through an analysis of these various mommy blog subgenres, I provide a sense of the range and diversity of the rhetorical work being done with regard to the redefinition of motherhood and challenges to the motherhood ideal, as well the interpretive communities called into being as these blogs hail their readers. Then, I examine the impact of consumerism into the mommy blogosphere as it has transitioned from a platform for personal narratives and interpersonal connection among mothers to a public marketplace for goods and services. I conclude that the recent move to "monetize," "brand," and "market" mommy blogs has had a significant impact on the radical potential of these blogs to remake motherhood, and has opened up both possibilities and limitations for positive social and political change within the motherhood community and society at large.

The Business of (Mommy) Blogging

The relatively short history of blogging begins in the mid-1990s when people began posting personal diaries or journals onto webpages. Initially referred to as Weblogs, blogs typically share a common format of daily observations or musings posted to the web and sorted by date with the newest on top and the rest archived for future use. Other characteristics of blogs that have evolved over the last decade include interlinked text (sometimes to other blog posts, often to news reports or to previous blog entries), repeated headings/tags that can become search terms, and, in recent years, photos, videos, and Twitter feeds.

The most defining aspect of blogs, especially in the last decade, is the comment feature in which readers can post their responses and reactions to posts. If the comment section is "open," readers can post not only to the blog author but to others' comments as well. Most blogs also include a blogroll, or a list of blogs they regularly read and recommend to other readers, which creates an interlinking online index of blogs that often coalesce around particular topics, such as motherhood/parenthood. In the early years of blogging, many scholars grappled with whether or not blogs actually could be considered a "virtual community." In 2004, Anita Blanchard argued that the comment feature (if used by the blog author to invite member interaction) and blogrolls that develop around particular topics have the potential to create a shared sense of community.[8] With the growth of social media more recently, many blogs also have buttons that allow readers to "share" blog content by recommending on Google, indicating that you "Like" the blog (and reposting) on Facebook, and also Tweeting or pinning it to Pinterest. These latest technological advances have further expanded the potential for blogs to tap into a sustainable, interactive, and mutually supportive virtual community across various technology platforms.

The blogger credited with revolutionizing the "mommy blog" genre—Dooce's Heather Armstrong—serves as a helpful example of how personal blogging began, evolved, and eventually became big business for the most prominent mommy bloggers. Armstrong began posting random thoughts on her personal website, which she titled Dooce (a reference to her frequent mistyping of "dude" in IM messages), while working as a web designer for an LA technology start-up in 2001. For the first month or so, she posted under the heading "Thinking," and those posts were often simple, one or two-line questions or observations. Later that year, she posted a diatribe against the Mormon Church, and her site found a growing community of ex-Mormon followers. The blog garnered even greater notoriety and popularity when she began venting about work and nicknaming her coworkers, a practice which eventually led to her firing and the entry of the word "dooced" into the Urban Dictionary (meaning "getting fired because of something you wrote in your Web log").[9] At that time, her web traffic was a steady 6,500 hits a day. Then, in April 2003, she announced she was pregnant and readership rose again.

It was not until Dooce began blogging about postpartum depression, which eventually led to a three-week stay in a psychiatric ward, that her blog traffic increased exponentially and she began making top blogger lists, such as Technorati's Top 100 for 2004 (at the time Technorati tracked over 5 million blogs).[10] By the end of that year, she and her husband decided to add some Google ads to their website, in order to pay for therapist-prescribed babysitting time for her daughter. Based on the amounts that advertisers were willing to pay to appear on Dooce's site (because of the amount of web traffic the site attracted daily), the Armstrongs decided to contract with Federated Media, an agency that recruits and manages advertising on websites. Dooce was a pioneer in this regard, becoming the first personal website to garner and provide significant advertising.[11] By 2009, Dooce was averaging 300,000 readers a day and courting such "blue chip" sponsors as McDonald's, AT&T, and Walt Disney, and she was ranked twenty-sixth in *Forbes* list of the most influential women in media.[12] By 2011, Dooce was receiving more than 5 million page views per month and thought to generate between $30,000 and $50,000 a month in advertising.

While Armstrong/Dooce may have blazed the trail, and undoubtedly has received more press coverage than any other mommy blogger, there are several million other mommy blogs that have emerged in the past decade. In what follows, I will consider a range of mommy blogs that rose to prominence between 2001 and 2009.[13] Mamma Pundit (Katie Allison Granju) actually outdates Dooce as the oldest mommy blog having begun posting about motherhood back in 2002. Momma Said's Jennifer Springer created her virtual network for mothers in 2003 from the corner of her New Jersey basement. While Finslippy (Alice Bradley), Girl's Gone Child (Rachel Woolf), The Bloggess (Jenny Lawson), and Amalah (Amy Storch) each began blogging between 2001 and 2004, they all gave birth to their first children in 2005, transforming their already existing blogs into the "mommy" category. Postpartum Progress (Katherine Stone) began in 2004, and in 2006 a wave of mommy blogs flooded the web, including Rage Against the Minivan (Kristen Howerton), Her Bad Mother (Catherine Connors), The Pioneer Woman (Ree Drummond), Pundit Mom (Joanne Bamberger), and Mom-101 (Liz Gumbinner). Jessica Gottlieb (also the title of her blog) and Because I Said So (Dawn Meehan) were both created in 2007, the year in which mommy blogging was recognized as an online phenomenon, and Scary Mommy (Jill Smokler), Cool Mom (Daphne Brogdon), Selfish Mom (Amy Oztan), and Resourceful Mommy (Amy Lupold Bair) each started in 2008. Finally, The Girl Who (Monica Beilanko) began her blog in 2005 charting her Mormon upbringing, her ex-Mormonism, her elopement to a rock guitarist two months after their first meeting, and her subsequent move from Salt Lake City to Manhattan. When Dooce linked to The Girl Who's blog, her following of readers surged, and in 2009 she became a mother and an official "mommy blogger" with the birth of her daughter.

Within this group of twenty blogs, all but three follow the general style/format of postings about motherhood, kids, life, and pets made famous by Dooce and the earliest mom bloggers (the exceptions are Pundit Mom, Postpartum Progress, and The Bloggess). Many of the bloggers are freelance or professional writers, or were former (or present) media/marketing executives and producers. Some of those who previously worked in graphic design or technology industries, such as Dooce and Girl's Gone Child, have very polished websites made up of serial posts accented with highly stylized photos of their children, dogs, and homes, which often conjure a story of their own. Other blogs, such as Amalah, Mamma Pundit, Her Bad Mother, and Rage Against the Minivan, include more amateur and/or smartphone photography to underscore or accentuate their personal essay-driven content. Most of the blogs are largely text-based in terms of content, use a single relevant photo, piece of clip art, or other web content as an accompanying visual, and stick to issues related to motherhood, children, the home, and so forth, including Momma Said, The Girl Who, Mom 101, Because I Said So, Scary Mommy, Selfish Mom, and Resourceful Mommy.

As many of these blogs have evolved, the themes and content of the blogs have expanded or, in some cases, become more focused. For example, Postpartum Progress began as a clearing house for information on postpartum depression culled from the Internet and posted by creator Katherine Stone, who suffered from a severe form herself. It has expanded to become the most widely read awareness and online support network for mental illness related to pregnancy and childbirth, is serviced by Stone's nonprofit organization focusing on perinatal mental health advocacy, and features both regular contributors and guest blogs. The Pioneer Woman has expanded to include separate but interrelated blogs on Cooking, (Motherhood) Confessions, Photography, Homeschooling, Entertainment, and Home and Garden. Filled with luxurious and digitally enhanced photography, The Pioneer Woman resembles a glossy high-end magazine more so than a typical blog. Pundit Mom, created by a DC journalist, is more closely aligned to a political blog than a traditional mommy blog, with a focus on political issues and current news/events from the perspective of a working mother with a young daughter.

A surprising number of blogs have developed various themes as the blogger and/or her family have faced personal issues varying from depression/anxiety (Dooce, Finslippy, The Bloggess, and The Girl Who), and becoming a single mom (Momma Said, Because I Said So, The Girl Who), to the challenges of adoption (Rage Against the Minivan) and developmental disorders (Amalah), to a devastating house fire (The Girl Who) and the drug addiction/death of a teenage child (Mamma Pundit). While these events may or may not be part of a "mommy blogger jinx" as Lisa Belkin pondered in her Motherlode blog in the *New York Times*, they have been instrumental in driving up "page views" for these bloggers.[14] Such personal crises and tragedies also have become an ongoing generator of content for many of these bloggers, and called forth a band of loyal readers, many of whom become entrenched in the unfolding drama. For many bloggers, these struggles further inspire them to articulate their own specialized "brand" of motherhood that cultivates a particular online community.

Remaking Motherhood One Post at a Time

While late twentieth- and early twenty-first-century mothers have had access to more information than any generation before them, this overload of advice about every aspect of motherhood, from trying to conceive to empty nest syndrome, has made us "more clueless and insecure about what we are doing and why we are doing it than perhaps any previous generation," according to Susan Maushart. Writing in the late 1990s, Maushart concluded that this insecurity had been fueled further by what she calls "the mask of motherhood" or "the public face of motherhood that conceals from the world and from ourselves the momentousness of our common undertaking." Mothers who individually sought information, approval, and solace in women's magazines, advice manuals, and parenting websites acutely experienced a "gap between image and reality, between what we show and what we feel," which Maushart argues "has resulted in a particular schizophrenia about motherhood."[15] In her *New York Times* bestselling book, *Perfect Madness: Motherhood in the Age of Anxiety*, Judith Warner referred to this syndrome as "the Mommy Mystique," in which many women "were suffering from a clash of expectations, popular rhetoric, and reality."[16] Warner writes that, "The mess of the Mommy Mystique—the belief that we can and should control every aspect of our children's lives, that our lives are the sum total of our personal choices, that our limitations stem from choosing poorly and that our problems are chiefly private, rather than public, in nature—is *not* an individual problem that individual women should have to scramble to deal with. It is a social malady—a perverse form of individualism, based on a self-defeating allegiance to a punitive notion of choice; a way of privatizing problems that are social in scope and rendering them, in the absence of real solutions, amendable to one's private powers of control."[17]

It is not surprising then that the seductive appeal of the mommy blog is that many of the earliest, and often most successful and enduring, blogs were constructed as online journals that were quite personal, confessional, and revelatory. As a response to the expectations and mythologies surrounding the cultural institution of motherhood, these women began to share their own psychological and emotional struggle to adjust to the unexpected realities of motherhood. Yet, through the seemingly contradictory *public* act of posting online for an expansive, and for the most part, unknown audience, blogging also brought about an awareness that these experiences were not part of an individual, or even a unique, reality experienced by one mother, but a reality shared by many mothers. The relative anonymity of that online community and the virtual relationships forged collectively between blogger/reader appealed to many of these mommy blog pioneers. Women such as Dooce, Mama Pundit, Momma Said, Finslippy, and all of the other forerunners were putting their parenting on display, flaws and all, for others to see. Through the act of publicly revealing their struggle, they found commonality and support in return and began to build a strong community of readers, as well as a growing community of bloggers. Melissa Gregg's study of blogs and the politics of gender notes that, for many women, blogs are a means of breaking out of the isolation many women have faced as primary caregivers, especially those that choose to stay at home with their children. Further, Gregg notes, "they are also used to reflect upon the responsibility of being a parent, acknowledging fears, seeking advice and gaining encouragement from other readers."[18]

As Belkin noted in an October 2011 *Huffington Post* Parents Blog post, titled "Mom Bloggers, A Force to Be Reckoned With," the power of these virtual conversations comes from the open window they provide into someone else's parenting choices, decisions, and philosophies (important since "each of us only knows the intimate workings of one or two households—specifically the ones in which we have lived"), as well as the fact that "they allow honesty through anonymity."[19] This was something most mothers didn't have access to before 2001, but as of 2012 more than 18.3 million mothers read blogs at least once a month (and some believe the statistic may be quite higher, because it has become more difficult to distinguish "blogs" from "websites").[20] Since the turn of the century, emerging technology has offered mothers a reliable space to share their anxieties and fears in a generally judgment-free zone (at least at the beginning). Now, through comment sections, Facebook shares, and Twitter feeds, mothers collectively work through solutions to the most serious, but more often banal, trials of parenting. Mommy blogs function as a community resource for many millennial moms, who have emerged as a supplement to, if not substitute for, the former dependence on "credentialed" experts and the traditional mothering advice industry.

Also, unlike mothering advice books and magazines, the blogging community offers an ongoing and constantly evolving view on motherhood with new offerings daily (or throughout the day depending on how many blogs one follows). Blogs are timely and relevant, often commenting on current events in the news, politics, or pop culture, while most parenting-advice books are already dated by the time they reach publication and distribution. Collectively, these mommy blogs also offer many and varied resources and perspectives generated by both the blogger and the interactive community built from the commentary of a vast population of readers. They may be a source of reflection, advice, humor, support group, or necessary distraction. As Finslippy (Alice Bradley) once posted (back in 2005), "That's what we're after (I think)—some representation of authentic experience that we're not getting elsewhere. . . . This is the service we try to provide—we share our lopsided, slightly hysterical, often exaggerated but more or less authentic experiences."[21]

Finslippy would go on to characterize mommy blogging as a "radical act" just a few months later at the first BlogHer conference, which would become a statement that would ignite debates throughout the blogosphere (and in a few academic articles) about the potential power and influence of this emerging genre. What many have come to understand as the most radical potential of these blogs is their ability to foster a community among mothers that previously did not exist, one without geographical or relational boundaries. According to Lisa Hammond, who was inspired by Bradley's pronouncement to analyze the function of mommy blogs as online communities, "That Bradley has chosen to represent blogging as a personal act with political implications points directly to the power of the Weblog to redefine maternal roles in self-defined communities of women—communities that have grown to spread a wide support network for mothers across the country and even worldwide."[22]

Rage Against the Minivan demonstrates the power of such defined communities when she explains how the community of adoptive parents that read and comment on her blog have helped her to better understand the dynamics of her own blended family. She wrote in June 2012: "It's also provided me with an amazing community of adoptive moms, with families that look like mine. I may not see them every day, but the beauty of our virtual community means that we can share struggles and ideas with each other, even though we are across the country. I think that I would feel really isolated in my own community if I didn't have these women to bounce ideas off, or email in the middle of the night because something happened that only they would understand."[23] For those navigating through parenting situations outside of the traditional model, blogs have provided a direct line into a community of other mothers who can easily relate because they are experiencing that same situation themselves in real time.

Mommy blogging is a two-way street, and the community that emerges around these blogs, as well as the comments generated therein, serve to create a virtual community through the shared reality of motherhood in day-to-day practice. As Andrea Buchanan eloquently observes, "Mothers who go online are finding a multiplicity of viewpoints, a real and humanized investigation of the complex and varied ways in which we mother, and mothers who recognize themselves in the writings of these mother-bloggers feel valid. They feel heard. And they feel empowered."[24] Mommy blogging has developed into a means of talking back to the media-generated parenting experts while at the same time allowing mothers to embrace their experiential expertise and empowerment.

Through blogging, these women have begun to reshape the contour of online conversations about the rewards and challenges of motherhood while also opening up new debates regarding the political and cultural significance of mothering, thus shifting the focus from outmoded patriarchal ideologies to the value of mothers sharing their lived experiences for women and children alike. Dooce emphasizes the impetus for blogging as a declaration that mothers' "voices matter," writing that, "We are an army of educated mothers who have finally stood up and said pay attention, this is important work, this is hard, frustrating work and we're not going to sit around on our hands waiting for permission to do so."[25] In this way, mommy blogging may be understood as a conscious expression of rhetorical agency, which Karlyn Kohrs Campbell defines as, "communal, social, cooperative, and participatory and, simultaneously, constituted and constrained by the material and symbolic elements of context and culture."[26] Further, Campbell claims that "agency emerges out of performances or actions that, when repeated, fix meaning through sedimentation" and "equally emerges in performances that repeat with a difference, altering meaning."[27] As an extremely popular form of symbolic action, these blogs have emerged as a means for reinventing the identities and language of motherhood as an institution and mothering as a collective practice.

It has been well established by several scholars that a significant contribution of mommy blogs is to the redefinition and revisioning of contemporary notions of motherhood. In her analysis of mommy blogs as communal constructions of maternal identities, Hammond argues that blogging mothers and readers form a "multiplicity of voices developing new cultural definitions of motherhood, definitions that are both individual and distinct, but also communal in nature, a collective memory through which women rewrite the roles of mothering in contemporary culture."[28] Also writing about the constitutive work of mommy blogs, Rebecca Powell asserts that the mommy blog is a rhetorical construction of identity that negotiates the discourses of motherhood from the good/bad mother dualism to intensive motherhood with a network of readers that then identify with, revise, and reinterpret those constructions.[29]

Through an analysis of three popular mommy blogs (including Dooce and Girl's Gone Child), Powell demonstrates that within the blog posts and reader comments, "constructions of motherhood and identity become more fluid and juxtapositions of complexity reign" while "meanings are contested, supported and complicated all within the frame of a screen and within minutes," and "mothers are encouraged to tell their stories and create new possibilities."[30] Powell concludes that these bloggers confront particular dualities of motherhood in far more complex and experiential ways than the good/bad mother and guilt-inducing intensive motherhood discourse allow. She observes that through their blogs, these mothers work against these discourses as well as in/with them through their own experiences, offering the following paradoxical interpretations: "Motherhood is isolating and motherhood is a community; motherhood is a favorite place and motherhood is torture; motherhood is almost perfect and motherhood is failure."[31]

What both Hammond and Powell effectively articulate, and what becomes clear after reading a number of blogs about mothering, many of which include thousands of posts and photos over a number of years, is that motherhood is never an either/or dichotomy, but always a both/and proposition. The blogs included in this chapter demonstrate a range of motherhoods, and many chart their evolution as mothers over the course of several years, multiple children, and changing personal circumstances. These unfolding narratives of motherhood developed over time and across a number of blogs not only emphasize the contradictions within motherhood for each woman who mothers (and blogs about it) but also expands our ideas of all that motherhood encompasses. According to Lori Lopez, "Women who blog about their children are transforming their personal narratives of struggle and challenge into interactive conversations with other mothers, and in doing so, are beginning to expand our notion of motherhood, women bloggers, and the mother's place within the public sphere. In this sense, showing the ugly side of motherhood has the potential to be liberating and beneficial to all women."[32]

For example, while Dooce typically focuses on the daily observations and often mundane aspects of motherhood in the witty and sarcastic style for which she has become famous, Girl's Gone Child (who became unexpectedly pregnant at 23) more often focuses on the betwixt and between of a life before and after motherhood and that fractured identity for women who have also become mothers. Momma Said's posts often work in opposition to media-proffered child-rearing advice that she believes has led to competitive and inauthentic parenting, while other blogs appear to be platforms for inviting entertainment, as well as therapeutic laughter, through the comical aspects of motherhood in the vein of great humorists such as Erma Bombeck or Nora Ephron (Cool Mom, The Bloggess). Most of the blogs considered in this chapter could be described as "confessional" as they each resist the media-defined image of a perfect or "intensive" motherhood ideal in their own ways, but some have made such confessions and embrace of "bad" mothering (and inviting the same from readers) their trademark (Selfish Mom, Scary Mommy, Her Bad Mother). Other bloggers try to engage larger sociopolitical issues relevant to their motherhood experience (biracial adoption in Rage Against the Minivan, feminist mothering and working motherhood in Mom-101, community service in Jessica Gottleib). When considered collectively, these blogs focus not so much on how to *be* a mother, as advice industry/news media has for so long, but on what *doing* motherhood means, from the mundane tasks to the most inspirational moments. What readers and bloggers alike also take from these blogs is that doing motherhood is easier when you are not trying to do it all alone.

From Community to Commodity: The Mommy Blog Becomes Big Business

At the same time that mommy blogs were emerging full force as a radical space for mothers making sense of motherhood through the cumulative wealth of shared life experiences, technology and marketing corporations began to recognize the collective nature of mommy blogs as a powerful online force. In a March 2010 report, *The New York Times* wrote that "Just as companies like Tupperware saw the untapped sales potential in the old-school kaffeeklatsch, advertisers now set their sights on mommy blogs, recognizing that anywhere women's eyes go in huge numbers—especially anywhere they might be discussing products they use—is prime real estate."[33]

Mommy blogs are more than just online sites with incredibly high page views. Some sites outpace major media websites by attracting readers in the millions each month. More significant than the high Internet traffic they generate is their function as places where relationships have been formed, perspectives are (largely) valued, and mothers gather to find solace for their real-world isolation through the commonality of their virtual connections. And it is precisely this community aspect of mommy blogs that have made them a unique place for marketing intervention. Lisa Belkin emphasizes in a report for *Adweek* that mommy blogs are "places to connect and be heard, they satisfy a need to belong to something larger than ourselves, and are an invisible but palpable scaffolding of support. Mom blog readers give and receive—and since the best advertising is a mention from a friend, strangers who feel like friends are marketing gold."[34] Yet, it is less the connection between blogger and readers and more the connection between blogging and business that has changed the face of mom blogging in the last five years.

When Dooce decided to monetize her site a decade ago (that is, allowing advertisers in for payment based on CPM, or cost per mille, which is a payment for every thousand impressions or page views), her blog became a model for those who wanted to merge their passion for mommy blogging with financial gain. Now it is difficult to find a popular mommy blog that *does not* feature advertising, sponsored posts, contests/giveaways, and other marketing tie-ins (each of the blogs included in this chapter have multiple advertising links and/or other marketing ventures associated with their site or blog content). What were once referred to by the long contested term "mommy blog" are now considered part of the powerhouse "woman-owned and operated media category," and their creators are now referred to as "women in social media" and "digital entrepreneurs." Writing for Babble.com, Mama Pundit (Katie Allison Granju) notes this transformation, and describes mommy blogging as "a brand new media business model" that merges a "uniquely interconnected and highly organic ecosystem of relationships and conversations" with the commercial marketplace in which those within that ecosystem also cultivate "meaningful online brands with engaged, loyal audiences of a size that would make many magazine publishers jealous."[35]

This merger between blogging and business has changed the dynamics of the blogger/reader community in a number of ways, and the form that this commercialization takes within that community is as diverse as the long list of mommy blogs themselves. Whether by choice, or because of a lack of sponsorship/profit opportunities, several of the blogs included in this chapter feature just one or two very discrete ads near the bottom of the page scroll. Blogs such as Mama Pundit, Her Bad Mother, Cool Mom, and Jessica Gottleib have managed to retain a format very close to the original WordPress or Blogger template, which includes a simple masthead with content tabs at the top, the latest blog post filling most of the center of the screen, archive links and perhaps a blogroll (blogs the blogger likes) listed on the right-hand side, and a few ads scrolling vertically to the far right. These blogs seem to be quaint reminders of what the blogosphere, and the original mommy blogs, once were. Yet, all twenty of the blogs considered here also include a tab at the top, or a link at the bottom, with some variation on "Advertising and Sponsorship," in which monthly page views and various blogger accolades are listed, as well as contact information regarding product reviews, sponsorship, and advertising deals.

On some of the more established and popular blogs considered here, the sponsorship on the website is nearly as plentiful as the blog content. Dooce's site, for example, features her content tabs and masthead across the top, and just below the masthead is a large ad banner flashing animated graphics (some of the ads featured in July 2012 included Kohler, The Olympics on NBC, Sweet & Low, Southwest.com, and Revlon cosmetics). Moving vertically down the right-hand side are several large ad blocks featuring brands such as Target, movie ads/preview trailers, various Google-sponsored ads that seem to be tailored to the reader's regional location, and a static ad for LiquidWeb, the blog-hosting site that powers Dooce.com. Many of the blogs follow this format to a greater or lesser degree (Girl's Gone Child, The Girl Who, Selfish Mom). Some blogs try to categorize sponsored or "paid" posts from their personal posts, creating a very delineated boundary between the commercial and noncommercial space. Momma Said, for example, has a large ad block for Target Home Catalogue parallel with her masthead at the top of the page (which announces her openness to sponsorship immediately to readers), then runs a list of product-review, sponsored, and guest posts down the left margin under a section titled "Linger," and lists her own nonsponsored posts in a middle section, titled "Laugh." Some mommy blogs have become billboards of sorts to advertise the bloggers' own wares, such as The Bloggess, whose page has become a virtual montage of advertisements, book signing announcements, reviews, and publicity for her recently published memoir and book tour.

Mommy blogs became controversial in 2009 when the boundaries between blog content and promotion became blurred, and bloggers were being accused of "blog-ola," or accepting goods and services or writing for sponsors without disclosure.[36] Some bloggers walk the line between sponsored content and noncompensated posts with little distinction within the formatting of their blog (although it is noted as such at the beginning of the post), including Girl's Gone Child, Cool Mom, and Mama Pundit. The posts on several other blogs, such as Rage Against the Minivan, Resourceful Mommy, The Girl Who, and Amalah, have a tendency to catch the reader off-guard since at times it is not clear until the end of the post (once the reader has finished reading) that the post is sponsored. For example, in a recent post from Rage Against the Minivan touting the benefits of podcasts, she explains how they allow for relaxation while still engaging in interactive parenting, and only at the end does she disclose that it was sponsored by the new Nokia Windows phone, which was photographed numerous times in the post showing it being used to play various podcasts. Unlike the flashing ads, these "sponsored posts" are more insidious as the reader only finds out at the end of the blog post that they are being hailed by advertisers. While these disclaimers have become common, and mandatory due to FTC regulations about the disclosure of paid product endorsements put in place in 2009, the merger of personal musings and marketing opportunities are quite blurry on a number of these blogs.[37]

It was this issue of blurred boundaries that inspired Selfish Mom to add a "Full Disclosure" tab to her masthead that explains the following policy: "This blog accepts many forms of compensation, including (but not limited to) paid posts, sponsorships, advertising, products, and trips. The compensation Amy receives may influence the advertising content, links, or post topics of this blog, but will never influence Amy's opinions on any subject or product." She also includes a breakdown of "compensation levels," which she numbers zero through seventeen in order to alert readers to the amount of compensation received for a post (if any), and the means in which it was acquired (payment for a post, sponsored post in which payment was received and talking points are suggested, running a contest, products/services provided for free in exchange for an online review, mention of a product associated with a company for whom the blogger works as a freelance writer, etc.)[38]

While disclaimers added to posts, and Selfish Mom's much more explicit compensation scale, may increase the transparency of the growing interconnectedness of blogging, advertising, and sponsorship, there are other aspects of the commercialization of blogs that are more opaque. One aspect, which is a logical consequence of the move toward professionalizing and commercializing one's blog, is that the blog is no longer considered a personal journal but instead becomes a manifestation of a "brand." In order to better court advertisers and other promotional opportunities, these mommy blogs need to find ways to distinguish their particular blog, and the demographic of readers they invite, from the rest of the mommy blog pack. In addition to a publishing network, such as BlogHer or Federated Media, which helps bloggers match their advertisers to their audience (and vice versa), many blogs now also employ public relations firms and brand consultants. As Dooce commented in April 2011, "It's the dirtiest word in the blogosphere: brand. It's even dirtier than SPONSORED BY."[39]

In a July 2011 post titled, "How To Talk About Succeeding in Blogging (Without Really Crying)," Her Bad Mother describes the mommy blogging enterprise this way: "It's a business. And it involves more than relying on the CPM advertising model—very few independent bloggers can make a go of things with this model. . . . It involves *work*—it's not just sitting down and tapping out posts. The content comes first, of course—I wouldn't have the 'brand' to capitalize on—yes, dirty words, these—if I didn't produce good content. But doing something with that content is work—roll up your sleeves and make the coffee at 6am *work*."[40] She goes on to explain that the establishment of her brand has also led to consultant and spokesperson contracts, as well as earnings from freelance writing also related to her "quote unquote brand," all of which have resulted in greater financial success than the CPM ad earnings generated from her blog. As Her Bad Mother points out, the business far exceeds the blog if one hopes to become a financial success through commercialization. A look at the session guide for the BlogHer '12 conference reveals many of the dynamics at play, including sessions on the Brand-Blogger Connection; Strategic Content Development Across Multiple Media: Onstage, Onscreen, and Online; Affiliate Marketing

Programs as Revenue Stream; and Beyond Guest Blogging: Pitching Media Outlets.[41]

In September 2010, The Pioneer Woman posted, "Ten Important Things I've Learned About Blogging," which included advice such as, "Be Yourself. Blog Often. Be Varied. Exercise More. Allow Your Boundaries to Set Themselves Up Naturally. Don't Be Afraid to Embarrass Yourself." Regarding the unprecedented popularity and growth of her website, Drummond commented to *ForbesWoman*, "I hate to say that it grew organically, but I didn't do anything to outright promote it—didn't take out ads or anything."[42] In fact, although the Pioneer Woman website is overflowing with images and content, the advertising is deeply imbedded into the content itself, and almost difficult to detect compared to a blog such as Dooce or Resourceful Mommy.

Surely, these homespun rules of blogging and humble beginnings alone could not have produced The Pioneer Woman's estimated 23.3 million monthly page views. Rather, *The New Yorker* profile from May 9, 2011, reveals that a very savvy businesswoman lurks behind the jeans and flannel appearance of this cattle-ranch mom, one who amassed ad revenue for 2010 that was "solidly one million" dollars and does not include the money she earns for book advances, royalties from her best-selling memoir *Black Heels to Tractor Wheels* and two cookbooks, her Food Network show, and the rights to her story for a Hollywood film.[43] Yet, to discuss the details of how she achieved such success would be to belie the brand that The Pioneer Woman has cultivated over the past five years. When asked what she thinks accounts for her blog's success, she offers, "It is a positive place on the Web. It may not be Susie Sunshine all the time, and I definitely have a sarcastically slanted sense of humor, but I think people know that when they come to my site they're not going to see griping or political debate. It's a few moments of lightness in a day."[44] Her blog clearly and consistently maintains that "branded" image of escapism, of a twenty-first century Harlequin romance heroine living the happily ever after, which is further reiterated impeccably across every celebrity appearance, book deal, and press interview.

While not all of the blogs considered in this chapter have quite the seamlessly articulated branding of The Pioneer Woman (not even Dooce has managed that), each has developed their own "brand" as their blogs have evolved over time. For example, Mama Pundit began blogging about her children in 2002, then about her "second family" post-divorce and second marriage back in 2007. But, with the 2010 death of her sixteen-year-old son from an addiction to painkillers and subsequent overdose, her blog now has become both support group for parents who have lost teens and advocacy against drug dealing, particularly through pain clinics. Resourceful

Mommy became a brand unto herself back in 2008 when she invented the "Twitter Party," described on her blog as: "a hashtagged social event with panelists and a conversational theme catering to the needs of clients ranging from e-commerce start-ups to nationally recognized trusted brands."[45] Recent Twitter Parties hosted through her blog and Twitter page include BJ's Wholesale, JCPenney's Salon, Norwegian Cruise Lines, and AT&T Mobile Safety. The Girl Who decided to capitalize on the popularity of her twelve-chapter "Mormon to Married in Manhattan" post, which chronicled her whirlwind romance and marriage to her rock-guitarist husband, by first inviting him to contribute to her blog with his own blog, ThunderPie, offering a male perspective on marriage and family. Then, in early 2012, the duo launched a new Babble.com/Babble Voices blog, titled "He Said, She Said with Serge and Monica Bielanko," which also generates much of the content for the The Girl Who blog.

The commercialization of the mommy blogosphere certainly has benefitted some of the women who have launched professional careers there, often leading to economic gain through not only ad revenue but by generating connections to secure freelance work in other social media and publishing outlets. The opportunity for entrepreneurship that mommy blogging affords also leads to women's empowerment through and within the realm of consumer culture. Though, the big trade-off of the move from blogging to branding may be that building a brand means less authenticity, and sometimes less honesty within the blog, and a performance of motherhood that fits the brand. Amalah comments on this unchartered territory in a post about 2011's BlogHer conference, writing, "I've gone on some nice trips, I've gotten some really nice gifts from companies, I've gotten laughably bad product pitches that I would never in a million years want or use or 'review.' I've alternated between being delighted by the attention and annoyed by the way it's changed our community, I've struggled to keep that balance between wanting my blog to be "successful" and wanting my blog to be . . . you know, MY STUPID LITTLE BLOG."[46]

Some bloggers find themselves uneasy with the media pitches and revenue streams, especially if they came to blogging as freelance writers rather than social media or advertising/marketing professionals, and so a few bloggers recently have begun to comment on the changes wrought by the professionalization of mommy blogging on their blogs. Finslippy wrote in June 2012: "Still, I've been uncomfortable with the marriage of blogging and advertising. I'm okay with ads (obviously) as long as they stay in their place. But the advertisers want in. They want to get into your posts. It's not because they're evil. They're smart. They know where people are looking. But once they're paying you to write, you work for them. That's fine if you're a copywriter, but if your 'copywriting' lands on your personal blog, that can get awfully weird. If your authenticity is being used to sell products, what does it mean, anymore?"[47]

Similarly, Belkin asks in her *New York Times* profile of Dooce "Queen of the Mommy Bloggers": "It is a question that hovers over all personal blogs—if they are based on trust, do you violate that trust by introducing commerce? Readers of personal blogs return again and again for the connection, the feeling they really know the writer—and ads can break the 'we're all friends here' mood."[48]

More than a few bloggers also have begun to reflect on what the competition has meant to the blogging community and the readers who support them. Scary Mommy, quoted in a *New York Times* report, laments, "I wish we could go back to where blogging was five years ago, when it was just about the writing and the connecting and none of the free stuff and the vacations and the swag bags. . . . I think it dilutes the point."[49] Similarly, Mom-101 wrote in a post titled "Mommybloggings Part Deux: The Marketers Are Here to Stay. Are We?" in May 2009: "I am also sad that the marketing is no longer a small part of the blog world but what seems to be the biggest part. I am sad that it's making some of the most authentic, talented writers on the web question their relevance. . . . I am most sad that marketing is pulling us apart."[50]

As mommy blog brands and their readers are "pitched" to advertisers, the advertising also comes to insidiously define the blogs, and by default begins to paint all mommy bloggers/readers with the same brush. The advertisers have a certain idea of the demographic they would like to reach, and if the blog does not cover those topics (most frequently household cleaning, décor, cosmetics, style, pets, and children's toys/accessories, for example), then the advertisers and media outlets will be less likely to seek them out. Pundit Mom, for example, responded to Granju's post about "How Much Do the 'Top Mommybloggers' Earn from Their Blogs" with the following: "I made/make virtually no money on ads on my blog that came through ad networks, so I finally just took them down. I make no money writing my blog. . . . It's a bit tougher for me to find 'sponsors' or people paying me for blog related things since I write about politics from a decidedly left-of-center point of view!"[51]

As Pundit Mom's experience demonstrates, bloggers have a choice to either forgo advertising revenue or to develop content and subsequent readers (or a "comment tribe" in blogging business terms) that advertisers are seeking out for their own brands. The most successful mommy blog brands, then, are those that most readily mesh with their sponsors' brands, such as Old Navy Kids, Target Home, Pampers, Edy's ice cream, and whichever big-budget animated film of the season is about to land in theaters. Both the blogger and the readers are defined as household shoppers, following a long history of women being associated with both domesticity and consumption.[52] The brands and sponsors most often associated with these blogs also reify traditional images of motherhood, that is, mom as the purchaser of back-to-school clothes, of home furnishings and décor, as well as food purchases and entertainment products. That consumer, the mother in charge of the household purchases, also harkens to an image of the domestic homemaker of a previous era who cleans the house, clothes the kids, and feeds her family but would not necessarily be the person making the big financial decisions about such things as cars, life insurance, financial plans, or more recently, technology. Mora Aarons-Mele commented on this retro-fitting of the feminine mystique in a *Huffington Post* editorial, asserting, "the current state of mom blogging plays into the most traditional gender roles. It's now a potentially lucrative way for women to earn money and wield power—from home. . . . As mom blogging grows as an industry fueled by ad dollars, I actually think it's taking us back to the days when a woman's worth was measured by the cleanliness of her kitchen floor."[53]

In addition to potentially fracturing the community of bloggers that already exists through increased competition and the selling of readers/comment tribe to advertisers, there is also the problem of brand building resulting in the further homogenization of mommy blogs. Already, the mommy blogosphere is fairly one-size-fits-all and the list of top blogs included in this chapter reflects that fact. A frequently reported study conducted by Scarborough Research in 2011 also reveals that the economic, social, and political reach of blogging moms far outpaced their non-blogging (or blog-reading) counterparts. Some of the key demographic statistics generated through this study indicate that of those mothers who had contributed to or read a mommy blog in the last month, the average age was 37, they were 52 percent more likely than other mothers to be college-educated, and their average household income was $84,000 a year ($14,000 higher than all moms). The study also reported that mommy bloggers are not only politically informed but also socially conscientious when spending their money on consumer products with blogging moms 69 percent more likely to buy organic food on a regular basis, 46 percent more likely to buy locally grown food, and 49 pecent more likely than other mothers to buy eco-friendly cleaning products.[54]

Writing for *Bitch Magazine*, Veronica Arreola asserts that the mommy blogosphere suffers from "sameness," explaining, "The lack of moms of color matters for the simple reason that our different backgrounds—e.g., ethnicity, class, religion—are reflected in the way we parent; this difference should be seen on blogs that claim to represent moms in general." Arreola blames this lack of diversity on a lack of recruitment of bloggers of color, and notes that while those in the mommy blogging community make claims on the value of a diversity of perspectives and network of support, "these communities only offer that if you fit into the community that is already there."[55] And in an essay titled, "Ain't I a Mommy?" Deesha Philyaw notes the aggrandizing effects of such a homongenized view of motherhood, arguing that, "The abundance of ink and airtime devoted to a vocal minority of women promotes the idea that this minority's experience is somehow universal. Low-income and working-class women, black women, and other women of color don't see their mothering experiences and concerns reflected in the mommy media machine, and we get the cultural message loud and clear: Affluent white women are the only mothers who really matter."[56]

The commercialization of the mommy blogosphere has real implications for whose voices coalesce to represent an authentic experience of motherhood, and from where those voices emanate—in this case, they are most often the voices of white, middle-class, well educated, heterosexual women who are writing from and about their home lives. In fact, it is quite revealing that Philyaw refers to this group as a "minority," considering that the women who comprise this demographic are some of the most empowered women in society. Yet, their limited numbers relative to the US population as a whole, and compared to the composition of mothers with very different profiles who make up the majority of that population, very much places the "typical" mommy blogger in the minority, even though their online presence belies this fact. Consequently, the community of blogging mothers is fairly narrowly defined along an axis of privilege (both ethnic and economic), which may impede their power as a collective and their rhetorical influence on the larger demographic of American mothers.

Another troubling aspect of the most successful mommy blogs (in terms of both popular and financial success) is their boundary-crossing status as personal expressions of rhetorical agency that invite public participation and influence, while being both enabled and constrained by the economic realm of advertising, marketing, and consumer culture. Casey Ryan Kelly suggests that "agency is the individual or collective capacity to recognize moments in which structures are open to reinterpretation and then act to resignify the social order."[57] Mommy blogs have clearly demonstrated the capacity to challenge dominant interpretations of motherhood and to respond with a more empowered, and collective, vision of mothering in the twenty-first century.

This work certainly has merits in terms of sociopolitical agency and perhaps may even be indicative of a new form of activism born of shared perspectives and experiences online.[58] However, Kelly also recognizes Campbell's arguments about the material limitations on authors/rhetors in his assertion that "rhetorical agents are linked to both culture and collectivities in ways that require negotiation within and against institutional power structures."[59] In this case, the rise of mommy blogs extend to mothers an opportunity to give voice to their own experiential expertise, to build participatory communities and harness their collective power, and to enhance their entrepreneurial profile within the economic realm. However, as Kelly notes, "exercising agency requires arduous work and involves direct challenges to patriarchal institutions and practices at both a material and symbolic level."[60] While these blogs present the possibilities of symbolic interventions that reinterpret and reimagine mothering, they also represent the limitations of reforming the social order in the face of the deep patriarchal structures of the economic realm, particularly the commodification of motherhood through the patriarchal institutions of advertising and consumer culture.

Conclusion

There has been much talk in recent years, both by bloggers and at blogging conferences, as to whether or not women bloggers are undervalued in the online marketplace. When the move was made to commercialize blogs, many mommy bloggers were willing to exchange services for gift cards, "swag" (free products to review), or for a link on a corporate brand's home page. Consequently, as of 2014, there still was no industry standard with regard to advertising rates, sponsorship deals, syndication, or public relations work. So, while mommy blogs have been targeted as an online force for marketers, on the whole they are regarded less seriously as a business venture than other blogs, which are thought to be more "professional." While the Internet was once thought to be a democratizing force, in many ways gender politics are alive and well behind the screen.

Part of the reason that mommy blogs have not garnered a high level of respect in either the blogosphere or the online marketplace is because, while all of the blogs considered here generate some level of income for their creators, most of these mommy bloggers do not talk about blogging as work or refer to themselves explicitly as working moms (two exceptions are Pundit Mom and Mom-101). Many bloggers also fail to regularly engage with issues happening outside the bounds of their own homes, families, and personal lives, thereby articulating their "authentic" experience of motherhood within the less valued realm of traditional gendered norms. That is, many blogging mothers' regular posts detail their labor within the home (with children, pets, domestic chores, and home remodeling/decorating), a practice that further reifies an image of motherhood as a domestic practice. According to Gregg, "the content of women's blogs is perceived by some to be less noteworthy than men's by virtue of their often domestic and personal sphere of reference, whereas men's blogs are often seen to be engaged more in political debate," which she argues leads to generalizations that "serve to confirm ingrained notions as to the proper participants in, and issues appropriate for, the public sphere."[61] The commercialization of blogs has increasingly repositioned this organic and "radicalized" mothering community back into the traditionalized and gendered bounds of the private/domestic sphere, thereby depoliticizing their potential for empowering the institution of motherhood.

The radical act of blogging becomes further delimited once bloggers turn their attention to courting advertisers, developing a brand, and creating content that will generate a reader community to match their sponsors' target demographic. The act of mommy blogging may be constitutive of a collectivity of mothers for those who participate in such online dialogue that works to reshape the traditional image of motherhood into the more empowered experience of mothering, yet the act of blogging has not necessarily liberated many of these bloggers into the realm of the political/public sphere. However, the unprecedented rise and impact of this blogging genre over the last five years, and the uncharted terrain of this new media business model for working mothers, could potentially reverse this trend as long as the women leading this blogging revolution work collectively to challenge gender politics and advocate social and political change for mothers and families, rather than just working on commodifying their brand. As Ronald Greene points out in his conceptualization of communicative labor and rhetorical agency, "rhetorical agency can no longer mediate the relationship between politics and economics, because politics and economics are no longer unique domains of social action."[62]

For those who have embraced the "blog as business model," these blogs already have become a source of political empowerment for the mothers who write them, both in terms of increased publishing opportunities that have allowed them a stronger public voice (from syndicated posts/editorials for outlets such as the *New York Times* and *Huffington Post* to book publishing contracts) and other entrepreneurial opportunities, such as the creation of cable television shows (home style and cooking mostly) and other social media outlets (such as Cool Mom Picks started by Mom-101 and Let's

Panic About Babies started by Finslippy). The popularity and economic success of some of these bloggers also has led to more collaborative blogging sites with an even larger audience share, such as Babble Voices (acquired by the Walt Disney Company in 2011, and a site on which many bloggers listed here contribute) and the Momversation project started by Cool Mom, which brings together prominent mommy bloggers in video "conversations" to talk about issues important to mothers, such as choosing the right school for your child, whether or not to breast-feed, and other hot-button topics. In this way, these bloggers with a proven record of revenue production have leveraged their own entrepreneurial success to launch more collaborative and wide-reaching blogging communities, which also have extended the network of support resources that mothers have available to them.

Other bloggers have used their blogs as a platform to initiate their own online campaigns for greater social good in recent years, from small scale movements (Because I Said So's "One Small Act of Kindness" series, with suggestions for committing random acts of charity) to increased health awareness, advocacy, and support (Mama Pundit and drug abuse, Postpartum Progress and pregnancy-related mental health, Her Bad Mother and muscular distrophy). During the Thanksgiving holiday season in 2011, for example, Scary Mommy raised $20,000 in one week to feed more than four hundred families, which led to the creation of Scary Mommy Nation, a grassroots organization of mothers helping mothers and families in financial need through a variety of projects. A number of bloggers included here also have used their growing celebrity status to join global initiatives to address mothers' and children's health in developing nations through the UN, Global Fund, and Every Mother Counts campaigns (Her Bad Mother, Dooce, and Jessica Gottlieb). After appearing on the Forbes 500 list, Dooce was invited to the White House in 2010 to participate in a forum on work-life/family issues for women entrepreneurs. These examples and others demonstrate how mommy blogs do not necessarily have to be constrained by the economic imperatives of capitalism and consumer culture, but rather they may flourish, in Greene's terms, as communicative labor or "a form of life-affirming constitutive power that embodies creativity and cooperation." Through these inroads into more collaborative projects that work toward greater collective mobilization and social justice work, the mommy blogosphere now has the capacity to, as Greene notes, "remodel rhetorical agency as communicative labor" that "extends beyond commodity production per se, to include communication's role in building social networks of all kinds."[63]

Although "mommy blogger" remains a contested term, and these bloggers feel compelled to constantly question and debate their "worth" (or lack thereof), while at the same time working more and more each year to professionalize the industry, the rhetorical impact of mommy blogging is undeniable. The collective act of mommy blogging has radically altered the conception of motherhood in the twenty-first century and brought forth a new and unabashed perspective on what doing motherhood really means. Most significantly, a vast online presence of mothers who practice motherhood every day have found a space to forge a community and to critically engage an identity that has been assumed to be a natural part of womanhood for generations. Perhaps as these blogging "radicals" continue to find ways to transcend the limits of commodification and broaden their community to include a diversity of moms and means of empowered mothering, this social media experiment may also get us closer to remedying the social malady that Warner calls the "mommy mystique" through blogging mothers uniting together to solve social problems (and leveraging their brands to do so) rather than battling them alone.

Notes

1. David Hochman, "Mommy (and Me)," *New York Times*, January 30, 2005.
2. Hochman, "Mommy," H6.
3. David White and Phillip Winn, "State of the Blogosphere 2008," *Technorati* (blog), October 13, 2009, http://technorati.com/social-media/feature/state-of-the-blogosphere-2008/.
4. "Mom Bloggers Voices and Votes Influence State of the Union," Scarborough Research, last modified October 2, 2011, accessed May 24, 2012, http://scarborough.com/press-release.php?press_id=mom-bloggers-voices-and-votes-influence-state-of-the-union&q_string=&s_string=/press.php.
5. I have chosen to use the term "mommy blog" here and throughout this essay despite its status as a highly contested and frequently debated term by many of those who have been labeled as such. Following blogger Catherine Connors, I employ the terms mommy blog and mommy blogger to signify an act of empowerment and ownership of the label as many (including many of the bloggers mentioned in this chapter) have done in their own embrace of it in recent years.
Gina Chen's study of twenty-nine blog posts in which the term "mommy blogger" was debated, "Don't Call Me That: A Techno-Feminist Analysis of the Term *Mommy Blogger*," *Mass Communication and Society, 16*, no. 4 (2013): 510–32.
6. Anna Marevska,"The Mommy Blog Phenomenon," *CisionNavigator* (blog), last modified October 29, 2009, accessed May 25, 2012, http://navigator.cision.com/The_Mommy_Blog_Phenomenon.aspx.
7. Stephanie Thompson, "Mommy Blogs: A Marketer's Dream," *Advertising Age*, February 26, 2007, http://adage.com/article/digital/mommy-blogs-a-marketer-s-dream/115194/.

8. Anita Blanchard, "Blogs as Virtual Communities: Identifying a Sense of Community in the *Julie/Julia Project*," in *Into the Blogosphere: Rhetoric, Community, and Culture of Weblogs*, eds. Laura J. Gurak, Smiljana Antonijevic, Laurie Johnson, Clancy Ratliff, and Jessica Reyman, 2004, accessed June 14, 2011, http://blog.lib.umn.edu/blogosphere/blogs_as_virtual.html.

9. Lisa Belkin, "Queen of the Mommy Bloggers," *The New York Times*, February 23, 2011.

10. Jeffrey Rosen, "Your Blog or Mine," *The New York Times*, December 19, 2004.

11. Belkin, "Queen."

12. Kiri Blakeley, "Dooce's Dilemma" July 15, 2009, http://www.forbes.com/2009/07/15/dooce-heather-armstrong-forbes-woman-power-women-blog.html.

13. Almost half of the blogs in this chapter were in the top ten list of Babble.com's Top 100 Mommy Blogs for 2011 (http://www.babble.com/mom/top-mom-bloggers/); others made it onto various other lists, such as *Working Mother* magazine's "Most Powerful Moms in Social Media" (http://www.workingmother.com/most-powerful-moms/most-powerful-moms-social-media-pictures).

14. Lisa Belkin, "The Mom Blog Jinx," *Motherlode*, January 14, 2011, http://parenting.blogs.nytimes.com/2011/01/14/the-mom-blog-jinx/?_php=true&_type=blogs&_r=0.

15. Susan Maushart, *The Mask of Motherhood: How Becoming a Mother Changes Everything and Why We Pretend It Doesn't* (New York: Penguin Books, 1999), 5–8.

16. Judith Warner, *Perfect Madness: Motherhood in the Age of Anxiety* (New York: Penguin, 2005), 51.

17. Warner, *Perfect Madness*, 56–57.

18. Melissa C. Gregg, "Posting with Passion: Blogs and the Politics of Gender," in *Uses of Blogs*, eds. Axel Bruns and Joanne Jacobs, eds. (Brisbane: Peter Lang, 2006), 152.

19. Lisa Belkin "Mom Bloggers, A Force To Be Reckoned With," *Huffington Post* (blog), October 31, 2011, http://www.huffingtonpost.com/lisa-belkin/mommy-bloggers_b_1067284.html.

20. Wendy Piersall, "16 Market Research Facts Proving Social Media Moms' Influence," *Wendy Piersall* (blog), February 18, 2011, http://www.wendypiersall.com/mom-blog-statistics/.

21. Alice Bradley, "Here's Where I Get All Preachy. You Can Skim This One, *Finslippy* (blog), February 20, 2005, http://alicebradley.net/blog/heres-where-i-get-all-preachy-you-can-skim-this-one.html.

22. Lisa Hammond, "'Mommy Blogging is a Radical Act': Weblog Communities and the Construction of Maternal Identities," in *Mothers Who Deliver: Feminist Interventions in Interpersonal and Public Discourse*, eds. Pegeen Reichert Powell and Jocelyn Fenton Stitt (New York: SUNY Press, 2010), 87.

23. Kristin Howerton, "How Has the Online Community Helped You as an Adoptive Mom?" *Rage Against the Minivan* (blog), June 26, 2012. http://www.rageagainsttheminivan.com/search?q=amazing+community+of+adoptive+moms&x=0&y=0

24. Andrea Buchanan, "The Secret Life of Mothers: Maternal Narrative, Momoirs, and the Rise of the Blog," *The Mothers Movement Online* (blog), February 2006, http://www.mothersmovement.org/features/06/02/a_buchanan_1.html.

25. Heather Armstrong, "Newsletter Month Fifty and Fifty-One," *Dooce* (blog), May 2, 2008, http://dooce.com/2008/05/02/newsletter-month-fifty-and-fifty-one.

26. Karlyn Kohrs Campbell, "Agency: Promiscuous and Protean," *Communication and Critical/Cultural Studies, 2*, no. 1 (2005): 3.

27. Campbell, "Agency," 7.

28. Hammond, "Mommy Blogging," 84.

29. For more on the good/bad mother discourse, see Shari L. Thurer, *The Myths of Motherhood: How Culture Reinvents the Good Mother* (New York: Penguin, 1994); Molly Ladd-Taylor and Lauri Umansky, eds. *Bad Mothers: The Politics of Blame in Twentieth Century America* (New York: New York University Press, 1998); Sharon Hays, *The Cultural Contradictions of Motherhood* (New Haven: Yale University Press, 1996); Susan J. Douglas and Meredith W. Michaels, *The Mommy Myth: The Idealization of Motherhood and How It Has Undermined All Women* (New York: Free Press, 2004).

30. Rebecca Powell, "Good Mothers, Bad Mothers and Mommy Bloggers: Rhetorical Resistance and Fluid Subjectivities" *MP: An Online Feminist Journal*, 2, no. 6 (2010), http://academinist.org/women-and-families, 41, 46.

31. Powell, "Good Mothers," 46.

32. Lori Kido Lopez, "The Radical Act of 'Mommy Blogging': Redefining Motherhood Through the Blogosphere," *New Media & Society*, 11, no. 5 (2009): 744.

33. Jennifer Mendelsohn, "Honey, Don't Bother Mommy. I'm Too Busy Building My Brand," *The New York Times*, March 12, 2010.

34. Lisa Belkin, "Babes No More," *Adweek*, February 27, 2012, http://www.adweek.com/news/advertising-branding/babes-no-more-138511.

35. Katie Allison Granju, "How Much Do 'Top Mommybloggers' Earn From Their Blog, and Is It Enough?" *Babble* (blog), March 31, 2011, http://blogs.babble.com/strollerderby/2011/03/31/how-much-do-top-mommybloggers-earn-from-their-blogs-and-is-it-enough/.

36. David Schaper, "Mom Bloggers Debate Ethics of "Blog-ola," NPR "All Tech Considered," July 27, 2009, http://www.npr.org/templates/story/story.php?storyId=111083779.

37. Douglas MacMillan, "Blogola: The FCC Takes on Paid Posts," *Bloomberg Business Week*, May 19, 2009, http://www.businessweek.com/technology/content/may2009/tc20090518_532031.htm.

38. For a more detailed reading of this list, sees: http://selfishmom.com/full-disclosure/.

39. Heather Armstrong, "A Peek Inside Our Day, The Fourth Hour," *Dooce* (blog), April 25, 2011, http://dooce.com/2011/04/25/peek-inside-our-day-fourth-hour

40. Catherine Connors, "How To Talk About Succeeding in Blogging (Without Really Crying)," *Her Bad Mother* (blog), July 29, 2011, http://herbadmother.com/2011/07/how-to-talk-about-succeeding-in-blogging-without-really-crying/

41. http://www.blogher.com/node/478218/schedule.

42. Meghan Casserly, "Home on the Range with the Pioneer Woman," *Forbes Online*, March 3, 2010, http://www.forbes.com/2010/03/03/blogger-pioneer-woman-ree-drummond-forbes-woman-time-food_2.html.

43. Amanda Fortini, "O Pioneer Woman!: The Creation of a Domestic Idyll," *The New Yorker*, May 9, 2011, http://www.newyorker.com/reporting/2011/05/09/110509fa_fact_fortini.

44. Casserly, "Home on the Range."

45. "About Resourceful Mommy" Resourceful Mommy (blog), http://resourcefulmommy.com/about-resourceful-mommy/

46. "Blogher, Part One" Amalah (blog), July 27, 2009, http://www.amalah.com/amalah/tantrums/page/3/#.U6WbdajUsdU

47. Alice Bradley, "On the Notion of Blogging as a Career" *Finslippy* (blog), June 15, 2012, http://www.finslippy.com/blog/tag/blogging.

48. Belkin, "Queen."

49. Mendelshon, "Honey, Don't."

50. Liz Gumbinner, "Mommybloggings Part Deux: The Marketers Are Here to Stay. Are We?" *Mom-101* (blog), May 27, 2009, http://mom-101.blogspot.com/2009/05/mommybloggings-part-deux-marketers-are.html.

51. Granju, "How Much Do Mommy Bloggers."

52. See Elizabeth Kowaleski-Wallace, *Consuming Subjects: Women, Shopping and Business in the Eighteenth Century* (New York: Columbia University Press, 1996); John Fiske, "Shopping for Pleasure: Malls, Power, and Resistance," in *The Consumer Society Reader*, ed. Juliet B. Schor and Douglas B. Holt (New York, The New Press, 2000); Hilary Radner, *Shopping Around: Feminine Culture and the Pursuit of Pleasure* (New York: Routledge, 1994); Erika Rappaport, *Shopping for Pleasure: Women in the Making of London's West End* (Princeton: Princeton University Press, 2001).

53. Morra Aarons-Mele, "Million-Dollar Mommy Blogging: Reinforcing the Feminine Mystique?," *Huffington Post* (blog), May 25, 2012, http://www.huffingtonpost.com/morra-aaronsmele/mommy-bloggers_b_829188.html.

54. "Mom Bloggers Voices."

55. Veronica I. Arreola, "Mommy & Me: Looking for the Missing Voices in the Burgeoning World of Mom Blogs," *Bitch Magazine* online, May 31, 2008, http://bitchmagazine.org/article/mommy-me.

56. Deesha Philyaw, "Ain't I a Mommy?," *Bitch Magazine*, June 27, 2008, http://www.alternet.org/story/89758/there%27s_something_missing_from_mommy_lit.

57. Casey Ryan Kelly, "Women's Rhetorical Agency in the American West: *The New Penelope*," *Women's Studies in Communication* 32, no. 2, (2009): 210–11.

58. I see such activist potential in a similar vein to how Stacey Sowards and Valerie Renegar have argued that rhetorical activism in contemporary feminism diverges from traditional understandings of rhetoric and social movements by "creating a private sphere through personal activism" through the process sharing, which "creates a network of experiences between women and acts as a story telling process that others can learn from if they so choose." See Stacey K. Sowards and Valerie

R. Renegar, "Reconceptualizing Rhetorical Activism in Contemporary Feminist Contexts," *The Howard Journal of Communications*, 17 (2006): 57–74.

59. Kelly, "Women's Rhetorical Agency," 210–11.

60. Kelly, "Women's Rhetorical Agency, 227.

61. Gregg, "Posting."

62. Ronald Walter Greene, "Rhetoric and Capitalism: Rhetorical Agency as Communicative Labor," *Philosophy and Rhetoric,* 37, no. 3 (2004): 189.

63. Greene, "Rhetoric," 201.

References

Arreola, Veronica I. "Mommy & Me: Looking for the Missing Voices in the Burgeoning World of Mom Blogs." *Bitch Magazine*, May 31, 2008. Accessed February 20, 2012. http://bitchmagazine.org/article/mommy-me.

Amalah Blog. http://amalah.com.

Babble Blog. http://www.babble.com/.

Belkin, Lisa. "Queen of the Mommy Bloggers." *The New York Times*, February 23, 2011. Accessed May 25, 2012. http://www.nytimes.com/2011/02/27/magazine/27armstrong-t.html?pagewanted=all.

Belkin, Lisa. "The Mommy Blog Jinx." *The New York Times*, January 14, 2011. Accessed May 10, 2012. http://parenting.blogs.nytimes.com/2011/01/14/the-mom-blog-jinx/.

Belkin, Lisa. "Babes No More." *Adweek*, February 27, 2012. Accessed May 25, 2012. http://www.adweek.com/news/advertising-branding/babes-no-more-138511.

Blakeley, Kiri. "Dooce's Dilemma." *Forbes*, July 15, 2009. Accessed February 10, 2012. http://www.forbes.com/2009/07/15/dooce-heather-armstrong-forbes-woman-power-women-blog.html.

Blanchard, Anita. "Blogs as Virtual Communities: Identifying a Sense of Community in the *Julie/Julia Project*." In *Into the Blogosphere: Rhetoric, Community, and Culture of Weblogs*, edited by Laura J. Gurak, Smiljana Antonijevic, Laurie Johnson, Clancy Ratliff, and Jessica Reyman. June 2004. Accessed June 14, 2011. http://blog.lib.umn.edu/blogosphere/blogs_as_virtual.html.

Campbell, Karlyn Kohrs. "Agency: Promiscuous and Protean." *Communication and Critical/Cultural Studies* 2 (2005): 1–19.

Casserly, Meghan. "Home on the Range with the Pioneer Woman," *Forbes Online*. March 3, 2010. Accessed February 20, 2012. http://www.forbes.com/2010/03/03/blogger-pioneer-woman-ree-drummond-forbes-woman-time-food_2.html.

Chen, Gina. "Don't Call Me That: A Techno-Feminist Analysis of the Term *Mommy Blogger*." *Mass Communication and Society* 16 (2013): 510–532.

Cision Blog. http://www.cision.com/us/tag/cision-navigator/.

Dooce Blog. http://dooce.com/.

Douglas, Susan J., and Meredith W. Michaels. *The Mommy Myth: The Idealization of Motherhood and How It Has Undermined All Women*. New York: Free Press, 2004.

Finslippy Blog. http://alicebradley.net/.

Fiske, John. "Shopping for Pleasure: Malls, Power, and Resistance." In *The Consumer Society Reader*, edited by Juliet B. Schor and Douglas B. Holt. 306–28. New York: The New Press, 2000.

Fortini, Amanda. "O Pioneer Woman!: The Creation of a Domestic Idyll." *The New Yorker*, May 9, 2011. Accessed February 20, 2012. http://www.newyorker.com/reporting/2011/05/09/110509fa_fact_fortini.

Girl's Gone Child Blog. http://www.girlsgonechild.net/.

Girl Who Blog, The. http://thegirlwho.net/.

Gregg, Melissa C. "Posting with Passion: Blogs and the Politics of Gender." In *Uses of Blogs*, edited by Axel Bruns and Joanne Jacobs, 151–160. Brisbane: Peter Lang, 2006.

Greene, Ronald Walter. "Rhetoric and Capitalism: Rhetorical Agency as Communicative Labor." *Philosophy and Rhetoric* 37 (2004): 188–206.

Hammond, Lisa. "'Mommy Blogging is a Radical Act': Weblog Communities and the Construction of Maternal Identities." In *Mothers Who Deliver: Feminist Interventions in Interpersonal and Public Discourse*, edited by Pegeen Reichert Powell and Jocelyn Fenton Stitt, 77–98. New York: SUNY Press, 2010.

Hays, Sharon. *The Cultural Contradictions of Motherhood*. New Haven: Yale University Press, 1996.

Her Bad Mother Blog. http://herbadmother.com.

Hochman, David. "Mommy (and Me)," *New York Times*, January 30, 2005. Accessed May 29, 2012. http://www.nytimes.com/2005/01/30/fashion/30moms.html?_r=0

Huffington Post Blog, The. http://www.huffingtonpost.com/.

Kelly, Casey Ryan. "Women's Rhetorical Agency in the American West: *The New Penelope*." *Women's Studies in Communication* 32 (2009): 201–231.

Kowaleski-Wallace, Elizabeth. *Consuming Subjects: Women, Shopping and Business in the Eighteenth Century*. New York: Columbia University Press, 1996.

Ladd-Taylor, Molly, and Lauri Umansky. *"Bad" Mothers: The Politics of Blame in Twentieth-Century America*. New York: New York University Press, 1998.

Lopez, Lori Kido. "The Radical Act of 'Mommy Blogging': Redefining Motherhood Through the Blogosphere." *New Media & Society* 11 (2009): 729–47.

MacMillan, Douglas. "Blogola: The FCC Takes on Paid Posts." *Bloomberg Business Week*, May 19, 2009. Accessed June 1, 2012. http://www.businessweek.com/technology/content/may2009/tc20090518_532031.htm.

Mama Pundit Blog. http://mamapundit.com/.

Maushart, Susan. *The Mask of Motherhood: How Becoming a Mother Changes Everything and Why We Pretend It Doesn't*. New York: Penguin Books, 1999.

Mendelsohn, Jennifer. "Honey, Don't Bother Mommy. I'm Too Busy Building My Brand." *The New York Times*, March 12, 2010. Accessed May 25, 2012. http://www.nytimes.com/2010/03/14/fashion/14moms.html?pagewanted=all&_r=0.

Mom 101 Blog. http://mom-101.com/.

"Mom Bloggers Voices and Votes Influence State of the Union," Scarborough Research, last modified October 2, 2011, accessed May 24, 2012, http://scarborough.com/press-release.php?press_id=mom-bloggers-voices-and-votes-influence-state-of-the-union&q_string=&s_string=/press.php.

Mothers Movement Online, The. http://www.mothersmovement.org/.

Philyaw, Deesha. "Ain't I a Mommy?" *Bitch Magazine*, June 27, 2008. Accessed February 20, 2012. http://www.alternet.org/story/89758/there%27s_something_missing_from_mommy_lit.

Powell, Rebecca. "Good Mothers, Bad Mothers and Mommy Bloggers: Rhetorical Resistance and Fluid Subjectivities." *MP: An Online Feminist Journal* 1 (2010): 37–50. Accessed May 24, 2012. http://academinist.org/wp-content/uploads/2010/02/03_Powell_Bloggers.pdf.

Radner, Hilary. *Shopping Around: Feminine Culture and the Pursuit of Pleasure*. New York: Routledge, 1994.

Rappaport, Erika. *Shopping for Pleasure: Women in the Making of London's West End*. Princeton: Princeton University Press, 2001.

Rage Against the Minivan Blog. http://www.rageagainsttheminivan.com/

Resourceful Mommy Blog. http://resourcefulmommy.com.

Rosen, Jeffrey. "Your Blog or Mine." *The New York Times*, December 19, 2004. Accessed May 24, 2012. http://www.nytimes.com/2004/12/19/magazine/19PHENOM.html

Schaper, David. "Mom Bloggers Debate Ethics of "Blog-ola." NPR "All Tech Considered," July 27, 2009. Accessed June 1, 2012. http://www.npr.org/templates/story/story.php?storyId=111083779.

Selfish Mom Blog. http://selfishmom.com.

Sowards, Stacey K., and Valerie R. Renegar. "Reconceptualizing Rhetorical Activism in Contemporary Feminist Contexts." *The Howard Journal of Communications* 17 (2006): 57–74.

Technorati Blog. http://technorati.com/.

Thompson, Stephanie. "Mommy Blogs: A Marketer's Dream." *Advertising Age*. February 26, 2007.

Thurer, Shari L. *The Myths of Motherhood: How Culture Reinvents the Good Mother*. New York: Penguin, 1994.

Warner, Judith. *Perfect Madness: Motherhood in the Age of Anxiety*. New York: Penguin, 2005.

Wendy Piersall Blog. http://www.wendypiersall.com/.

6
Mompreneurs

Homemade Organic Baby Food and the Commodification of Intensive Mothering

Kara N. Dillard

Amy Ballon and Danielle Boterell were MBA degree holders and Bay Street executives when they both became pregnant.[1] Rather than return to full-time employment after their respective maternity leaves had ended, both Ballon and Boterell quit their corporate jobs and became stay-at-home mothers.[2] Ballon and Boterell's decision is not surprising. Any decision to opt-out of the workforce is based on a multitude of factors. However, the justifications expressed by opt-out mothers that garner the most media coverage draw on and normalize the "prefeminist notions of mothering and family care" associated with intensive mothering.[3] According to Sharon Hays, intensive mothering is a socially constructed phenomenon in which mothers view parenting as a child-centered, expert-guided, emotionally absorbing, labor intensive, and financially expensive undertaking.[4]

The precepts of intensive mothering seemingly counter the profit-maximizing marketplace in which women work. Indeed, as markets continue to encroach and absorb the private sphere, mothers function even more as the cultural symbolic anchor meant to stem the tide against the destabilizing effects of capitalism on the family.[5] Thus, mothers live at the convergence of several conflicting social ideologies, including: (1) that the career woman is the unfettered, totally committed worker; (2) the working world is more valuable than the domestic world; and (3) the best mothering is the hands-on, intensive type.[6] More importantly, these competing logics hold equal social status.[7] This presents an interesting paradox for mothers as they face unappealing and often mutually exclusive choices: leave the careers they have spent years developing for full-time motherhood or stay in the workplace and strain to maintain a position of intensive mothering. But, as Linda Seidel writes, "if the relationship of intensive mothering to capitalism can be described as 'paradoxical' that is because intensive mothering, while seeming to espouse different values, was produced by a capitalist society and, arguably, helps sustain it."[8] Intensive mothering is consistent with a neoliberal regime that places the risks of family life on the shoulders of mothers. The logic of the neoliberal marketplace often divides people into "mothers" or "others."[9]

Women have attempted to redefine mothering in a variety of ways.[10] Some have begun to challenge the cultural practices involved in meeting the "good mother" standard.[11] For example, Allison Pugh notes the growth of developmental toy sales in which "women are sold the notion that a certain product allows them to do the work of mothering well despite competing social directives."[12] Pugh's research illustrates a new trend of how mothers engage the competing exigencies of working and mothering. Instead of contesting the cultural construction of what motherhood means, women are now able to purchase and consume the ideal vision of "good," intensive motherhood, albeit in ways that tend to reinforce the concerns and luxuries of white, middle-class, heterosexual mothers.[13]

The switch from contesting motherhood to consuming products that enable women to be both productive workers and "good" mothers has led to new avenues of challenging the mother/worker dichotomy. In this relatively recent trend, women are choosing both stay-at-home motherhood and full-time employment by becoming mompreneurs. The rise of the "mompreneur," a term coined by authors Patricia Cobe and Ellen Parlapiano of www.momrepreneur.com, represents the relatively new movement of moms running trademarked, often Internet-based home-businesses geared toward selling other mothers child-based products.[14] Mompreneurs are typically highly educated twenty- and thirty-something women who resigned from their corporate jobs when they became mothers. From designing and selling items like baby blankets, baby shoes, and baby toys, mompreneurship allows mothers to apply their management, organizational, and social media savvy into thriving baby and child-based businesses while continuing to fulfill their traditional mother roles.[15] Networked through social media, mompreneurs are often seen as leading the charge into the "mommy industry." One such industry ripe for mompreneurs is in organic baby foods. Because the types of food mothers serve is seen as an especially salient measure of "good" mothering, the homemade organic baby food market presents a unique illustration of motherhood as a commodity and how mompreneurs market that ideology to other mothers.[16]

This chapter examines the rise of mompreneurs in online companies that sell homemade organic baby food such as Sweetpea, HappyBaby, Petite Palate, Petit Cuisine, and Jack's Harvest. The stories told within these sites reinforce the socially constructed role of intensive mothering through the production and consumption of specialized organic baby food. This research explores the ways in which mothers themselves commercialize identities for other mothers to consume. Whereas Brittany Lopez and Lori Lee have studied the impact of new media technologies on motherhood and Pugh has examined the consumption patterns of mothers, little research has examined this powerful online community of mompreneurs and their commercialization of intensive mothering ideals.[17] Recent literature has focused on how working and middle-class mothers have justified the process for purchasing certain foods, but such research does not examine how products are marketed and how that marketing can impact a mother's justification for purchasing food.[18] This chapter thus adds to the emerging literature on motherhood and consumer culture by highlighting how the commitment to intensive mothering is shared by both those who make and purchase the product.

In order to investigate how mompreneurs promote the commercialization and consumption of motherhood, I examined the product websites of the five mompreneur-based organic processors listed above, including Sweetpea, HappyBaby, Petite Palate, Petit Cuisine, and Jack's Harvest. I examined the company homepages—surveying bios of founders and owners, the company history and Frequently Asked Questions (FAQ) pages but focusing on sections where ingredients and cooking procedures are discussed. In these sections, I tracked the degree to which the rationale emphasized the health/nutritional benefit to the child and/or convenience/cost for the mother. I identified a number of key themes and strategies linked to intensive mothering, such as the importance of organics in developing healthy children, how homemade food is healthier than conventionally processed food, and how mompreneurs themselves came from the workforce into the baby food business. Those themes guided my evaluation and subsequent structuring of this chapter.

In this chapter, I argue that through the commodification of homemade organic baby food, mompreneurs have found a way to package and commercialize a mother's cultural need to satisfy the standards of intensive mothering in a risk society. Implicit in the stories and marketing campaigns of these mompreneur-led companies is a recognition of what Lake and collegues call an "enduring gender divide in food responsibility."[19] Starting with the decision to breast-feed or not, mothers are perceived to have primary control over their children's consumption patterns and are held accountable for providing food with the least-possible health risks. Mompreneurs promote a type of mothering ideal based around the notion that organic, homemade baby food is best. Embedded in the production of such products is a symbolic message that the standard of intensive mothering must be met either by adopting the lifestyle or purchasing proxy products. While mompreneurs themselves are challenging the mother/worker dynamic, the products they sell to other mothers reify the necessity of consumption as a means to solidify one's motherhood status. It is within this dynamic that mothers as consumers "live out motherhood in and through, as well as against, ideologies and practices of consumption."[20] When culture becomes commodified, the commodity and culture become disconnected from the socioeconomic conditions that frame such products.[21] The unfortunate conclusion is that, as in the case of homemade organic baby food, such culturally required purchases are often financially unaffordable to many middle- and working-class families.

Understanding the Politics of Moms' Plates

Starting with the decision to breast-feed or bottle-feed, decisions over what and how to feed children are seen as having nutritional, economical, and moral consequences. Moms are the primary purchasing agent for families and thus shoulder the burden of consumption and judgment regarding their decisions.[22] In an article from the *Denver Post* featuring mothers who make their own baby food, one mother states: "'I want total control,' says Kim Barry of Denver's Stapleton neighborhood. She uses organic ingredients almost exclusively to make mushy meals for her roly-poly six-month-old daughter, Kaitlyn. 'I want to know exactly what I'm putting in her.'"[23] In this context, "total control" is not so much the ability of mothers to choose what types of food they eat but how that food is grown, where it is grown, how it was produced, and what, if any, additives were put into it.

The global recession of 2007–2009, which had significant effects on unemployment and family savings, devastated the US organic food industry. Organic food revenue had averaged $17 billion annually, with 60 percent of all US households purchasing organic items.[24] In the wake of the Great Recession, sales of organic fruit, vegetables, and bread slumped nearly 13 percent from a record high in 2009, while meat dropped 22.7 percent.[25] This marks an overall reversal of fortunes for the organics industry, which has seen nearly a decade of double-digit growth. Only two products were able to defy the declining sales trend: organic milk and organic baby food. Organic baby food saw its market share increase by double digits, indicating that there was still a sustainable market willing to pay premium prices for such products. To illustrate, a week's worth of 3.5 ounce stage one (mostly liquid) organic baby food is $84.00 at Petit Cuisine's online store compared to seven days of 2.5 ounce stage one organic prunes from Gerber Baby retailing for less than $10.00.

That specialty food systems like organic baby foods are experiencing an explosion of popularity despite economic downturns signifies a change in how consumers relate to food. Much of this can be attributed to changes in values, norms, and customs that have challenged long-held assumptions about food and the agricultural production process. Two interdependent transformations in the mid-twentieth century set the stage for an alternative food renaissance. First, the cheap food policies of the postwar era, which brought plentiful and inexpensive canned, frozen, and preprepared foods to the supermarket shelves, also created a sense of trust in farmers, nutritionists, corporations, and agribusinesses tasked as food oversight experts.[26] Letting the experts take charge, as Wynne Wright and Gerad Middendorf argue, had the effect of switching American's consciousness about health and food safety away from the biological and social basis of production. Consumers were told that large-scale food production was providing people with nutritious food and that food scientists were using state-of-the-art technology to mitigate any food safety issues. At the same time, changes in the types of food families chose to eat resulted in a significant shift in women's labor force participation.[27] As women moved into the workplace and spent more time outside the household during the 1970s and 1980s, canned, frozen, and preprepared foods increased in availability. The end of the twentieth century and the beginning of the twenty-first century has again seen a shift in trends, this time back toward health and food safety.[28] Consumers now seem more focused on the potential risks they take when eating certain foods than they did thirty years ago.

The commodification of intensive motherhood relies on the exaggeration of certain cultural practices associated with "good" mothering. Discourses of risk often contribute to the construction of intensive parenting as an ideology based on expert-induced uncertainty that, in turn, leads to increased fears of parents, especially mothers, for the safety of their children. Motherhood often becomes associated with the norms of "good" or intensive parenting through exposure to "expert" discourse, which directs mothers to nurture children in specific, intensive ways.[29] In a risk society, mothers are encouraged to organize their behavior as responsible and rational responses to empirical data.[30] As Cairns and collegues note, such calls create an individualization of risk of which mothers—as the primary parent associated with the care of children—traditionally bear the burden. Thus, the neoliberal discourses of risk operate to enlist mothers in strategies that strive for but cannot achieve absolute control over childhood.[31] One mode that mothers use to achieve control and navigate risk is through various consumption practices. When considering whether to breast-feed or bottle-feed, how to diversify types of food offered or making educational toy choices, mothers strive to achieve control through consumption. As Daniel Thomas Cook notes, "contemporary motherhood cannot usefully be understood apart from commercial life and its extensions."[32]

Given the imperative to minimize risk, consumers both wary of corporate food and more informed about child nutrition have see-sawed between the convenient products manufactured by industrial agriculture firms (dubbed Big Baby) and more labor-intensive food they could make themselves.[33] Organic baby food marketers argue that the reticence consumers feel stems from justifiable concerns over pesticides and hormones found in conventional baby foods, which they frame as toxic to maturing infant systems. A *Consumer Reports* study states that baby food is filled with sugar and additives and lacks essential nutrients.[34] Iron, an essential nutrient for growth and development in infants and toddlers, is left out of many baby foods because the USDA bans it. Because attempts to minimize risk guide consumer food choices, many purchase organics to avoid food safety risks.[35] While Big Baby battles to defend their market-share against the emerging homemade organics market, definitions of safety, value, and risk are being redefined in the process.

Looking to capitalize on risk fears, industrial agriculture has moved into the organic baby food market. Producers such as Earth's Best and Healthy Times have developed organic baby food product lines that are made with organic fruits and vegetables, a lower level of contaminants, and high levels of iron. More importantly, these conventional processors emphasize the relative inexpensiveness of their foods compared to other organic products. But one method of reducing "risk" and rejecting industrial agriculture is the consumption of "homemade" foods.[36] Enter the mompreneurs, the mothers with food processors and fresh organic produce that Big Baby identifies as a growing challenge to their market share. Mompreneurs of companies such as Sweetpea Baby Food, HappyBaby Food, Petit Cuisine, Petite Palate, and Jack's Harvest differentiate their products (and channel skepticism about industrial agriculture) by contrasting their approach to baby food processing. These companies not only criticize Big Baby's jarring process, which heats foods until the jar is sterile and can produce a stale taste, but also raise concerns over the common practice of adding minerals and vitamins to foods. In so doing, momprenuers emphasize the impersonality of Big Baby's production process. Organic products made by Big Baby are grown in a far-off field, picked, pureed, and jarred by unknown persons. In contrast, organic baby food moms pick only the best foods, and are deeply involved in the recipes in which the food is made. Most mompreneurs note how their food testers (i.e., their own children) are vital to making sure the food is just right for other babies.

Niche market products, such as organic baby foods, succeed because they are able to capitalize on anxieties about the quality of food, creating a perennial search for ways to exploit the conflict between a mother's concern for her child and the consumption of child-based products claiming to assuage those concerns.[37] Indeed, the preparation and consumption of "homemade" foods is one mode of reducing risk and rejecting Big Baby's production methods.[38] Using this idea, the organics industry and organic baby food in particular has succeeded largely by creating an upscale clientele willing to pay a premium for the quality and status that purchasing organics affords, and by association, assuaging concerns about their child's health.[39] The child-centered, labor-intensive, and financially expensive dictates of intensive mothering are precisely the characteristics posited by the mompreneurs-led organic baby food industry as its hallmarks. It is the freshest, most natural food farmed and packaged specifically with children's best health in mind and, consequently, is more expensive than traditional baby food. Thus, the climate of risk seems integral to the market success of organic baby food and the business success of mompreneurs. Specifically, the mother-oriented consumerism targeted by mompreneurs is defined by a need to provide expert knowledge, control, and convenience, which, in turn, allows mothers to feel they are adhering to the contemporary standards of "good" mothering.[40]

The Production and Consumption of Motherhood

At the heart of any business is the story of how the company came to be—what factors led the entrepreneur to develop the product or exploit the niche that is now the core to their success. For mompreneurs in the organic baby food business, the story of their businesses is the same: each night, mothers slaved over the food processor grinding up fresh, organic foods for their babies. Whether they needed less time in the kitchen or were too busy to continually make fresh food daily, the women at the heart of these companies found that the process of searching for the best ingredients and then making baby food was a time consuming process. Going to the local grocery store was not an option either; the jarred baby food sold there could not measure up in terms of quality and taste to the homemade food mothers were making in their own kitchens. Noting the lack of market share for fresh, non-jarred organic food for the littlest of mouths, these mothers began online businesses marketing fresh, organic baby food for the working or health-conscious mom that comes straight from the kitchen of another, caring mother. For some organic baby food mompreneurs, their narrative begins from the point-of-view as a stay-at-home mother; for others, the narrative starts from the harried, working full time mom who wishes to hand prepare their children's food after coming home at night. Either narrative directly appeals to the logic of intensive mothering. The lives of mompreneurs are child-centered; they engage in the labor intensive and financially draining project of homemade organic baby food.

A key commonality among the narratives of baby food mompreneurs is their corporate backgrounds. Of the SweetPea Baby Food founders, Eryn Green is a former corporate consultant and Tamar Wagman is a former event planner. When Wagman's son was born, she took her eight-month maternity leave. During her leave she and her professional chef husband made their own organic baby food. After Wagman's maternity leave was over, she realized that she could not maintain her baby food-making schedule while holding down a full-time job. Grocery store and online foods were not "equally healthy and delicious" as the baby food she was making at home.[41] Three weeks later, Wagman quit her event planning job. After meeting her best friend Green for lunch one day, they decided to start a business on their own terms.[42]

Heather Schoenrock of Jack's Harvest was a former computer consultant who quit her job when she became a mother. After having her first child, she began making her own organic baby food. Connie Pope, Schoenrock's friend and a former marketing consultant, was too busy to cook her own baby food, so she asked Schoenrock to make some for her children. Much like the creation of SweetPea, the two women decided to start an organic baby food business, because alternatives such as conventional jarred baby foods were not palatable.

Shazi Visram was a marketing and media consultant before she developed HappyBaby. While in business school, Visram listened to a friend's difficulty finding time to make her own baby food while caring for her child and working full time. Visram did some research and found that, like the SweetPea founders, there was no market for homestyle baby food in the New York City area. While Visram herself was not a mother when she started HappyBaby, listening to women struggling with the demands of intensive parenting gave her the idea to start a homemade baby food company.

Lisa Beels and Christine Naylor, two friends who bonded during their children's playdates, set out to be professional chefs before turning to the organic baby food business. Over those playdates, Beels and Naylor experimented with cooking different types of infant food, and once their mutual friends started asking for the baby food they were making, Beels and Naylor came up with Petite Palate.

The humble beginnings of the mompreneur is a story of the commodification of motherhood culture. The themes running through the narratives of these businesses are two-fold: making homemade baby food is integral to the cultural practices of intensive mothering and that there are other entrepreneurial women who are looking out for working moms who cannot make the time and resource-intensive food themselves. These themes then become a mechanism in which mompreneurs reproduce the material conditions that permit intensive mothering.[43] Working women need not fear returning to work or, if staying at home, sacrifice time with their children so they can prepare high-quality food. In the commodity frontier, purchasing of organic homemade baby food is the equivalent of purchasing the intensive mothering practices expected in neoliberal life.

One intended consequence of the commodification of intensive mothering is the legitimation of such cultural practices and the businesses created to profit from it.[44] The narratives of mompreneur businesses specifically highlight their mother status (or the role mothers played in influencing the ideas of HappyBaby's Visram), which reaffirm the intensive mothering requirement that, despite running successful companies, mompreneurs are first and foremost child-centered. In fact, these companies were inspired because a mother's day-to-day job "is, above all, to respond to a child's needs and wants."[45] In following their children's leads, these mompreneurs developed organic baby food businesses so their children could have the food they demanded—palatable, fresh food—and so that other mothers could also follow their children's lead in giving them the food they demand.

One of the ways risk discourse is deployed by mompreneurs is through a critique of adequate food choices for babies. The women of SweetPea, Wagman in particular, decries the lack of easily purchasable foods that are of comparable quality to food made by stay-at-home mothers. HappyBaby's website notes that just five years ago, "processed foods or homemade baby food—which can be time consuming for busy families—were the only options."[46] Petit Cuisine founder Veronica Rives states that her business was "born out of necessity."[47] As a new mother, she found herself looking at all the foods available in grocery stores and realized they were not fresh. Schoenrock of Jack's Harvest began looking for the "healthiest, most nutritious and delicious baby food." Like Wagman, unable to find such food in the grocery store, she began making it herself, and now "it is [her] passion to share it with you."[48] Mompreneurs, by framing their company stories as an attempt to bring the types of products that they want for their children to others, are able to articulate a compelling reason for mothers to purchase homemade organics. As Carrigan and collegues find, mothers perceive homemade foods as an antidote for Big Baby, because they safeguard against problems of industrial agriculture.[49] Mompreneurs draw attention to the lack of quality foods available by contrasting what is sold in stores by conventional producers—HappyBaby specifically describes the food as "processed"—with homemade foods from parents.[50] By framing baby food dichotomously, either processed or fresh, mompreneurs leave little choice of what type of food to purchase if mothers wish to adhere to the intensive mothering ideology: mothers risk feeding their children inferior food if they choose not to purchase homemade organics.

Mompreneurs frame their version of organic baby food as a healthier alternative with the essential ingredients needed to promote growth and development for babies who are just now developing their taste buds. These mompreneurs wish to develop the child's appreciation of a variety of food as well as discourage parents from purchasing products with additives and fillers that they claim are harmful to infants and toddlers. Citing unnamed research, Schoenrock writes, "Pesticides, fertilizers, hormones and other yucky stuff do NOT belong in our children's bodies. That's why Jack's Harvest organic baby food is made with no artificial ingredients, additives, preservatives or fillers—and with no added salt, modified starches or sugar."[51] Petit Cuisine's mompreneur looked at available baby foods and asked herself "Are they fresh? Do they contain common allergens? Is the container safe? I found that I only had half a solution—But is it fresh? The answer, no matter how hard I looked was 'NO.' "[52] Rives continues, "Store bought organic baby food is not fresh and most contain preservatives such as citric acid and ascorbic acid to give their product shelf life. Moreover, many store bought organic baby food containers are unsafe, using petroleum-based plastics, which can leak into your baby's food."[53] Health risks as well as taste risks drive mompreneurs in their marketing language.

Petite Palate's mompreneurs want to change the way mothers feed their infants and toddlers. They note that most parents start out by giving their children jarred foods. They claim the jarring process of heating both food and jar to high temperatures to ensure shelf life destroys the food's naturally occurring nutrients and vitamins. Petite Palate also packages their baby food in eco-friendly paper cups so mothers do not have to worry about BPA levels in glass jars the food is typically found in, calling paper "a natural choice."[54] Schoenrock cites the fact that all of Jack's Harvest food is prepared in small, gently cooked batches in an organic kitchen.[55] The implication is that this is how homemade food is prepared—with care and in small, almost on-demand doses. She even brands her environmentally friendly consciousness by noting that all fruit and vegetable peels left over from cooking are composted.

To counter the growing risks posed by jarred baby foods, whether conventional or organically processed, mompreneurs frequently cite their own technical training or collaborations that guide their recipes and ingredient selections. HappyBaby works with Dr. Robert W. Sears, the famed baby-advice book author and pediatrician, "to ensure the healthiest formulations possible for baby's growing body. We work together to create products that he feels good about recommending to his patients and you."[56] Beels and Naylor of Petite Palate feature their formal chef training as a reason to purchase their food. Wagman at SweetPea cites how she and her husband, a former executive chef now currently the company's executive chef, used to experiment with unique food combinations when making baby food at home.[57] With the exception of HappyBaby, the expert influence and guidance of these mom-based companies is described as a family-type affair. Either the moms themselves are chefs, and thus experts at creating great tasting, quality baby food, or someone in their family or social network is an expert in the culinary arts.

Alternatively, mompreneurs often rely on their status as mothers and the underlying assumption that mothers know best when it comes to feeding. Rives of Petit Cuisine writes that when she began making all of her own baby's food (with the help of grandma), she chose from all natural, fresh, and organic vegetables, fruits, and meats. As a child, Rives suffered from food allergies and so, as a mompreneur, she carefully selects ingredients to avoid such allergies. The mompreneurs of Petite Palate claim, "We are mothers who are trained chefs. We not only understand children, we understand food."[58] In comparison, Schoenrock has no formal training in culinary arts, but the company began because of her own food experimentations and her research into what foods young children should be eating. These narratives create an image of mother-scientists who are using their kitchens as baby food laboratories complete with beakers full of pureed peas, peaches, and sweet potatoes. The allusion to the scientifically trained mother armed with research briefs constructing baby food recipes endows these mompreneurs with an aura of professionalism or "expert" status that is based on risk threats.[59] Even though these women were professionals before motherhood, using science and risk-based discourse to describe their products creates the mompreneur-as-expert. This is also, according to Hays, a hallmark of normative mothering practices.[60] Purchasing homemade organic baby food from expert mompreneurs alleviates mothers from having to do their own research on healthy infant and toddler foods or from having to revert back to organic chemistry lessons to create the 'healthiest formulations possible.' Instead, mother-consumers can purchase food made by mothers with specialized expertise and similar values, which, by extension affirms their own adherence to the dominant intensive mothering paradigm.

By highlighting their unique fusion of mothering know-how and professional expertise, mompreneurs maximize their authority in direct appeals to mother-consumers. Petite Palate describes their baby food as being produced with the finest organically grown produce available, adding that this maintains the health and well-being of children and the environment. They write that "the food we create is part of an unbroken chain of clean handling: from grower to us and then to you."[61] Petite Palate's philosophy discusses the need to nurture children's taste buds from the first taste of solid foods in order to develop a positive relationship with food. By encouraging taste bud development with smaller meals that have more flavor than typically found in jarred foods, children are less likely to grow up obese and more likely to choose nutritious foods over processed ones. Thus, by purchasing organic baby food, mothers are "setting healthy habits for their [children's] entire lives."[62]

The core tasks of mothering Sara Ruddick highlights—preservation, nurturing, and training—are strongly highlighted in the narrative about the quality of mompreneur's homemade, organic baby food.[63] Protecting children from the ill effects of poor quality, processed baby food is a hallmark of mompreneur-based "expert"-made baby food. Among the items noted as risky is the practice of sterilizing jars to ensure shelf life, which has the impact of eliminating vital nutrients and minerals from food, the additives and preservatives mixed into the foods, and BPA found in glass jars and plastic containers. These health issues are framed around the issue of risk control—Schoenrock of Jack's Harvest would never willingly let her child eat not-natural foods and Rives of Petit Cuisine felt she had no control over what exactly was in the baby food she was buying. Even the interview detailed in the previous section, in which mom Kim Barry from Denver wants to know what exactly is in her child's food—she demands total control of all her child's consumption practices. Ruddick summarizes—"protection without control would be a horror."[64] And so, mompreneurs frame their companies' narratives around themes of control. In these narratives, processed foods that contain sodium and preservatives that are unhealthy to infants and toddlers signify risk whereas homemade baby foods that are fresh, natural, and without additives signify control.

Organic baby foods from mompreneurs also normalize intensive mothering by advertising how their products are an equivalent to nurturing, because they help children develop healthy bodies. Many mothers engaged in intensive parenting are involved in socializing their children into healthy consumption habits by making them aware of what constitutes "good" food.[65] Mompreneurs claim the boldness of their fresh ingredients will help children develop complex taste buds that will help them have an appreciation for healthier foods. Petit Cuisine's meals contain potassium and antioxidants that keep children healthy; SweetPea lists several reasons to prefer their baby food, including that it protects children's developing immune systems and against the onset of harmful diseases, and reduces children's exposure to herbicides and pesticides. Jack's Harvest cautions against conventional produce since the organophosphates have been linked to possible neurological disorders. Petite Palate warns about the use of DHA as an additive, then states, "this is why we decided NOT to add ANYTHING to our baby food but the food itself—this includes DHA."[66] Mompreneurs expand on the theme of nurturing by also making arguments about how organics help protect the environment. SweetPea writes that using organics protects the environment from soil erosion and water quality issues, making it safe for the next generation. Jack's Harvest composts and Petite Palate uses ecofriendly natural paper cups. The threat of purchasing the wrong food that could cause significant health issues for little children draws strong attention toward the developmental benefits of organics.

Training, according to Ruddick, is also an integral component to maternal thinking. In the context of food, training means teaching children to eat the "correct" foods, such as whole grains, vegetables, fruits, and the like—all the items emphasized by mompreneurs as core to their products. By taking the initiative and purchasing the correct foods, mothers train their babies how to develop healthy eating habits for the rest of their lives. Again, this training is placed squarely on the shoulders of mothers and hinges on a cause-effect commercial logic with nutritional and moral consequences. First, mothers are responsible for choosing food for infants. If they make the wrong choice and train their children to eat the wrong foods then their children will lead unhealthy lives. If mothers purchase homemade, organic baby foods from mompreneurs then their children will be not only healthier but also more discerning consumers in the future. Implicit in the relationship between intensive mothering and capitalism is the notion that if mothers uphold these standards then they can keep their children safe, happy, and competitive in a world defined by economic and environmental risk.[67]

Resolving the Paradoxes of the Commodification and Commercialization of Motherhood

The ideology of intensive mothering has a strong hold on American culture. Such practice is the norm despite its impracticality for working women, because, paradoxically, many see it as the "last best defense" against a capitalist economy hostile to families.[68] According to Hays, American mothers feel solely responsible for ensuring their children's development, despite a culture that values work outside the home over domestic labor.[69] This chapter addressed two recent developments that seek to resolve this contradiction: (1) the advent of the mompreneur who combines the qualities of intensive mothering while working in a child-based business and (2) the subsequent drive to purchase products that promote an ideology of intensive mothering. Mompreneurs attempt to manage the divide between being mothers and workers by combining motherhood with a profit-making but child-directed business.[70] In seeking to reconcile this contradiction, however, mompreneurs foster a new hierarchy between mothers who are aware of the risks of industrially produced baby food and *invest* in their children's health as opposed to those mothers who lack knowledge of the risks and/or cannot afford the investment in homemade organic food.[71]

The power of risk discourses to create a sense of consumer agency is, as Cairns and collegues, note, "substantial," but the "actual" potential for change is limited when politics is undertaken within the marketplace.[72] The perception of children consuming healthful, high-quality food provides mothers with a sense of cultural distinction or status.[73] Despite the appeals from mompreneurs who tout nutrient-rich foods that promote refined palates, such idealized notions of the "organic child" require significant cultural and economic capital that many families do not have. Indeed, the "organic child" assumes a standard of food provision that is not universally attainable.[74] Due to higher prices, organic products are often out of the economic reach or unavailable in the stores where working-class families shop.[75] By naturalizing the individualization of risk, mother-oriented consumerism obscures the constraints that many poor and working-class women face when feeding their children. While some mothers are able uphold the standards associated with intensive mothering and the "organic child" through coupon clipping, price comparison shopping, and watching for sales, such cost-cutting strategies do not apply to the online-only niche organic baby food market, which situates itself as less risky than Big Baby's industrially processed organic baby food.[76] Thus, when mompreneurs play on risk discourse to market their products, their branding contributes to a neoliberal framework that obscures the role of structural socioeconomic inequality in the availability of quality food options for families.

In her study of the baby toy industry, Pugh laments the anxieties that might fester within any mother clinging to the dictates of the intensive mothering ideology, wondering if she is doing enough to properly develop her child.[77] The same concern applies here, too. Indeed, this analysis shows that mompreneurs play upon such anxieties. Consuming commodities is an important avenue for mothers to achieve the self-respect and identity in the social world.[78] So much so that Clarke argues women can be "made" into mothers through their consumption choices.[79] The organic baby food companies helmed by mompreneurs certainly seem to recognize—and attempt to capitalize—on this. Mompreneurs try to blunt the "tainting" of consumer capitalism by using their status as mothers to make appeals to their mother-customers.[80] By emphasizing their own working-mother status and their previous corporate backgrounds, mompreneurs package their products with the assumption that all mothers, particularly working mothers, strongly adhere to the intensive mothering ideology while participating in the workforce. Commodification is presented as a shortcut for managing the work/family life balance. As Hochschild notes, the "existence of such market substitutes becomes a form of societal legitimation for this ambivalence."[81]

The major implication of such commodification is the increasing dependence on consumption as a means of creating identity. Mothering is based upon individual experiences that women have in striving toward the "moral imperative" of meeting the needs of their children.[82] Mompreneurs frequently emphasize the impact of mother-oriented consumerism as highly individualistic. For example, HappyBaby frames the purchasing choice as solely a parent's decision: "You are the parents that demand that your children get foods that truly nourish their bodies and support their growth as healthy happy individuals for the years to come."[83] To be sure, the mompreneurs marketing examined in this chapter individualizes social risks.[84] The individualized experiences emphasized by mompreneurs occur within the context of intensive mothering, whether they are consistent with the realities of motherhood or not.[85] Indeed, the lack of knowledge working mothers may have regarding the actual risks posed by their food choices not only enhances the marketing appeals but also positions consumption as a convenient and risk-averse option.[86]

One additional disadvantage of the commercialization of intensive mothering is a renaturalization of child rearing as a mother's job. Mompreneurs frame their products and visualize their corporate origin-stories by emphasizing the importance of mothers in developing life-long skills in children.[87] Because mothers shoulder the burden of consumption for their children, the intensive mothering practices commodified in homemade organic baby foods are targeted squarely toward women.[88] While fathers often assume supportive roles in shopping and choosing foods for children, the labor involved in researching and planning food decisions for the family is conceptualized by these companies as an extension of a mother's role as child protector and nurturer.[89] Playing upon the concern that male partners "don't know how to do [child-rearing] right," mompreneur's products are not marketed toward fathers.[90] The process of renaturalizing child-rearing as a mother's job through the consumption of a culturally created commodity questions whether mothers who consume such products are effectively challenging the "mother"/"other" dichotomy.

Culturally speaking, commercializing intensive motherhood through homemade organic baby food has created a self-perpetuating cycle where the more legitimate a product (and business model) becomes, the stronger the demand for the product and thus the cultural practice.[91] As of yet, neither mompreneurs nor their products are effective forms of cultural resistance against the worker/mother dichotomy that has come to define the business of motherhood in American economic and family life.

Notes

1. Bay Street is the Canadian version of the United States' Wall Street.

2. A. Brouwer and A. Wilson, "Food That Doesn't Suck For People Who Still Do," *The Financial Post*, April 3, 2010, *http://life.nationalpost.com/2010/04/03/shelf-life-food-that-doesn%E2%80%99t-suck-for-people-who-still-do/.*

3. Eileen Boris, "Mothers Are Not Workers: Homework Regulation and the Construction of Motherhood, 1948–1953," in *Mothering: Ideology, Experience, and Agency*, eds. Evelyn Nakano Glenn, Grace Chang, and Linda Rennie Forcey (New York: Routledge, 1994), 161–80.

4. Sharon Hays, *The Cultural Contradictions of Motherhood* (New Haven: Yale University Press, 1996).

5. Arlie R. Hochschild, ""The Commodity Frontier," in *Self, Social Structure, and Beliefs: Essays in Sociology*, eds. Jeffrey T. Alexander, Gary T. Marx, and Christine L. Williams (Berkeley: University of California Press, 2004), 38–56.

6. Ibid; Alison J. Pugh, "Selling Compromise: Toys, Motherhood, and the Cultural Deal," *Gender & Society* 19 (2005).

7. Ibid, 20.

8. Linda Seidel, *Mediated Maternity: Contemporary American Portrayals of Bad Mothers in Literature and Popular Culture* (Lexington Books, 2013).

9. Joan Williams, *Unbending Gender: Why Family and Work Conflict and What To Do About It* (Oxford University Press, 2001), 59.

10. Evelyn Nakano Glenn, "Social Constructions of Mothering: A Thematic Overview," in *Mothering: Ideology, Experience, and Agency*, eds. Evelyn Nakano Glenn, Grace Chang, and Linda Rennie Forcey (New York: Routledge, 1994) 1–31; Lynet Uttal, "Custodial Care, Surrogate Care, and Coordinate Care: Employed Mothers and the Meaning of Childcare," *Gender & Society* 10 (1996).

11. Mary Blair-Loy, *Competing Devotions* (Cambridge: Harvard University Press, 2003); Arlie Hochschild, *The Time Bind* (New York: Metropolitan Press, 1997).

12. Pugh, "Selling Compromise," 729–49.

13. Sara Ruddick, *Maternal Thinking: Toward a Politics of Peace* (Boston: Beacon Press, 1989).

14. Adrienne Bower, "Meet the Mompreneurs," *Time Magazine*, June 25, 2005, *http://www.time.com/time/connections/article/0,9171,1053667,00.html.*

15. Tony Wanless, "Baby Food Firm Grows Through Word of Mouth," *Financial Post*, March 28, 2011, *http://business.financialpost.com/2011/03/28/baby-food-firm-grows-through-word-of-mouth/.*

16. The Mompreneurs Online facebook site, found at www.facebook.com/pages/Mompreneurs-Online/68940135438, has 2,638 fans as of September 23, 2013; Daniel Thomas Cook, "Semantic Provisioning of Children's Food: Commerce, Care and Maternal Practice," *Childhood*, 16 (2009) 317–34.

17. Brittney D. Lee, "Mommy Blogs: Identity, Content, and Community" (masters thesis, University of Arkansas, 2011); Lori Kido Lopez, "The Radical Act of 'Mommy Blogging': Redefining Motherhood through the Blogosphere," *New Media and Society* 11 (2009); Pugh, "Selling Compromise," 729–49.

18. Sara Afferback, Shannon K. Carter, Amanda Koontz Anthony, and Liz Grauerholz, "Infant-feeding Consumerism in the Age of Intensive Mothering and Risk Society" *Journal of Consumer Culture*, 13 (2013) 387–405; Kate Cairns, Josee Johnston, and Norah MacKendrick, "Feeding the 'Organic Child': Mothering Through Ethical Consumption" *Journal of Consumer Culture*, 13 (2013) 97–118; Daniel Thomas Cook, "Semantic Provisioning of Children's Food"; Josee Johnston, Michelle Szabo, and Alexandra Rodney, "Good Food, Good People: Understanding the Cultural Repertoire of Ethical Eating" Journal of Consumer Culture, 11 (2011) 293–318; Risto Moisio, Eric J. Arnould, and Linda L. Price, "Between Mothers and Markets: Constructing Family Identity Through Homemade Food" Journal of Consumer Culture, 4 (2004) 361–384; Elizabeth Murphy, "Risk, Responsibility and Rhetoric in Infant Feeding" *Journal of Contemporary Ethnography*, 29 (2000) 291–325.

19. Andrew J. Mathers, Rugg-Gunn, Charlotte E. Wood, and Ashley J. Adamson, "Food Shopping and Preparation among 30-somethings: Whose Job is It? (The ASH30 Study)," *British Food Journal* 108, no. 6(2006): 475

20. Janelle S. Taylor, "Introduction," in *Consuming Motherhood*, eds. Janelle S. Taylor, Linda L. Layne and Danielle F. Wozniak (Piscataway, NJ: Rutgers University Press, 2004), 1–16.

21. Regina Austin, "Kwanzaa and the Commodification of Black Culture," in *Rethinking Commodification: Cases and Readings in Law and Culture*, eds. Martha M. Ertman and Joan C. Williams (New York: New York University Press, 2005), 178–190.

22. Daniel Thomas Cook, "The Mother as Consumer: Insights from the Children's Wear Industry, 1917–1929," *The Sociological Quarterly* 36 (1995), 505–22; Hays, *The Cultural Contradictions of Motherhood*, 99.

23. Christine Tatum, "Mmm Mmm Good, Mom! Making Baby Food From Scratch Is Easy and Nutritious," *The Denver Post*, March 22, 2006, http://www.denverpost.com/food/ci_3622558.

24. Sue Stock, "Organics Craze Is Still Going," *The News & Observer*, April 2, 2008, accessed on March 15, 2011, http://www.soyatech.com/news_story.php?id=7794.

25. Rebecca Smithers, "Organic Sales Slump for the First Time: Bread, Meat, and Chilled Beans Hit Hardest," *The Guardian (London)*, April 12, 2010, accessed March 1, 2011, *http://www.guardian.co.uk/environment/2010/apr/12/organic-food-recession-shopping.*

26. Wynne Wright and Gerad Middendorf, "Introduction," in *The Fight Over Food: Producers, Consumers, and Activists Challenge the Global Food System*, eds Wynne Wright and Gerad Middendorf (University Park, PA: The Pennsylvania State University Press, 2008) 1–26.

27. David Goodman and Michael Redclift, *Refashioning Nature: Food, Ecology, and Culture* (London: Routledge, 1991) 1–46.

28. Marion Nestle, *Food Politics: How the Food Industry Influences Nutrition and Health* (Berkeley: Univesity of California Press, 2002).

29. Ulrich Beck and Elisabeth Beck-Gernsheim, *The Normal Chaos of Love* (Cambridge: Policy Press, 1995); Lesley Murray, "Motherhood, Risk, and Everyday Mobilities," in *Gendered Mobilities*, eds. Tanu Priya Uteng and Tim Cresswell (Burlington, VT: Ashgate Publishing Company, 2008), 47–85.

30. Murphy, "Risk Responsibility" 292.

31. Cairns, Johnston and MacKendrick, "Feeding the Organic Child," 100; Cindi Katz, "Childhood as Spectacle: Relays of Anxiety and the Reconfiguration of the Child," Cultural Geographies, 15 (2008) 5–17.

32. Cook, "Semantic Provisioning," 317.

33. Bower, "Meet the Mompreneurs."

34. Consumer Reports. "Better for Baby? Our Analysis Finds Organic is Better for Baby," *Consumer Reports*, January 2006, accessed March 15, 2011, *http://www.consumerreports.org/health/healthy-living/diet-nutrition/healthy-foods/consumer-reports-why-organic-baby-food-is-safer-106/overview/index.htm.*

35. Afflerback et al., "Infant-feeding Consumerism" 387–405.

36. Moisio, Arnould, and Price, "Between Mothers and Markets," 361–84.

37. Cook, "The Mother as Consumer," 505–22; Josee Johnston, "Counterhegemony or Bourgeoisie Piggery? Food Politics and the Case of Foodshare," in *The Fight over Food: Producers, Consumers, and Activists Challenge the Global Food System*, eds. Wynne Wright and Gerad Middendorf (University Park: The Pennsylvania State University Press, 2008) 93–120.

38. Moisio, Arnould, and Price, "Between Mothers and Markets," 361–84.

39. Wright and Middendorf, *The Fight over Food*, 1–26.

40. Afflerback et al., "Infant Feeding Consumerism," 387–405.

41. "The SweetPea Story," *SweetPea Baby Food*, accessed April 5, 2011, http://*.sweetpeababyfood.com/sweetpeababyfood.php.*

42. Ibid.

43. Austin, "Kwanzaa and the Commodification of Black Culture" 178–90.

44. Ibid.

45. Hays, *The Cultural Contradictions of Motherhood*, 98–108.

46. "About Us," *Happy Baby Food*, accessed April 5, 2011. http://happybabyfood.com/about-us

47. "Who We Are," *Petit Cuisine*, accessed April 5, 2011. *http://petitcuisine.com/who.htm.*

48. "Our Chef," *SweetPea Baby Food*, accessed April 5, 2011. *http://sweetpeababyfood.com/sweetpeababyfood.php.*

49. Marilynn Carrigan, Isabelle Szmigin, and Sheena Leek, "Managing Routine Food Choices in UK Families: The Role of Convenience Consumption" *Appetite*, 47 372–83.

50. "About Us," *Happy Baby Food.*

51. "Our Chef," *SweetPea Baby Food.*

52. "Who We Are," *Petit Cuisine.*

53. Ibid.

54. "Why Choose?" *Petite Palate*, accessed April 5, 2011. http://petitepalate.com/pp/why.html

55. "Our Process," *Jacks Harvest*, accessed April 5, 2011http://www.jacksharvest.com/jacks-kitchen/our-process/

56. "Our Promise To You," *Happy Baby Food*, accessed April 5, 2011. *http://happybabyfood.com/about-us/our-promise.*

57. "The SweetPea Story," *SweetPea Baby Food.*

58. "Homepage," *Petite Palate*, accessed April 5, 2011. http://petitepalate.com/pp/index.html.

59. Murray, "Motherhood, Risk, and Everyday Mobilities." Shari L. Thurer, *The Myths of Motherhood: How Culture Reinvents the Good Mother* (New York: Penguin Books, 1994).

60. Hays, *The Cultural Contradictions of Motherhood*, 9.

61. "Why Choose?" *Petite Palate.*

62. "Our Philosophy," *Petite Palate*, accessed April 5, 2011. *http://petitepalate.com/pp/about.html.*

63. Ruddick, *Maternal Thinking, 61–126.*

64. Ibid, p. 72

65. Cairns, Johnston, and MacKendrick., "Feeding the 'Organic Child'," 106.

66. Beck, *Risk Society*; "Why Choose?" *Petite Palate.*

67. Hays, *The Cultural Contradictions of Motherhood*, 162–65; Seidel, *Mediated Maternity*, 19, 36.

68. Ibid

69. Hays, *The Cultural Contradictions of Motherhood*, 108.

70. Williams, *Unbending Gender*, 59.

71. On the lack of food knowledge, see Gordon in this volume.

72. Cairns, Johnston, and MacKendrick, "Feeding the Organic Child," 113.

73. Johnston, Szabo, and Rodney, "Good Food, Good People," 312.

74. Cairns, Johnston, and MacKendrick, "'Feeding the Organic Child," 111.

75. Barbara Ehrenreich,"Food Worship," in *The Worst Years of our Lives: Irreverent Notes from a Decade of Greed*, ed. Barbara Ehrenreich (New York: Pantheon Books, 1985), 1–25; William Friedland,"The New Globalization: The Case of Fresh Produce," in *From Columbus to ConAgra: The Globalization of Agriculture and Food*, ed. Alessandro Bonanno, Lawrence Busch, William H. Friedland, Lourdes Gouveia, and Enzo Mingioner (Lawrence: University of Kansas Press, 1994), 210–31; Terry Marsden and Alberto Arce, "Constructing Quality: Emerging Food Networks in the Rural Transition," Environment and Planning 27 (1995); Wright and Middendorf, "Fighting Over Food," 1–26.

76. Afflerback et al., "Infant Feeding Consumerism," 402.

77. Pugh, "Selling Compromise," 729–49.

78. Taylor, "Introduction," 1–16.

79. Allison J. Clarke, "Maternity and Materiality: Becoming a Mother in a Consumer Culture," in *Consuming Motherhood*, eds. Janelle S. Taylor, Linda L. Layne, and Danielle F. Wozniak (Piscataway: Rutgers University Press, 2004), 55–71.

80. Taylor, "Introduction," 1–16

81. Hochschild, "Commodity Frontier," 22

82. Simon Duncan and Rosalind Edwards, *Lone Mothers, Paid Work, and Gendered Moral Rationalities* (London: Macmillan Press, 1999); Tina Miller, *Making Sense of Motherhood* (Cambridge: Cambridge University Press, 2005).

83. "About Us," *Happy Baby Food.*

84. Beck, *Risk Society*, 53–55.

85. Deborah Connolly, "Mythical Dichotomies of Good and Evil: Homeless Mothers in the United States," in *Ideologies and Technologies of Motherhood: Race, Class, Sexuality, Nationalism*, eds. Helena Ragone and Frances Winddance Twine (New York: Routledge, 2000), 264–94; Murray, "Motherhood, Risk, and Everyday Mobilities," 47–85.

86. Beck, *Risk Society*, 53.

87. Annette Laureau, *Unequal Childhoods: Class, Race and Family Life* (Berkeley: University of California Press, 2003); Pugh, "Selling Compromise." 729–49

88. Cook, "The Mother as Consumer," 505–22.

89. Cairns, Johnston, and MacKendrick, "Feeding the 'Organic Child,'" 109

90. Hays, *The Cultural Contradictions of Motherhood*, 104.

91. Austin, "Kwanzaa and the Commodification of Black Culture," 178–90.

References

Afferback, Sara, Shannon K. Carter, Amanda Koontz Anthony, and Liz Grauerholz, "Infant-feeding Consumerism in the Age of Intensive Mothering and Risk Society" *Journal of Consumer Culture* 13 (2013): 387–405.

Austin, Regina. "Kwanzaa and the Commodification of Black Culture." In *Rethinking Commodification: Cases and Readings in Law and Culture*, edited by Martha M. Ertman and Joan C. Williams, 178–90. New York: New York University Press, 2005.

Beck, Ulrich, and Elisabeth Beck-Gernsheim. *The Normal Chaos of Love*. Cambridge: Policy Press, 1995.

"Better for Baby? Our Analysis Finds Organic is Better for Baby," *Consumer Reports*, January 2006. Accessed March 15, 2011, http://www.consumerreports.org/health/healthy-living/diet-nutrition/healthy-foods/consumer-reports-why-organic-baby-food-is-safer-106/overview/index.htm.

Blair-Loy, Mary. *Competing Devotions*. Cambridge: Harvard University Press, 2003.

Boris, Eileen. "Mothers Are Not Workers: Homework Regulation and the Construction of Motherhood, 1948–1953." In *Mothering: Ideology, Experience, and Agency*, edited by Evelyn Nakano Glenn, Grace Chang, and Linda Rennie Forcey, 161–80. New York: Routledge, 1994.

Bower, Adrienne. "Meet the Mompreneurs," *Time Magazine*, June 25, 2005. Accessed October 1, 2011. http://www.time.com/time/connections/article/0,9171,1053667,00.html.

Brouwer, A., and A. Wilson, "Food That Doesn't Suck For People Who Still Do," *The Financial Post*. April 3, 2010. Accessed March 15, 2011. http://life.nationalpost.com/2010/04/03/shelf-life-food-that-doesn%E2%80%99t-suck-for-people-who-still-do/.

Cairns, Kate, Josee Johnston, and Norah MacKendrick, "Feeding the 'Organic Child': Mothering Through Ethical Consumption" *Journal of Consumer Culture* 13 (2013): 97–118.

Carrigan, Marilynn, Isabelle Szmigin, and Sheena Leek, "Managing Routine Food Choices in UK Families: The Role of Convenience Consumption" *Appetite* 47 (2006): 372–83.

Clarke, Allison J. "Maternity and Materiality: Becoming a Mother in a Consumer Culture." In *Consuming Motherhood*, edited by Janelle S. Taylor, Linda L. Layne and Danielle F. Wozniak, 55–71. Piscataway, NJ: Rutgers University Press, 2004.

Connolly, Deborah. "Mythical Dichotomies of Good and Evil: Homeless Mothers in the United States." In *Ideologies and Technologies of Motherhood: Race, Class, Sexuality, Nationalism*, edited by Helena Ragone and Frances Winddance Twine, 264–94. New York: Routledge, 2000.

Cook, Daniel Thomas. "Semantic Provisioning of Children's Food: Commerce, Care and Maternal Practice" *Childhood* 16 (2009): 317–34.

———. "The Mother as Consumer: Insights from the Children's Wear Industry, 1917–1929" *The Sociological Quarterly* 36 (1995): 505–22.

Duncan, Simon, and Rosalind Edwards, *Lone Mothers, Paid Work and Gendered Moral Rationalities*. London: Macmillan Press, 1999.

Ehrenreich, Barbara. "Food Worship." In *The Worst Years of Our Lives: Irreverent Notes from a Decade of Greed*, edited by Barbara Ehrenreich, 1–25. New York: Pantheon Books, 1985.

Friedland, William. "The New Globalization: The Case of Fresh Produce." In *From Columbus to ConAgra: The Globalization of Agriculture and Food*, edited by Alessandro Bonanno, Lawrence Busch, William H. Friedland, Lourdes Gouveia, and Enzo Mingioner, 210–31. Lawrence: University of Kansas Press, 1994.

Glenn, Evelyn Nakano. "Social Constructions of Mothering: A Thematic Overview." In *Mothering: Ideology, Experience, and Agency*, edited by Evelyn Nakano Glenn, Grace Chang, and Linda Rennie Forcey, 1–31. New York: Routledge, 1994.

Goodman, David, and Michael Redclift, *Refashioning Nature: Food, Ecology, and Culture*. London: Routledge, 1991.

Happy Baby Food. "About Us." Accessed April 5, 2011. http://happybabyfood.com/about-us.

——. "Our Promise To You." Accessed April 5, 2011. http://happybabyfood.com/about-us/our-promise.

Hays, Sharon. *The Cultural Contradictions of Motherhood*. New Haven: Yale University Press, 1996.

Hochschild, Arlie R. "The Commodity Frontier." In *Self, Social Structure, and Beliefs: Essays in Sociology*, edited by Jeffrey T. Alexander, Gary T. Marx, and Christine L. Williams, 38–56. Berkeley: University of California Press, 2004.

——. *The Time Bind*. New York: Metropolitan Press, 1997.

Jacks Harvest. "Our Process." Accessed April 5, 2011. http://www.jacksharvest.com/jacks-kitchen/our-process/.

Johnston, Josee. "Counterhegemony or Bourgeoisie Piggery? Food Politics and the Case of Foodshare." In *The Fight over Food: Producers, Consumers, and Activists Challenge the Global Food System*, edited by Wynne Wright and Gerad Middendorf, 93–120. University Park: The Pennsylvania State University Press, 2008.

Johnston, Josee, Michelle Szabo, and Alexandra Rodney. "Good Food, Good People: Understanding the Cultural Repertoire of Ethical Eating." Journal of Consumer Culture 11 (2011): 293–318.

Katz, Cindi, "Childhood as Spectacle: Relays of Anxiety and the Reconfiguration of the Child." *Cultural Geographies* 15 (2008): 5–17.

Lake, Amelia A., Robert M. Hyland, John C. Mathers, Andrew J. Rugg-Gunn, Charlotte E. Wood, and Ashley J. Adamson. "Food Shopping and Preparation among 30-somethings: Whose Job is It? (The ASH30 Study)." *British Food Journal* 108 (2006): 475–86.

Laureau, Annette. *Unequal Childhoods: Class, Race and Family Life*. Berkeley: University of California Press, 2003.

Lee, Brittney D. "Mommy Blogs: Identity, Content, and Community." Masters thesis, University of Arkansas, 2011.

Lopez, Lori Kido. "The Radical Act of 'Mommy Blogging': Redefining Motherhood through the Blogosphere." *New Media and Society* 11 (2009): 729–47.

Marsden, Terry, and Alberto Arce, "Constructing Quality: Emerging Food Networks in the Rural Transition." *Environment and Planning* 27 (1995): 1261–79.

Miller, Tina. *Making Sense of Motherhood*. Cambridge: Cambridge University Press, 2005.

Moisio, Risto, Eric J. Arnould, and Linda L. Price. "Between Mothers and Markets: Constructing Family Identity Through Homemade Food." Journal of Consumer Culture 4 (2004): 361–84.

Murphy, Elizabeth. "Risk, Responsibility and Rhetoric in Infant Feeding." *Journal of Contemporary Ethnography* 29 (2000): 291–325.

Murray, Lesley. "Motherhood, Risk, and Everyday Mobilities." In *Gendered Mobilities*, edited by Tanu Priya Uteng and Tim Cresswell, 47–85. Burlington, VT: Ashgate Publishing Company, 2008.

Nestle, Marion. *Food Politics: How the Food Industry Influences Nutrition and Health*. Berkeley: University of California Press, 2002.

Petit Cuisine. "Who We Are." Accessed April 5, 2011. http://petitcuisine.com/who.htm.

Petite Palate. "Homepage." Accessed April 5, 2011. http://petitepalate.com/pp/index.html.

——. "Our Philosophy." Accessed April 5, 2011. http://petitepalate.com/pp/about.html.

——. "Why Choose?" Accessed April 5, 2011. http://petitepalate.com/pp/why.html.

Pugh, Alison J. "Selling Compromise: Toys, Motherhood, and the Cultural Deal." *Gender & Society* 19 (2005): 729–49.

Ruddick, Sara. *Maternal Thinking: Toward a Politics of Peace*. Boston: Beacon Press, 1989.

Seidel, Linda. *Mediated Maternity: Contemporary American Portrayals of Bad Mothers in Literature and Popular Culture*. Lanham, MD: Lexington Books, 2013.

Smithers, Rebecca. "Organic Sales Slump for the First Time: Bread, Meat, and Chilled Beans Hit Hardest." *The Guardian (London)*, April 12 2011. Accessed March 15, 2011. http://www.guardian.co.uk/environment/2010/apr/12/organic-food-recession-shopping.

Stock, Sue. "Organics Craze Is Still Going." *The News & Observer*, April 2, 2008. Accessed March 15, 2011. http://www.soyatech.com/news_story.php?id=7794.

SweetPea Baby Food. "Our Chef." Accessed April 5, 2011. http://sweetpeababyfood.com/sweetpeababyfood.php.

——. "The SweetPea Story." Accessed April 5, 2011. http://.sweetpeababyfood.com/sweetpeababyfood.php.

Tatum, Christine. "Mmm Mmm Good, Mom! Making Baby Food From Scratch Is Easy and Nutritious." *The Denver Post*, March 22, 2006. Accessed March 15, 2011. http://www.denverpost.com/food/ci_3622558.

Taylor, Janelle S. "Introduction." In *Consuming Motherhood*, edited by Janelle S. Taylor, Linda L. Layne, and Danielle F. Wozniak, 1–16. Piscataway: Rutgers University Press, 2004.

Thurer, Shari L. *The Myths of Motherhood: How Culture Reinvents the Good Mother*. New York: Penguin Books, 1994.

Uttal, Lynet. "Custodial Care, Surrogate Care, and Coordinate Care: Employed Mothers and the Meaning of Childcare." *Gender & Society* 10 (1996): 291–311.

Wanless, Tony. "Baby Food Firm Grows Through Word of Mouth." *Financial Post*, March 28, 2011. Accessed March 15, 2011. http://business.financialpost.com/2011/03/28/baby-food-firm-grows-through-word-of-mouth/.

Williams, Joan. *Unbending Gender: Why Family and Work Conflict and What To Do About It*. Oxford: Oxford University Press, 2001.

Wright, Wynne, and Gerad Middendorf. "Introduction." In *The Fight Over Food: Producers, Consumers, and Activists Challenge the Global Food System*, edited by Wynne Wright and Gerad Middendorf, 1–26. University Park: The Pennsylvania State University Press, 2008.

7
Maternal Crime in a Cathedral of Consumption

Sara Hayden

On June 16, 2007, Bridget Kevane dropped three young children, ages eight, seven, and three, at the local mall in the care of her twelve-year-old daughter and the daughter's twelve-year-old friend; she was subsequently charged with child endangerment.[1] This story would have gone unnoticed if it were not for an article authored by Kevane and published in *Brain, Child: The Magazine for Thinking Mothers* two years after her arrest. In the article, Kevane, a professor at Montana State University, recounts the events that led up to the charge as well as her efforts to fight back against what she saw as the overzealous efforts of law enforcement and a prosecutor who viewed Kevane as a well-educated and wealthy outsider. Kevane's essay was later discussed by *New York Times* columnist Judith Warner, who cast Kevane's plight as evidence of "our country's resentment, and even hatred, of well-educated, apparently affluent women."[2] The response to Warner's column was robust, garnering over 450 comments in twenty-four hours.

In this chapter I offer a rhetorical criticism of the comments responding to Warner's article in an effort to tease out assumptions about mothering, shopping malls, and class represented in this body of discourse. Rejecting the totalizing implications of the "shopping malls as cathedrals of consumption" metaphor, John Fiske argues that consumers, and particularly female consumers, may engage shopping malls in ways that resist both patriarchy and capitalism. "The mall," he writes, "is where women can be public, empowered, and free, and can occupy roles other than those demanded by the nuclear family."[3] Fiske appeals to de Certeau's discussion of "the trickster" to support his argument, maintaining "tricks and ruses are the art of the weak that enables them to exploit their understanding of the rules of the system, and to turn it to their advantage. They are a refusal to be subjugated."[4] Yet Jessica Stewart and Greg Dickinson suggest that opportunities for resistance are limited. Focusing specifically on the design and structure of a mall, they argue that individual's abilities to transform the identities offered to them are "colonized," "structuring what might otherwise be a resistive meaning."[5] In this essay, I argue that the responses to Kevane's story support Stewart and Dickinson's argument, offering a specific case that illuminates of the limitations of "trickster" resistance.

Intensive Mothering

In the contemporary United States, mothers are expected to practice a form of parenting that scholars alternately have dubbed "intensive mothering,"[6] "patriarchal motherhood,"[7] and "the new momism."[8] The assumptions underlying this form of mothering include: "1) children can only be properly cared for by the biological mother; 2) this mothering must be provided 24/7; 3) the mother must always put children's needs before her own; 4) mothers must turn to the experts for instruction; 5) the mother is fully satisfied, fulfilled, completed, and composed in motherhood; and finally, 6) mothers must lavish excessive amounts of time, energy, and money in the rearing of their children."[9] The roots of intensive mothering can be found in post–World War II efforts to urge women—especially white, middle-class mothers—to give up the public-sector jobs they had assumed during the war and turn their energies to full-time homemaking. Yet intensive motherhood did not fully blossom until the wake of second wave feminism when an increasing number of middle-class women chose to pursue careers before—and sometimes instead of—starting families.[10]

Susan Douglas and Meredith Michaels explain why intensive mothering took hold at this time and with this demographic. As they point out, professional women in the 1970s and 1980s had to prove themselves. "Being an overachiever simply went with the territory of breaking down barriers," they write, "so it wouldn't be surprising to see these women bring the same determination to motherhood."[11] Other scholars have offered insights into why this form of mothering has remained the norm. As Andrea O'Reilly suggests, mothering intensely may be a way for some working mothers to assuage the guilt that stems from the fact that they have careers they enjoy.[12] Further, for many women, embracing intensive mothering means upholding a set of values they cherish and that are in contradistinction to the values of the working world. "The ideology of intensive mothering is protected and promoted," Sharon Hays argues, "because it holds a fragile but nonetheless powerful cultural position as the last best defense against what many people see as the impoverishment of social ties, communal obligations, and unremunerated commitments."[13] Central to the construction of intensive mothering is the value placed on loving relationships—values that stand in profound distinction to the rules of paid work and the market economy.

Significantly, however, to argue that the ideology of intensive mothering stands in contrast to the market calculations that mark interactions in the public world is not to suggest that motherhood can be performed separate from the marketplace. Although intensive mothering has an uneasy relationship with consumption, consumerism nonetheless plays an integral role in its practice.[14] As Douglas and Michaels observe, "Our homes are supposed to be havens from the everything-has-a-price, everyone-is-defined-by-commodities values of the marketplace. . . . Our kids are priceless, their value to us completely outside market calculations. And yet, our devotion as mothers, our commitment to our kids not falling through the cracks, our kids' own sense of self-worth and our love for them, all have been and are measured by how many and what kinds of goods and services we buy for them."[15]

Thus shopping for one's children—choosing the educational toys that will enhance their development; purchasing clothes that are both practical and attractive; nabbing the hard-to-find, trendy gadget one's child "must have"—all these tasks and more fall to women in their roles as mothers, and one of the central institutions in which much of this shopping occurs is the mall.

Intensive Mothering and the Mall

Above I argued that intensive mothering is rooted in post–World War II efforts to move middle-class women out of wartime jobs and back into the home. These mid-twentieth-century efforts, of course, had their own precedents; most directly, they were part of a movement to reinstate the separation between the public and private spheres that accompanied mid-nineteenth-century industrialization.

With industrialization, factory work replaced family farms and businesses, and male wage labor was distinguished from female domestic work. Concurrently, men were understood to occupy public spaces; they "enjoyed the freedom to move in the crowds of modernity."[16] A woman's place, on the other hand, was said to be the home. This material shift was accompanied by an ideological one: The public world was marked "as cold, competitive, and individualistic" and so too were the men who inhabited it. The home, in turn, "was valorized as warm, nurturing, and communal."[17] Thus the attributes that would come to be associated with the idealized intensive mother—her nurturance, selflessness, and caring—were directly linked to the place she was said to occupy.

Although most of the public world was deemed off limits to the middle-class nineteenth-century woman, there were a few public institutions into which she might venture. One of those institutions was the department store. "Because the department store interiorized the public street and transformed it into a private space, it became an acceptable extension of the home that the bourgeois woman could enter alone."[18] Today, of course, women are no longer prohibited from participating in the public world; nonetheless, shopping malls, like the department stores that preceded them, are designed largely for female shoppers.

Like nineteenth-century department stores, malls are "quasi-public spaces," neither fully public nor fully private.[19] Indeed, according to Staeheli and Mitchell, malls are designed to function as a kind of "new town square."[20] Yet unlike traditional town squares in which any member of a community is invited to voice her opinions, to interact, and to deliberate with others, "the public/private spaces of the mall are cleansed of those people whom 'legitimate' members of the public find offensive or worrying or, more specifically, the mall is cleansed of those people who may challenge social norms and expectations related to civility (and perhaps to consumption)."[21] Thus malls are designed to be safe and welcoming to "legitimate" guests; the vast majority of these guests are consuming women.

Liz Ferrier writes that the mall "offers public conveniences, free buses, parking, toilets, entertainment, free samples, competitions. In the [mall], women have access to public space without the stigma or threat of the street."[22] Malcolm Voyce similarly notes that "The mall is constructed to form a predictable controlled environment which acts like a prison in reverse: to keep deviant behavior on the outside and to form a consumerist form of citizenship inside."[23] Thus the ambience of a mall is designed to be "warm, safe, convenient, friendly, and welcoming . . . in other words . . . feminine."[24]

Both reflecting and extending the feminine characteristics of malls, the female consumer is invited to purchase a wide array of products linked to traditional femininity, including her role as wife and mother. In the mall a woman can buy clothing and toys for her children; bath, kitchen, and decorative items for her home; and products that mark her own femininity such as clothing, shoes, makeup, and lingerie. Indeed, on average, a shopping mall will include five times as many women's clothing stores and three times as many women's shoe stores as there are for men.[25]

That malls are aimed largely at women is not surprising; worldwide, women do the majority of shopping.[26] Yet it is important to recognize that a mall—and indeed, any kind of organized public space—is not simply a place in which activities occur. Instead, malls are "spaces in which people form their identities and interact with one another."[27] Jeanne Van Eeden argues that "malls can be read as texts sited within the ideology of capitalism that articulate ideas concerning space, identity, class, race, and gender."[28] In other words, not only do malls welcome women shoppers in their roles as wives and mothers; they also function to *create* those roles while simultaneously inviting women to *assume particular iterations of those identities.*

A great deal of scholarship has been devoted to the ways traditional femininity—including intensive mothering—is bad for women.[29] Drawing on the work of Susan Faludi and Naomi Wolf, O'Reilly maintains that norms of contemporary femininity function as a backlash discourse. "Just as the self-hate produced by the beauty myth undercuts and undermines women's sense of achievement in education or a career, the current discourse of intensive mothering gives rise to self-doubt, or more specifically guilt, that immobilizes women and robs them of their confidence as both workers and mothers."[30] Thus through their promotion of traditional femininity and intensive mothering, malls serve an oppressive function, enjoining women to enact behaviors and assume identities that are fundamentally disempowering.

As Michel Foucault has taught us, however, where there is power, there is also resistance.[31] And indeed, while some scholars reflect on the oppressive functions of malls, others explore their liberating possibilities. John Fiske argues that "shopping, while apparently addressing women precisely as disempowered domestic consumers, may actually offer opportunities to break free not just from these meanings, but from the structure of binary oppositions that produces them."[32] These opportunities, he maintains, come in the form of feminine "trickery" whereby the weak "use the resources provided by the strong in their own interests, and to oppose the interests of those who provided the resources in the first place."[33]

Fiske notes, for example, that people often enter shopping malls for purposes other than to shop. Mothers, he points out, will sometimes take children to malls during the extreme heat of the summer, thereby enjoying the comfort of a controlled environment without planning to participate in the economic activity that environment is designed to promote.[34] Of course, even if they do not *plan* to make purchases, by entering a mall, the mothers referred to by Fiske make themselves available to the enticement of products and the feminine identities they promote. Yet Fiske maintains that the moment of consumption itself can be empowering. "Any one single act of buying," he argues, "involves multiple acts of rejection—many commodities are rejected for every one chosen, and rejecting the offerings of the system constitutes adopting a controlling relationship to it."[35]

Nancy Backes builds on Fiske's argument, suggesting that it is not just through the *purchasing* of products that women are empowered but also in their *use*. One of the ways malls invite women to enact roles of traditional femininity is through the promotion of beauty products, yet Backes argues that "fashion and cosmetics are tools of fantasy," and these tools may enable "women 'to pretend to escape from the routine trivia of everyday life, by making believe that they look and live like someone they are not, but would like to be'. . . . 'In short, through these pretend maneuvers, [women] try to convince others that [they] have transcended the constraints of everyday life, and that the life [they] live is interesting, adventurous, and exciting.'"[36] Additionally, Backes maintains that there is a practical element to a woman's use of beauty products. "The way a woman presents herself can be seen as a form of control, a means of disciplining the look directed toward her."[37]

That the subordinated have means to resist the power structures that oppress them is a well-worn theme in contemporary scholarship, and Fiske and Backes offer reasonable arguments regarding women's use of malls such that both capitalism and patriarchy are challenged. Moreover, as Fiske notes, there are limitations to acts of resistance; as such, he makes an effort to offer a balanced discussion of the ways power relations unfold as women shop. He writes: "Shopping can never be a radical, subversive act; it can never change the system of a capitalist-consumerist economy. Equally, however, it cannot be adequately explained as a mere capitulation to the system."[38] In spite of his desire to be balanced, following Stewart and Dickinson, I maintain that the limitations to "trickery" are more pronounced than Fiske acknowledges. Indeed, I suggest that the resistance central to trickery is necessarily paired with the reinforcement of the power structures against which "tricks" are played, a pairing that is made apparent through an analysis of the discourse surrounding the case of Bridget Kevane.

The Case

Kevane's Apologia: "Guilty as Charged"

Roughly two years after dropping the children at the mall, Kevane wrote an article recounting the event and its aftermath. Titled "Guilty as Charged" and published in *Brain, Child: The Magazine for Thinking Mothers*, the article serves largely as an apologia. Kevane insists that she did nothing wrong and she maintains that although she is not perfect, she is a good mother. Here is an overview of what she wrote:

On June 17, 2007, Kevane's daughter asked to go to the mall with her friend. Kevane told her she could go, but only if she took the younger children along. Kevane notes that on that particular day she was "exhausted," a state she attributes to her varied responsibilities as mother, wife, pet owner, and professor. She also points out that her daughter and her daughter's friend were both experienced and knowledgeable babysitters, having completed a babysitting course sponsored by a local hospital. "The plan for the day,"

Kevane writes, "was for the kids to have lunch and walk around a bit. I told the girls the rules. They could not leave the younger kids unsupervised. They could not make a ruckus. They had to behave. . . . The three-year-old had to stay in her stroller." The girls had a cell phone and could call Kevane if they needed her. Before dropping the children off, Kevane checked with her husband, who was at work, and the other child's mother. Everyone agreed to the plan. Kevane drove the children to the mall, told them she'd pick them up in a couple of hours, and went home to nap.

The older girls did not obey the rules. At one point they left the three younger children by the cosmetics counter in Macy's to try on some shirts. Employees spotted the three young children unattended and called mall security. Mall security, in turn, called the local Bozeman police, who contacted Kevane and her husband, insisting that they "come down to the mall immediately." Although Kevane and her husband were allowed to take the children home, the police filed a report, and in turn, the city attorney charged Kevane with criminal neglect.

Kevane and her lawyer soon came to realize that the prosecutor would accept nothing short of a guilty plea. Reluctant to plead guilty to actions she did not consider a crime, Kevane and her lawyer prepared to fight the charge. However, after the results of a mock trial indicated they could not win, Kevane's lawyer worked out a deferred prosecution agreement through which Kevane was placed on probation and ordered to attend parenting classes. Kevane ends her essay with the following passage: "I do feel guilty about what happened. Not because I committed a crime according to the legal definition, but because no parent has confidence that they have been completely successful, ever. For all the times I was not the 'good' parent, I am guilty; for all the times that I did not respond perfectly to my children's needs, I am guilty. For all the times that I've not given them enough of me, I am guilty. For feeling constantly torn between so many daily demands, trying to make it all work, but knowing that I sometimes fall short, I am guilty. But of knowingly putting my children in harm's way by letting them go the mall alone? Not guilty."

Apologia Redux: From "Guilty as Charged" to "Dangerous Resentment"

Nine days after Kevane's essay was published in *Brain, Child*, Judith Warner recounted the story in "Domestic Disturbances," her recurring *New York Times* column. Whereas Kevane's essay served to explain and justify Kevane's actions, Warner is somewhat more reserved in her assessment. She suggests that while the decision to leave the children at the mall without adult supervision may be questionable, it did not warrant the charges proffered. Indeed,

Warner is less interested in defending Kevane than she is in exploring what the responses of the police and prosecutor suggest about contemporary attitudes toward women, especially women who are highly educated and financially comfortable. "What really sent my head spinning after reading Kevane's story" Warner writes, "was the degree to which it drove home the fact that our country's resentment, and even hatred, of well-educated, apparently affluent women, is spiraling out of control."

Warner provides details from Kevane's essay to support her class-based thesis. She recounts a meeting in which the prosecutor told Kevane's lawyer that "she believed professors are incapbable of seeing the real world around them because their 'heads are always in a book.'" She cites a letter to Kevane's lawyer in which the prosecutor wrote: "I just think that even individuals with major educations can commit this offense, and they should not be treated differently because they have more money or education." And Warner reiterates Kevane's conclusions about the role class played in her prosecution: "I now realize that [the prosecutor's] pressure—her near obsession with having me plead guilty—had less to do with what I had done and more to do with her perception of me as an outsider who thought she was above the law, who had money to pay her way out of a mistake, who thought she was smarter than the Bozeman attorney because of her 'major education.' This perception took hold even though I had never spoken one word to her directly. . . . I was visible but silent, and thus unable to shake the image that the prosecutor had created of me: a rich, reckless, highly educated outsider mother who probably left her children all the time in order to read her books." According to Warner, then, the treatment Kevane experienced is indicative of a pervasive and "simmering" resentment aimed at highly educated, financially comfortable women in the contemporary United States, leading her to conclude her essay with an admonishment: "The hatred of women—in all its archaic, phantasmagoric forms—is still alive and well in our society, and when directed at well-educated women, it's socially acceptable too. Think of this for a second the next time you're inexplicably moved to put an 'elite' woman in her place."

Readers' Response

Intensive Mothering and Social Class

As noted above, more than 450 comments to Warner's article were posted within 24 hours of its publication. Significantly, the majority of readers disagreed with Warner's claims, rejecting both her assessment of Kevane's actions as well as her arguments about social class.

Whereas Warner sought to minimize a discussion of Kevane's behavior, a large number of readers seized the opportunity to pass judgment, and for the most part, the judgments passed were negative. The adjectives readers use to describe Kevane's actions are sometimes colorful and often cruel. Her behaviors are portrayed as "lunatic," "criminal," "not smart or safe," "idiotic," "ridiculous," "foolish," "dangerous," "a recipe for disaster," "close to irrational," "boneheaded," and "wack." She is found to have shown a "major lapse in judgment," "appalling lack of sound judgment," an "enormous lack of judgment," a "serious error in judgment." Her "decision" is deemed "terrible," "awful," "poor," and "bad." Her "mistake" is called "very major and stupid," "dumb and illegal;" her "offense" is said to be "grave."[39]

Readers not only cast aspersions on Kevane's actions but also offered negative assessments of her character. The most common terms used to depict Kevane are "neglectful," "selfish," and "stupid." She also is described as a "fool," an "idiot," a "lazy, ignorant, self-absorbed narcissist," "a dunderhead," "a complete nut," "crazy," "reckless," "wrong," "odd," "abusive *and* paranoid." According to one reader, "Prof. Kevane doesn't have the sense God gave a goose."

In part, readers seem to be responding to both Kevane's and Warner's insistence that Kevane's actions did not constitute child endangerment. Identifying himself as "a former case worker for child protection services" "andrew b" writes "I would definitely consider the mother's actions to be endangerment." Others insist that Kevane's behaviors constituted "endangerment, pure and simple," "public endangerment of a child, PERIOD," "child abuse," "abandonment," and "neglect." Indeed, one reader insists that her behavior was analogous to "leaving your baby in a hot car while the mother goes into the bar for a few drinks."

In addition to rejecting Warner's assessment of Kevane and her actions, many posters resist Warner's contention that the prosecutor "pursued her child endangerment case ultra-zealously" because of Kevane's class status. To the contrary, a large number of readers insist that a poor woman in a comparable situation would have been treated similarly, or even more harshly by the state. Kathy writes, "If a young, less-educated mom or dad had dumped children of this age at the mall, she or he would have been treated exactly the same way (or worse), and we wouldn't have been hearing this slant on the story." Azul Perez asserts, "I don't buy this for a moment. I don't believe they were going after this mom for her education and affluence but for her poor parenting decision. . . . This article is not written in a manner that persuades me otherwise or that she was pursued more aggressively than a meth mom that would do the same." And SB writes "Wow, a majorly poor judgment on the part of a parent who should have known better. I can see why the authorities would want to prosecute her. They would hardly have done any different if she had been a [sic] unemployed welfare mother."

Interestingly, although neither Warner nor Kevane mention Kevane's nationality or race, a number of readers assume she is white and native-born, and they pair race and class, contrasting the treatment Kevane received to what a poor woman of color and/or a non-native woman might have encountered. Scott Baboyian writes, "If the offender was poorly educated and/or darkly skinned, one can easily imagine not only an arrest, but also extensive media coverage." William offers a hypothetical counterexample: "If it was a Colombian nanny that pulled that move with the kids there's a fair chance she'd have been fired at least and jailed at worst." And Josie maintains, "If this had been a poor minority woman she would have been not only arrested, but her children most likely would have been taken from her and put in foster homes."

In offering up judgments of Kevane's behaviors and character, readers articulate a set of beliefs related to good and bad mothering. Specifically, they call on the first two criteria of intensive mothering identified above: that "children can only be properly cared for by the biological mother" and that "this mothering must be provided 24/7." By leaving her children in the care of others—even an older sibling and friend—readers insist that Kevane violated both of these tenets.[40] Through their discussion of the comparable treatment received by poor women and minorities, readers *reinforce* these assumptions. To be clear, the readers who argue that poor women and/or women of color would be treated similarly or worse than Kevane may very well be correct. Douglas and Michaels offer a detailed account of what they dub "the war against welfare mothers," a combination of punitive public policies and sensational media depictions. Moreover, they argue that the negative treatment poor mothers receive is a fundamental part of intensive mothering. "For momism to work as a new norm," they write, "there had to be delinquents who dramatized what happened to those who failed to comply."[41]

Yet, it is important to notice that while readers may insist that poor and/or minority women would be subject to treatment similar to or worse than the treatment Kevane received, they do *not* challenge the state's fundamental practice of scrutinizing mothers. To the contrary, the majority of readers suggest that law enforcement's oversight of mothers' parenting is both appropriate and necessary. Thus steven iler admonishes, "I hope you are not saying that an advanced degree or some other measure of achievement should confer some sort of immunity in a case like this. This system is, after all, intended to protect children." And Jane similarly asserts, "I'm glad to see this prosecutor holding all parents, regardless of income or education, accountable for breaking laws that concern the welfare of children." Indeed, according to Matilda, Kevane's case is a "perfect example of equal treatment;" or in the words of Judi L. Green, "in this case, equal justice prevailed."

Indeed, many readers suggest that Kevane's relative wealth and education *heighten* the expectation that she should enact intensive mothering. Because she has greater ability, readers suggest she has more responsibility to be a "good mom." Euripedes923 asserts, "This particular woman's behavior is indefensible, all the more so particularly because of her level of education, not in spite of it." Brian similarly maintains, "'For those to whom much is given, much is expected.' If Prof. Kevane did indeed benefit from a 'major education' and enjoys some affluence then she ought to have known better." According to Defender Dick, "I agree with your premise that in general, women are held to a different and often an unfair standard when it comes to child care and that well-educated women often must measure up to an even higher standard, but really, shouldn't they? After all, a women [sic] as well educated as Ms. Keane [sic] is expected to show judgment and a sense of responsibility consistent with her education and status as a teacher and professor."

Douglas and Michaels argue that poor and wealthy mothers inhabit two sides of "the maternal media diptych."[42] Poor women serve as representative anecdotes, as maternal delinquents. Their poverty precludes them from meeting the demands of intensive mothering, thus they often are forced to undergo the scrutiny of the child welfare system, sometimes losing their children to foster care. Wealthier women, on the other hand, are expected to uphold intensive mothering's key tenets, including tending to one's children 24/7. Because Kevane did not comply with the latter dictum, readers suggest the treatment she received was not only appropriate but perhaps more lenient than she deserved.

Intensive Mothering and Consumer Culture

As noted above, another demand of intensive mothering is that a mother must expend extensive amounts of time, energy, and money on her children, and shopping malls facilitate this mandate. Not only are malls designed to be safe and welcoming to women, in malls, women encounter a myriad of products that help them enact their roles as mothers and wives. Consistent with Lynn Staeheli and Don Mitchell's argument that people are invited to gather in malls as long as they "conform to norms of civility,"[43] however, readers commenting on Warner's article suggest that malls are "safe and welcoming" if and only if women/mothers obey the rules. When a mother leaves her children at a mall and absents herself from the premises, malls are best understood as dangerous.

Readers insist that malls are filled with "sexual predators," "gangs," "pervs," "crazies," "pedophiles," "snatchers," "child predators," and "potentially creepy strangers." Many readers invoke scenarios of what might have happened, including that the three-year-old might have been "snatched out of her stroller," she and/or the other children might have been "kidnapped," "molested," "abducted," or "sexually assaulted." Leslie ends her post by insisting that "Anything could have happened!" gblico maintains that Kevane's actions could have "resulted in tragedy . . . such as serious injury or death." The child abduction/murder cases of Etan Patz and Adam Walsh are recounted a number of times,[44] and Jackie writes, "If this person read only a few books about crimes against children she might learn to be more cautious."

Indeed, according to many readers, Kevane was "lucky" nothing happened to her children. Sarah insists, "Sure, the kids were fine, but they were plain lucky. I shudder to think of the things that could have happened." Linda Simpson Spratt asserts, "She is very fortunate to have only the judge/attorney to contend with and not the emergency room, mortician, kidnapper, or lawsuit from other children's parents." And rac maintains "it is amazing her children survived being abandoned at the mall." To frame the safety of the children as a matter of luck—to be *amazed* that they survived—implies that it was *likely* that the children would come to some harm—an implication that is patently untrue. In her article, Kevane describes Bozeman as a "safe community" and the mall as a "safe place." She notes that "no one has ever been kidnapped or molested at the mall." Her assertions are supported by crime statistics. Crime rates in Bozeman are generally low, and there was not a single murder in Bozeman in 2007.[45]

Douglas and Michaels identify overblown fears of "threats from without" as one of the reinforcing factors of intensive mothering. "By the early 1980s," they note, "there was the seemingly new and horrid phenomenon of the missing child. As soon as you let your kid out of your sight, he or she was in danger of being abducted."[46] The sudden belief that children were the potential and even likely victims of abduction and other horrible crimes was in large part a media creation. Starting in the late 1970s, both "infotainment" and "hard" news programs began sensationalizing crimes against children—Douglas and Michaels point to stories covering Etan Patz and Adam Walsh as emblematic of this phenomena—while also grossly exaggerating the number of such incidents. Of course, any case of child abduction or murder is tragic; what was problematic, however, was the way in which a few horrific crimes were presented as if they reflected a common and everyday threat. Through such reporting, mothers were told that their children were at constant risk and that mothers—and only mothers—were responsible for ensuring their children did not come to harm. That readers of Warner's column spoke about the grave dangers the children faced in the mall—and that a number of readers referenced the by-then decades-old cases of Patz and Walsh—indicates that "fears from without" continue to discipline contemporary mothers.

Adding insult to injury, a number of readers maintain that through her actions Kevane not only placed the children in danger but she simultaneously violated rules governing the mall as a site of consumption. By leaving her children alone at the mall, many readers complain that Kevane burdened *others* with the responsibility of seeing after the children's wellbeing. Malls, numerous readers assert, are neither "babysitters," nor "day care centers." According to joe, when Kevane dropped her children there she "infringe[d] upon the community, the other mall customers, the mall tenets [sic] and the security forces private and public." "Why," Mary asks, "should the mall employees be in charge of watching anybody's children?" James asserts, "Leaving kids unattended in a mall is outsourcing your parenting duty to the Mall security." Staeheli and Mitchell note that "mall owners are clear that malls are first and foremost spaces of consumption . . . [as such] they are unlikely to allow functions that will interfere with commerce."[47] As the readers quoted above see it, by dropping her children off at the mall, Kevane violated this fundamental rule. She used a quasi-public space to care for her children, and by absenting herself from the site she imposed on other adults to assume her caregiving responsibilities while simultaneously hindering their participation in the exchange of goods.

For many readers, the reason Kevane gives—and Warner repeats—for leaving the children at the mall only exacerbates the crime. Des Johnson responds with incredulity at the fact that Kevane dropped the children at the mall and *went home to nap*. "My first reaction on reading Kevane had just gone home for a rest was 'what??!?'" Tom similarly writes, "Let's focus on the facts. A grown woman (educated or not) drover [sic] her kids to a shopping mall and left them there to fend for themselves while she went home to take a nap. GIVE ME A BREAK!" Others deploy sarcasm to indicate their dismay. TW, for example, writes that she (or he) is "sorry Ms. Kevane's nap time was interrupted by the Bozemen police, but let's quit sniveling." Leeza C maintains, "Oh, okay, she left the kids because she was tired—that works." And punning on the title of one of Warner's books, Norman asserts "any parent who leaves not only her own children but others' [sic] alone in a mall because she wants to 'drive home to rest' is indeed an example of 'perfect madness.'"[48] Thus in contrast to the rules of intensive mothering and the norms governing behavior in malls, on the day in question Kevane neither put the children's needs ahead of her own nor did she shop. Instead, according to readers, she dropped her children off and went home to rest, thus imposing upon mall customers and staff to care for her children, subsequently interfering with the consumptive activities a mall is designed to promote.

The Limitations of Trickery

Above I referenced scholarship that explores how women engage malls in ways that challenge both patriarchy and capitalism. Moreover, I noted that the means through which women accomplish such challenges is through "trickery." Fiske also refers to such acts as "guerrilla tactics," noting that they "are often most successful when the guerrillas do not wear the uniform of 'the enemy.'"[49] In other words, key to being a trickster is hiding one's tricks. Thus, for example, women who use the mall as an escape from the heat but do not shop *appear* to be enacting the role of consumers; as such, their challenges to patriarchy and/or capitalism fly under the radar. Rather than seeming to challenge these power structures, they *look like* they are reinforcing both.

As I also noted, Fiske qualifies the extent to which acts of trickery challenge systems of power. When discussing women's use of fashion he writes, "For a woman in patriarchy, commodities that enable her to be 'in fashion' enable her to relate to the social order in a way that grants her access to the progressive and the public. Such a move may not be radical in that it does not challenge the right of patriarchy to offer these pleasures to men more readily than women, but it can be seen as both progressive and empowering insofar as it opens up masculine pleasures to women."[50] Thus, Fiske asserts that although patriarchy may provide men more varied opportunities to participate in the public sphere, women nonetheless can utilize the potential provided by fashion in order to present themselves in ways that suggest their lives are glamorous and successful. In this, he argues, women have access to pleasures typically reserved for men.

What Fiske does not acknowledge, however, is that by using fashion in this way—by assuming the role of tricksters—women not only *appear* to be reinforcing patriarchy and capitalism; *in some ways they are doing just that.* Those women who purchase fashion and cosmetics may enjoy the fantasy the products provide, nonetheless, through their actions they simultaneously reinforce the belief that a woman's worth is linked to the consumption of products that enhance her appearance while literally buying into institutions whose policies and practices privilege men.[51] Similarly, as noted above, when women use malls in order to escape the summer heat, they make themselves available to the enticement of products, many of which promote traditional feminine roles. As such, these summer outings might very well lead to acts of consumption that reinforce patriarchy and capitalism.

Unlike the tricksters discussed by Fiske, Kevane made no effort to disguise her "transgression." Rather than masquerading her actions through subterfuge and guile, Kevane transparently confronted the rules of intensive mothering and consumer culture. Moreover, she broadcast her behavior, justifying her actions in the article in *Brain, Child.* Had Kevane been more careful to disguise her actions, numerous readers suggest, there would have been no problem. According to Cherie Ernest, it would have been permissible for the twelve-year-olds to watch the younger children at the mall, but only if Kevane was there, too. "To have them 'baby-sit" in the mall for a brief period while Mom was on the premises would have been one thing, to leave them alone there was inviting disaster." Of course, it's hard to understand how Kevane being on the premises but presumably not staying with the five children would have stopped the situation from unfolding as it did. What would have been different was that Kevane would have remained in the mall, shopping in relatively close proximity to her children, thus *appearing* to be a good mother and good consumer. She, like the women who use fashion and cosmetics in a resistive function, would have enacted the role of a trickster rather flaunting the rules.

Other readers suggest that Kevane could have gotten her rest at home—if she had kept the children there, too. MJ insists "leaving kids of mixed ages to play in ones' [sic] backyard while you took a light mid-day nap is kind of the most one would do—but driving them over and leaving them in a mall is stupid." Steffi Hartley offers a similar perspective based on her own experiences: "When my son was three, we had a fifteen year old come into the house for a couple hours a day, several days a week so I had a little time off. Most of that time I remained in the house and though relaxing or resting, I listened—hard to turn those 'mother ears' off." Thus according to these readers, it is permissible for mothers to use the private sphere to tend to their own needs, but only if they are not too obvious, and only if they arc poised to resume intensive mothering at any moment. Again, such behaviors are permissible if they are shrouded in trickery.

In addition to offering suggestions about what Kevane "could" or "should" have done, each of the readers cited above identifies herself as *similar* to Kevane. MJ notes, "I grew up as a feminist, I'm educated, I hold a respectable outside-the-home job and all, but after I had my kids my perspective totally changed." Steffi Hartley likewise identifies herself as "a highly educated woman and a mother," and Cherie Ernest defines herself as "an ardent feminist and the holder of a doctorate who raised two children." These women are not alone in both identifying with Kevane's background and status while insisting they would not do what she did. Doris Lewis writes, "For the record, I am a woman, I have a PhD, and I have never at any time dumped my children at the mall while I napped." Maria exhorts "As a well educated woman with a PhD in child psychology and the parent of two children now ages 24 and 21, I can only say that this parent was in fact neglectful of her children." Gloria asserts, "I am a college educated professional woman, with three children. I would never dump my children in a mall so 'I can rest.'"

The passion with which these readers compare themselves to Kevane while simultaneously denouncing her behaviors is indicative of the hold intensive mothering continues to have on many women—and perhaps especially those who self-identify as well-educated and affluent. In an effort to distinguish their own parenting from Kevane's, the readers cited above seem to be saying "yes, I am well-educated and have a job in the public sphere, but I am still a good mother." As such, they embody a perspective O'Brien Hallstein refers to as a "split subjectivity." Caught between old and new gender norms, they embrace their professional identities while also performing a maternity that assumes a mother's whole life revolves around her children.[52] Indeed, through their efforts, these readers imply that unlike Kevane, they follow the rules of intensive mothering—and in doing so they draw attention to the fact that *intensive mothering itself can be seen as a form of trickery.*

Through their posts, the women cited above suggest that while they may be participating in the public world as workers, the ideological separation between the public and private spheres remains intact. They may be in the public sphere and they may enjoy the opportunities the public sphere provides, but they continue to engage in the caregiving work assigned to women who occupy the private sphere. Thus like those women who use shopping malls to escape the heat and/or to purchase products that allow them to pretend their lives are different than they actually are, women who engage in intensive mothering challenge the power structure inherent in the public/private split—they venture into the public world as economic actors comparable to men. At the same time, however, they engage in behaviors that simultaneously *reinforce* that power structure. They draw attention away from the fact that their actions challenge men's power in the public world by continuing to play the role of "good moms." As such, the enactment of intensive mothering allows male privilege to remain in place.[53]

Unlike the tricksters who enact intensive mothering, Kevane did not try to disguise her challenge to patriarchy or capitalism. She did not (appear to) care for her children and she did not (appear to) shop. Instead, she put her oldest daughter in charge and cared for herself. As such, Kevane's challenges to both patriarchy and capitalism are both more visible and pointed than are the challenges of a trickster; too pointed, it seems, for either the state or many of her peers to accept.

Voices of Opposition

Although the vast majority of readers' comments reflect negatively on Kevane's actions and/or Warner's column, there were, of course, alternate views expressed.[54] These voices of opposition suggest that Kevane is not alone in her challenge to intensive mothering. For example, reflecting on their own experiences as children and teens, several readers note that the rules of intensive mothering are a relatively new phenomena. fd writes "I was myself frequently supervised by older siblings when I was growing up and started making money as a babysitter when I was in the fourth grade—no one ever accused those families of child endangerment." The Angry Geologist similarly notes "If this lady abandoned her children, then my brother and I were practically abused. We weren't by the way."

Others readers place Kevane's story in historical perspective. Kathleen James-Chakraborty recounts what she learned in a college anthropology class: "almost no mothers in any culture before the time of the industrial revolution . . . had focused on childcare, which was instead left to grandmothers, older children (not necessarily siblings) and, in those households who could afford them, servants." And charles points out, "100 years ago children were given far more responsibility than a little 3 year old [sic] watching at he [sic] mall with cell phones. On farms a 12 year old [sic] had chores they did independently that would be considered dangerous, and therefore abuse now."

In addition to calling attention to the ways in which assumptions underlying "good motherhood" have become more demanding over the years, some readers seek to debunk the myth that children are in constant, grave danger. Joseph asks, "About abductions—how many children have been abducted and killed in the last decade from the closest mall to your house. (For 99% of people the answer will be 0). In the 1950 [sic] it was common for mothers to leave babies in a baby carriage in front of the store while they went in. . . . Violent crime rates have gone down since then, and yet we are more fearful?" Lev Bronstein concurs, writing that "Americans are really hysterical about The [sic] molesters and predators that exist mostly in their fevered imaginations." And riverdaughter recalls "in all my years of babysitting, starting at age 12, I never heard of an incident of a toddler's life endangered or a child mistreated by another babysitter. What has changed is our attitude, which has meant hyper-vigilance of our kids, hours of intense supervision duties for stressed out working parents and no real child with growing responsibilities and independence."

Like riverdaughter, numerous people express concern about the effects contemporary child rearing norms have on children, and some of these readers simultaneously identify the sexism such norms reflect and help maintain. Jennifer laments the fact that "our culture has moved toward an almost pathological over-protectiveness of children, while reestablishing the responsibility for enforcing all that hovering to mothers." And smw insists, "The idea that a woman should spend her life toddling after toddlers is a very recent and very silly one, fueled in equal parts by not-so-archaic stereotypes of women . . . and the media hysteria that has talked folks into seeing pedophile kidnappers behind every corner."

Thus like Kevane and Warner, the readers discussed above reject intensive motherhood as a culturally constructed and recent phenomena that functions to keep women in positions of subordination. The presence of these voices suggests that the ideology of intensive mothering does not have total hold in the contemporary United States. Indeed, these readers speak to the truth of Fiske's assertion that "hegemony can never finally relax in victory" as it is regularly resisted by those who are constructed as subjects within it.[55] Nonetheless, the profound imbalance between the number of comments in support of Kevane and the number who judge her negatively speaks to the limitations of such resistance. There were some readers who agreed with Warner's arguments and joined with Kevane to challenge intensive mothering, but the majority of readers took the opposite stance, illustrating just how powerful a place intensive mothering continues to hold in contemporary society.

Conclusions

As Fiske, Backes, and others have argued, malls trade in cash and fantasy. People use malls to purchase the mundane products necessary for everyday life; however, these scholars also emphasize the numerous ways malls offer opportunities to transcend the everyday. Malls provide opportunities for trickery, allowing people to use the tools of the powerful for their own benefit and in contrast to the interests of those in power. Malls provide the means, however temporary and illusory, to cross social boundaries linked to gender and class.

Yet whereas Fiske and others highlight the liberating potential of trickery, following Stewart and Dickinson, in this chapter I have argued that Kevane's case illustrates the limitations of such tactics. Trickery involves disguising one's behaviors, and while one may partially challenge the powerful through these disguises, successful tricks necessarily involve the partial reinforcement of the power structures against which they are deployed. Thus when women use malls to escape from the heat, and/or to engage in the fantasy that fashion provides, they may access pleasures typically restricted to men and hence challenge patriarchy and capitalism, but they do so only through their participation in consumer culture, partially reinforcing those same structures of power. Similarly, women may shroud the challenge to patriarchy that their professional lives entail by enacting intensive mothering; in doing so, however, they simultaneously reinforce the gendered power differential that underlies the separation of the public and private spheres.

In contrast to those tricksters who use shopping malls to engage in fashion-based fantasies or who enact intensive mothering in order to disguise the ways their professional success challenges men, Bridget Kevane directly confronted both patriarchy and capitalism. She dropped five children at a mall and went home to nap, breaking rules linked to consumer culture and intensive mothering. Because she did not try to masquerade the violation of these rules through trickery, she was disciplined—by the security forces at the mall, by the power of the state, as seen in the actions of the Bozeman police and prosecutor, and by the majority of people who responded to Warner's recounting of the incident. "Functioning as the new town squares," Staeheli and Mitchell write, "shopping malls may effectively exercise [a] kind of control . . . creating a qualitatively different 'civic' or 'community' space in which only certain kinds of people, ideas, and behaviors are acceptable in public."[56] Staeheli and Mithell are particularly concerned with malls' abilities to limit political speech; moreover, they investigate the explicit disciplinary mechanisms that mall owners' employ to exert such control. This case study suggests a more subtle, but no less troubling, exercise of control. The fierce intensity with which mall security, the state, and much of the public responded to Kevane's actions speaks to the powerful hold rules of consumption combined with intensive mothering have in contemporary US society. Concurrently, these responses illustrate that in the current climate, only limited challenges to these power structures are tolerated.

Notes

1. Two of the younger children were Kevane's, the other was the child of a friend.

2. Judith Warner, "Dangerous Resentment," *The New York Times*, 9 July 2009, accessed July 10, 2009, http://warner.blogs.nytimes.com/2009/07/09/don't-hate-her-because-shes-educated/?emc=eta1.

3. John Fiske, "Shopping for Pleasure: Malls, Power, and Resistance," in *The Consumer Society Reader*, ed. Juliet B. Schor and Douglas B. Holt (New York: The New Press, 2000), 311.

4. Fiske, "Shopping for Pleasure," 309.

5. Jessie Stewart and Greg Dickinson, "Enunciating Locality in the Postmodern Suburb: FlatIron Crossing and the Colorado Lifestyle, *Western Journal of Communication*, 72, (2008): 294.

6. Sharon Hays, *The Cultural Contradictions of Motherhood* (New Haven:Yale University Press, 1996); D. Lynn O'Brien Hallstein, "Public Choices, Private Control: How Mediated Mom Labels Work Rhetorically to Dismantle the Politics of Choice and White Second Wave Feminist Successes," in *Contemplating Maternity in an Era of Choice: Explorations into Discourses of Reproduction*, ed. Sara Hayden and D. Lynn O'Brien Hallstein (Lanham, MD: Lexington Press, 2010).

7. Andrea O'Reilly, *Rocking the Cradle:Thoughts on Motherhood, Feminism, and the Possibility of Empowered Mothering* (Toronto: Demeter Press, 2006).

8. Susan J. Douglas and Meredith W. Michaels, *The Mommy Myth: The Idealization of Motherhood and How It Has Undermined Women* (New York: Free Press, 2004).

9. O'Reilly, *Rocking the Cradle*, 43.

10. Ibid.

11. Douglas and Michaels, *The Mommy Myth*, 9.

12. O'Reilly, *Rocking the Cradle*, 42.

13. Hays, *The Cultural Contradictions of Motherhood*, xiii.

14. Janelle S. Taylor, Linda L. Layne, and Danielle F. Wozniak, eds., *Consuming Motherhood* (New Brunswick: Rutgers University Press, 2004).

15. Douglas and Michaels, *The Mommy Myth*, 273.

16. Jeanne van Eeden, "The Gender of Shopping Malls," *Communicatio* 32, (2006): 44.

17. Hays, *The Cultural Contradictions of Motherhood*, 33.

18. van Eeden, "The Gender of Shopping Malls," 46; also see Nancy Backes, "Reading the Shopping Mall City," *Journal of Popular Culture*, (1997): 1–17.

19. Malcolm Voyce, "Shopping Malls in Australia: The End of Public Space and the Rise of 'Consumerist Citizenship'?" *Journal of Sociology*, 42, (2006): 269–86.

20. Lynn A. Staeheli and Don Mitchell, "USA's Destiny? Regulating Space and Creating Community in American Shopping Malls. *Urban Studies*, 43 (2006): 982.

21. Staehali and Mitchell, "USA's Destiny," 987.

22. As cited in Fiske, "Shopping for Pleasure," 313.

23. Voyce, "Shopping Malls in Australia," 273.

24. van Eeden, "The Gender of Shopping Malls," 50.

25. Backes, "Reading the Shopping Mall City," 9.

26. van Eeden, "The Gender of Shopping Malls," 50.

27. van Eeden, "The Gender of Shopping Malls," 38; also see Backes; Stewart and Dickinson.

28. van Eeden, "The Gender of Shopping Malls," 38.

29. Douglas and Michael, *The Mommy Myth*; O'Reilly, *Rocking the Cradle*.

30. O'Reilly, *Rocking the Cradle*, 43.

31. Michel Foucault, *The History of Sexuality: An Introduction* (New York: Random House, 1990).

32. Fiske, "Shopping for Pleasure," 315.

33. Ibid., 314.

34. Ibid., 309.

35. Ibid., 316.

36. Ibid., 9.

37. Ibid., 9.

38. Ibid., 317.

39. All readers' comments can be found in Warner.

40. As Hays points out, "A framework for caretaking by older, independent siblings . . . is apparently not currently available in the United States," 21.

41. Douglas and Michaels, *The Mommy Myth*, 177.

42. Ibid., 81

43. Staeheli and Mitchell, "USA's Destiny?" 985.

44. Both stories involved the disappearance of children that became fodder for media frenzy.

45. Bozeman Crime Statistics, accessed June 1, 2011, http://bozeman/areaconnect.com/crime1.htm.

46. Douglas and Michaels, *The Mommy Myth*, 92.

47. Staeheli and Mitchell, "USA's Destiny?," 983.

48. Warner is the author of *Perfect Madness: Motherhood in the Age of Anxiety* (New York, Riverhead, 2005).

49. Fiske, "Shopping for Pleasure," 317.

50. Ibid., 328.

51. Although women outnumber men in the fashion industry, male designers are featured more prominently in magazines and television and receive more industry awards. See Eric Wilson, "In Fashion, Who Really Gets Ahead?," *New York Times*, December 8, 2005, g1, g11. Additionally, hiring practices in clothing stores select for conventionally beautiful women and mannequins reinforce unhealthy body images; both factors, then, reinforce the problems of "the beauty myth." See Julia Wood, *Gendered Lives: Communication, Gender, and Culture* (Boston: Wadsworth, 2011).

52. Lynn O'Brien Hallstein, *White Feminism and Contemporary Maternity: Purging Matrophobia* (New York: Palgrave, 2010)

53. According to Wood, "although the vast majority of heterosexual families today have two wage earners, the housework and the care of children, parents, and other relatives continue to be done primarily by women" Wood, *Gendered Lives*, 223.

54. There were 468 separate comments submitted. Three hundred forty of the comments included judgments of Kevane's behaviors. Of these, 267, or 78 percent, judged Kevane's behavior negatively while 73, or 15 percent, defended Kevane. Forty-five readers mentioned class specifically; each disagreed with Warner's class-based argument.

55. Fiske, "Shopping for Pleasure," 307.

56. Staeheli and Mitchell, "USA's Destiny?" 982.

References

Backes, Nancy, "Reading the Shopping Mall City," *Journal of Popular Culture*, (1997). 1–17.

Douglas, Susan J., and Meredith W. Michaels, *The Mommy Myth: The Idealization of Motherhood and How It Has Undermined Women* (New York: Free Press, 2004).

Fiske, John, "Shopping for Pleasure: Malls, Power, and Resistance," in *The Consumer Society Reader*, ed. Juliet B. Schor and Douglas B. Holt, 306–28. New York: The New Press, 2000. Originally published in John Fiske, *Reading Popular Culture* (London: Routledge, 1989).

Foucault, Michel, *The History of Sexuality: An Introduction* (New York: Random House, 1990).

Hays, Sharon, *The Cultural Contradictions of Motherhood* (New Haven: Yale University Press, 1996).

O'Brien Hallstein, D. Lynn, "Public Choices, Private Control: How Mediated Mom Labels Work Rhetorically to Dismantle the Politics of Choice and White Second Wave Feminist Successes," in *Contemplating Maternity in an Era of Choice: Explorations into Discourses of Reproduction*, ed. Sara Hayden and D. Lynn O'Brien Hallstein (Lanham, MD: Lexington Press, 2010), 5–26.

——, *White Feminism and Contemporary Maternity: Purging Matrophobia* (New York: Palgrave, 2010).

O'Reilly, Andrea, *Rocking the Cradle: Thoughts on Motherhood, Feminism, and the Possibility of Empowered Mothering* (Toronto: Demeter Press, 2006).

Staeheli, Lynn A., and Don Mitchell, "USA's Destiny? Regulating Space and Creating Community in American Shopping Malls. *Urban Studies*, 43 (2006): 977–92.

Stewart, Jessie, and Greg Dickinson, "Enunciating Locality in the Postmodern Suburb: FlatIron Crossing and the Colorado Lifestyle, *Western Journal of Communication*, 72, (2008): 280–307.

Taylor, Janelle S., Linda L. Layne, and Danielle F. Wozniak, eds. *Consuming Motherhood* (New Brunswick: Rutgers University Press, 2004).

van Eeden, Jeanne, "The Gender of Shopping Malls," *Communicatio*, 32, (2006): 38–64.

Voyce, Malcolm, "Shopping Malls in Australia: The End of Public Space and the Rise of 'Consumerist Citizenship'?" *Journal of Sociology*, 42, (2006): 269–86.

Warner, Judith, "Dangerous Resentment," *The New York Times*, 9 July 9, 2009. Acccessed July 10, 2009. *http://warner.blogs.nytimes.com/2009/07/09/don't-hate-her-because-shes-educated/?emc=etal.*

Wilson, Eric, "In Fashion, Who Really Gets Ahead?," *The New York Times*, December 8, 2005, g1, g11.

Wood, Julia, *Gendered Lives: Communication, Gender, and Culture* (Boston: Wadsworth, 2011).

8
"Don't Worry, Mama Will Fix It!"
Playing with the Mama Myth in Video Games

Shira Chess

For many, video game characters call to mind various representations of masculinity: the criminals of the *Grand Theft Auto* series, the soldiers of *Halo* games, or the masculine absurd in the land of *Super Mario Bros.* Within these masculine playspaces, feminine representations are generally the hypersexualized Lara Crofts, or else the helpless princess being saved.[1] This, in large part, has to do with audience: until recently video games were created for primarily masculine audiences. While this audience has begun to shift in the past decade, white masculinity still remains the primary mode of gaming.[2] With recent marketing attempts from Nintendo specifically targeting women audiences, it seems that more mothers are being targeted as potential game players (or, in the very least, game *consumers*).[3] This consumerist move of gaming companies to commodify the feminine player (and character) has created new genres, styles, and characters meant to appeal to this emerging audience.

With this emerging market, new characters have begun to seep into our cultural milieu, redefining both who is permitted to play and who we are permitted to play *with* (i.e., the video game avatars and key characters). At the same time, it is important to remember that games are not just play spaces but also consumer spaces—games that are sold in attempts to appeal to feminine audiences often reproduce and commodify the tastes of women, often (re)constructing a kind of white, middle-class, femininity. As evidence, recent game franchises such as the *Diner Dash, Cake Mania*, and *Cooking Mama* (all of which are guided by desexualized, white, middle-class, feminine avatars) have leapt in popularity, in part due to the expanding market.

The following addresses one such game—the *Cooking Mama* series. The series features its title character, Mama, who instructs players how to cook an endless menu of virtual meals. More than teaching cooking, however, the game-space specifically teaches the practice of motherhood and mothering in gender-specific ways, making motherhood not only playable but also commodifiable. By simplifying the tasks of motherhood in distinct ways, *Cooking Mama* turns motherhood into commodifiable production. In the game, motherhood becomes simplified to domestic tasks and to practices of melodrama. In turn, the cultural (re)production of motherhood both allows for changes in a shifting market (the emergence of more female players) and, through its main character, assigns specific kinds of problematic play.

Mama's (re)production of motherhood is, however, pure performance. Motherhood, in this series, becomes a performance of melodramatic mother-subject who sacrifices her own needs and desires for those of the player. The player, in turn, becomes both mother and child—rewarded and chastised by Mama's capricious moods and ultimately trained to conform to an idealization of "the mommy myth" (or the Mama Myth). In this, Mama reproduces white, middle-class motherhood and trains players to perform this form of motherhood, reinforcing the Mama Myth through melodrama and overvaluation of domesticity. While it does these things playfully and with some humor, the reproduction of the Mama Myth still has resonance because of the game series' cultural importance. The game itself could not function without the driving influence of the Mama Myth. Given the dearth of mother characters in video games, it becomes a rich place to explore the inherent tensions between motherhood and gaming specifically, and also gender and gaming in a more general sense. At the same time, Mama's performance of motherhood is a form of commodification: her reductive practices make mothering a commodity meant to be sold to the aforementioned emerging market of feminine gamers. In what follows, I contextualize the game in relation to the evolving video game industry and the Mama avatar to its Anime roots. My analysis examines how the game series commodifies practices of motherhood by focusing on how players reproduce mothering practices and interact in domestically defined games spaces. These dynamics of game play reflect the prevalence of melodrama (common to representation of motherhood in film and television) as well as the Mama Myth associated with intensive mothering.

Situating Cooking Mama in the Video Game Industry

In considering individual video games and video game series, it becomes important to consider the political economy of the video game industry as a whole. Casey O'Donnell explains, "Game development is a creative collaborative process involving numerous disciplines rooted in a particular culture producing creative, artistic, and culturally important works," but in this the video game sits at the precipice of art and commerce.[4] Video games, like other forms of mass media, develop at the intersection between the artistic endeavors of creators/designers and the economic interests of publishers. According to Peter Zackariasson and Timothy Wilson, the participants in this system include developers, consumers, producers, and IP-owners, among others. Using Actor Network Theory, Zackariasson and Wilson continue to suggest that "these participants could be described as making up the core of the value chain in video game development—from developer to consumer—where each actor contributes and adds value to the video game."[5] But one can assume that as both art and commerce, a video game is able to add not only financial value to a game but also can serve as a guidepost of both larger cultural and industry-centric values.

And, indeed, the video game industry's values are already complicated both in terms of female players as well as female developers. The video game industry is primarily composed of a male workforce. At last survey, only about 11 percent of the video game industry's workers were women.[6] At the same time, industry statistics report about 45 percent of all gamers as women.[7] Within this disconnect lies part of the problem—very few women are actually making and designing video games for women audiences. Often this boundary is described by a division between "hardcore" versus "casual" gaming—hardcore games are considered big-budget, expensive video games that are often geared toward male audiences, whereas casual games often refer to games played on mobile devices or quick downloadable computer games. This dichotomy, as I have written elsewhere, is a false one. Both men and women play games that fit into both categories, and play styles often overlap.[8]

In recent years, feminist scholarship has begun to question the practices and values underlying the video game industry, not only in terms of both how it promotes more female gamers but also how it treats women that work in video game development.[9] For example, a hashtag (#1reasonwhy) became viral on Twitter when women who currently or previously had worked in the video game industry offered examples of sexism as the "one reason why" there were not more women video game developers.[10] At the same time, organizations such as Penny Arcade have repeatedly been accused of promoting sexist and gender-insensitive topics in their industry talks and web comics. Anastasia Salter and Bridget Blodgett write that because of shifting audiences, "Increasing presence of female gamers is met at the contentious boundary by pushing femininity to the outskirts of gaming spaces, thus reaffirming the role of the masculine with hardcore gamer identity."[11]

Given this recurring theme of "pushing femininity to the outskirts" in gaming, it seems both curious and compelling to have a primary character embroiled in the complexities of mothering and motherhood. As an ultrafeminine figure, Mama plays an important role in both figuring out how the ordinary woman is seen within the larger scope of the masculine dominated video game industry and also as an important character to understanding how motherhood is commodified and fetishized for audiences.

The primary function of Mama, the games' protagonist, is to instruct players how to cook an endless menu of virtual meals. Mama is featured as the main character in several food-related games for the Nintendo DS and Nintendo Wii (*Cooking Mama: Dinner with Friends*, *Cooking Mama: Chop and Shop*, *Cooking Mama: Cook Off*, and *Cooking Mama: World Kitchen*) as well as an increasing number of non-culinary games (*Gardening Mama*, *Crafting Mama*, *Babysitting Mama*). In fact, the producer of the *Cooking Mama* games reported that over a million copies had sold by 2007 in Europe alone.[12] Additionally, with fan sites suggesting *Cooking Mama*–themed crafts,[13] and an "unauthorized" PETA version of the game,[14] the series clearly has cultural resonance that exceeds gaming spaces. With recent additions to the series and a Facebook version, the popularity of this game is undeniable. While her name shifts in each game (i.e., "Cooking Mama" becomes "Gardening Mama" depending on which game you are playing), "Mama" herself remains a consistent force throughout the franchise, guiding characters in gameplay with maternal panache. Mama, herself, remains completely unchanged in design and character throughout these games. Thus, despite the moniker "Cooking Mama" within some games, she is simply "Mama" within the context of the entire franchise (and throughout the remainder of this paper).

Who's Your Mama?

In considering the primary avatar of the *Cooking Mama* series, it is worth discussing common constructions of women's bodies in video games. In part, because video games are so often designed and programmed by men, the images of women characters (both playable and nonplayable) in popular video games often physically align with gendered stereotypes. This is particularly the case in aforementioned "hardcore" gaming. Female characters are often either damsels in distress or hypersexualized. Nina Huntemann explains, "The sexualization of women's bodies in video games has parralled advances in game technology. As the graphics capabilities of computers and video game consoles have improved, game designers have increased the visual detail of backgrounds, objects, and characters."[15] To this end, so-called hardcore video games often feature women characters that are buxom, small-waisted, and adorned in tight clothing. Casual gaming, in turn, often features less-sexualized and physically nonthreatening characters, such as Flo in *Diner Dash*.[16]

It is with this in mind that it is worth considering Mama's physical form. A cherubic, Caucasian, nonsexualized character, Mama is garbed in aprons and pastel colors and both advises and chastises players on their virtual domestic chores. In some ways, Mama appears to be a white mammy. Yet, as I will discuss later in this essay, race plays a far more complicated and pivotal role in the construction of this character. Regardless, Mama's initial appearance is nonthreatening. Mama is typically depicted from the chest upwards, wearing a blue apron and a scarf in her hair. She wields no weaponry beyond a spatula, and she is clearly meant to be physically comforting in appearance—much like one would expect from a mother character. Most notable is Mama's facial expression—her smile is a large semicircle and eyes are shown with large diamond-shaped sparkles in them. In many ways, Mama embodies the myth of perfect femininity—her whiteness and lack of sexuality makes her nonthreatening, and the domestic tasks she teaches are both gendered and racially defined. Completely consumed with domestic affairs and designed with a surplus of pink, she is a white, feminine caricature.

The game itself is mostly without narrative structure, and the player is given dish after dish to prepare using a variety of movements such as chopping, mixing, using a blender, and frying. The player performs these actions either with a stylus, Wii-remote, or other interface (depending on the version of the game). The actions are often monotonous but still require a certain degrees of speed, skill, and dexterity: stirring pots quickly, chopping with precision, pouring things accurately, and adding ingredients at the precise moment. Each recipe (referred to as a "dish" in the game) is composed of several actions that cumulate to form the final food product. Points are given at the end of the recipe to determine the player's score, and when foods are properly cooked the player is given new dishes to prepare. Primarily, the variety and interest in the game derives from the different cookable dishes, and unlocking new foods. The food choices range from American comfort foods to Japanese fare (the game originated in Japan) to other international fare (although generally limited to American, European, or East Asian menus). Dishes that the player can cook include such exotic culinary delights as Udon, Chili Sauce Shrimp, meatballs, brioche, and many more. Players can also practice tasks, combine recipes, and design Mama's clothing and kitchen in various versions of the game. In more recent versions, the player is able to compete against other players. Early versions of the game did not directly involve purchasing goods, although later versions of the game have taken more consumerist routes. For example, in *Cooking Mama: Chop and Shop*, players are asked to purchase goods they will later use as ingredients. Thus, as newer games are released, players have been asked to correlate Mama's domestic tasks to consumerist tasks.

Mama stands at a point of judgment with all of the in-game actions—she functions as both the game's coach as well as the game's avatar. Because we never see a game avatar cooking (beyond hands), the player is bound to associate her own actions with the actions of Mama. This complicated relationship between the player and Mama means that (to some extent) the player is both the cook and the judge of the in-game cooking they are partaking in. In one version of the game, *Cooking Mama: Cooking with Friends*, players are given the option to cook for Mama or for one of Mama's friends. In this version, the game characters function more as audience than as helper—and an easily disgruntled audience at that. While the player cooks, Mama continues to appear with words of encouragement and criticism. Alternatively, when cooking for so-called "friends," they patiently wait to be served each kind of food (each game character has their own preferences). If the food is not to their liking, the friends reject the player's food—not unlike real-life picky family members.[17] Thus, cooking in *Cooking Mama*, in many ways, resembles a domestic experience that many women have at home—endless work and only mild appreciation. Mama's experience is similar to many women's experiences, and the never-ending set of menus and tasks shows a routinizing of feminine work.

More important are Mama's remarks when a task is completed. In each of the *Mama* games (regardless of the version) there are three possible outcomes for a player's cooking efforts. When successful, Mama exclaims to the player, "Perfect! Just as skilled as Mama." If a player does average, she applauds the player and remarks, "Good job. Keep going!" Finally if a player fails a task they are scolded, "Don't worry, Mama will fix it." For this final answer, Mama's sparkling eyes and big smile are replaced by burning eyes and a frown. With these responses the player is being judged by, and against, Mama. These responses will be discussed in more detail later in this essay, but the rejoinders are constantly judging the player in terms of her abilities to keep up with Mama within the drudgery of domesticity. Even the response, "Keep going!" reminds the player of the never-ending tasks of motherhood.

There are certainly many ways to look at the Mama games, and different audience members will pull in their own different experiences to enhance potential interpretations. Jesper Juul, for example, discusses the game as being pure abstraction. He explains, "*Cooking Mama*, like other representational games, has a *level of abstraction*—the player can only act on a certain level, outside which the world is either crudely implemented as in the case of the ingredients, simply represented as in the case of the table cloth, or simply absent, as in the case of the world outside the kitchen."[18] These abstractions, according to Juul, define the game play and structure how the player sees and understands the game world.

The complexities of the game are manifold, though—particularly where race is concerned. Because (as already noted) the game was originally Japanese and later introduced to American popular culture, depictions of race are ambiguous even while appearing to be Caucasian. Mia Consalvo[19] mentions *Cooking Mama* in a discussion of how Japanese culture affects American gaming. She explains that the gaming industry has "historical and cultural roots" and "strong business interests" in Japanese culture. She elaborates, "That influence and power extends to Japanese companies (such as Nintendo, Sega, CapCom, and Square Enix), Japanese visual styles (such as super-deformed characters and anime-like images), as well as an extensive list of games that have influenced successive generations of game designers around the world."[20]

In considering Mama's physical appearance it becomes essential to think of her in terms of her relationship to her Anime roots. On one hand, despite being a Japanese character, Mama is undeniably a caricature of not just motherhood but also of whiteness and *white motherhood*. This is complicated because of ways that Anime and Japanese visual culture often integrates white features into cartoon characters. But, on the other hand, Anime scholar Susan Napier[21] also warns to be careful in critiques of this whiteness. She explains that many who critique what appears to be "non-Japanese" or "Western" depictions of characters do not always understand the larger cultural implications of this style. Napier explains, "In fact, while many anime texts do include figures with blond hair, it is perhaps more to say that rather than a 'Western' style of figuration, the characters are drawn in what might be called 'anime' style. This style ranges from the broadly grotesque drawing of characters with shrunken torsos and oversized heads of some anime comedy to the elongated figures with huge eyes and endless flowing hair that populate many romance and adventure stories."[22] Rather than being a question of whiteness, Napier argues, this visual style offers "an alternative world to its Japanese audiences."[23] Analyzing the complexities of Anime style and the relationship to race is well beyond the scope of this essay, but it is important to recognize that Mama's whiteness is a multicultural whiteness.

At the same time, whiteness and class are ever-present themes in the game. The character's relationship to domestic chores makes her both privileged and beholden. The character's focus on domestic chores and "happy housewife" perspective makes the chores and domestic tasks appear to be easy and fun. Mama, of course does not have to worry about fitting her cooking schedule in between a full-time job (or jobs), making her whiteness appear to be a form of privilege. At the same time, she is constantly beholden to her domestic chores—cooking on demand, she cannot escape them and is not permitted to be anything beyond them. She is, in essence, a domestic slave, making her kerchief and "mammy"-like appearance a bit more noteworthy. Additionally, given her Japanese roots and popularity with American audiences, Mama appears to be a kind of "whiteface," playing the role of whiteness (if not actually white) because it gives her a racial ambiguity that makes her whiteness entirely invisible. Thus, in terms of both race and class, Mama remains complex and ultimately ambivalent.

At the same time, it is impossible to ignore that the game reproduces this white, middle-class motherhood and domesticity in ways that are clearly meant to be compelling to female audiences. While both men and women play the game, it is clearly marketed to have appeal to girl and women audiences, given its white, feminine main character, pink packaging, and domestic gameplay. It is, then, relevant to ask how meaning and abstractions gleaned from how the game (re)produces and commodifies practices of motherhood. This question will be addressed throughout the remainder of this essay.

Mama as Mother Figure

Mama's role of mother in the game series comes through in her mothering practices. The game places a heavy emphasis on the relationship between mother and child—the caregiver and the person who is cared for. In the *Cooking Mama* games, Mama certainly takes on the role of the caregiver, the person who is performing "mothering" through guidance and guidelines. This puts the player in the role of child—the one who is being "mothered." At the same time, when being tasked to cook for others (Mama's "friends") the player is taking on the role of mother, as well, feeding and capitulating finicky eaters. Throughout the games, the role of who plays "mother" shifts between the player and Mama. This is clearest when the player gets responses from Mama, who declares, "Perfect! Just as good as Mama!" and "Don't Worry, Mama will fix it!" When successful, the player transforms into Mama, whereas failure reminds the player that they are being mothered and that the task must be "fixed" by the real mother.

Motherhood, in the game, is entirely linked to consumptive practices—in order to be mother, you must purchase and play mother. Motherhood has been commodified here, and the practices of mothering are something purchasable and replicatable. While there are several cooking games on the market, what is unique and identifiable about the *Cooking Mama* series is not the foods, but is Mama—she (and the motherhood she performs) is what is being bought and sold. Mama is the brand of motherhood.

To understand the distinction between actual motherhood versus Mama's commodified representation of motherhood, it is useful to consider Judith

Butler's concept of "performativity."[24] With this term Butler is not referring to conscious performance but rather repurposing Louis Althusser's notion of "interpellation."[25] By interpellation, Althusser was referring to ways that individuals get hailed by specific ideologies that already resonate with them, making them subjects of that ideology. Because these ideologies already have previous resonance, he insists that at the moment of interpellation the individual is "always already" a subject of that ideology. In *Gender Trouble*, Butler uses Althusser's notion of interpellation for gender construction, which she insists is "always already" a person's sex, meaning that perhaps sex and gender are not necessarily culturally distinct. Gender, she insists, is produced "performatively" and regulated through social constructions of gender. Essentially, despite the agency that sounds inherent in the term "performativity," it shows how little agency we have when it comes to gender: while we might perform our genders, we are not able to choose them. And just as gender can be understood as a performance of expectations of sex difference, there is a distinction between actual motherhood and the performance of motherhood, done by Mama.

Mama's role is not just as mother but as *performing* motherhood. Her performativity is not shown through being a birth mother but rather through domesticity, caregiving, and melodrama: her performance teaches players what motherhood should look like. So while the aforementioned distinction between birth and cultural mother implies that boys and men, too, can take on the role of mothering and motherhood, the hyperfeminine depiction of Mama reinforces a feminine symbolic mother. This performance of motherhood becomes the commodified product of the game. With her clothing, face, and body, as well as her actions, Mama is not just a mother, she is a caricature of motherhood. She is an objectified construction of motherhood that reinforces white, middle-class stereotypes of motherhood and denies the player any other version of motherhood. The player, in turn, is being virtually asked to reproduce and perform this motherhood back to the game. Through the performance of motherhood, the game essentializes all mothering practices down to a purchasable product.

The performance of motherhood in the game is reinforced by the player's reproduction of mothering practices. Nancy Chodorow[26] has argued that mothering (in the nongame world) is "reproduced on a number of different levels. . . . Women's capacities for mothering and abilities to get gratification from it are strongly internalized and psychologically enforced, and are built developmentally into the feminine psychic structure."[27] The mothering in *Cooking Mama* is similarly complex, because it is reproduced and shared between the Mama and the player. Through being trained by Mama (the idealized mother), the player learns how to play mom, and then reproduces the practices when cooking for Mama's friends. By being both nurtured by and nurturing in-game characters the player is deftly being trained in the role of Mama. And because Mama is being commodified, as this transfer takes place, the player's reproduction of motherhood, too, becomes part of this commodification. Regardless of who is playing, the practices and internalization of motherhood becomes symbolically transferred throughout the games.

Performing Mom, Playing Domesticity

Mama's domestic "expertise" helps to reinforce her reproduction of motherhood. All of the games deal with domestic tasks to varying extents (cooking, shopping, crafting, gardening, and babysitting). Obviously, both men and women are capable of doing these tasks (and often do). Yet, collectively in the games, they combine to form a set of domestic (and feminine) chores. Because these domestic chores replicate many of the things women commonly have to do, the play space becomes full of ambiguities, and play is minimized to everyday, mundane responsibilities. Domestic tasks have long been linked to women's work, and thus, women's oppression. According to Ruth Schwartz Cowan in *More Work for Mother*: "The allocation of housework to women is . . . a social convention which developed during the nineteenth century because of a specific set of material and cultural conditions. It is a convention so deeply embedded in our individual and collective unconsciousnesses that even the profound changes wrought by the twentieth century have not yet shaken it."[28] Thus, while many women have found careers out of the household in the past fifty years, domestic work is still often associated with femininity. For many women domesticity comes with implications of guilt and anxiety.

Certainly, motherhood is more nuanced than a set of tasks or chores. However, by not allowing Mama to have a role that exceeds these domestic tasks and chores (or teaching the tasks and chores to the player), we are left with the impression that her sense of being "Mama" is inextricably linked to the fact that she cooks, shops, gardens, crafts, and babysits. By her name we are told that she is a "mama," and by her expertise we are taught what a "mama" is good at. And just as the player is being asked to reproduce motherhood, she is also being asked to reproduce it through (primarily) domestic chores.

Cooking Mama, in many ways, is a rarity: it is uncommon to see game spaces where domesticity plays such an integral role. In the paper "A Game of One's Own," the Ludica Group[29] suggests that domestic spaces are often absent in video games and that inclusion of these spaces might instigate more gender-inclusive game design. But the authors also warn that, "Although domestic space can be a site of play and pleasure . . . it can also connote stifling captivity for women."[30] Thus the domestic settings of *Cooking Mama* create potentially ambivalent game spaces for feminine players: on the one hand they provide a space that might be familiar and comfortable, while on the other hand they can create anxieties, because of the expectations between femininity, domesticity, and motherhood.

Cooking and food, in particular, have implications in terms of the domestic performance in the Cooking Mama games.[31] Food, cooking, and the serving of food is wrought with gendered anxiety. In *Food Is Love: Advertising and Gender Roles in Modern America*, Kathleen Parkin[32] explains how advertising food long has been used to suggest that "food is love" in the domestic sphere. According to Parkin, food products are historically marketed to women as a means of garnering familial love. She explains: "Food advertisers . . . exploited the connection between food preparation and love toward women, enlisting mild allusions, floating hearts and pecks on the cheek to demonstrate how her food selection accorded her affection. The message was clear: when she chose such a high quality, tasty product she was entitled to receive love and credit for her pains."[33] Similarly, the interface of *Cooking Mama* suggests that virtual food, too, is love. Littered with similar "floating hearts" and involving the affection of nonplayer characters when a food is properly cooked, the game helps to reinforce the "food is love" message found in other forms of popular culture and advertising. Even though the player is not actually cooking real food, she reproduces Mama's performance of motherhood through the act of cooking. And just, as with advertising, this generates simplistic representation of love (from Mama and from her friends). As the player gains expertise and *becomes* Mama ("Perfect! Just as good as Mama!"), "food is love" themes become ingrained in the core gameplay and the commodifiable performance of mothering.

Melodrama Mama

Just as domesticity and caregiving are essential parts of how motherhood is represented, so is the importance of melodrama in representations of motherhood. Melodrama is a dramatic genre that according to E. Ann Kaplan[34] is particularly relevant to maternalism. She explains, "Centered on the female protagonist and on ostensibly female concerns (love, seduction, motherhood, marriage, children, abandonment, jealousy, role-conflicts, etc), maternal melodramas . . . address the female spectator in ways other genres rarely do."[35] The melodrama is characterized by feminine style, extreme emotionalism, changing roles, and (most importantly) the role of the mother. Kaplan explains that melodrama centralizes the "mother-as-subject"[36] in many Hollywood films.

Throughout the *Cooking Mama* games, the player is embroiled in melodrama. She is constantly negotiating between her role as child and role as mother, dealing with the extreme emotional responses of Mama, and involving a form of self-denial characterized by sacrificial motherhood. This use of maternal melodrama allows the game to turn "motherhood" into a fragile subject-object, where the player is permitted to interact with the melodrama in a superficial way: the melodrama is purely on the surface and does not deal with any real emotional strife. At the same time the game objectifies this kind of motherhood: Mama (in her anger and praise) is overly cute and her threat is contained.

Primarily, *Cooking Mama*'s melodrama is a result of the player's actions and success or failure in properly cooking dishes. As already noted, when the player is successful at cooking Mama declares, "Perfect! Just as good as Mama!" at which point she transforms into the mother-subject. But upon failure to cook something properly, Mama scolds the player, "Don't worry, Mama will fix it." Judging verbally alone, this might seem to be a soothing remark that a mother might say to a child (again reinforcing that Mama is parenting the player in the player's reproduction of motherhood). But upon this failing rejoinder, Mama's facial expression becomes disturbingly angry for the first time in the game, eyes ablaze and her wide smile turned into a disapproving frown. The menacing and angry look on Mama's face in this response implies a threat—more like "Don't make Mama come fix that!" She appears almost to be a frustrated authority figure. With her fists raised in the air, Mama's previous caricature of femininity is now consumed with melodrama and resentment. Underlying these melodramatics is her own frustration: because the player failed at their reproduction of motherhood (via cooking tasks) she has now forced Mama to do the work for her and "fix it." Mama's previously gentle coaching transforms into the cry of a woman always tasked with fixing the mistakes of others. As exemplar, she must take on the burdens of all, as is the burden of being the exemplar "mama."

Secondarily, the role of melodrama in the game is apparent through the self-denial of creating virtual, inedible food. The tasks of both Mama and the player, alike, are in creating the food that others will ultimately eat. While the player is given descriptions of these foods and spends the majority of gameplay time constructing these foods, they are impotent to enjoy the food for the function one general cooks: eating. Instead, the player must be in a constant mode of self-denial, cooking things that will never touch their lips.

This form of self-denial of appetite is a central part of constructions of femininity, according to Susan Bordo.[37] Bordo discusses the "cultural containment of the female appetite" where, "women are most gratified by feeding and nourishing *others*, not themselves."[38] As such, the *Cooking Mama* games reinforce this ideological stronghold where women are expected to deny themselves the enjoyment of sustenance. Mama and the player share a stance of self-denial: neither will ever enjoy the abstracted food that they cook but must watch others enjoy the efforts of their labor. This self-denial maintains the game's melodrama: Mama never gets anything and does everything for others. Melodrama, thus, serves to reinforce both the roles and expectations of motherhood for the player. It helps to reinforce what I will characterize in the next section as the *Mama Myth*.

The Mama Myth

In many ways, Mama neatly folds into what Susan Douglas and Meredith Michaels refer to as an affect of "the new momism."[39] They explain that new momism constitutes the "mommy myth," in which "the insistence that no woman is truly complete or fulfilled unless she has kids, that women remain the best primary caretakers of children, and that to be a remotely decent mother a woman has to devote her entire physical, psychological, emotional, and intellectual being 24/7, to her children. The new momism is a highly romanticized and yet demanding view of motherhood in which the standards for success are impossible to meet."[40] According to Douglas and Michaels, the effects of pernicious momism creep into all forms of popular culture (film, television, advertising, celebrity culture, etc.) to normalize the assumption that all women should not only be mothers but also meet impossible standards in their mothering skills. Within the mommy myth, motherhood itself becomes commodified—while being the perfect mother is not something one can achieve, women can purchase products that help one be a "better" mother.

The *Cooking Mama* games stand at an interesting place in light of the momist culture that Douglas and Michaels are referring to. If the player is understood to be Mama's representative child (being trained into motherhood) then she fits neatly into the mommy myth—her goal, her entire raison d'être, is making sure that the player-as-child is fulfilled and (more importantly) is ultimately on track to take over Mama's role. Her perfectionism and diligence in making sure the player learns the value of domesticity, importance of melodramatic motherhood, and importance of caregiving (as opposed to care of oneself) is central to the game's dynamics. As a commodified version of motherhood, the game becomes yet another product to teach mothering practices. In essence, the game could not function without the Mama Myth.

The connection between the Mama Myth and the Mommy Myth is most overt in one of the noncooking games: *Babysitting Mama*.[41] In this Nintendo Wii version of the game, the player is given a baby doll to wrap around the Wii-remote. To play the game properly, the player must coddle, rock, and hold the doll as one would an actual child. The *Babysitting Mama* website explains of the game play, "Babysit and care for 6 different babies while playing 40 fun activities including peek-a-boo, teaching baby to walk, chasing a puppy and more!" Easily, the Mama Myth here is equivalent to the Mommy Myth, suggesting that the player juggle six babies at once. As symbolic mother, the player is expected to conflate the difficulties of motherhood with "40 fun activities" and that "teaching baby to walk" is on par with "playing peek-a-boo." Literally, the game is training players to perform and reproduce motherhood. While players obviously might have their own individual experiences (and their own agency in how they play the game), they are constantly being asked to confront and play with (and as) these troublesome stereotypes.

Conclusion

In *The Myths of Motherhood: How Culture Reinvents the Good Mother* Shari Thurer[42] deftly provides a history of how the mother has been formed and reformed: "For thousands of years, because of her awesome ability to spew forth a child, mother has been feared and revered. She has been the subject of taboos and witch hunts, mandatory pregnancy and confinement in a separate sphere. She has endured appalling insults and perpetual marginalization. She has also been the subject of glorious painting, chivalry, and idealization. Through it all, she has rarely been consulted. She is an object, not a subject."[43] This objectification of motherhood helps to foster unrealistic expectations, sexism, and idealization. Popular culture depictions help to reinforce the objectification of motherhood and provide a means of maintaining this marginalization.

One could argue that while the *Cooking Mama* games do not sexually objectify the main character, there is an equally problematic objectification at play through commodification—motherhood itself becomes what is being sold by the game. While previously in this paper Mama has been referred to as the mother-subject, perhaps more accurately she can be referred to as mother-object. The two-dimensional character (both literally and figuratively) reaffirms historical reproductions of motherhood in art, media, and culture. But while the character, Mama, is a two-dimensional mother-object, the player, transformed into mother through the process of the game, is truly the mother-subject. In reproducing tropes of motherhood through domestic chores, melodrama, and becoming the embodiment of the Mama Myth, it ceases to matter whether the player is a mother in the real world, or for that matter is female, male, adult or child: all are able to equally reproduce Mama's tasks commodifying (and simplifying) the complexities of motherhood.

Notes

1. Sheri Graner Ray, *Gender Inclusive Game Design Expanding the Market* (Charles River Media, 2004), http://site.ebrary.com/id/10061187.

2. Janine Fron et al., "The Hegemony of Play," in *Situated Play*, 2007.

3. Shira Chess, "A 36–24–36 Cerebrum: Productivity, Gender, and Video Game Advertising," *Critical Studies in Media Communication* 28, no. 3 (2011): 230–52.

4. Casey O'Donnell, "This Is Not a Software Industry," in *The Video Game Industry: Formation, Present State, and Future*, ed. Peter Zackariasson and Timothy L. Wilson (New York: NY: Routledge, 2012).

5. Peter Zackariasson and Timothy L. Wilson, "Introduction," in *The Video Game Industry: Formation, Present State, and Future*, ed. Peter Zackariasson and Timothy L. Wilson (New York: Routledge, 2012).

6. *Game Developer Demographics: An Exploration of Workforce Diversity* (International Game Developer's Association, October 2005), http://archives.igda.org/diversity/IGDA_DeveloperDemographics_Oct05.pdf.

7. Dan Hewitt, *Women Comprise Nearly Half of Gamer Population* (Entertainment Software Assocation, July 11, 2013), http://www.theesa.com/newsroom/release_detail.asp?releaseID=202.

8. Shira Chess, "Youthful White Male Industry Seeks 'Fun'-loving Middle-aged Women for Video Games—no Strings Attached," in *The Routledge Companion to Media & Gender*, ed. Cynthia Carter, Linda Steiner, and Lisa McLaughlin (New York: Routledge, 2014), 168–78.

9. O'Donnell, "This Is Not a Software Industry."

10. Betsy Isaacson, "#1 ReasonWhy Reveals Sexism Rampant in the Gaming Industry," *Huffington Post*, November 29, 2012, http://www.huffingtonpost.com/2012/11/29/1reasonwhy-reveals-sexism-gaming-industry_n_2205204.html.

11. Anastasia Salter and Bridget Blodgett, "Hypermasculinity & Dickwolves: The Contentious Role of Women in the New Gaming Public," *Journal of Broadcasting & Electronic Media* 56, no. 3 (2012): 401–16, doi:10.1080/08838151.2012.705199.

12. Emma Boyes, "Cooking Mama Serves up 1 Million," *Gamespot UK*, December 6, 2007, http://www.gamespot.com/ds/puzzle/cookingmama/news.html?sid=6183713.

13. Earnest Cavalli, "Custom Cooking Mama Apron Trumps Official Swag," *Wired*, April 28, 2008, http://geekcrafts.com/cooking-mama-apron.

14. PETA, "Cooking Mama Responds to Peta Parody," *PETA*, November 20, 2008, http://www.peta.org/b/thepetafiles/archive/2008/11/20/cooking-mama-responds-to-peta-parody.aspx.

15. Nina B. Huntemann, "Pixel Pinups: Images of Women in Video Games," in *Race/Gender/Media*, ed. Rebecca Ann Lind (Boston: Allyn & Bacon, 2010).

16. Shira Chess, "Going with the Flo," *Feminist Media Studies* 12, no. 1 (2012): 83–99, doi:10.1080/14680777.2011.558350.

17. In this particular game, despite the game's international origins, all of the "friends" are Caucasian. In later games (such as *Cooking Mama: World Kitchen*) a handful of Asian characters are introduced. That said, for the most part the games feature primarily Caucasian characters.

18. Jesper Juul, "A Certain Level of Abstraction" (presented at the DiGRA: Situated Play, Tokyo, 2007), http://www.jesperjuul.net/text/acertainlevel/.

19. Mia Consalvo, "Visiting the Floating World: Tracing a Cultural History of Games through Japan and America" (presented at the DiGRA: Situated Play, Tokyo, 2007), http://www.digra.org/digital-library/publications/visiting-the-floating-world-tracing-a-cultural-history-of-games-through-japan-and-america/.

20. Ibid., 136.

21. Susan Napier, *Anime from Akira to How's Moving Castle* (New York: Palgrave Macmillan, 2005).

22. Ibid., 25.

23. Ibid.

24. Judith Butler, *Gender Trouble: Feminism and the Subversion of Identity* (New York: Routledge, 1990).

25. Louis Althusser, "Ideology and Ideological State Apparatuses," in *Cultural Theory & Popular Culture*, ed. John Storey, 3rd ed. (London, England: Pearson, 1971).

26. Nancy Chodorow, *The Reproduction of Mothering: Psychoanalysis and the Sociology of Gender* (Berkeley: University of California Press, 1978).

27. Ibid., 39.

28. Ruth Cowan, *More Work for Mother: The Ironies of Household Technology from the Open Heart to the Microwave* (New York: Basic Books, 1999), 150.

29. Janine Fron, Tracy Fullerton, Jacquelyn Ford Morie, Celia Pearce, "A Game of One's Own: Towards a New Gendered Poetics of Digital Space," (Proceedings from perthDAC, 2004).

30. Janine Fron et al., "A Game of One's Own: Towards a New Gendered Poetics of Digital Space," 2004, 5, http://lmc.gatech.edu/~cpearce3/PearcePubs/LudicaDAC07.pdf.

31. Here, I am specifically referring to the cooking games, and not the gardening, crafting, or babysitting games in the franchise.

32. Kathleen Parkin, *Food Is Love: Advertising and Gender Roles in Modern America* (Philadelpha: University of Pennsylvania Press, 2006).

33. Ibid., 40.

34. E. Ann Kaplan, "Sex, Work, and Motherhood: Materal Subjectivity in Recent Visual Culture," in *Representations of Motherhood*, ed. D. Bassin, M. Honey, and M.M. Kaplan (New Haven, CT:Yale University Press, 1992).

35. Ibid., 70.

36. Kaplan, "Sex, Work, and Motherhood," 256.

37. Susan Bordo, *Unbearable Weight: Feminism, Western Culture, and the Body* (Berkeley, Calif.: University of California Press, 2003).

38. Ibid., 118.

39. Susan J Douglas and Meredith Michaels, *The Mommy Myth:The Idealization of Motherhood and How It Has Undermined All Women.* (New York, NY: Simon & Schuster, 2004).

40. Ibid., 4.

41. Unquestionably, *Babysitting Mama* is meant for younger girl demographics (even the game advertising shows a young girl playing the game). While this game is less universally relevant than the *Cooking Mama* games (which appeal to broader demographics), it seems relevant to consider how motherhood functions in this game.

42. Shari Thurer, *The Myths of Motherhood: How Culture Reinvents the Good Mother* (New York, NY: Penguin Books, 2004).

43. Ibid., 229.

References

Althusser, Louis. "Ideology and Ideological State Apparatuses." In *Cultural Theory & Popular Culture*, edited by John Storey, 3rd ed. London, England: Pearson, 1971.

Bordo, Susan. *Unbearable Weight: Feminism, Western Culture, and the Body*. Berkeley, Calif.: University of California Press, 2003.

Boyes, Emma. "Cooking Mama Serves up 1 Million." *Gamespot UK*, December 6, 2007. http://www.gamespot.com/ds/puzzle/cookingmama/news.html?sid=6183713.

Butler, Judith. *Gender Trouble: Feminism and the Subversion of Identity*. New York: Routledge, 1990.

Cavalli, Earnest. "Custom Cooking Mama Apron Trumps Official Swag." *Wired*, April 28, 2008. http://geekcrafts.com/cooking-mama-apron.

Chess, Shira. "A 36–24–36 Cerebrum: Productivity, Gender, and Video Game Advertising." *Critical Studies in Media Communication* 28, no. 3 (2011): 230–52. doi:10.1080/15295036.2010.515234.

——. "Going with the Flo." *Feminist Media Studies* 12, no. 1 (2012): 83–99. doi:10.1080/14680777.2011.558350.

——. "Youthful White Male Industry Seeks 'Fun'-loving Middle-aged Women for Video Games—no Strings Attached." In *The Routledge Companion to Media & Gender*, edited by Cynthia Carter, Linda Steiner, and Lisa McLaughlin, 168–78. New York: Routledge, 2014.

Chodorow, Nancy. *The Reproduction of Mothering: Psychoanalysis and the Sociology of Gender*. Berkeley: University of California Press, 1978.
Consalvo, Mia. "Visiting the Floating World: Tracing a Cultural History of Games through Japan and America." Tokyo, 2007. http://www.digra.org/digital-library/publications/visiting-the-floating-world-tracing-a-cultural-history-of-games-through-japan-and-america/.
Cowan, Ruth. *More Work for Mother: The Ironies of Household Technology from the Open Heart to the Microwave*. New York: Basic Books, 1999.
Douglas, Susan J, and Meredith Michaels. *The Mommy Myth: The Idealization of Motherhood and How It Has Undermined All Women*. New York, NY: Simon & Schuster, 2004.
Fron, Janine, Tracy Fullerton, Jacquelyn Ford Morie, and Celia Pearce. "A Game of One's Own: Towards a New Gendered Poetics of Digital Space," 2004. http://lmc.gatech.edu/~cpearce3/PearcePubs/LudicaDAC07.pdf.
——. "The Hegemony of Play." In *Situated Play*, 2007.
Game Developer Demographics: An Exploration of Workforce Diversity. International Game Developer's Association, October 2005. http://archives.igda.org/diversity/IGDA_DeveloperDemographics_Oct05.pdf.
Graner Ray, Sheri. *Gender Inclusive Game Design Expanding the Market*. Charles River Media, 2004. http://site.ebrary.com/id/10061187.
Hewitt, Dan. *Women Comprise Nearly Half of Gamer Population*. Entertainment Software Assocation, July 11, 2013. http://www.theesa.com/newsroom/release_detail.asp?releaseID=202.
Huntemann, Nina B. "Pixel Pinups: Images of Women in Video Games." In *Race/Gender/Media*, edited by Rebecca Ann Lind. Boston, MA: Allyn & Bacon, 2010.
Isaacson, Betsy. "#1ReasonWhy Reveals Sexism Rampant in the Gaming Industry." *Huffington Post*, November 29, 2012. http://www.huffingtonpost.com/2012/11/29/1reasonwhy-reveals-sexism-gaming-industry_n_2205204.html.
Juul, Jesper. "A Certain Level of Abstraction." Tokyo, 2007. http://www.jesperjuul.net/text/acertainlevel/.
Kaplan, E. Ann. "Sex, Work, and Motherhood: Materal Subjectivity in Recent Visual Culture." In *Representations of Motherhood*, edited by D. Bassin, M. Honey, and M.M. Kaplan. New Haven, CT: Yale University Press, 1992.
Napier, Susan. *Anime from Akira to How's Moving Castle*. New York, NY: Palgrave Macmillan, 2005.
O'Donnell, Casey. "This Is Not a Software Industry." In *The Video Game Industry: Formation, Present State, and Future*, edited by Peter Zackariasson and Timothy L. Wilson. New York, NY: Routledge, 2012.
Parkin, Kathleen. *Food Is Love: Advertising and Gender Roles in Modern America*. Philadelpha, PA: University of Pennsylvania Press, 2006.
PETA. "Cooking Mama Responds to Peta Parody." *PETA*, November 20, 2008. http://www.peta.org/b/thepetafiles/archive/2008/11/20/cooking-mama-responds-to-peta-parody.aspx.

Salter, Anastasia, and Bridget Blodgett. "Hypermasculinity & Dickwolves: The Contentious Role of Women in the New Gaming Public." *Journal of Broadcasting & Electronic Media* 56, no. 3 (2012): 401–16. doi:10.1080/08838151.2012.705199.

Thurer, Shari. *The Myths of Motherhood: How Culture Reinvents the Good Mother.* New York, NY: Penguin Books, 2004.

Zackariasson, Peter, and Timothy L. Wilson. "Introduction." In *The Video Game Industry: Formation, Present State, and Future*, edited by Peter Zackariasson and Timothy L. Wilson. New York, NY: Routledge, 2012.

9

Motherhood and the Necessity of Invention

The Possibilities of Play in a Culture of Consumption

Christine Harold

Roughly two and a half millennia ago, Plato handed down one of our most pervasive and central clichés about mothering, noting in *The Republic*, "The true creator is necessity, who is the mother of our invention."[1] This dictum has long been a rhetorical commonplace, one that found new life in the early days of the industrial revolution, when invention had a very tangible meaning. For industrial capitalists, the phrase promised innovation; it connoted a belief that out of apparent need would come apparent solutions. For critics of capitalism, it was quite the other way around. Early twentieth-century sociologist and economist Thorstein Veblen, for example, suggested that, in fact, "invention is the mother of necessity," as evidenced by the early efforts of advertisers to orchestrate mass desire for the products of increasingly prolific factories.[2] In both instances, the figure of the mother is seen as a creator, a figure that signifies birth and innovation.

One assumes this legacy status for motherhood derives from the mother's role in rearing her young, of nurturing and guiding them, a role that is less stridently maternal these days, shared as it is between various configurations of mothers and fathers alike. Nonetheless, the conviction that the young must be mothered, which is to say "invented," through proper parenting continues to hold sway over the literature providing parenting advice to anxious moms and dads. This vast body of literature offers different perspectives, to be sure, but it also enjoys certain remarkable consistencies. In the spirit of Veblen's reversal of Plato, we might say today that mothers (and by proxy, fathers) are defined by the *necessity of invention*—specifically, the invention of the agency of the child, who will one day grow into their subjectivity in a way concordant with his or her parenting.[3]

Of course, the journey into subjectivity that is child development never takes place in a vacuum, nor is it free from the imprints of the cultural biases from which it emerges. In this era of beyond-late-capitalism, childhood is increasingly inflected by or infected with the hallmarks of commerce and the assumptions about gender, race, and economic privilege that come with it. Toothbrushes boast a bevy of Nickelodeon characters, T-shirts sport NFL mascots, and higher end chain stores like Pottery Barn Kids make it abundantly clear that the choices for girls' rooms are pink ballerinas and show ponies, while boys should embrace robots, the solar system, or golden-era baseball. Disney Princesses now come in a variety of skin tones, but all are equally doe-eyed with luxurious hair and impossibly pinched waistlines.

But the relationship between childhood and consumption operates at a level far more essential than merely the interpenetration of youth and brand affiliation. The more fundamental concern, the connective tissue that tethers childhood development to the eventual subject-position of consumer, is not just early brand identification but the developmental process itself. In this chapter, I suggest that the dominant ways in which parents are supposed to rear their young is to invent them as agents; that is, as subjects for whom the inventional process is invented for them. It is this compulsion, this assumption that mothering (indeed, parenting in general) is the necessity to "invent" our children that I contend knots together childhood, agency, and consumption. As such, it also directs our attention to where and how we might start untangling these ties, freeing children to have a bit more control over the invention of their own agency. The central question of this chapter is: what are the conditions and practices through which children can imagine themselves creators of their world, rather than merely consumers of it?

In what follows, I first will identify two "channels" that operate as mutual reinforcements on the invention of childhood as an "agent-in-need-of-agency." The first stakes its claim on the role of parents themselves, either as strict disciplinarians or nurturing supporters. Although these approaches differ radically at the level of ideology, rhetoric, and practice, they converge on the premise that the role of the parent is essentially to invent the child through a correct set of mothering protocols. Although one of these strands of parenting advice (such as the best-selling books by James Dobson, founder of Focus on the Family) advocates compliance through strict structure, and the other advocates for gentle guidance through attachment parenting (exemplified by the Sears Parenting Library series), both foreground parents' responsibility as the primary shapers of the child. This insistence on parents' inventional responsibility has proven incredibly lucrative. Parenting advice literature and its related products and programs have become a multi-billion dollar industry.[4] The second channel announces itself in the marketing of toys and educational tools, the play objects that comprise much of children's activity. Parents are still figured prominently here, but their success is measured by how faithfully they make purchasing decisions in line with the latest "scientific" expertise about child development.

As I hope will become evident, a homology is at work between both channels such that the rhetorical core remains the same in both instances: childhood is a series of critical stages, or windows of opportunity, and how the parents parent (what "program" they buy into), and what commercial products are supplied to the child, determine the future of that child's inventional capacities, from political inclinations to intellectual acumen and beyond. Agency begins at the top, and is then carefully grafted onto the child. Socioeconomic class certainly influences what kinds of resources parents can access in this process, but as Anne Teresa Demo notes in her introduction to this volume, "economic privilege cannot be reduced to a class-based determinism—the rich buy and the poor don't—because why we buy, borrow for, or boycott is informed by intersecting norms of consumer culture and motherhood within particular communities and cultures."[5] Although the content of what parents buy may differ, the consumer mindset—the underlying assumption that good parenting is, in part, the proper enactment of consumer practices—is prevalent across traditional class lines.[6]

In contrast to the channels offered by commercial parenting literature and education toys, I will highlight a third approach, advocated by an increasingly vocal collection of scholars and educators, that emphasizes a child's innate affinity for *play* as the genesis of their own agency. This approach values the parent-child relationship, but encourages parents to remove themselves and the bevy of commercial products from center stage and allow children to do what they do best. By exploring the arguments about the importance of free play, I hope to suggest that although the rhetoric promoting play does not escape a potential bias toward those with an abundance of time and money, a perspective that defines childhood by its freedom to play offers a significant philosophical and practical challenge to the logic of consumption and entertainment that so dominates childhood today.

Inventing Children: Parenting Advice in the Twenty-First Century

The parenting advice industry is booming. Five times as many parenting books were published in 2005 as in 1970, peddling programs for sleep, diet, and discipline to increasingly anxious and overworked parents seeking a magic wand for producing happy, well-adjusted children.[7] Although they differ in particulars and prose, two approaches dominate much of the popular discourse on parenting. On one hand are experts promoting a structured and disciplined style symbolized by so-called "Ferberization," among other methods. On the other is the responsive and baby-centered "attachment parenting" popularized by pediatricians William Sears and T. Berry Brazelton among others.

Richard Ferber is a prominent figure in the parenting advice industry. His "Ferber method" featured in the best-selling *Solve Your Child's Sleep Problems* is seen as either a godsend to sleep-deprived parents looking for relief or a borderline abusive strategy inflicting permanent emotional damage on babies forced to "cry-it-out" (CIO). Although CIO as a method predates Ferber by decades, his method is often erroneously equated with the strategy. In fact, Ferber advocates a somewhat modified version of CIO, in which parents put their baby down to sleep in his or her own bed and then return in progressively increased intervals to comfort the crying child without picking the child up. Over the course of several nights, the parents are advised to extend the length of time before entering the child's room. The goal is a child who "self soothes" and puts him or herself to sleep without parental assistance.

Although Ferber is a Harvard neurologist who studies pediatric sleep disorders, his method is often associated, perhaps unfairly, with those advocating a more generalized and rigid structure to childrearing beyond just sleep. A much more severe model is the popular "Babywise" method advocated by Gary Ezzo. This Bible-based program promotes what Ezzo calls "structured parenting" in which parental authority must be established from birth and "spoiling" must be avoided at all costs. The Babywise program includes a strict feeding schedule, CIO sleep inducement, and corporal punishment as part of its disciplinary repertoire.[8] Evangelist James Dobson, founder of Focus on the Family, has published several best-selling parenting books, such as *Dare to Discipline*, that advocate clear structure and unequivocal parental authority. Dobson, like Ezzo, reminds readers that spanking is biblically sanctioned and that the rod should not be spared when it comes to disciplining disobedient children. In *The Strong-Willed Child*, he writes, "Some strong-willed children absolutely demand to be spanked, and their wishes should be granted. . . . Two or three stinging strokes on the legs or buttocks with a switch are usually sufficient to emphasize the point, 'You must obey me.'"[9] This approach celebrates compliance as the first step toward any other positive "outcome" of the child-parent relationship.

Ferber, Ezzo, and Dobson, to wildly varying degrees, are just three of the more prominent advocates of a "tough love" approach to parenting that positions the strong, dominant parent as the centerpiece of a functional family. Structured parenting, however, has found audiences beyond just white Bible

Belt conservatives. Modified, more mainstream versions are routinely advocated in the pages of popular parenting magazines by experts encouraging, for example, "time outs," in which children are sent to some version of a "naughty corner" as punishment for wrongdoings. The popularity of the strict parent approach can be seen by the recent onslaught of books in the genre: *Don't Be Afraid to Discipline; Parents in Charge; Parent in Control; Taking Charge; Back in Control*; *Disciplining Your Preschooler—and Feeling Good About It; 'Cause I'm the Mommy, That's Why*; *Laying Down the Law*; *Guilt-Free Parenting*; *The Answer is No* and so on.[10] This approach has been popularized by best-selling author Jo Frost, known to TV audiences as the *Supernanny*. Like her method, Frost's show follows a strict formula. Each week, she pops into the homes of stressed parents (overwhelmingly middle-class whites) who have lost control of their children and, with an arsenal of reward charts, punitive measures, and a healthy dose of the word "naughty" helps restore order to parents' lives. Frost's persona, with her neat chignon and tailored suits, is that of the warm but strict British school marm, offered as a bracing antidote to American overindulgence. *Supernanny* inevitably ends with grateful parents singing the praises of Frost's tough love approach. As one mother puts it: "It's kind of a slap in the face, but it's what [we] needed."[11]

The *Supernanny* and other proponents of structured parenting beseech parents to reclaim their place at the top of a power hierarchy. To do so, successful parents must firmly and consistently impose a structure of rewards and punishments on children. A stark instantiation of this position became a cultural lightening rod in early 2011 when *The Wall Street Journal* published an excerpt entitled "Why Chinese Mothers are Superior," from Yale law professor Amy Chua's parenting memoir *Battle Hymn of the Tiger Mother*. In it, Chua explains why Chinese families seem to produce such academically successful children: "Chinese parents demand perfect grades because they believe that their child can get them. If their child doesn't get them, the Chinese parent assumes it's because the child didn't work hard enough. That's why the solution to substandard performance is always to excoriate, punish and shame the child. The Chinese parent believes that their child will be strong enough to take the shaming and to improve from it. (And when Chinese kids do excel, there is plenty of ego-inflating parental praise lavished in the privacy of the home.)"[12]

This stringent parenting philosophy bears many similarities to what George Lakoff describes as the metaphorical frame governing political conservatism: the "strict father."[13] In the strict father model, people are thought to be essentially errant and hence need to learn morality and obedience by way of discipline—often in the form of corporeal punishment. Inspired, specifically, by the influence of James Dobson, Lakoff explains that "the rationale behind physical punishment is this: When children do something wrong, if they are physically disciplined . . . they will develop internal discipline . . . so that in the future they will be obedient and act morally. Such internal discipline has a secondary effect. It is what is required for success in the difficult, competitive world."[14] When extended to politics, government's job is to remain relatively hands-off unless disobedient citizen-children require a firm punitive hand. Whether applied to civic life or family life, success in this model is assumed to be an outcome of one's moral worth, both the "parent's" and the "child's." This is a philosophy in which control is definitively in the hands of the parents, as they play the crucial role in inventing upstanding individuals ready to face the harsh realities outside the childhood home.

If structured parenting is about gaining compliance through rewards and punishments, attachment parenting prioritizes a strong emotional bond between parent and child as the key to producing secure, independent adults. Popularized by pediatrician and author William Sears through his lucrative Sears Parenting Library series, attachment parenting promotes mother's close physical proximity and availability in the early years of a child's life. Only when a young child's innate need for attachment is satisfied, say parenting advocates, will they develop the security required for independence as an adult. Breast-feeding "on demand," regularly wearing baby close to the body, and co-sleeping in a "family bed" are main strategies used to encourage this deep attachment. Whereas structured parenting encourages parents to teach independent self-soothing by allowing sleep-resistant infants to "cry it out," attachment parenting proponents decry the practice as borderline abusive. Leaving baby to cry it out may "work" at getting baby to eventually quiet down, they say, but only by seriously undermining the parent-child bond. As Sears argues in his best-selling guide for new parents, *The Baby Book*, "Baby loses trust in the signal value of her cues, and parents lose trust in the ability to read and respond to baby's cues. . . . The basis of baby training is to help babies become more 'convenient.' It is based upon the misguided assumption that babies cry to manipulate, not to communicate."[15]

Discipline in the attachment parenting model looks quite different as well. Programs such as Becky Bailey's "Loving Guidance," Marshall Rosenberg's "Non-Violent Communication," or the myriad books and websites devoted to "gentle discipline" advocate nonpunitive discipline strategies such as redirection, modeling, and natural consequences to socialize children.[16] Above all, attachment parents strive to form a strong parent-child relationship by attending to the specific needs of their child based on their individual developmental stage. A common assertion is that it is often unrealistic parental expectations, not unruly children, at the root of discipline "problems." Author Scott Noelle argues, for example, that for many cultures in which parent-child relationships are less authoritarian, the "terrible twos" and "terrible teens" stages of rebellion endured by parents in the West are nonexistent.[17] Rather, these are just two phases of development in which healthy humans make a "quantum leap in personal autonomy." But, he writes, "in our anti-nature, control-oriented culture, parents are expected (if not required *by law*) to oppose or control children's natural developmental impulses toward personal empowerment, which guarantees the terribles!"[18]

Like Lakoff's notion of the "Nurturant Parent," the metaphor he attributes to political progressives, attachment parenting, and others of its sort assume that a just society (civic or personal) requires caring, attentive leadership that strives to meet the needs of its wards.[19] A culture of care and respect for self and others is believed to provide sufficient boundaries and incentives to guarantee a well-functioning child and thereby society at large. Indeed, from this perspective, it is only when people's needs are not adequately met or when authority is too coercive that people feel the need to rebel. A morality based on care of self and others dominates what Lakoff describes as the nurturant parent model.

It is likely many readers, especially the parents among us, have already identified themselves with one or the other model described thus far. Depending upon our politics, our disposition, and indeed, our own upbringing, one or the other feels more "right" as an approach to parenting in both its actual and metaphoric senses. Both approaches undoubtedly have hiccups on their road to better children and advanced social outcomes. Any compliance achieved through strict parenting, for instance, is by no means assured absent the authoritative presence of the parent. In fact, authoritative parenting often results in rebellion. And, conversely, many feel that attachment parenting will produce children who retain a sense of entitlement amidst a real dependency on outside assistance. For many feminists, the baby-centered focus of attachment parenting yokes women too tightly to the proverbial hearth, undermining the hard-earned strides toward advancing women's roles in every sphere of social life. *New York Times* columnist Judith Warner voices this concern in her book *Perfect Madness: Motherhood in the Age of Anxiety*, suggesting that the popularity of attachment parenting contributes to a "culture of total motherhood" that places undue and unrealistic expectations on women.[20]

It is worth noting, too, that a full commitment to the dictates of attachment parenting assumes a mother who has an ample supply of emotional capital including time, patience, and other resources to spend attending to the needs of her child. Although not explicitly economic, these resources are often more plentiful in families who enjoy economic privileges such as childcare, time for recreation, vacations, and one-parent incomes. In fact, total "buy in" to attachment parenting requires a mother who does not work outside the home; this is not an arrangement that is financially possible for many families. Even if a working mother is committed in principle to attachment parenting values, nursing on demand, attending to baby's needs throughout the night, and allowing baby to spend most of his or her day in a cozy sling are luxuries that may not be possible for someone who must work full time to support her family. As Katha Pollitt puts it in her critique of attachment parenting in *The Nation*, "Dr. Bill Sears, guru of attachment parenting and, not incidentally, a devout Christian, is fairly explicit that mothers shouldn't have jobs—he even suggests that couples borrow money from their parents to enable the wife to stay home. (That Romney-esque suggestion shows how class-based attachment parenting is.)"[21] Partisan politics aside, the economic barriers to fully implementing an attachment parenting lifestyle are significant. That said, as critics such as Warner and Pollitt suggest, the mainstreaming of so-called "total motherhood" advice may, especially for women already struggling to balance the demands of work and home life, add yet another message pressuring them to do more still.

Different as they may be, both of the above approaches to parenting are bolstered by two implicit and antecedent assumptions. First, they hold a firm conviction in the power of rewards and punishments (even if they conceptualize reward and punishment differently at the level of content). Attachment parents are full of praise and affirmation. Structured parents are full of boundaries and discipline based on obedience. The ultimate goal of both is a strong and coherent child identity, often measured against a backdrop of educational or developmental achievement.

Second, each approach assumes that agency is a privilege that is gifted to the child, bequeathed so to speak, through the implement of proper parenting. Motherhood, or parenting in general, is thus defined by the expectation or the obligation to invent their children, and not just in the biological sense. Albeit in very different ways, both place a heavy emphasis on mothering (or, parenting in general) as an act of unilateral production, of this or that kind of person. In this, they both align with what Dana Cloud has termed "therapy rhetorics" in that they promote the realization of the true, autonomous self and consider the primary shaper of that self the parent-child relationship.[22]

The assumption that parents are ultimately responsible for creating their children has offered fertile ground for advertisers and producers of children's toys and media who have profited greatly from anxious parents understandably eager to "get it right." Most parents, regardless of political ideology, preferred parenting method, or economic standing, are simply trying their best to provide their child with the best emotional and material resources they can. The desire to avail ourselves and our children of every opportunity for success and happiness is shared by good parents, regardless of race, faith, or economic means. Especially in an age when our traditional social ties have shifted, we rely as much on experts, websites, magazines, and even marketers for advice about parenting as we do on the wisdom of our own parents and community elders. Understandably, it is particularly easy to be seduced by claims for products touting the best that science and technology have to offer.

Consuming Play: Commercial Toys in an Achievement-Oriented World

Like parenting advice literature, educational toys are a growth industry. Now a $1-billion-dollar-a-year business, "educational toys" for babies and young children are everywhere, with brand names like Baby Einstein (which includes Baby Van Gogh and Baby Shakespeare), IQ Baby, Baby Genius, Baby Wow, Jumpstart Baby, Baby Boost, Your Baby Can Read!, and Brainy Baby.[23] Foreign language DVDs, classical music CDs, and computer programs for toddlers all promise to stimulate young brains before it is too late. One website selling baby flashcards on topics ranging from Picasso masterpieces to bones of the human body and even Euclidean Geometry urges parents to "provide a lot of visual stimulations between 0 to 6 years before the right brain window shuts down."[24]

This rhetoric of critical "windows" during which the brain is receptive to certain data pervades popular discourse about baby brains. As Davi Johnson Thornton explains, these "critical periods are windows of access, providing an opening during which parents can shape and control the brain through appropriate stimulation" and "they are windows of opportunity, in the sense that they are 'once in a lifetime' chances to get things right."[25] This line of rhetoric capitalized on the buzz around the so-called "Mozart effect," a theory that may have reached its popular apex in the late 1990s, when then Georgia governor Zell Miller proposed legislation requiring his state to produce and distribute classical music CDs to all new parents. These "windows of opportunity" offer potent *topoi* for producing anxiety in new parents. They imply both parents' capacity and responsibility to influence a child's future success and the fear that this opportunity may be wasted, for once lost it is lost forever.

Further, according to several consumer products marketed to parents-to-be, this responsibility begins earlier and earlier. Books with titles like *Pre-Parenting*, *The Secret Life of the Unborn Child*, and *The Prenatal Person* now teach parents how to give their offspring a competitive edge before they even leave the womb.[26] The book *Prenatal Parenting* has a chapter called "On Becoming a Brain Architect" and teaches parents to help aid "proper nerve and brain development" in their unborn child. Baby Plus, a sonic device expectant mothers wear on their bellies, is just one of a host of gadgets offering unborn babies "auditory exercises" intended to increase early learning and socialization. As the company's website puts it: "You're never too young to learn. (In fact, you don't even have to be born!)."[27] The inventor of the Baby Plus system has even made his own contribution to the prenatal parenting mini-boom with his self-published *Learning Before Birth*. This increased focus by marketers on "windows of opportunity" in brain development, and the appeal to parents to become "brain architects" before baby even leaves the womb all contribute to the presumption that parenting is a process of inventing the child in an appropriate way, that our job is to create the child as agent in the world. Certainly parents do and *should* play a significant role in a child's development, but so much of the rhetoric aimed at separating parents from their money casts the child as parental *project*. And, again, the pressure to get the project "right" is powerful indeed.

The merits of the products offered by the so-called baby achievement industry are hotly contested in the scientific community. The Baby Einstein line of DVDs offers a particularly stark case in point. The Disney Corporation bought the line in 2001 and expanded it to include not just *Baby Mozart* and *Baby Galileo* DVDs but flash cards, books, and clothing. Following a 2006 complaint to the Federal Trade Commission (FTC) by the Campaign for a Commercial Free Childhood (CCFC), Disney scaled back its claims about its products' effectiveness at developing baby brains. At issue for CCFC was that Baby Einstein intentionally misled consumers and that its claims were in direct contradiction to recommendations by the American Association of Pediatrics (AAP), which recommends "no screen time for children under two."[28] Childhood development researchers at the University of Washington added weight to the CCFC's position in 2007 when *The Journal of Pediatrics* published their findings that infants exposed to DVDs such as Baby Einstein actually scored lower on standardized language tests than those who did not. Although the Disney Corporation initially challenged the findings, it now offers refunds to customers who bought Baby Einstein products between 2004 and 2009 under what the company calls an "enhanced consumer satisfaction guarantee."[29]

Despite controversies such as that surrounding Baby Einstein, the appeals of products promising better baby brains have resonated deeply with American parents of all stripes and has made millions for the educational products and services industry. The "god term" for those marketing educational toys and media seems to be "structure." This appeal suggests that if parents can fill their children's time with enrichment activities and classes, and transform play into learning via sophisticated, technologically advanced toys, then children will become hardwired for success—structured time, structured play, structured brain. And despite skepticism from the pediatric community, the popularity of Baby Einstein products and the like means they appeal to parents of all kinds, not just the structure-loving disciplinarians among us. (Indeed, *The New York Times* cited a 2003 study claiming that one-third of American babies between the ages six months to two years old had at least one Baby Einstein video).[30] In its mainstream form, structured parenting makes a "better-living-through-science" promise that if we diligently follow an expertly sanctioned pedagogical regime, our experiment will produce the desired outcome. We might call this mothering by way of "inventional correctness."

Except perhaps at their extremes, neither mainstream parenting literature nor baby achievement products are necessarily harmful to families. They also do not exhaust the field of possible approaches to parenting. As dominant as these approaches seem to be, a third approach, by no means new, is increasingly making its way into the mainstream parenting conversation. This approach, what we might call "creative play," is not mutually exclusive with either of the above, but it does operate from a different set of assumptions and encourage significantly different outcomes. Above all, I will argue in the following section that a commitment to open, free-form play provides children not with agency bequeathed from on high through strict guidelines, sufficient attachment, or careful consumption, but rather that play, at its best, allows children to experiment, invent, and create their own agency—to develop their own capacity to act in the world.

Creating Play: The Conditions of Invention

The fast-track, early academics trend is being challenged by some of the most prominent voices in pediatrics and child development, many of whom are arguing that children need less intellectual "stimulation" and more time to do the real work of childhood: play. These play advocates contend that the structured-learning approach that is so breathlessly promoted by the baby achievement industry not only fails to achieve its high-achieving objective, but may even make that achievement less likely. "Education is not a race where the prize goes to the one who finishes first" urges the Alliance for Childhood, a play advocacy group. Wendy Grolnick, coauthor of *Pressured Parents, Stressed-Out Kids*, warns that if parents try too hard to manage their children's successes, kids are denied the opportunity to explore and experiment with their world: "Showing a child the 'right' way to play with a toy or filling her every hour with activities can reduce internal motivation and creativity, both key to long-term success in life."[31]

Experts promoting free play urge parents to trust in children's ability to seek out the kinds of play that will serve them best. What a child's brain needs, they say, is not flashcards, computers, and music classes, but time, space, and patience for it to explore and satisfy its own curiosities. "By making children dependent on others to schedule and entertain them, we deprive them of the pleasures of creating their own games and the sense of mastery and independence they will need to enjoy running their own lives" say child development scholars Kathy Hirsh-Pasek and Roberta Michnick Golinkoff in their book *Einstein Never Used Flashcards*.[32]

Instead, Hirsh-Pasek and Michnick Golinkoff argue that Mother Nature has brain development "pretty much covered" thanks to millions of years of evolution in which the human brain has learned to respond to everyday experiences: "Unless it is severely deprived of these experiences, the brain will build itself. It doesn't rely on parental architects who put each experience in place for the young rat or the young child."[33] In short, parents (and marketers) overestimate their own agency and responsibility to improve in one generation what evolution has been perfecting over millennia. Instead of externally imposed structure, play advocates suggest that good old-fashioned play is "the crucible of learning."[34]

So, what do we mean by "play"? For child development researchers, play has at least five characteristics: It is enjoyable; it has no extrinsic goals; it is spontaneous and voluntary; it involves active engagement; and it involves make-believe.[35] At its base, the case for play suggests that whereas early academics emphasizes mastery or memorization of *content* (ABCs and 123s, for example), free play hones a far more important facet of the intellect: creative invention, or *make-believe*. Israeli psychologist Sara Smilansky concluded after a lengthy study that a capacity for make-believe play was directly linked to later academic success: "For example, problem solving in most school subjects requires a great deal of make-believe: visualizing how the Eskimos live, reading stories, imagining a story and writing it down, solving arithmetic problems, and determining what will come next. History, geography, and literature are all make believe. All of these are conceptual constructions never directly experienced by the child."[36] Unfortunately, say many child development scholars, in the prevailing culture of "outcomes" and "standards," nonlinear activities like fantasy play are too often seen as a waste of precious learning time.

Even many toy manufacturers are attempting to offer parents a way to assess the educational outcomes of play. Fisher-Price, for example, has developed a detailed taxonomy of developmental skills presumably bolstered by the company's products. Through a system of color-coded pictographs, parents can identify which category of skills—physical, cognitive, or social-emotional—each toy promotes. Each category has several skill sets within it (for example "gross motor," "self-expression and confidence," and "thinking and problem solving") each with its own pictograph. Fisher-Price labels toy packages with two to three relevant pictographs so parents can see what skills will be promoted by the product inside. Fisher-Price also offers a detailed explanation of outcomes as they relate to products on their website, all searchable by developmental stage. Adjacent to descriptions of the pictograph system, the Fisher-Price website offers quotes from a host of PhDs and MDs about the educational value of play.

Fisher-Price's attempt to lend scientific ethos to their products by aligning them with research on child development is likely a well-intentioned attempt to highlight the educational benefits of their products. The harms, if there are any, of Fisher-Price doing so are negligible. Rather, the company's practice of explicitly focusing on the outcomes of play objects is simply a symptom of our culture's larger tendency to *instrumentalize* play, to measure the worth of play based on how well, or how fast it advances a child along a progressive path. Unfortunately, this tendency often undervalues (and even deems wasteful) forms of play such as make-believe that play experts insist contribute powerful and important resources to the developing child, even if these resources are less linear or quantifiably educational.

Indeed, the trend toward targeting younger and younger children for enrichment and stimulation indicates that, for some, there is not a moment to spare when it comes to "educating" babies and children. As we have seen from the examples above, for some parents and marketers, even the prenatal life of the fetus could be put to more productive use. "What we are in danger of doing" by focusing on outcomes rather than the process of play, writes educator and scholar Vivian Gussin Paley, "is delegitimatizing mankind's oldest and best-used learning tool."[37] Perhaps it is because parents often feel so obligated to invent their children, to grant them agency, that we are susceptible to the lure of standards and measures that presume to tell us if we are successfully doing so.

Creative play benefits from a set of conditions that differ from those found in the parenting approaches outlined thus far. Parents still have an important role to play, of course, but that role is less to *bestow* agency than to help facilitate the conditions in which agency can flourish. First, one must consider the character of the *objects* provided for play. Although commercial toy culture suggests quite the opposite, play advocates encourage parents to choose objects that are simple and invite imaginative play. A common rule of thumb is that play should be "10 percent toy and 90 percent child," meaning that learning happens best when the child has to do more cognitive work to engage the toy. The Waldorf education model based on the philosophy of early twentieth-century scholar Rudolf Steiner, for example, provides small children with baskets containing everyday items like sea shells, pine cones, and wool to aid their play. The idea is that these open-ended objects allow for multiple uses and do not over-determine one type of play over another. A clamshell can function as a toy car in one play scenario, money in another, and a doll's cradle in yet another. The formal simplicity of a clamshell does not impose itself on play as much as more explicitly mimetic toys. It does not bring with it an *a priori* script, the way, say, a small toy car might. Surely children can and do reimagine commercial products in all kinds of ways, and use them in ways radically different from the intentions of their producers. But many contemporary toys, with their internal microchips and their intricately detailed surfaces, often encourage children to adapt their play to what the toy apparently "wants," rather than vice versa. And although learning to adapt to technology has a certain value, this value is limited if the goal of play is for children to think in an open, creative, inventive way. To turn a clamshell into a car requires a child to exercise more creative muscle and, in turn, grants them more agency over their play.

Walt Whitman gets at the profound relationship between children and their material surroundings in his poem "There was a Child Went Forth," from *Leaves of Grass*:

> There was a child went forth every day;
> And the first object he look'd upon, that object he became;
> And that object became part of him for the day, or a certain part of
> the day, or for many years, or stretching cycles of years.[38]

Whitman goes on to catalogue the lilacs, sow's litter, apple blossoms, and the fragrance of salt marsh that will become a part of the child who went forth. But of course today's children are as likely to be shaped by Disney Princesses and Thomas the Tank Engine as they are the "song of the phoebe-bird" Whitman admires. Countless commentators, parents, and scholars have decried the heavily branded world in which today's children grow up. Increasingly, childhood throughout the world is wallpapered with the imagery of (usually American, often white) licensed characters—Barbie sneakers, Lego Movie lunchboxes, and Transformers backpacks. The degree to which the cultural landscape is saturated with brands is concerning, to be sure. As branding so often does, it renders objects disposable vehicles of some transitory commercial message. But increasingly, those transitory commercial messages are the building blocks of young people's sense of self and their relationship to others. Scholars Juliet Schor and Susan Linn have thoroughly and convincingly demonstrated the many negative effects that have emerged at the intersection of commerce and childhood.[39] In her book *Born to Buy*, Schor documents the ways in which childhood has been so inundated with commercial values that consumption has become for children, as it has for adults, their primary mode of identity formation. But it is not only the way children's products are branded and marketed that merits our attention. It is the *form* of the objects themselves.

Psychologist Fergus Hughes, in his book *Children, Play, and Development*, describes several studies that have shown a direct relationship between the development of problem-solving skills and the nature of play objects. In one study, for example, subjects were divided into two groups. One group was given *convergent* materials to play with, such as a puzzle that had only one correct solution. The other group was given *divergent*, or open-ended materials, such as wooden blocks that can be assembled in countless ways. Later, the children in the two groups were asked to solve a variety of problems. "The children who had engaged in divergent object play," reports Hughes, "were found to be more flexible and more original in their problem-solving approaches.[40] For example, they were quicker than those in the convergent play group to abandon ineffective approaches to solving problems and to come up with new approaches." He continues: "Playing with open-ended materials . . . may tell a child that numerous approaches can be taken to any problem and the possibilities for the use of one's creative imagination are limitless."[41] In other words, divergent play materials make children more *inventive*.

As is the case with adult consumer products, products marketed to children are increasingly high tech and many are embedded with microchips, making it possible for toys to perform a variety of complex actions. David Elkind, child development researcher and author, argues that the technological sophistication of today's toys inhibits children's natural curiosity, in part because they are functionally unable to see how their own toys work. Electronic toys, such as handheld computer games and the like, are essentially black-box technologies that make it impossible for children to tinker under the hood, so to speak. "Even young children may be amazingly adept in using technology," Elkind writes: "but the ability to use something well doesn't necessarily require an understanding of how it works," and "children's curiosity should still be encouraged and supported through the provision of toys that can satisfy their curiosity about how things work."[42] Indeed, a key part of any technological or material literacy is the ability to take something apart and understand the mechanisms that animate it. Media educators teach media literacy by teaching students how to make their own advertisements and films so they can see firsthand how persuasion and storytelling function. An apprentice in an auto shop takes apart and reassembles an engine in order to understand how the pieces work together. We become makers by first understanding the mechanisms and processes by which things are made. Becoming an agent in the world is a status one must acquire for oneself, through the trial-and-error experiences that come with invention and exploration.

Elkind's concern, that contemporary toys are turning children into users rather than creators, was anticipated by Roland Barthes in the chapter "Toys," in his well-known *Mythologies* essays written in the 1950s. In this short but powerful indictment of French toys, Barthes writes, "French toys *always mean something*," in that they tend to merely reproduce the adult world in miniature: armies, doctor's kits, beauty parlors, for example.[43] "The fact that French toys *literally* prefigure the world of adult functions obviously cannot but prepare the child to accept them all, by constituting for him, even before he can think about it, the alibi of a Nature which has at all times created soldiers, postmen, and Vespas."[44] It is not just the imitative quality of modern toys that is so problematic, he suggests, but their literalness.

The form of most toys encourages, *a priori*, the way a child should play with them. The child's task, then? To represent in her play, as convincingly as possible, the world of adults. And, what we adults so often find charming are the little slippages in our children's attempts to represent adequately this world: the wobbly smear of lipstick meant to look like mama's, for example, or the little boy attempting to work "just like daddy." "How cute!" we say, our amusement unintentionally bordering on condescension and the hope they will one day perfect the transition to being just like us. But for Barthes, the cost of this representational play is high: "faced with this world of faithful and complicated objects, the child can only identify himself as owner, as user, never as creator; he does not invent the world, he uses it: They are, prepared for him, actions without adventure, without wonder without joy."[45]

In contrast, Barthes, like many contemporary play researchers, argues that simple, open-ended toys, such as blocks "appeal to a spirit of do-it-yourself" that is crucial to one's development. He writes, "The merest set of blocks, provided it is not too refined, implies a very different learning of the world: Then the child does not in any way create meaningful objects, it matters little to him whether they have an adult name; the actions he performs are not that of a user, but those of a demiurge. He creates forms which walk, which roll, *he creates life, not property*."[46] Of course mimetic toys have a certain value in the socialization process; children must learn about the world they will inherit. But when the form of toys risks over-determining play such that experimentation is reduced to minor adaptations on a theme, children are left with play experiences in which the possibilities for innovation are limited. The parallel to consumerism should be clear: a consumer is one who can make certain choices from a predetermined set of options and can piece products together in somewhat novel ways, but consumers are typically users of products, not creators of them.

Second, in addition to considering the objects of play, this approach considers the context, or *environment*, that best promotes free play. This includes both the time and the space in which play occurs. For creativity to flourish best, play advocates argue that children need long expanses of unscheduled time in which to explore their interests. Time that is too fragmented, too scheduled with adult-led, goal-oriented "enrichment activities," deprives children of the freedom to follow their own interests. As in Montessori education, play advocates believe that left largely to their own devices, and provided the time and resources, children will gravitate to those things that are developmentally appropriate and challenging. This approach openly opposes two trends in American children's culture intended to bolster academic achievement: the reduction (and, often, elimination of) recess, and the staggering popularity of classes, workshops, for-profit learning centers (such as Kumon and Sylvan), and other extracurricular activities designed to accelerate learning.[47]

In addition to significant free time, creativity begins, as art critic Bernard Berenson suggests, "with the natural genius of childhood and the 'spirit of place.'"[48] The Montessori method, for example, encourages teachers and parents to establish an orderly "prepared environment" in which toys and other learning objects are neatly organized and available for children to engage on their own. In a typical Montessori classroom, everything is child size—desks and chairs, but also sinks, counters, bookcases, brooms, and other supplies. The Waldorf classroom is also carefully prepared to encourage free, child-led play. Waldorf play objects are made of only natural materials (wood, wool, silk) and are organized neatly in baskets on child-level shelves. Unstructured outdoor play is a big part of the Waldorf curriculum. For Richard Louv, author of the naturalist manifesto *Last Child in the Woods*, nature provides the best physical environment for play, noting that "Natural spaces and materials stimulate children's limitless imaginations and serve as the medium of inventiveness and creativity observable in almost any group of children playing in a natural setting."[49] Although they differ somewhat in pedagogical method, the goal of the Montessori, Waldorf, and naturalist models is that the environment must be open enough to facilitate children's independence and creativity.

In addition to the objects and environment, the *parent's role* in a play-focused model shifts as well, and here we see how play serves as an alternative path to either structure or attachment as disciplinary models or as educational templates. However, as I will discuss, this model also assumes ample resources of time and parent involvement. Just as the formal design of objects, schedule, and environment must not impose themselves too much on child's play, the parent or teacher's role recedes in prominence as well. In Montessori schools, for example, teachers are considered part of the prepared environment—a resource for the child to draw upon as she might any other materials in the room. They offer demonstrations of how to use a particular learning object, then largely get out of the way of the child's experimentation.

Although not a "play advocate" per se, the work of education reformer Alfie Kohn is instructive here. Kohn's many books, including *Unconditional Parenting*, *Punished by Rewards*, and *Beyond Discipline* argue stridently against the ways in which American children are "incentivized" to learn through heavy-handed parent and teacher intervention. Citing an extensive body of child development research, Kohn suggests that the prevailing trends—both the strict disciplinary model and the praise-heavy nurturant model—rob children of the internal motivation required to develop fully into ethical, creative citizens. "External regulations" he writes, "can interfere with the development of internal regulation" when it comes to ethical and moral behavior. A heavy-handed parenting style does nothing to promote, and actually may undermine, children's moral development. Those who are pressured to do as they are told are unlikely to think through ethical dilemmas for themselves."[50]

His critique of the counter-productivity of corporeal punishment is perhaps easiest to concede. Spanking children is discouraged in mainstream American society. But, for Kohn, all punishment is problematic because it essentially encourages selfishness. By punishing children for wrongdoings, parents miss important opportunities to teach values like empathy or responsibility to community and instead teach children to avoid unpleasantness for themselves. For example, if Amber hits Joey on the playground and is given a "time out" for doing so, any lesson learned for Amber is a self-interested one: "Next time I won't hit Joey so I won't get a time out." Any consideration of the effects of Amber's behavior *on others* is left out of the equation. Further, any opportunity for both Amber and Joey to address the situation creatively is missed. Certainly adults must not stand idly by in the face of playground violence, but by stepping in simply to dole out punishments, they deny children their own response-ability, their own capacity to respond inventively to the ethical situation in which they find themselves. Punishment might curb behavior in the short-term, but it also renders children "bully" or "victim" rather than citizens responsible to others in their community.

It may surprise some that Kohn considers positive incentives to be as problematic as punitive ones. Kohn argues against conventional rewards for performance—grades, "gold stars," and even traditional praise. Since incentives, positive or negative, are external, there is no innate reason for children to behave appropriately when they think they can get away with doing so or when the rewards run out. The point for Kohn and other supporters of child-led learning is that judgmental commentary of any kind can disrupt the playful "work" of children. The authors of a popular Montessori book for parents, for example, write: "commenting or clapping for children's accomplishments can break their absorption with the experience and draw their attention to you. Further, parental cheerleading, if overdone, can interfere with the child's independence and create the expectation of an audience for even normal accomplishment."[51] Instead, they suggest, a simple warm smile can go along way toward sharing a child's pleasure in her accomplishments: "Such a low-key response indicates that you are happy for your child because you know that he his happy. You are not happy because your child is a 'super baby.'"[52] For Kohn, conditionality (the notion that acceptance must be earned) is the greatest stumbling block to the healthy development of a child's agency.

If the goal of open-ended play is to promote experimentation, creativity, and independence, then parents might consider refraining from conditional judgment (positive or negative) in favor of descriptive commentary that allows children to lose themselves in the give-and-take of play and to draw their own conclusions about the experience. Parents might also keep play objects and schedules open enough to promote experimentation and innovation to allow children to discover for themselves what works and what does not in any particular play scenario. Much of the advice and products we are offered as parents situate the parent as the inventor of children's agency; the child becomes who they are because the parent makes it so, either by adhering to the correct parenting model or purchasing the right consumer products. In each model, *motherhood* is the necessity of this invention.

Conclusion

I suspect it is possible to take play too seriously. As I write, I wonder if this encomium to creative play does not itself run the risk of mandating yet another parenting method as *the* way to best invent our children. As David Elkind reminds us in *The Power of Play*: "Mark Twain had Tom Sawyer say that 'work is what a body is obliged to do, and play is what a body is not obliged to do.' When play becomes an obligation it is no longer play."[53] Approaching play as yet another *strategy* in the project of "properly creating our children as agents" perpetuates the problematic dynamic that over-obligates parents as the inventors of children rather than allowing children to invent themselves in a safe and loving environment. Further, not all families have the resource of ample time for free, open-ended play. While some parents may over-schedule kids with sports, music lessons, and other enrichment activities to give them a competitive edge, others place their children in after-school programs, vacation Bible school, or other activities out of sheer economic necessity. Further still, the style of play advocated by programs like Waldorf and Montessori are hardly free from commercial motivations. Catalogues like *Magic Cabin*, *Nova Natural Toys*, and *For Small Hands* cater to largely upper-middle-class families with money to spend on $100 Waldorf dolls and sustainably harvested, handcrafted wooden blocks. And tuition for the schools themselves is often prohibitively expensive for many families, resulting in self-selected student bodies that barely resemble their surrounding communities.

In the United States, Waldorf (and, to a lesser degree, Montessori) schools and products have become luxury brands of a sort, or status symbols targeting educated, often liberal upper-middle-class families for whom "opting out" of a high tech childhood in favor of a hands-on, customized education is increasingly prevalent. A recent article in *the New York Times*, for example, highlights the booming popularity of the Waldorf School of the Peninsula, located in the heart of Silicon Valley. Many employees of high-tech firms like Google, Apple, and Hewlett-Packard are sending their children to the nearly $18,000-a-year private school where the students work with knitting needles, not computers.[54] That Waldorf and Montessori have become somewhat elite private schools is ironic, given the histories of their respective creation. Rudolf Steiner opened his first school to serve the children of factory employees at the Waldorf-Astoria cigarette company in Stuttgart, Germany. His educational approach has been adopted by schools serving children from a wide range of social classes and abilities throughout Germany and Europe. Maria Montessori, one of the first female physicians in Italy, developed her pedagogical method—allowing children the liberty to act freely within a prepared environment—by working with mentally disabled and poor children in urban Rome, many of whom were considered uneducatable. Montessori argued that intelligence was not a privilege of elites, and that many of the barriers to educational success were due to the conditions of poverty—inadequate nutrition, disease, and unsupportive living environments, for example.

Rather than play as a mandate adding yet another obligation for parents to meet, perhaps *playfulness* can offer a perspective that helps parents explore and experiment as they develop their own selves as parents. Playfulness—flexibility, making-do, creative exploration—may be just the recipe for creating for ourselves an agency that responds to others, including our children, in a spirit that is noninstrumental, engaged, and of the moment. In this, play has as much potential as a set of ethical principles as many more seemingly sophisticated philosophies.

Not only is play philosophical, but philosophical thinking is play. In his book *Philosophy and the Young Child*, philosopher Gareth B. Matthew writes, "Philosophy may indeed be motivated by puzzlement. But to show that and stop there is to suggest, quite mistakenly, that philosophy is inevitably about something terribly serious. In fact it is often play, conceptual play."[55] Here, Matthew hints at something he explores throughout his work on philosophy and children: that children have an inherent capacity for philosophical thought, "higher order" inventive thinking that is so often considered the domain of learned adults.

If play is indeed the intellectual work of childhood, then we must be careful that it does not become denigrated as a superfluous distraction from academics, nor usurped as the domain of advertisers and toy manufacturers, nor as one more parenting program to be followed to the letter. In contrast and at its best, play offers a practicum in *kairos*, a child-like absorption in the present moment. A "playful" parent might help create the conditions for children to develop their own agency, to cultivate a sense of "self" through engaged practice rather than bequeathal from on high, benevolent or otherwise. Perhaps joining our children in play, giving ourselves over to the kairotic, unpredictable world of childhood, may be just the thing for (re)inventing ourselves as parents. Child psychologist Lawrence J. Cohen writes in his book *Playful Parenting*, "If we don't play, we miss out on more than fun. Play is where children show us the inner feelings and experiences that they can't or won't talk about. We need to hear what they have to say, and they need to share it. That's why we have to join children where *they* live, on *their* terms."[56] Invention is not about creating something utterly original in a vacuum, it is about negotiating existing relationships in novel, collaborative, even childish, ways. As Jean Piaget famously asserted, "play is the answer to the question, how does anything new come about?"[57]

Notes

1. Plato and Paul Shorey, *The Republic. Books I-V Books I-V* (Cambridge: Harvard University Press, 1937).

2. Thorstein Veblen, *The Instinct of Workmanship: And the State of the Industrial Arts* (Viking, 1943), 314.

3. In the rhetorical tradition, invention is the first of the five classical canons of rhetoric, the generative moment in the art of discovering and developing one's argument. In rhetorical studies today, scholars have complicated and expanded the scope of invention such that it is largely understood not just as the first step in a process controlled by an intentional rhetorical agent, but as a host of critical and interpretive approaches we deploy as we navigate the rhetorical world in which we live. That is, rather than just understanding invention as a strategy of *production*, contemporary rhetoric scholars are exploring invention as a strategy of interpretation, or *reception*. Invention still performs its generative function, but it is no longer seen as the first in a series of steps the rhetor controls. As I will suggest in this chapter, much commercial rhetoric aimed at parents assures them they are very much in control (indeed, responsible) for inventing their children. See, for a discussion of contemporary rhetorical invention: Janet M. Atwill and Janice M. Lauer, *Perspectives on Rhetorical Invention*, University of Tennessee Press, 2003.

4. For a detailed study, see Paul, Pamela, *Parenting, Inc.: How the Billion Dollar Baby Business Has Changed the Way We Raise our Children* (New York: Holt: 2009)

5. Anne Teresa Demo, "Introduction."

6. For example, child psychologist David Elkind notes in *The Power of Play* that the sheer *quantity* of toys children now own has increased exponentially, regardless of socioeconomic privilege. David Elkind, *The Power of Play: Learning What Comes Naturally* (Cambridge; London: Da Capo Lifelong ; Perseus Running [distributor], 2007), 23.

7. Karen Goldberg Goff, "Parenting pundits proliferate," *The Washington Times*, January 16, 2005, D01.

8. Gary Ezzo and Robert Bucknam, *On Becoming Babywise: Giving Your Infant the Gift of Nighttime Sleep* (Sisters, OR: Parent-Wise Solutions, Inc.: 2006).

9. James Dobson, *The Strong-Willed Child*, (Carol Stream, Il: Tyndale House Publishers, Inc.) 53–54.

10. Alfie Kohn, *Unconditional Parenting* (New York: Atria Books, a division of Simon and Schuster, 2006), 4. See also, Ruth Allen Peters, *Don't Be Afraid to Discipline* (New York: Golden Books, 1999); Gregory Bodenhamer, *Parent in Control* (New York: Simon and Schuster, 1995); Mitch Golant and Susan K Golant, *Disciplining Your Preschooler and Feeling Good About It* (Los Angeles; Chicago: Lowell House/ Contemporary Books, 1989); Donna Black, "*Cause I"m the Mommy (that's Why)!* ([Bridgeport, CT]: Hysteria, 1995); Ruth Allen Peters, *Laying Down the Law: The 25 Laws of Parenting to Keep Your Kids on Track, Out of Trouble, & (pretty Much) Under Control* ([Emmaus, Pa.]; [New York]: Rodale ; Distributed to the book trade by St. Martin's Press, 2003); Robert G. Bruce, Debra Bruce, and Ellen W. Oldacre, *Guilt-free Parenting* (Nashville: Dimensions For Living, 1997); Cynthia Whitham, *The Answer Is No: Saying It and Sticking to It* (Los Angeles: Perspective Pub., 1994).

11. Leigh Edwards, "Supernanny: British Nanny Invation," PopMatters website, http://www.popmatters.com/tv/reviews/s/supernanny-2005.shtml, retrieved February 10, 2009.

12. Amy Chua, "Why Chinese Mothers Are Superior," *Wall Street Journal*, January 8, 2011, sec. The Saturday Essay, http://online.wsj.com/article/SB100014240527487 04111504576059713528698754.html.

13. George Lakoff, *Moral Politics: How Liberals and Conservatives Think* (Chicago [u.a.: University of Chicago Press, 2002). It is important to note that although Lakoff is a cognitive linguist, not a communication scholar, his family metaphor has proven fruitful for rhetorical scholars. See, for example, Sara Hayden, "Family Metaphors and the Nation: Promoting a Politics of Care through the Million Mom March," *Quarterly Journal of Speech*, 89, no.3 (2003): 196–215.

14. George Lakoff, *Don't Think of an Elephant!: Know Your Values and Frame the Debate: The Essential Guide for Progressives* (White River Junction, Vt.: Chelsea Green Pub. Co., 2004).

15. William Sears, Martha Sears, Robert Sears, and James Sears, *The Baby Book: Everything You Need to Know About Your Baby from Birth to Age Two* (New York: Little-brown and Co., 2003), 9.

16. Becky Bailey, "About," Conscious Discipline: Loving Guidance, http://consciousdiscipline.com/about/dr_becky_bailey.asp (accessed September 13, 2013); Marshall Rosenberg, "About," Non-Violent Communication, accessed September 13, 2013, http://www.cnvc.org/about/marshall-rosenberg.html.

17. Scott Noelle, "Terrible Two's and Rebellious Teens . . . Not!" Enjoy Parenting weblog, http://www.enjoyparenting.com/daily-groove/terrible-not, retrieved February 10, 2009.

18. Ibid.

19. For example: Attraction parenting (Scott Noelle), continuum concept (Jean Liedloff), and natural parenting (various, including *Mothering* magazine).

20. Judith Warner, *Perfect Madness: Motherhood in the Age of Anxiety* (New York: Riverhead Trade, 2006).

21. Pollitt, Katha, "Attachment Parenting: More Guilt for Mother" *The Nation http://www.thenation.com/article/167928/attachment-parenting-more-guilt-mother#.*

22. Dana Cloud, *Control and Consolation in American Culture and Politics: Rhetorics of Therapy*, (Thousand Oaks, CA: SAGE Publications, 1997).

23. Kathy Hirsh-Pasek and Roberta Michnick Golinkoff, *Einstein Never Used Flashcards: How Our Children Really Learn—and Why They Need to Play More and Memorize Less*, (Emaus, PA: Rodale Books, 2003).

24. Baby Flashcards website, http://www.babyflashcards.org/download/, retrieved February 20, 2009.

25. Davi Johnson Thornton, *Brain Culture: Neuroscience and Popular Media*, 104. For an extensive analysis of the baby brain movement, see especially chapter four, "Babies, Blank Slates, and Brain Building."

26. Thomas R. Verny and John Kelly, *The Secret Life of the Unborn Child* (New York: Dell Pub. Co., 1988); Norman M Ford, *The Prenatal Person: Ethics from Conception to Birth* (Malden, Mass [u.a.: Blackwell, 2002); Thomas R. Verny and Pamela Weintraub, *Pre-parenting: Nurturing Your Child from Conception* (New York: Simon & Schuster, 2003).

27. "You're Never Too Young To Learn!," accessed September 28, 2013, http://blog.babyplus.com/blog/babyplus-customer-service/youre-never-too-young-to-learn-v3.

28. Ari Brown, "Media Use by Children Younger Than 2 Years," *Pediatrics* 128, no. 5 (November 1, 2011): 1040–45, doi:10.1542/peds.2011–1753.

29. Tamar Lewen, "No Einstein in Your Crib? Get a Refund," *The New York Times*, October 23, 2009.

30. Ibid.

31. Shinn, Lora, "Slow Parenting in a Sliding Economy," ParentMap March 2009, 33.

32. Hirsh-Pasek and Michnick Golinkoff, *Einstein Never Used Flashcards*, 11

33. Ibid., 28

34. Ibid.

35. Ibid., 210–211.

36. Elkind, 211.

37. Vivian Gussin Paley, *A Child's Work: The Importance of Fantasy Play* (Chicago: Chicago University Press, 2005) 8.

38. Walt Whitman, *Leaves of Grass* (1855; reprint, Wilder Publications, 2007).

39. Susan Linn, *Consuming Kids: The Hostile Takeover of Childhood* (New York; London: New Press : distributed by W. W. Norton & Co., 2004); Juliet Schor, *Born to Buy: The Commercialized Child and the New Consumer Culture* (New York: Scribner, 2004); Susan Linn, *The Case for Make Believe: Saving Play in a Commercialized World* (New York; London: New Press ; Turnaround [distributor], 2009).

40. Fergus P Hughes, *Children, Play, and Development* (Los Angeles: Sage, 2010).

41. Ibid.

42. David Elkind, *The Power of Play: Learning What Comes Naturally* (Cambridge, MA; London: Da Capo Lifelong ; Perseus Running [distributor], 2007), 23.

43. Roland Barthes, *Mythologies* (New York: Noonday Press, 1972).

44. Ibid., 53.

45. Ibid., 53–54.

46. Ibid., 53.

47. According to Hirsh-Pasek and Michnick Golinkoff, 40 percent of American school districts have eliminated recess. One significant strain of the "play movement" is devoted to defending recess. For more on this issue, see: Kathy Hirsh-Pasek and Roberta Michnick Golinkoff, *Einstein Never Used Flashcards: How Our Children Really Learn—and Why They Need to Play More and Memorize Less* (Emaus, PA: Rodale Books, 2003); Dirk Johnson, "Many Schools Putting an End to Child's Play," *New York Times* April 7, 1998, accessed September 28, 2013, http://www.nytimes.com/1998/04/07/us/many-schools-putting-an-end-to-child-s-play.html?pagewanted=all&src=pm; Anthony Pellegrini and Patricia Davis, "Relations Between Children's Playground and Classroom Behavior," *British Journal of Educational Psychology* 63 (1993), 88–95

48. Quoted in Richard Louv, *The Last Child in the Woods: Saving Our Children from Nature Deficit Disorder* (Chapel Hill, NC: Algonquin Books, 2008) 85.

49. Ibid, 86.

50. Kohn, *Unconditional Parenting: Moving from Rewards and Punishment to Love and Reason* (New York: Atria Books, 2006) 59.

51. Paula Polk Lillard and Lynn Lillard Jessen, *Montessori from the Start: The Child at Home, from Birth to Age Three* (Random House LLC, 2008).

52. Kohn, *Unconditional Parenting*, 100–101

53. David Elkind, *The Power of Play: How Spontaneous Imaginative Activities Lead to Happier, Healthier Children* (Cambridge: DeCapo Lifelong Books), 70.

54. Matt Richtel, "A Silicon Valley School that Doesn't Compute," *The New York Times*, October 22, 2011.

55. Gareth B Matthews, *Philosophy and the Young Child* (Cambridge: Harvard University Press, 1980), 11.

56. Lawrence J. Cohen, *Playful Parenting* (New York: Ballantine, 2001), p. 17.

57. Quoted in David Elkin, *The Power of Play: Learning What Comes Naturally* (New York: Da Capo Press, 2007).

References

Atwill, Janet, and Lauer, Janice M. *Perspectives on Rhetorical Invention*. Knoxville: University of Tennessee Press, 2003.

Baby Flashcards website. Accessed February 20, 2009. http://www.babyflashcards.org/download/

Barthes, Roland. *Mythologies*. New York: Noonday Press, 1972.

Brown, Ari. "Media Use by Children Younger Than 2 Years," *Pediatrics* 128, no. 5 (November 1, 2011): 1040–45.

Chua, Amy. "Why Chinese Mothers Are Superior," *Wall Street Journal*, January 8, 2011. Accessed September 27, 2014. http://online.wsj.com/article/SB10001424052748704111504576059713528698754.html.

Cloud, Dana. *Control and Consolation in American Culture and Politics: Rhetorics of Therapy*. Thousand Oaks, CA: SAGE Publications, 1997.

Cohen, Lawrence J. *Playful Parenting*. New York: Ballantine, 2001.

Dobson, James. *The Strong-Willed Child*. Carol Stream, Il: Tyndale House Publishers, Inc. 1992.

Edwards, Leigh. "Supernanny: British Nanny Invation," *PopMatters*. Accessed February 10, 2009. http://www.popmatters.com/tv/reviews/s/supernanny-2005.shtml.

Elkind, David. *The Power of Play: Learning What Comes Naturally*. Cambridge, Mass.; London: Da Capo Lifelong ; Perseus Running [distributor], 2007.

Ezzo, Gary, and Robert Bucknam. *On Becoming Babywise: Giving Your Infant the Gift of Nighttime Sleep*. Sisters, OR: Parent-Wise Solutions, Inc., 2006.

Goldberg Goff, Karen. "Parenting pundits proliferate," *The Washington Times* January 15, 2005. Accessed September 27, 2014. http://www.washingtontimes.com/news/2005/jan/15/20050115–100349–3912r/?page=all

Gussin Paley, Vivian. *A Child's Work: The Importance of Fantasy Play*. Chicago: Chicago University Press, 2005.

Hirsh-Pasek, Kathy, and Roberta Michnick Golinkoff. *Einstein Never Used Flashcards: How Our Children Really Learn—and Why They Need to Play More and Memorize Less*. Emaus, PA: Rodale Books, 2003.

Hughes, Fergus P. *Children, Play, and Development*. Los Angeles: Sage, 2010.

Johnson Thornton, Davi. *Brain Culture: Neuroscience and Popular Media*. New Brunswick: Rutgers, 2011.

Kohn, Alfie. *Unconditional Parenting*. New York: Atria Books, 2006.

Lakoff, George. *Moral Politics: How Liberals and Conservatives Think*. Chicago: University of Chicago Press, 2002.

———. *Don't Think of an Elephant!: Know Your Values and Frame the Debate: The Essential Guide for Progressives*. White River Junction, VT: Chelsea Green, 2004.

Lewen, Tamar. "No Einstein in Your Crib? Get a Refund," *The New York Times*, October 23, 2009.

Linn, Susan. *Consuming Kids: The Hostile Takeover of Childhood*. New York; London: New Press : distributed by W.W. Norton & Co., 2004.

Linn, Susan. *The Case for Make Believe: Saving Play in a Commercialized World*. New York; London: New Press, 2009.

Louv, Richard. *The Last Child in the Woods: Saving Our Children from Nature Deficit Disorder*. Chapel Hill, NC: Algonquin Books, 2008.

Matthews, Gareth B. *Philosophy and the Young Child*. Cambridge: Harvard University Press, 1980.

Noelle, Scott. "Terrible Two's and Rebellious Teens . . . Not!" *Enjoy Parenting* weblog. Accessed February 10, 2009. http://www.enjoyparenting.com/daily-groove/terrible-not.

Paul, Pamela. *Parenting, Inc.: How the Billion Dollar Baby Business Has Changed the Way We Raise our Children*. New York: Holt: 2009.

Plato, and Paul Shorey. *The Republic. Books I-V Books I-V*. Cambridge: Harvard University Press, 1937.
Polk Lillard, Paula, and Lynn Lillard Jessen. *Montessori from the Start: The Child at Home, from Birth to Age Three*. New York: Random House, 2008.
Pollitt, Katha. "Attachment Parenting: More Guilt for Mother," *The Nation*, June 4, 2012, Accessed September 27, 2014. *http://www.thenation.com/article/167928/attachment-parenting-more-guilt-mother*
Richtel, Matt. "A Silicon Valley School that Doesn't Compute," *The New York Times*, October 22, 2011.
Schor, Juliet. *Born to Buy: The Commercialized Child and the New Consumer Culture*. New York: Scribner, 2004.
Sears, William, Martha Sears, Robert Sears, and James Sears. *The Baby Book: Everything You Need to Know About Your Baby from Birth to Age Two*. New York: Littlebrown and Co., 2003.
Shinn, Lora. "Slow Parenting in a Sliding Economy," *ParentMap*. March 2009.
Veblen, Thorstein. *The Instinct of Workmanship: And the State of the Industrial Arts*. New York: Viking, 1943.
Warner, Judith. *Perfect Madness: Motherhood in the Age of Anxiety*. New York: Riverhead Trade, 2006.
Whitman, Walt. *Leaves of Grass*. 1855; Reprint, Wilder Publications, 2007.
"You're Never Too Young To Learn!," *Baby Plus* website. Accessed September 28, 2013, http://blog.babyplus.com/blog/babyplus-customer-service/youre-never-too-young-to-learn-v3.

10
Choosing to Consume

Race, Education, and the School Voucher Debate

Lisa A. Flores

Public education. In crisis. It has been a topic for news, television, and film, as well as policy, politics, and law. Reports list rising dropout rates combined with lowered levels of basic skills in reading and math. Accounts of the crisis name varied consequences, ranging from increasing unemployment and crime to national security. Consider, for instance, a report issued by the Council on Foreign Relations, identifying public education as a "national security crisis."[1] With too many dropouts and too many youngsters allegedly undereducated, overweight, and even carrying criminal records, the nation is raising American youth who will be ineligible for military service and unable to complete globally.[2] Or, concluded in the White House Position Paper published by the *Boys and Girls Club of America*: "It is manifestly clear that our nation is facing a dropout crisis."[3] Local and national communities across the country are debating and deliberating the state of public education.

Consistent in such conversations are commentaries that pinpoint both race and class, noting that far too often those most dramatically undereducated are either poor and/or nonwhite. For instance, a recent *Time* magazine article announces that the high school graduation rate for "Hispanics" is at 64 percent, and college entrance is at "a shockingly low 7%."[4] Reported statistics for African Americans are generally lower, with only 47 percent of black males graduating from high school and 53 percent of all African Americans earning their high school diploma.[5] Though these figures are markedly different from those published elsewhere, which list that 10 percent of blacks and 15 percent of Latinos will drop out, the larger message that race (and class) are linked to school success remains.[6]

While the debate varies in its intensity, with some reports seemingly more hyperbolic than others in their insistence on "crisis," there is considerable agreement that public education needs attention and reform. Not surprisingly, the national conversation about public education often turns to questions of problem and solution. At fault is everything from federal underfunding to school misuse of funds, from bad government policy, such as No Child Left Behind, to teachers unions and their allegedly misguided, if not selfish, attempts to protect the tenure of bad teachers at the expense of students. Solutions, too, range. Some argue for more federal funding, while others suggest greater competition, mostly in the form of alternatives to public education, namely charter, online, and private schools. One such solution—vouchers—has recently gained considerable attention.

Vouchers, also often termed "opportunity scholarships" or "choice scholarships," offer scholarships, money, or credit that can be used by families toward private school tuition. Regulations on eligibility vary by state or even region. Many are linked to income, while a few target specific populations, such as students with disabilities. The choice *du jour*, voucher programs have been proposed and passed in cities and states across the country, garnering so much attention that 2011 was deemed "The Year of the Voucher,"[7] with more than fifty-two voucher proposals emerging across thirty-six states.[8] Often heated, the voucher debate, with its emphasis on using federal funds to send students to private schools, sits at the intersections of questions of education, race/ethnicity/class, and the turn to privatization and consumption. Indeed, proponents of vouchers, typically representing a more politically conservative population, couch their arguments explicitly in race and/or class equity, arguing that vouchers and school choice may well be the "civil rights" issue of the current moment.[9] That this turn to the salience of race and class appears at a time many have identified as mired in a narrative of postracial triumph is curious. It also taps into consumption, remaking education from public good to consumer good. Marshalling the figure of an empowered, individualist parent newly situated to purchase their child's education, the voucher debate likens the choice of school to the choice of mobile telephone providers. Parents should be able to—indeed, parents become constituted as needing to—pick the best.[10]

In this essay, I turn to the pro-voucher discourse and its centering of race/ethnicity/class. I argue that race, class, and choice intersect in what Peter Bansal identifies as a "conceptual coupling" that positions the privatization of education as the best and most equitable solution to the education crisis crippling underserved populations.[11] Mobilizing racialized and class-laded characterizations, the "choice" for vouchers utilizes a race- and class-specific narrative that relies upon emotional caricature as a means to consolidate public support for privatized education. In this way, the prochoice debate personalizes a political argument. As I will argue in the conclusion, it marshalls as well a consumerist mentality of mothering and parenting in which as good parents, we must buy our children the very best. Across the essay, I detail the ways that choice functions to normalize not only the privatization of education but also how that normalization relies upon and reproduces privilege, particularly race- and class-based privilege. Though my arguments here mostly emerge out of my analysis of the public discourse, they are also reflective of my struggles as a mother with considerable choice over my children's education. To account for my personal investment in contemporary debates about public education and social privilege, I pause throughout my analysis to offer moments of auto-ethnographic reflection. In this way, I hope, as Carolyn Ellis argues, to "connect the autobiographical and personal to the cultural, social, and political."[12]

Resituating Race

It is, by now, passé to suggest that race, class, and education are linked. After all, it is only a few years since the nation celebrated the fiftieth anniversary of Brown v. Board of Education, a case that many mark as a crucial turning point in US racial history. The Supreme Court declined the opportunity to rule on Fisher v. the University of Texas in 2013, a case that would have prohibited public colleges and universities from considering race in admissions.[13] Nonetheless, if discourse surrounding the case is any indicator then the provoucher discourse should come as a surprise. For here, the problem to be fixed is one in which a racialized figure takes center stage, not as the opportunist greedily taking a seat that he or she did not earn but instead as the impoverished and disadvantaged victim of greedy teachers and politicians who consistently put their own interests above those of marginalized student populations. Coming amidst a larger neoliberal climate in which to name race is to be racist, the rhetorical force of the racialized narrative that supports the provoucher argument needs critical attention.

Per most scholarly accounts, "race" has been and remains publicly off-limits, at least as a marker of societal stratification. Across many different conversations and a range of venues, we, as a society, allegedly perpetuate racism when we consistently name race. Darrel Enck-Wanzer, for instance, notes that in contemporary politics, the language of race has become both antiquated and taboo.[14] To see it or to speak it is to situate ourselves with an outdated and unproductive politic. That is, of course, to speak race *and* racism, to assert that racial status may continue to be linked to experiences of racism, or more directly, to claim that racism continues to pervade US social and political culture, is taboo. In what Jodi Melamed names "neoliberal multiculturalism," the language of race today mostly operates strategically to represent the contemporary accomplishments of diversity, seen perhaps in mediated narratives of success, while simultaneously obscuring the persistent materialities of racism.[15] Consider, for instance, the range of racialized bodies that populate contemporary television, occupying enviable positions of authority. These representational politics of race narrate a Cosby Show–like postracial America of equality.[16] Functioning within a neoliberal context, race-as-representation serves simultaneously to assuage guilt while it also fosters fears—that people of color really are taking over. It thus serves to accentuate that taboo that Enck-Wanzer identifies, for if a working-class black woman with a marked Southern accent can become America's Next Top Model, it is because US society has achieved racial equity.[17] The logic of neoliberal multiculturalism suggests that when we name race and link it to racism, we are playing opportunist victim.

And yet, for all that the language of race has been disciplined into submission, its workings remain. Indeed, as Roopali Mukherjee so beautifully illustrates, since the 1960s and despite varying political contexts in which race and gender have been contested and (re)defined, we continue to witness the "undulating but abiding racial order of the post-soul era."[18] For instance, in attacks upon affirmative action, ethnic studies programs, and immigration, race and gender have been and continue to be contested and regulated. Mukherjee continues, "these assaults . . . confirm that politico-economic practices are not necessarily rational nor always merit-based. They suggest, to the contrary, that hiring and admissions decisions are deeply intertwined with cultural imaginaries about women and nonwhites."[19] And yet, despite persistent economic and political backlash against efforts to erase structural inequalities, neoliberal multiculturalism regulates conversations about race (and gender) to depoliticize difference and contain it in the private sphere.[20]

It is to this merger of race, politics, and the private that this essay turns. In naming the relationship between multiculturalism and neoliberalism, Melamed argues, "it legitimates as it obfuscates."[21] The specificity of racialized and class-based difference—mostly taboo in public and political discourses—claims center stage in the analysis that follows. In a highly emotive tale of disadvantage and greed, difference becomes the politicized move that justifies the depoliticized privatization of education.

Racing to Choose, Erasing Choice

> We sit at dinner, and I casually mention some of what emerged early that day, as I worked on this essay, "according to one article I read, kindergarteners enter knowing a few letters of the alphabet." I offer this tidbit with considerable skepticism, sure that it is overstating the case.

> After all, my almost four year old could count to ten when she was two, in English and Spanish. Now, she easily counts to thirty and most days can count to one hundred or as high as my patience allows, with a bit of help. She knows most of her letters and can write her name. She knows that $2 + 2 = 4$ and $7 - 5 = 2$. My partner, whose position requires that she be more versed in the "realities" of public education responds to my skepticism, "That's true of most public kindergartners. Kids whose parents don't or can't pay what we do for preschool, don't know their letters." I'm stunned. I recall a day last week when my daughter and I walked to the car after school, and I overheard her friend tell her mother, $9 + 9 = 18$. My partner continues by reminding me that dropout rates are high and that students are graduating high school with elementary-school reading levels. Will we send our children to public schools? Or will we participate in what often appears to me as the hyper-elite, madly consumerist rush to private or charter or magnet schools? And, regardless of our choice, how will our beautiful, multiracial, dark-skinned daughters of queer parents be treated?

The racialized characters—or caricatures—of public discourse are all too familiar. The welfare queen, the pregnant single mother, and the affirmative action scholarship student have populated public discourse at least since the Reagen era. Typically cast in a familiar tale of opportunism, these caricatures have been the carriers of race and racism, evidence of the dangers of government programs that allegedly foster dependency at taxpayer expense. They appear mostly as anecdotal evidence of the widely proclaimed structural problem of affirmative action, the figures who deplete the nation of its promise through their overconsumption of public goods. They are typically used to illustrate why it is that middle-class white men, for the most part, are the ones with legitimate cause for concern, as they are—or so they claim to be—today's disadvantaged population. So how is it that those arguing for vouchers, which would effectively undermine public education by privatizing K–12 education, relay a different racial tale in which the poor and nonwhite students and families are experiencing the material effects of structural and institutional racism and segregation?

Consider the plight of Ingrid Campbell, a black mother, seemingly a single parent, whose children's participation in the Washington, DC, voucher program is depicted as at risk: "My middle child is the one I'm fighting for all the way, because I might have to put her back in public school next year if we lose the vouchers. . . . I would get two or three jobs to keep her in her private school."[22] Or Claudia Correa, explicitly named a single mother, who moved her children from public school to private: "Correa had no idea her daughter was two years behind in reading [while in public school]."[23] Or the experience recounted by Philadelphia's former schools superintendent Arlene Ackerman after she spoke in favor of vouchers, when parents "gave me a big hug and just said 'No one is going to listen to us.' . . . I felt their frustration. I was kind of sad."[24] Or finally, what about the children who attend "the schools that are ranked at the bottom 5 percent academically and are among the most violent. State Department of Education statistics show 5,430 violent incidents occurred on students and staff at these schools during the 2008–09 school year, including seven rapes, 554 weapons charges and 1,983 assaults on students."[25]

> We're at the dinner table, playing with Aliana, teaching her "shush . . . it's a secret," as we put a finger up to our lips. Amaris interjects—"Secrets are mean." Caught off guard, I say, "sometimes, but not always." She continues by explaining that, at school, some of the girls tell secrets, and they don't tell her. I see—and feel—her hurt. My sweet baby, already navigating such dynamics. She seems to struggle with friendships, and I wonder, is it race? Her dark body marked in a school that is almost all-white? If I fear what I try to dismiss as mostly typical negotiations of gender, race, and friendship for my children, how would I respond if her school was marred by violence, weapons, assault, rape. Wouldn't I then give anything for choice?

Attending schools that are overpopulated, failing, and have populations that are eligible for free or reduced lunch, students depicted as the ones who would likely benefit from vouchers emerge as non-white, probably black or Latino, and poor. Though extended examples offering details about particular families appear only occasionally in the public discourse supporting vouchers, what does occur with regularity are accounts that emphasize race and class. For instance, that many voucher programs link eligibility to income is made evident: "During its first year, 3,919 students participated in the program statewide, with nearly 85 percent of them on the free and reduced lunch program, according to School Choice Indiana."[26] In addition, income and class intersect with race, as in this typical commentary: "about 98 percent of participating students are black or Hispanic. . . . The average household income of students was $23,401 in 2010. The federal poverty line for a family of four was $41,347.50 last year."[27]

What occurs in this discourse is a different mobilization of race than what most scholars have identified as the more traditional neoliberal account. Here race and class are regularly named. Moreover, they are connected such that to be African American or Latino is also to be poor and disadvantaged. This recognition of the material intersection of race and class begins to name a structural pattern—that race/class segregation may indeed exist in the United States. Indiana's secretary of public instruction goes so far as to state that "demographics do not determine a child's ability to grow academically and should not determine the educational opportunities offered to any student."[28] Expressing a similar sentiment, school board member in Florida's Pinellas County, Glenton Gilzean, argued, "We need to make sure all children, regardless of race, color or where they live have the opportunity to get the best education."[29]

The move to identify the structural occurs implicitly as well, through a metaphor of being trapped. Articulating the need for vouchers, one article writer claims, "they have no solution to provide immediate help to these trapped kids,"[30] while in another article Tennessee Governor Bill Haslam is quoted as saying "We should offer alternatives to low-income students and their parents who may feel stuck in failing schools."[31] New Jersey Governor Chris Christie frames it this way, "'We need to give choice and hope to those students and parents trapped in failing school districts,"[32] and Minnesota state Senator Nienow asks, "They probably don't have any options. . . . Why should we lock them into failure?"[33]

The combination of the emphases on race and class with the metaphor of being trapped functions rhetorically to create a narrative in which the public education crisis is about choice, or more precisely, the lack of it. That is, because some populations are "trapped" or "stuck," they do not have the choice that, to many, is fundamental to ideals of American mobility and freedom. It is likely not coincidental that vouchers are often referred to as "choice scholarships," nor that the language of choice permeates this debate. Emerging across numerous cultural conversations, the ideology of choice has become a generative force with particular gendered, and I would argue, raced and classed implications. Virginia McCarver, for instance, argues that choice emerges in contemporary gendered debates as a means through which feminism is made individual and the structural forces of patriarchy become a "relic of the 1960s."[34] Similarly, Mary Douglas Vavrus concludes that in mothering "opt-out" discourse, "stories confidently conclude that any gender imbalance in workplaces or society in general is directly attributable to mothers' choices."[35] Centering the individual while noting, perhaps casually, the larger forces of gender, race, or class, choice participates in a consumerist ideology in which all individuals are made equal, for we all have choice.

Though relying on narrowly constrained scripts and limited options, "choice" discourse highlights individual agency as the promised response to structural forces. As Bansel concludes, with choice, "citizens, in the name of their own self-interest, are to take responsibility for their own conduct and its consequences."[36] Herein, the rhetorical force and related danger of the neoliberal multiculturalism that Melamed identifies begins to emerge. Freedom and choice, within neoliberalism at least, function rhetorically to embue individuals with the agency that is heralded as foundational to American democracy. Bansel explains, "A discourse of choice, for example, adheres to a discourse of freedom in such a way that choice is valorized as a personal and social good, and as a mode of taking one's place within a democracy (providing of course the 'right' choices are made)."[37] In other words, if certain populations are structurally trapped, via race, class, and education, they are denied the freedom to choose the options that would situate them more fully within American democracy. Moreover, not only are the structural concerns raised above eliminated, but, as Bansel hints at here, individuals are responsible for making the *right* choices. Education becomes a commodity and parents the consumers. Sounds logical, if not imperative.

> For wasn't it, in part, that very imperative of educational choice coupled with our responsibility as mothers to secure for our children the best education that motivated our move from a diverse urban Denver school district, where schools scored poorly on the various governmental measures, to the seemingly all-white Golden suburbs, and their high-scoring schools? We chose to move to a more elite neighborhood in a better school district. We chose to give our children what we deemed to be the very best that we could, for what more can we offer them than love and education. As mothers, isn't that our responsibility? Education is choice; it is freedom. This belief guides my life. But it is also, perhaps, that very stance which reveals my own social location, firmly ensconced in middle-class white ideologies of mothering. Byrne, in her analysis of middle-class mothers' emphasis on sending their children to the "right" school, concludes: "The cultural and social capital they [mothers] were seeking to preserve and pass on to their children was white as well as middle-class."[38] My ideologies of mothering steeped in larger cultural practices of consumption and whiteness, merged as choice.

In the debate at play, freedom of choice is possible with the privatization of education that occurs with vouchers. And it is not just freedom of choice but mobility and access that are promised by pro-voucher arguments. For instance, Christopher Knight, superintendent of schools for the Catholic Diocese of Toledo, states, "We support school choice. The legislation reaches out to lower-income and middle-class families. It's about choice and access."[39] Speaking similarly Denise Lessow, executive director of a private school in Indiana, proclaims, "I'm excited about it as a tool that gives families more options."[40] An account of the proposed legislation in Pennsylvania situates it this way: "The governor's proposal is not about shutting down the public school system. It is about empowering parents to have the economic freedom to choose the best school for their children."[41] Across these and other similar discussions is a consistent linking of vouchers with choice, freedom, access, and parental empowerment. Vouchers offer agency to those depicted in the metaphor of the trap, as most lacking it. Bansel argues that neoliberalism functions discursively by linking abstract ideals such as freedom and choice, mobility and flexibility.[42] These "conceptual couplings," he argues, work to sustain neoliberalism via the relationship that seems natural to the coupling—one necessitates the other. Freedom requires choice. As a result, the individual, the parent-made-consumer, responsible for and empowered to choose, becomes the locus for seemingly structural change.

The connections that emerge in the pro-voucher discourse, between and among race/class/educational trap and freedom/choice/mobility/access function to situate the privatization of education—via vouchers—as the equitable solution. In the words of Representative Bill Dunn, who sponsored the Knoxville proposal, the voucher proposal "allows parents to 'make decisions' and 'focuses on children who don't have a choice to flee failing public schools.'"[43] In this way, the privatization of education becomes the new public good, a good that is designed to remedy the structural disadvantage of race and class segregation. Indeed, as Arlene Ackerman, Philadelphia's former schools superintendent, speaking in support of vouchers, proclaims, school reform is the "civil-rights movement of our generation."[44] Not an isolated sentiment, the linkage of vouchers to civil rights appears and justice emerges regularly. Indiana Governor Mitch Daniels states: "It's a matter of social justice. Before this program arrived, most of these folks did not have the options of those with more means,"[45] while another article announces, "Make no mistake, school vouchers is the civil rights issue of our generation."[46] If readers had doubts about the centrality of race and class to arguments in support of vouchers, such connections erase those doubts. Mobilizing the language of social justice, voucher supporters imbue the debate with a political and emotional urgency that plays off the centrality of race and choice, coupled here in ways that allow good citizens, those already enjoying choice, to extend their privilege to others.

In her analysis of war discourse, Dana Cloud argues that contemporary war rhetoric relies upon the rhetorical creation of an "affected public . . . an irrational artificial social construct that enforces emotional identification over heterogeneity and dissent."[47] Catherine Chaput, too, identifies affect, noting that the social connectivity of affective energy produced through communicative labor helps explain the persuasive capacity of these reaches.[48] Though their projects are different, both Cloud and Chaput identify the rhetorical force of affect and its connections to neoliberal discourse. As Chaput argues, "theorizing neoliberalism demands a structural reorganization in the way we think about political-economic and cultural practices within capitalism from situation to transsituation and a new understanding of rhetoric as continuously moving through and connecting different instantiations within this complex structure."[49] Considered alongside Bansel's notion of conceptual couplings, what Chaput and Cloud help illuminate are the ways in which the complex and contradictory discourses of race and class, education and access, public and private, social justice and civil rights intersect such that the plight of the racialized and impoverished family trapped in a violent and failing school system replaces the demonized quota queen and welfare queen of the 1980s and 1990s. Citing Jackie Jones, Mukherjee argues that in the "the post-soul" era of race and raciality, static caricatures of blacks and Latinos mostly emerge in public discourse within the "space of the accused."[50] They serve as the evidence of a nation gone awry, overly concerned with racial- and class-based disadvantages and too quick to offer faulty and misguided governmental reform that ultimately created its own system of reverse racism. She continues: "With deliberate disregard of race as a systemic factor in economic life, the operation of racism as an invisible system of economic hierarchies and oppressions is muted. Systemic privileges associated with whiteness and structural burdens faced by the black poor remain veiled."[51] And yet, in the machinations of the voucher debate, DC Council Chairman Kwame Brown, testifying in support of vouchers, argues, "I cannot look a working mother in the eye and tell her that she deserves less choice, not more."[52] A vilified welfare queen no more, Ingrid Campbell, the black mother worried about the future of her three children, reemerges as a disadvantaged single mother who needs and seemingly deserves our help, public help. Importantly, however, that public help is privatized education.

The rhetorical question, then, is how is it that the long-disparaged and reviled welfare queen becomes Ingrid Campbell, seemingly single mother whose children need and *deserve* help? Arguments for vouchers mobilize support via these complex narrative intersections. Heightened in the discourse is an emphasis on disparity—some parents have choices and others do not—and hypocrisy, suggesting that those who oppose vouchers do so despite the fact that their own children are protected from the crisis that is public education. For instance, one article recounts what are described as the two key questions asked by voucher supporters that opponents cannot answer: "Would you send your child—the one you love with all of your heart—to any of these schools where violence and mayhem are the golden rule? What is your plan to immediately help the third-grade student trapped in a violent, failing school whose future is slipping away day by day [waiting] for a solution?"[53] Another situates the debate thusly: "What speaks volumes as hypocrisy to parents whose kids are trapped in failing schools is that many of our well paid representatives opt out of public education for theirs while at the same time are adamant in denying the same option to parents who can't afford to."[54] Together, these fragments cement the social justice/civil rights argument of structural disparity, of haves and have nots, of access and barrier. They do so through affect, in part relying on the guilt of race and class privilege.

The emphasis on the structural within the voucher debate names the very real educational disparities that exist. There is considerable evidence that suggests that public schools are indeed in trouble. Dropout rates are too high, reading levels are too low, particularly for poor, black, and Latino populations, as well as for recent immigrants. Structural barriers, such as race- and class-based segregation, exist, and the impact that they have on our society is unquestionable. Rising rates of poverty, unemployment, and imprisonment threaten the well-being of communities of color. And to varying degrees, middle-class and white populations can *choose*, if not private school, at least neighborhood. With greater access to flexibility in their jobs and to the personal transportation that would allow them to drive their children to private, charter, or other non-neighborhood and thus non-school-bus schools, some parents can make individual decisions about what educational opportunities to offer their children. As the article referenced above asks, "Would you send your child—the one you love with all of your heart—to any of these schools where violence and mayhem are the golden rule?" Of course not. And as Lauren Berlant so powerfully argues, compassion functions crucially in the rhetorical discourse of neoliberalism.[55]

> It's Saturday morning, my favorite morning, when the girls and I typically enjoy a "breakfast snack" in bed, while they get to watch television and I leisurely drink coffee. But today, Mary Ann is at work again, and the girls' school is hosting a session for parents on how to make educational choices after Montessori. I make the misguided decision to go, which means getting the girls up, dressed, and fed, and thus foregoing our one morning of nothing-to-do together-time. Before long,

as I sit with the sixty or so other parents in the room, listening to the Montessori expert speaker talk about schools, pedagogical theories, and gifted children, my heart begins to race, seemingly alongside all the other parents in the room. The anxiety is palpable, and it emerges in the barrage of frantic and impassioned questions, in which we all ask in our own way, "But what about the special-ness of my child? How do I ensure the right school?" The assumption seems to be that neighborhood public schools are not likely to be "right" for our special children. Instead, parents mention schools across the Denver metro area, suggesting their willingness and ability to drive twenty miles or more to take their children to school. A parent next to me inquires about her energetic son and fears he will be disciplined and labeled ADD in a public school. I know her and her son. I know he is multiracial. I ask about Amaris, who often prefers reading and working on projects alone. Will she be ignored in her quiet independence or praised for being a good girl. We both assume our children are "gifted and talented." We both tell gendered stories about our children. I suspect that had an educational consultant been at the session most of the parents, myself included, would have scheduled appointments then and there. Credit cards out, our children's futures secured.

The invocation of affect into this debate intersects with the turn to the privitized solution, one that is allegedly not only about choice and educational opportunity but also, crucially, requires that voters turn away from *public* education. In this way, the voucher debate taps into what Giroux calls the "neoliberal fervor for unbridled individualism and its disdain for community, public values, and the public good."[56] Within the voucher debate, such fervor taps into what may well be a public education system in crisis and, rather than arguing for greater public funding of education, suggests that the solution is a market-based approach to education in which public tax money is diverted from public schools and sent to private ones. Indeed, voucher, proponents are clear that the public school crisis is due to government regulation and bureaucracy: "When monopolies continue unchecked without choice and competition, they will do what all monopolies do—offer their customers an inferior product at a higher cost. But unlike other monopolies, the education monopoly produces results that are far more disastrous for all of us. Children drop out and end up unemployed and on state and federal assistance programs. Competition—through school choice—is the only real force to improve learning. If we shop for a mobile phone, we have ample, ever-improving providers and a variety of plans to choose from.

We usually select the plan that provides us the highest quality service at the best price. The same would happen for Pennsylvania parents if they are given more options through charter schools, vouchers and an expanded tuition tax-credit program."[57] Importantly, here, these arguments for competition situate public schools as governmental, coupling them to larger latent discourses about government as forced and controlled.

In its emphasis on choice versus control, the debate becomes, in many accounts, about big—read, bad—government and irresponsible unions. Opponents to school choice are depicted as invested in themselves at the expense of students. For instance, public school teachers who oppose vouchers are described as against it because of the threats it represents to their job security and their retirement: "as more students choose private educational alternatives, the need for public-sector employees diminishes a welcome development for legislatures looking to reduce compensation and pension payments for state workers. Of course, that's exactly what has motivated teachers unions to keep vouchers at bay for decades."[58] Not surprisingly, President Obama earns some criticism as well, for his alleged conspiracy with DC–area teachers unions. For instance, one writer notes, "Because the president's teachers union allies are opposed to school choice for poor people, Mr. Obama ignores or downplays these findings [of voucher program success],"[59] while another accuses, "Nowhere is President Obama's allegiance to public-sector unions—to the detriment of the people they serve—on more stunning display than in his bid to defund what's hailed as one of the best school-voucher programs in the country."[60]

The problems—government bureaucracy, schools in crisis, students at risk, potentially, even, a nation at risk. The solution—choice. Intersecting discourses that come together and, as Chaput notes, stimulate a circulation of "material values" that ultimately "forms the backbone of capitalist production."[61] Within a larger national climate of consumption and parenting, where "intensive mothering" dictates the ways that mothers parent as it also categorizes mothers into good and bad, often along lines of race, class, and education, the raced and classed subject of the voucher debate prompts a consumer model of private education.[62] This consumer model of education and its reliance on narratives of mothers—whether that mother is Ingrid Campbell working three jobs to keep her children in private school or me paying for quality Montessori as I prepare my next semester syllabi—and our choices takes rhetorical hold amidst what Judith Warner names the "perfect madness" of the "Mommy Mystique." This mystique, she explains, is feminism within neoliberalism, individual control and (limited/bad) choice. Or, as Warner explains, it is "the belief that we can and should control every aspect of our children's lives, that our lives are the sum total of our personal choices, that our limitations stem from choosing poorly and that our problems are chiefly private, rather than public, in nature."[63] If Warner's assessment of the contemporary narrative of motherhood is correct, then the seemingly inconsistent shift in the gendered/racial/classed narratives that I identified in the introduction, the move from welfare queen to deserving mother, makes perfect rhetorical sense. The voucher argument, grounded in choice, emerges at the intersections of neoliberalism and feminism. Within that intersection, power and empowerment are at least reliant on if not made equivalent to choice, individualism, and effort. If we can just send our children to the right schools, then everything will be okay.

Conclusion

In her analysis of contemporary mediated representations of race and gender, Amy Adele Hasinoff states, "It is crucial to understand how the links between racial representation and neoliberalism might contribute to the production of new racisms."[64] She argues that this new racism of neoliberalism is one in which we celebrate and promote a racial self-transformation that occurs through "personal responsibility, choice, and flexibility."[65] In many ways, the new racism that is emerging here is a new twist on an old racism. Individualized and privatized, the racial subjects of the voucher debate, both the struggling single mother and her neglected child trapped in a failing and violent school, are situated as deserving in ways that have rarely been allowed within neoliberal multiculturalism. Yet they are made deserving in ways that highlight the structural only to use that structural to justify strengthening and enhancing private education at the expense of public. Moreover, for all their triumphant claims about equity and choice, voucher proponents provide very little information about the difference between the amount of the vouchers and the tuition costs of participating schools. Too often, that disparity is prohibitive for most students, meaning that very few impoverished students will actually be able to participate. As Joshua Akers notes, in the case of school choice in post-Katrina New Orleans, "The choice is the ability to opt out of public education, open to all, and select from private offerings, closed to many by a wide range of variables."[66] Moreover, recent voucher proposals have dramatically changed their income requirements. For instance, in a recent Ohio bill, students were eligible regardless of their school's rating and with family incomes under $95,000.[67] Colorado's Douglas County, a wealthy school district with high-performing schools, recently proposed a voucher program. Though ultimately deemed unconstitutional, the program had significant local support, seemingly from financially stable families who wished to send their children to private schools.[68] Here, the consumerist ideology becomes vividly clear; vouchers participate in what George Lipsitz names the larger "social warrant of competitive consumer citizenship [that] encourages well off communities to hoard their advantages, to seek to have their tax base used to fund only themselves and their interests."[69]

Across such proposals, the rhetorical and material implications of the voucher programs emerge. Bradley Jones and Roopali Mukherjee writing about the recent University of Michigan anti-affirmative action case, conclude: "affirmative action policies are doubly intolerable in the neoliberal imagination because they require recognition of social difference in the political realm, and, moreover, because they insist that such difference should direct state efforts in the redistribution of resources and opportunities."[70] In the new racist twist, privatization and consumption are the new affirmative action, the new social justice, the civil rights solution, and they are made rhetorically amenable through a discourse that tokenizes the disadvantaged poor. By depoliticizing education, the voucher debate pulls into play shifting discourses, producing a citizenship invested in individual accountability, with the effect that "an economic subject is conflated with a moral subject."[71] That is, morality and choice are wedded together.

The role of affect, emergent in this discourse both in the reinscription of welfare queen to deserving single mother *and* in the invocations of privilege and choice with guilt, is a key rhetorical player in this new twist on the old racism. Our rhetorical attention to the force of neoliberalism requires that we understand not the static subjects of identity politics, either as emergent in nationalist raced and gendered rhetorics or in calls of reverse racism and white male victims, but instead subjects with "fluctuating identities."[72] It is these fluctuating identities that provide the rhetorical force of the pro-voucher arguments; they are racialized and classed subjects seeking, not to evade their social responsibility as they allegedly were in Reagan-era discourse, but instead constituted as "families that desperately want their children to succeed. . . . They want to access the American dream, and that is through education."[73]

Public education and school choice couple competing discourses that situate race, class, and education with *and* against parenting, consumption, and privatization. As consumers and as mothers and parents, we are constituted within this discourse, asked to do what is right not only for our children but for all children. Voucher programs no doubt help individual students and families. This discourse asks us, as citizens and parents, to choose Ingrid Campbell, Claudia Correa, and their children. But of course, when those of us who already have choices make the pro-voucher choice we are consuming, yet again, as individuals rather than as citizens.

It's my night to put the little one to bed. I'm tired, and I want nothing more than for both of my kids to be asleep so that I can either go back to work or maybe, actually, just relax. I ask Aliana, eighteen months old, to get her book, and she toddles over to her books, looks through them, and brings me one. We read it, and off she goes to pick her second book. Just as we finish and I ask her to put it away, Amaris comes in, hoping to get to listen to her sister's books. I tell her we just finished, and she asks, "What books did you read?" I can see the disappointment in her eyes. But, I have a two-book rule for bedtime. At bedtime, I typically just want the day to be over. Aliana picks up Piglet and Mama, and I say, "OK, today we can read one more book." They negotiate their spots on my lap, each trying to scoot the other over to get more space. We read as piglet looks all over the farm, calling, "Mama!" I know that, regardless of whether voucher programs continue, my own location within whiteness and my own access to privilege means that I will have choices. And I hope that I will make good choices.

Notes

1. Nat Hentoff, "From These Schools, Lifelong Informed Voters," *The Fort Morgan Times*, April 5, 2012, accessed May 21, 2012, http://proquest.umi.com/pqdweb?did=2627076881&sid=1&Fmt=3&cl ientId=18938&RQT=309& VName=PQD.

2. "Public Education Crisis Extends Widely," *Florida Times Union*, March 27, 2012, A8, accessed May 21, 2012, http://jacksonville.com/opinion/editorials/2012-03-27/story/public-education-crisis-extends-widely.

3. "Our Nation's Dropout Crisis is Everyone's Problem: Why Boys & Girls Clubs are Part of the Solution," Boys & Girls Clubs of America, September 2010, 2, accessed May 21, 2012, http://www.bgcbentoncounty.org/2010/09/the-drop-out-crisis-facing-our-nation/

4. Andrew J. Rotherham, "The Education Crisis No One is Talking About," *Time*, May 12, 2011, accessed May 21, 2012, http://www.time.com/time/nation/article/0,8599,2070930,00.html.

5. "Black History Month Brings Calls for School Equity," *Call & Post*, February 11, 2009, 3B, accessed May 22, 2012, http://proquest.umi.com/pqdweb?did=1666515191&sid=3&Fmt=3&cl ientId=18938&RQT=309&VName=PQD.

6. "High School Drop Out Rates," *Child Trends Data Bank*, accessed May 22, 2012, www.childtrendsdatabank.org.

7. Marcus A. Winters, "Why 2011 is the Year of the School Voucher," *The Ex-*

aminer, November 17, 2011, 43, accessed March 28, 2012, http://proquest.umi.com/pqdweb?did=2514502911&sid=-1&Fmt=3&c lientId=18938&RQT=309& VName=PQD.

8. Peter Schrag, "Vouchers: They're *Baaaaaack*!" *The Nation*, July 20, 2011, 25–26, accessed May 24, 2012, http://web.ebscohost.com/ehost/pdfviewer/pdfviewer?vid=8&hid=15&sid=b64ac9ea-a094-45a4-918b-8b9d435a2632%40sessionmgr14.

9. Morgan Zalot, "Now, For Vouchers—Ackerman Says School Reform is New 'Civil-Rights Movement,'" *McClatchy—Tribune Business News*, November 7, 2011, accessed March 28, 2012, http://proquest.umi.com/pqdweb?did=2504376491&sid=-1&Fmt=3&c lientId=18938&RQT=309& VName=PQD.

10. Joshua M. Akers, "Separate and Unequal: The Consumption of Public Education in Post-Katrina New Orleans," *International Journal of Urban and Regional Research* 36 (2012): 29–48.

11. Peter Bansel, "Subjects of Choice and Lifelong Learning," *International Journal of Qualitative Studies in Education* 20 (2007): 283–300.

12. Carolyn Ellis, *The Ethnographic I: A Methodological Novel about Autoethnography* (Walnut Creek, CA: AltaMira Press, 2004), xix.

13. Adam Liptak, "Justices Take Up Race as a Factor in College Entry," *New York Times*, February 21, 2012, A1, accessed May 22, 2012, http://www.nytimes.com/2012/02/22/us/justices-to-hear-case-on-affirmative-action-in-higher-education.html?pagewanted=all.

14. Darrel Enck-Wanzer, "Barack Obama, the Tea Party, and the Threat of Race: On Racial Neoliberalism and Born Again Racism," *Communication, Culture & Critique* 4 (2011): 23–30.

15. Jodi Melamed,"The Spirit of Neoliberalism: From Racial Liberalism to Neoliberal Multiculturalism," *Social Text* 24 (2006): 1–24

16. Herman Gray, *Watching Race: Television and the Struggle for Blackness* (Minneapolis: University of Minnesota Press, 1995).

17. Amy Adele Hasinoff, "Fashioning Race for the Free Market on America's Next Top Model," *Critical Studies in Media Communication* 25 (2008): 324–43.

18. Roopali Mukherjee, *The Racial Order of Things: Cultural Imaginaries of the Post-Soul Era* (Minneapolis: University of Minnesota Press, 2006), 33.

19. Ibid, 27.

20. Bradley Jones and Roopali Mukherjee, "From California to Michigan: Race, Rationality, and Neoliberal Governmentality," *Communication and Critical/Cultural Studies* 7 (2010): 401–22.

21. Melamed, "The Spirit of Neoliberalism,"14.

22. Quoted in Zach Miners. "Washington's Voucher Program Dilemma," *U.S. News & World Report* January 2010, 39–40, accessed May 24, 2012, http://web.ebscohost.com/ehost/detail?vid=9&hid=15&sid=b64ac9ea-a094-45a4-918b-8b9d435a2632%40sessionmgr14&bdata=JnNpdGU9ZWhvc3QtbGl2ZQ%3d%3d#db=aph&AN=47092529.

23. Megan Boldt, "At the Capitol: In Fight Over School Vouchers, It's Promise

vs Performance," *Pioneer Press* March 3, 2012, accessed May 21, 2012, www.twincities.com/education/cl_20090583.

24. Quoted in Zalot, "Now for Vouchers."

25. Dawn Chavous, "Should State Approve School Choice Plan? Parents Have a Right to Pick Child's School," *Morning Call*, November 27, 2011, A27, accessed March 28, 2012, http://proquest.umi.com/pqdweb?did=2521830291&sid=-1&Fmt=3&c lientId=18938&RQT=309& VName=PQD.

26. April Toler, "Court Battle Delays Full Impact of School Vouchers," *McClatchy—Tribune Business News*, December 24, 2011, accessed March 28, 2012, http://proquest.umi.com/pqdweb?did=2546456281&sid=-1&Fmt=3&c lientId=18938&RQT=309& VName=PQD.

27. Lisa Gartner, "Enrollment in D.C. School Voucher Program Surges," *The Examiner*, November 23, 2011, 44, accessed March 28, 2012, http://proquest.umi.com/pqdweb?did=2518245421&sid=-1&Fmt=3&c lientId=18938&RQT=309& VName=PQD.

28. J. K. Wall, "School-Voucher Program Growing Fast," *Indianapolis Business Journal*, November 7, 2011, A9, accessed March 28, 2012, http://proquest.umi.com/pqdweb?did=2506397011&sid=-1&Fmt=3&c lientId=18938&RQT=309& VName=PQD.

29. Rebecca Catalanello, "Newly Appointed to the School Board, Glenton Gilzean Backs School Vouchers," *Tampa Bay Times*, January 25, 2012, B1, accessed March 28, 2012, http://proquest.umi.com/pqdweb?did=2569798261&sid=-1&Fmt=3&c lientId=18938&RQT=309& VName=PQD.

30. Chavous, "Should State Approve School Choice Plan."

31. Andy Sher, "Study of School Vouchers Needed Before Legislation, says Tennessee Gov. Bill Haslam," *McClatchy—Tribune Business News*, December 15, 2011, accessed March 28, 2012, http://proquest.umi.com/pqdweb?did=2538084431&sid=-1&Fmt=3&c lientId=18938&RQT=309& VName=PQD.

32. Quoted in Andrew Kitchenman, "Kean Prepares New Version of the School Vouchers Bill," *NJBIZ* February 27, 2012, 10, accessed March 28, 2012, http://proquest.umi.com/pqdweb?did=2602353481&sid=-1&Fmt=3&c lientId=18938&RQT=309& VName=PQD

33. Quoted in Boldt, "At the Capitol."

34. Virginia McCarver. "The Rhetoric of Choice and 21st-Century Feminism: Online Conversations about Work, Family, and Sarah Palin," *Women's Studies in Communication* 34 (2011): 22.

35. Mary Vavrus, "Opting Out Moms in the News: Selling New Traditionalism in the New Millennium," *Feminist Media Studies* 7 (2007): 51.

36. Bansel, "Subjects of Choice and Lifelong Learning," 285.

37. Ibid 284.

38. Bridget Byrne, "In Search of a 'Good Mix': 'Race," Class, Gender and Practices of Mothering," *Sociology* 40 (2006): 1008.

39. Nolan Rosenkrans, "Bill to Expand School Vouchers Called Attack on Public

Schools," *The Blade*, November 19, 2011, A1, accessed March 28, 2012, http://search.proquest.com/docview/1008949630?accountid=14503

40. Quoted in Toler, "Court Battles Delay."

41. John W. Storey, "Is Corbett's Education Plan with Vouchers a Smart One?" *Morning Call*, October 27, 2011, A19, accessed March 28, 2012, http://proquest.umi.com/pqdweb?did=2496509751&sid=-1&Fmt=3&c lientId=18938&RQT=309&VName=PQD

42. Bansel, "Subjects of Choice and Lifelong Learning," 287.

43. Quoted in Andy Sher, "Fight Builds Over School Vouchers," *Chattanooga Times Free Press*, November 2, 2011, A1, accessed March 28, 2012, http://proquest.umi.com/pqdweb?did=2500823801&sid=-1&Fmt=3&c lientId=18938&RQT=309& VName=PQD.

44. Quoted in Zalot, "Now for Vouchers."

45. Quoted in Margaret Fosmoe, "Daniels Sees Voucher Effect," *South Bend Tribune*, November 17, 2011, A1, accessed March 28, 2012, http://proquest.umi.com/pqdweb?did=2514883991&sid=-1&Fmt=3&c lientId=18938&RQT=309&VName=PDQ.

46. Chavous, "Should State Approve School Choice Plan."

47. Dana L. Cloud, "Therapy, Silence, and War" Consolation and the End of Deliberation in the 'Affected' Public," *POROI*, 2 (2003): 130.

48. Catherine Chaput, "Rhetorical Circulation in Late Capitalism: Neoliberalism and the Overdetermination of Affective Energy," *Philosophy & Rhetoric*, 43 (2010): 8.

49. Ibid, 5.

50. Mukhurjee, *The Racial Order of Things*, 62.

51. Ibid, 64.

52. Quoted in Gartner, "Enrollment in D.C. School Voucher Program Surges."

53. Chavous, "Should State Approve School Choice Plan."

54. Daniel J. Colgan, "Does Moul Back School Choice or Not?" *The Evening Sun*, December 2, 2011, accessed March 28, 2012, http://proquest.umi.com/pqdweb?did=2525297531&sid=-1&Fmt=3&c lientId=18938&RQT=309&VName=PQD.

55. Lauren Berlant, *Compassion: The Culture and Politics of an Emotion* (New York: Routledge, 2004).

56. Henry A. Giroux, "The Crisis of Public Values in the Age of the New Media," *Critical Studies in Media Communication* 28 (2011): 8.

57. Robert Enlow, "Evidence Shows Voucher Programs Help," *The Daily News*, November 22, 2011, accessed March 28, 2012, http://proquest.umi.com/pqdweb?did=2517556081&sid=-1&Fmt=3&c lientId=18938&RQT=309&VName=PQD.

58. Winters, "Why 2011 is the Year of the School Voucher."

59. Jason L. Riley, "Obama's War on School Vouchers: The President Downplays School Choice in His New $3.8 Trillion Budget," *Wall Street Journal (Online)*, February 15, 2012, accessed March 28, 2012, http://proquest.umi.com/pqdweb?did=2585842671&sid=-1&Fmt=3&c lientId=18938&RQT=309&VName=PQD.

60. "Killing Vouchers," editorial, *McClatchy—Tribune Business News*, February 22,

2012, accessed March 28, 2012, http://proquest.umi.com/pqdweb?did=2591428541&sid=-1&Fmt=3&c lientld=18938&RQT=309& VName=PQD.

61. Chaput, "Rhetorical Circulation in Late Capitalism," 14.

62. Amy Romagnoli and Glenda Wall, "'I Know I'm a Good Mom':Young, Low-Income Mothers' Experiences with Risk Perception, Intensive Parenting Ideology and Parenting Education Programmes," *Health, Risk, & Society* 14 (2012): 273–89.

63. Judith Warner, *Perfect Madness: Motherhood in the Age of Anxiety* (New York: Riverhead Books, 2005).

64. Hasinoff, "Fashioning Race," 339.

65. Ibid, 326.

66. Joshua M. Akers, "Separate and Unequal," 42.

67. "School, Legislative Leaders Speak Out Against Voucher Bill," *McClatchy—Tribune Business News*, November 18, 2011, accessed March 28, 2012, http://proquest.umi.com/pqdweb?did=2514618581&sid=-1&Fmt=3&c lientld=18938&RQT=309& VName=PQD.

68. Carlos Illescas and Liz Navratil, "Judge halts Douglas County school voucher program," *The Denver Post*, August 13, 2011, accessed May 28, 2012, http://www.denverpost.com/news/ci_18673490.

69. George Lipsitz, "Learning from New Orleans: The Social Warrant of Hostile Privatism and Competitive Consumer Citizenship," *Cultural Anthropology* 21 (2006): 455.

70. Jones and Mukherjee, "From California to Michigan,"403.

71. Bansel, ""Subjects of Choice and Lifelong Learning," 236.

72. Chaput, "Rhetorical Circulation in Late Capitalism," 5.

73. Dahlman, quoted in Boldt, "At the Capitol."

References

Akers, Joshua M. "Separate and Unequal: The Consumption of Public Education in Post-Katrina New Orleans," *International Journal of Urban and Regional Research* 36 (2012): 29–48.

Bansel, Peter. "Subjects of Choice and Lifelong Learning," *International Journal of Qualitative Studies in Education* 20 (2007): 283–300.

Berlant, Lauren. *Compassion: The Culture and Politics of an Emotion* (New York: Routledge, 2004).

"Black History Month Brings Calls for School Equity," *Call & Post*, February 11, 2009, 3B, accessed May 22, 2012, http://proquest.umi.com/pqdweb?did=1666515191&sid=3&Fmt=3&cl ientId=18938&RQT=309&VName=PQD.

Boldt, Megan. "At the Capitol: In Fight Over School Vouchers, It's Promise vs. Performance," *Pioneer Press,* March 3, 2012, accessed May 21, 2012, www.twincities.com/education/cl_20090583.

Byrne, Bridget. "In Search of a 'Good Mix': 'Race," Class, Gender and Practices of Mothering," *Sociology* 40 (2006): 1001–17.

Catalnello, Rebecca. "Newly Appointed to the School Board, Glenton Gilzean Backs

School Vouchers," *Tampa Bay Times*, January 25, 2012, B1, accessed March 28, 2012, http://proquest.umi.com/pqdweb?did=2569798261&sid=-1&Fmt=3&c lientId =18938&RQT=309& VName=PQD.

Chavouos, Dawn. "Should State Approve School Choice Plan? Parents Have a Right to Pick Child's School," *Morning Call*, November 27, 2011, A27, accessed March 28, 2012, http://proquest.umi.com/pqdweb?did=2521830291&sid=-1& Fmt=3&c lientId=18938&RQT=309& VName=PQD.

Chaput, Catherine. "Rhetorical Circulation in Late Capitalism: Neoliberalism and the Overdetermination of Affective Energy," *Philosophy & Rhetoric*, 43 (2010): 1–25.

Cloud, Dana L. "Therapy, Silence, and War" Consolation and the End of Deliberation in the 'Affected' Public," *POROI*, 2 (2003): 125–42.

Colgan, Daniel J. "Does Moul Back School Choice or Not?" *The Evening Sun*, December 2, 2011, accessed March 28, 2012, http://proquest.umi.com/pqdweb?did =2525297531&sid=-1&Fmt=3&c lientId=18938&RQT=309& VName=PQD.

Ellis, Carolyn. *The Ethnographic I: A Methodological Novel about Autoethnography* (Walnut Creek, CA: AltaMira Press, 2004).

Enck-Wanzer, Darrel. "Barack Obama, the Tea Party, and the Threat of Race: On Racial Neoliberalism and Born Again Racism," *Communication, Culture & Critique* 4 (2011): 23–30.

Enlow, Robert. "Evidence Shows Voucher Programs Help," *The Daily News*, November 22, 2011, accessed March 28, 2012, http://proquest.umi.com/pqdweb?did =2517556081&sid=-1&Fmt=3&c lientId=18938&RQT=309& VName=PQD.

Gartner, Lisa. "Enrollment in D.C. School Voucher Program Surges," *The Examiner*, November 23, 2011, 44, accessed March 28, 2012, http://proquest.umi.com /pqdweb?did=2518245421&sid=-1&Fmt=3&c lientId=18938&RQT=309& VName =PQD.

Giroux, Henry A. "The Crisis of Public Values in the Age of the New Media," *Critical Studies in Media Communication* 28 (2011): 8–29.

Gray, Herman. *Watching Race: Television and the Struggle for Blackness* (Minneapolis: University of Minnesota Press, 1995).

Hasinoff, Amy Adele. "Fashioning Race for the Free Market on America's Next Top Model," *Critical Studies in Media Communication* 25 (2008): 324–43.

Hentoff, Nat. "From These Schools, Lifelong Informed Voters," *The Fort Morgan Times*, April 5, 2012, accessed May 21, 2012, http://proquest.umi.com/pqdweb?did =2627076881&sid=1&Fmt=3&cl ientId=18938&RQT=309& VName=PQD.

"High School Drop Out Rates," *Child Trends Data Bank*, accessed May 22, 2012, www.childtrendsdatabank.org.

Illescas, Carlos, and Liz Navratil, "Judge halts Douglas County school voucher program," *The Denver Post*, August 13, 2011, accessed May 28, 2012, http://www .denverpost.com/news/ci_18673490.

Jones, Bradley, and Roopali Mukherjee, "From California to Michigan: Race, Rationality, and Neoliberal Governmentality," *Communication and Critical/Cultural Studies* 7 (2010): 401–22.

"Killing Vouchers," editorial, *McClatchy—Tribune Business News*, February 22, 2012, accessed March 28, 2012, http://proquest.umi.com/pqdweb?did=2591428541&sid=-1&Fmt=3&c lientId=18938&RQT=309&VName=PQD. Accessed March 28, 2012.

Kitchenman, Andrew. "Kean Prepares New Version of the School Vouchers Bill," *NJBIZ* February 27, 2012, 10, accessed March 28, 2012, http://proquest.umi.com/pqdweb?did=2602353481&sid=-1&Fmt=3&c lientId=18938&RQT=309&VName=PQD

Lipsitz, George. "Learning from New Orleans: The Social Warrant of Hostile Privatism and Competitive Consumer Citizenship," *Cultural Anthropology* 21 (2006): 451–68.

Liptak, Adam. "Justices Take Up Race as a Factor in College Entry," *New York Times*, February 21, 2012, A1, accessed May 22, 2012, http://www.nytimes.com/2012/02/22/us/justices-to-hear-case-on-affirmative-action-in-higher-education.html?pagewanted=all.

McCarver, Virginia. "The Rhetoric of Choice and 21st-Century Feminism: Online Conversations about Work, Family, and Sarah Palin," *Women's Studies in Communication* 34 (2011): 20–41.

Melamed, Jodi. "The Spirit of Neoliberalism: From Racial Liberalism to Neoliberal Multiculturalism," *Social Text* 24 (2006): 1–24

Miners, Zach. "Washington's Voucher Program Dilemma," *U.S. News & World Report* January 2010, 39–40, accessed May 24, 2012, http://web.ebscohost.com/ehost/detail?vid=9&hid=15&sid=b64ac9ea-a094-45a4-918b-8b9d435a2632%40sessionmgr14&bdata=JnNpdGU9ZWhvc3QtbGl2ZQ%3d%3d#db=aph&AN=47092529

Mukherjee, Roopali. *The Racial Order of Things: Cultural Imaginaries of the Post-Soul Era* (Minneapolis: University of Minnesota Press, 2006).

"Our Nation's Dropout Crisis is Everyone's Problem: Why Boys & Girls Clubs are Part of the Solution," Boys & Girls Clubs of America, September 2010, 2, accessed May 21, 2012, http://www.bgcbentoncounty.org/2010/09/the-drop-out-crisis-facing-our-nation/

"Public Education Crisis Extends Widely," *Florida Times Union*, March 27, 2012, A8, accessed May 21, 2012, http://jacksonville.com/opinion/editorials/2012-03-27/story/public-education-crisis-extends-widely.

Riley, Jason L. "Obama's War on School Vouchers; The President Downplays School Choice in His New $3.8 Trillion Budget," *Wall Street Journal (Online)*, February 15, 2012, accessed March 28, 2012, http://proquest.umi.com/pqdweb?did=2585842671&sid=-1&Fmt=3&c lientId=18938&RQT=309&VName=PQD.

Romagnoli, Amy, and Glenda Wall, "'I Know I'm a Good Mom': Young, Low-Income Mothers' Experiences with Risk Perception, Intensive Parenting Ideology and Parenting Education Programmes," *Health, Risk, & Society* 14 (2012): 273–89.

Rosenkrans, Nolan. "Bill to Expand School Vouchers Called Attack on Public Schools," *The Blade*, November 19, 2011, A1, accessed March 28, 2012, http://search.proquest.com/docview/1008949630?accountid=14503

Rotherham, Andrew J. "The Education Crisis No One is Talking About," *Time*,

May 12, 2011, accessed May 21, 2012, http://www.time.com/time/nation/article/0,8599,2070930,00.html.

"School, Legislative Leaders Speak Out Against Voucher Bill," *McClatchy—Tribune Business News*, November 18, 2011, accessed March 28, 2012, http://proquest.umi.com/pqdweb?did=2514618581&sid=-1&Fmt=3&c lientId=18938&RQT=309& VName=PQD.

Schrag, Peter. "Vouchers: They're *Baaaaaack*!" *The Nation*, July 20, 2011, 25–26, accessed May 24, 2012, http://web.ebscohost.com/ehost/pdfviewer/pdfviewer?vid=8&hid=15&sid=b64ac9ea-a094-45a4-918b-8b9d435a2632%40sessionmgr14.

Sher, Andy. "Fight Builds Over School Vouchers," *Chattanooga Times Free Press*, November 2, 2011, A1, accessed March 28, 2012, http://proquest.umi.com/pqdweb?did=2500823801&sid=-1&Fmt=3&c lientId=18938&RQT=309& VName=PQD.

———. "Study of School Vouchers Needed Before Legislation, says Tennessee Gov. Bill Haslam," *McClatchy—Tribune Business News*, December 15, 2011, accessed March 28, 2012, http://proquest.umi.com/pqdweb?did=2538084431&sid=-1&Fmt=3&c lientId=18938&RQT=309& VName=PQD.

Storey, John W. "Is Corbett's Education Plan with Vouchers a Smart One?" *Morning Call*, October 27, 2011, A19, accessed March 28, 2012, http://proquest.umi.com/pqdweb?did=2496509751&sid=-1&Fmt=3&c lientId=18938&RQT=309& VName=PQD

Toler, April. "Court Battle Delays Full Impact of School Vouchers," *McClatchy—Tribune Business News*, December 24, 2011, accessed March 28, 2012, http://proquest.umi.com/pqdweb?did=2546456281&sid=-1&Fmt=3&c lientId=18938&RQT=309& VName=PQD.

Vavrus, Mary Douglas. "Opting Out Moms in the News: Selling New Traditionalism in the New Millennium," *Feminist Media Studies* 7 (2007): 47–63.

Wall, J. K. "School-Voucher Program Growing Fast," *Indianapolis Business Journal*, November 7, 2011, A9, accessed March 28, 2012, http://proquest.umi.com/pqdweb?did=2506397011&sid=-1&Fmt=3&c lientId=18938&RQT=309& VName=PQD.

Warner, Judith. *Perfect Madness: Motherhood in the Age of Anxiety* (New York: Riverhead Books, 2005).

Winters, Marcus A. "Why 2011 is the Year of the School Voucher," *The Examiner*, November 17, 2011, 43, accessed March 28, 2012, http://proquest.umi.com/pqdweb?did=2514502911&sid=-1&Fmt=3&c lientId=18938&RQT=309& VName=PQD.

Zalot, Morgan. "Now, For Vouchers—Ackerman Says School Reform is New 'Civil-Rights Movement,'" *McClatchy—Tribune Business News*, November 7, 2011, accessed March 28, 2012, http://proquest.umi.com/pqdweb?did=2504376491&sid=-1&Fmt=3&c lientId=18938&RQT=309& VName=PQD.

Suggested Readings

Bennetts, Leslie. *The Feminine Mistake: Are We Giving Up Too Much?* New York: Hyperion, 2007.

Bobel, Chris. *The Paradox of Natural Mothering*. Philadelphia: Temple University Press, 2002.

Buchanan, Lindal. *Rhetorics of Motherhood*. Carbondale ; Edwardsville: Southern Illinois University Press, 2013.

Chávez, Karma R., and Cindy L. Griffin, eds. *Standing in the Intersection: Feminist Voices, Feminist Practices in Communication Studies*. Albany: SUNY Press, 2012.

Crittenden, Ann. *The Price of Motherhood: Why the Most Important Job in the World Is Still the Least Valued*. New York: Henry Holt & Company, 2001.

Cook, Daniel Thomas. "The Missing Child in Consumption Theory." *Journal of Consumer Culture* 8 (2008): 219–43.

Davey, Moyra. *Mother Reader: Essential Writings on Motherhood*. New York: Seven Stories Press, 2001.

Douglas, Susan J. and Meredith W. Michaels. *The Mommy Myth: The Idealization of Motherhood and How It Has Undermined All Women*. New York: Free Press, 2004.

Ehrenreich, Barbara and Deirdre English. *For Her Own Good: Two Centuries of the Experts' Advice to Women*. Rev. ed. New York: Anchor House, 2005.

Ginsburg, Faye D., and Rayna Rapp. *Conceiving the New World Order. The Global Politics of Reproduction*. Berkeley: University of California Press, 1995.

Glenn, Evelyn Nakano, Grace Chang, and Linda Rennie Forcey, eds. *Mothering: Ideology, Experience, and Agency*. New York: Routledge, 1993.

Goodwin, Michele Bratcher, ed. *Baby Markets: Money and the New Politics of Creating Families*. Cambridge: Cambridge University Press, 2010.

Hall, Ann C., and Mardia Bishop. *Mommy Angst: Motherhood in American Popular Culture*. New York: Praeger, 2009.

Hanauer, Cathi, ed. *The Bitch in the House: 26 Women Tell the Truth About Sex, Solitude, Work, Motherhood, and Marriage*. New York: Harper, 2003.

Hays, Sharon. *The Cultural Contradictions of Motherhood*. New Haven: Yale University Press, 1996.

Hochschild, Arlie Russell. *The Commercialization of Intimate Life: Notes from Home and Work*. Berkeley: University of California Press, 2003.

Jolly, Margaret. "Divided Mothers: Changing Global Inequalities of 'Nature.'" In *The Globalization of Motherhood: Deconstructions and Reconstructions of Biology and Care,* edited by Maher and Chavkin, 154–79. New York: Routledge, 2010.

Kinser, Amber E. *Mothering in the Third Wave*. New York: Demeter Press, 2008.

Ladd-Taylor, Molly, and Lauri Umansky. *"Bad" Mothers: The Politics of Blame in Twentieth-Century America*. New York: New York University Press, 1998.

Laureau, Annette. *Unequal Childhoods: Class, Race and Family Life*. Berkeley: University of California Press, 2003.

Layne, Linda L., ed. *Transformative Motherhood: On Giving and Getting in a Consumer Culture*. New York: New York University Press, 1999.

Littler, Jo. "The Rise of the 'Yummy Mummy': Popular Conservatism and the Neoliberal Maternal in Contemporary British Culture." *Communication, Culture & Critique* 6, no. 2 (June 1, 2013): 227–43. doi:10.1111/cccr.12010.

Lury, Celia. *Consumer Culture*. New Brunswick: Rutgers University Press, 1996.

Martens, Lydia, Dale Southerton, and Sue Scott. "Bringing Children (and Parents) into the Sociology of Consumption: Towards a Theoretical and Empirical Agenda." *Journal of Consumer Culture 4(2)* (2004): 155–82.

O'Brien Hallstein, D. Lynn. "She Gives Birth, She's Wearing a Bikini: Mobilizing the Postpregnant Celebrity Mom Body to Manage the Post–Second Wave Crisis in Femininity." *Women's Studies in Communication* 34, no. 2 (September 2011): 111–38. doi:10.1080/07491409.2011.619471.

O'Reilly Andrea, ed. *Feminist Mothering*. Albany: State University of New York Press, 2008.

——. *Mother Outlaws: Theories and Practices of Empowered Mothering*. Toronto: Women's Press, 2004.

——. *Twenty-First-Century Motherhood: Experience, Identity, Policy, Agency*. New York: Columbia University Press, 2010.

Pugh, Allison J. *Longing and Belonging: Parents, Children, and Consumer Culture*. Berkley: University of California Press, 2009.

Rich, Adrienne. *Of Woman Born: Motherhood as Experience and Institution*. Rev. ed. New York: W. W. Norton & Company, 1986.

Sandilands, Catriona. "On 'Green' Consumerism: Environmental Privatization and 'Family Values.'" *Canadian Woman Studies* 13.3 (1993): 45–47.

Sassatelli, Roberta. *Consumer Culture: History, Theory and Politics*. Thousand Oaks, CA: Sage Publications, 2007.

Schor, Juliet B. *Born to Buy: The Commercialized Child and the New Consumer Culture*. New York: Scribner, 2004.

Seiter, Ellen. *Sold Separately: Children and Parents in Consumer Culture*. New Brunswick: Rutgers University Press, 1993.

Spar, Debora L. *The Baby Business: How Money, Science, and Politics Drive the Commerce of Conception*. Boston: Harvard Business School Publishing Corporation, 2006.

Rothman, Barbara Katz. *Recreating Motherhood: Ideology qnd Technology in a Patriarchal Society*. New York: Norton, 1989.

Taylor, Janelle S., Linda L. Layne, and Danielle F. Wozniak. *Consuming Motherhood*. New Brunswick: Rutgers University Press, 2004.

Thomas, Susan Gregory. *Buy Buy Baby: How Consumer Culture Manipulates Parents and Harms Young Minds*. Boston: Houghton Mifflin Company, 2007.

Thornton, Davi Johnson. "Neuroscience, Affect, and the Entrepreneurialization of Motherhood." *Communication and Critical/Cultural Studies* 8, no. 4 (2011): 399–424. doi:10.1080/14791420.2011.610327.

Thurer, Shari L. *The Myths of Motherhood: How Culture Reinvents the Good Mother*. New York: Penguin, 1994.

Warner, Judith. *Perfect Madness: Motherhood in the Age of Anxiety*. New York: Riverhead Books, 2006.

Vavrus, Mary Douglas. "Opting Out Moms in the News." *Feminist Media Studies* 7, no. 1 (March 2007): 47–63. doi:10.1080/14680770601103704.

Vandenbeld Giles, Melinda, ed. *Mothering in the Age of Neoliberalism*, first edition (Bradford, Ontario: Demeter Press, 2014).

Zukin, Sharon. *Point of Purchase: How Shopping Changed American Culture*. New York: Routledge, 2005.

Contributors

Jennifer L. Borda is an associate professor of communication at the University of New Hampshire. Her research focuses on how discourse and ideologies about women, work, motherhood, and identity have been constructed and challenged in the mass media. She is the author of *Women Labor Activists in the Movies: Nine Depictions of Workplace Organizers, 1954–2005* (McFarland, 2010). Her work has been published in several scholarly anthologies and various journals, such as *Text & Performance Quarterly*, *Feminist Media Studies*, *Women's Studies in Communication*, and *Communication Quarterly*.

Shira Chess is an assistant professor of mass media arts at Grady College of Journalism and Mass Communication at the University of Georgia. Her research examines gender and media, gaming culture, and digital storytelling. She is the coauthor, along with Eric Newsom, of *Folklore, Horror Stories, and the Slender Man: The Development of an Internet Mythology* (Palgrave Pivot). Her other research has been published in *Critical Studies in Media Communication*, *Feminist Media Studies*, *New Media & Society*, *Games and Culture*, and *Information, Communication & Society* as well as several essay collections.

Anne Teresa Demo is an assistant professor in the Department of Communication Arts and Sciences at Pennsylvania State University. Her work explores the relationship between visual/digital rhetoric, identity, and US cultural politics. A past recipient of the National Communication Association's Golden Monograph award, her articles have appeared in the *Quarterly Journal of Speech*, *Critical Studies in Media Communication*, *Rhetoric and Public Affairs*, and *Women's Studies in Communication*. She is the coeditor of *Rhetoric, Remembrance, and Visual Form: Sighting Memory* (Routledge, 2012).

Kara N. Dillard is an assistant professor in the Department of Sociology at the University of Alaska Fairbanks. Her research interests are in the areas of public sphere and democracy, social movements, and the political economy of food and agriculture. Her articles have been published in the *Journal of Ap-*

plied Communication Research and the *International Journal of Communication.* She is mother to Christian, who loves to garden.

K. Animashaun Ducre is associate professor and chair in the Department of African American Studies at Syracuse University and a 2011 Fulbright Scholar at the Institute for Gender and Development Studies at the University of the West Indies, St. Augustine. A committed advocate for environmental justice, she combines her experiences on the frontlines of the environmental justice movement and academic training in geographic information systems and demography for a unique perspective on economic and environmental inequality. She is author of *Bearing Witness: Gender Race, Space, and Justice in Syracuse* (Syracuse University Press, 2012).

Lisa A. Flores is associate professor in the Department of Communication at the University of Colorado. Her research and teaching interests lie in rhetoric, critical race studies, and gender. She has published in *Text and Performance Quarterly*, *Communication and Critical/Cultural Studies*, and the *Quarterly Journal of Speech*. Her current work examines the rhetorical logics of race and the intersections of race, nation, and belonging.

Cynthia Gordon is associate professor in the Department of Linguistics at Georgetown University. In 2012–2013 she was a fellow at the Center for Advanced Study in the Behavioral Sciences at Stanford University. She is author of *Making Meanings, Creating Family: Intertextuality and Framing in Family Interaction* (Oxford, 2009) and coeditor (with Deborah Tannen and Shari Kendall) of *Family Talk: Discourse and Identity in Four American Families* (Oxford, 2007).

Christine Harold is associate professor in the Department of Communication at the University of Washington, Seattle. She is author of the book *OurSpace: Resisting the Corporate Control of Culture* (University of Minnesota Press, 2007) as well as several scholarly articles and chapters on consumerism and cultural politics. Among other venues, her work has appeared in *Public Culture*, *Rhetoric and Public Affairs*, *Critical Studies in Media Communication*, and *JAC*. She is mother to Helena, Liam, and Josephine.

Sara Hayden is professor of communication studies at the University of Montana. Her research focuses on the rhetoric of women's health, sexuality, and maternity and has been published in several scholarly anthologies and various journals including the *Quarterly Journal of Speech*, *Communication and Critical/Cultural Studies*, *Journal of Applied Communication Research*, and *Women's Studies in Communication*. She is coeditor, with D. Lynn O'Brien Hallstein, of *Contemplating Maternity in an Era of Choice: Explorations into Discourses of Reproduction* (2010, Lexington), which received the 2011 Outstanding Edited Book Award from the Organization for the Study of Communication, Language, and Gender.

Karen Hvidtfeldt Madsen is associate professor at the University of Southern Denmark. She heads the research group Cultural Analysis of Health, Reproduction, Gender and the Body, which works in the border area between humanities and health sciences, and examines how cultural analytical methods may be applied to issues related to health, disease, reproduction, sexuality, gender, and the body. She also participates in the research project titled (Trans)Formations of Kinship: Travelling in Search of Relatedness (KinTra), which is funded by the Danish Research Council on the Humanities (2011–2014). She has conducted research on transnational surrogacy and has published her work in several scholarly anthologies and Scandinavian journals.

Charlotte Kroløkke is associate professor at the University of Southern Denmark and heading the research project titled (Trans)Formations of Kinship: Travelling in Search of Relatedness (KinTra), which is funded by the Danish Research Council on the Humanities (2011–2014). Kroløkke has conducted research on the marketing and branding of Danish sperm and three-dimensional ultrasound technology. In her latest work she inquires into fertility travel, most notably Danish women and couples who travel to Spain or the Czech Republic for egg donation as well as Scandinavian infertile individuals who go to India for surrogacy. She is theoretically informed by feminist communication scholarship, and her work has been published in various journals such as *The Journal of Consumer Culture, Women's Studies in Communication, Cultural Politics*, and *Text and Performance Quarterly*.

Index